D0915572

COGNITIVE LEARNING IN CHILDREN
Theories and Strategies

EDUCATIONAL PSYCHOLOGY

Allen J. Edwards, Series Editor
Department of Psychology
Southwest Missouri State University
Springfield, Missouri

Phillip S. Strain, Thomas P. Cooke, and Tony Apolloni. Teaching Exceptional Children: Assessing and Modifying Social Behavior

Donald E. P. Smith and others. A Technology of Reading and Writing (in four volumes).

> Vol. 1. *Learning to Read and Write: A Task Analysis (by Donald E. P. Smith)*

Joel R. Levin and Vernon L. Allen (eds.). Cognitive Learning in Children: Theories and Strategies

In preparation:

Donald E. P. Smith and others. A Technology of Reading and Writing (in four volumes).

> Vol. 2. *Criterion-Referenced Tests for Reading and Writing (by Judith M. Smith, Donald E. P. Smith, and James R. Brink)*
> Vol. 3. *The Adaptive Classroom (by Donald E. P. Smith)*
> Vol. 4. *Preparing Instructional Tasks (by Donald E. P. Smith)*

Gilbert R. Austin. Early Childhood Education: An International Perspective

Vernon L. Allen (ed.). Children as Teachers: Theory and Research on Tutoring

António Simões (ed.). The Bilingual Child: Research and Analysis of Existing Educational Themes

Erness Bright Brody and Nathan Brody. Intelligence: Nature, Determinants, and Consequences

COGNITIVE LEARNING IN CHILDREN
Theories and Strategies

EDITED BY

Joel R. Levin
Department of Educational Psychology
University of Wisconsin
Madison, Wisconsin

Vernon L. Allen
Department of Psychology
University of Wisconsin
Madison, Wisconsin

ACADEMIC PRESS   New York   San Francisco   London   1976

A Subsidiary of Harcourt Brace Jovanovich, Publishers

ACADEMIC PRESS, INC.
111 Fifth Avenue, New York, New York 10003

United Kingdom Edition published by
ACADEMIC PRESS, INC. (LONDON) LTD.
24/28 Oval Road, London NW1

Library of Congress Cataloging in Publication Data

Main entry under title:

Cognitive learning in children.

    (Educational psychology series)
    "This book presents several programs of research and
development conducted at the Wisconsin Research and
Development Center for Cognitive Learning."
    Includes bibliographies.
    1.   Educational psychology.   2.   Cognition (Child
psychology)   I.   Levin, Joel R.   II.   Allen, Vernon L.,
Date   III.   Wisconsin Research and Development
Center for Cognitive Learning.
LB1067.C56   370.15′2   75-40610
ISBN 0–12–444850–X

PRINTED IN THE UNITED STATES OF AMERICA

Contents

06999

PART II   STRATEGIES FOR IMPROVING COGNITIVE LEARNING

Chapter 4   What Have We Learned about Maximizing What Children Learn?   105
Joel R. Levin

Chapter 5   The Role of Metaphor and Analogy in Learning   135
Robert E. Davidson

Chapter 6   Prerequisites for Learning to Read
Richard L. Venezky

PART III   STRATEGIES FOR IMPROVING CLASSROOM INSTRUCTION

Chapter 7   Instructional Design and the Teaching of Concepts   191
Herbert J. Klausmeier

Chapter 8   Research and Development in Training Creative Thinking   219

Gary A. Davis

Chapter 9   Children Helping Children: Psychological Processes in Tutoring   241

Vernon L. Allen

List of Contributors

Numbers in parentheses indicate the pages on which the authors' contributions begin.

Vernon L. Allen (241), Department of Psychology, University of Wisconsin, Madison, Wisconsin

Robert E. Davidson (135), Department of Educational Psychology, University of Wisconsin, Madison, Wisconsin

Gary A. Davis (219), Department of Educational Psychology, University of Wisconsin, Madison, Wisconsin

Elizabeth S. Ghatala (61), Weber State College, Ogden, Utah

Herbert J. Klausmeier (5, 191), Department of Educational Psychology, University of Wisconsin, Madison, Wisconsin

Gisela Labouvie-Vief (31), *Department of Educational Psychology, University of Wisconsin, Madison, Wisconsin

Joel R. Levin (61, 105), Department of Educational Psychology, University of Wisconsin, Madison, Wisconsin

Richard L. Venezky (163), Department of Computer Sciences, University of Wisconsin, Madison, Wisconsin

*Now at Department of Psychology, Wayne State University, Detroit, Michigan.

Preface

This book presents several programs of research and development conducted at the Wisconsin Research and Development Center for Cognitive Learning. The Center is located on the campus of the University of Wisconsin, in Madison. Funded by the National Institute of Education, the Wisconsin Center is mandated to conduct research, development, and implementation activities related to the educational problem of cognitive learning in children. All the chapters contained in this book were written by persons who are now or were formerly associated with the Center. Researchers from a wide range of academic disciplines are involved in the research and development work of the Center.

Since its inception in 1964, the Wisconsin Center has generated a number of highly visible educational "products," including its well-known alternative to the traditional age-graded system of schooling, Individually Guided Education (IGE). At the present time, over 2000 schools across the United States have adopted the IGE model. The intent of this book is not to promote IGE or any other educational product. We do hope, however, that this volume will demonstrate the value of targeted educational research and development activities, for it is such research and development that frequently forms the basis for innovative educational products used in the classroom.

The book is directed toward three major groups. First, it should be of interest to researchers and scholars in the university community, especially those persons concerned with human learning, human development, and curriculum and instruction. Second, it should be useful to teachers and practitioners who want to apply research findings to classroom settings. Third, we hope the book will demonstrate to policymakers and critics of educational research and development that a large amount of useful knowledge can be accumulated in a comparatively short time by targeted educational research and development.

xi

Many persons have helped us during the course of the preparation of this book. We should like to express our appreciation, in particular, to James Harritt of the Wisconsin Research and Development Center for Cognitive Learning for his aid in developing this volume; to Lynn Sowle for typing a goodly number of pages; and to the staff of Academic Press for their part.

Introduction

Over the years severe criticism has been directed toward the public schools from many quarters. Critics from the political right, left, and center have charged the schools with being guilty of a multitude of sins. Criticism has come both from laymen in the community and from professional educators. It has often been said that we expect too much of our schools; many problems facing the schools are, in part, attributable to broader problems that exist in the society at large. Whether a reasonable expectation or not, still our schools are expected to succeed in areas where other institutions of society (e.g., the family) have failed.

Once caught up in the whirlwind of complex social and political turmoil, it is only too easy to lose sight of the basic responsibility of the school—the enhancement of children's cognitive learning. However, even in the area of basic cognitive learning, schools have not escaped criticism for the level of performance typically attained by children after many years of instruction. Many critics have charged that the schools should be performing much better in the teaching of the basic cognitive skills necessary for participation in a complex technological society.

EDUCATIONAL RESEARCH AND DEVELOPMENT

Clearly there is a gap between the aspirations set for the schools by its critics and children's academic performance at the present time. Yet, to some degree this gap can be bridged by psychological research concerned with children's learning in educational contexts. The goal of educational research in the teaching—learning process is to identify instructional methods and materials that will optimize learning for all children. Research and development activities are dictated by theories related to children's cognitive operations (i.e., how children learn), as well as strategies related to instruction (i.e., how to improve children's learning). Although it is abundantly clear that program implementation per se is foremost in the minds of citizens and legislators concerned with effecting immediate changes in the present educational system, it is obvious to others that such efforts represent only the tip of the iceberg. That is to say, educational products devoid of underlying theory and strategy are not likely to contribute toward the substantial long-term improvement of schooling.

Two arguments can be advanced for the importance of research on theories and strategies in cognitive learning, as opposed to hasty efforts to implement tangible products. First, educational products are often born out of faddish social and political concerns, rather than out of enduring educational problems; as a consequence, such products constitute short-sighted and stop-gap solutions. For example, the now dying "free school" movement of the last 10 years (including a variety of "laissez-faire" or student-choice alternatives) apparently did not fulfill its promise. Second, it is reasonable to expect that formative versions of educational products will not work as well as anticipated; invariably, unexpected difficulties are encountered which require solution— especially when the initial novelty of a program has dissipated.

In the absence of an underlying research base from which to draw, refinement of a product generally proceeds as a stumbling, trial-and-error process. On the other hand, the availability of a research base serves to systematize product refinement; components of the relevant instructional theory or strategy can be examined, and suggestions for corresponding changes in practice may emerge. In some cases, practical outcomes from using a procedure or product may also suggest modifications of existing theory and strategy, modifications which can in turn be cycled back into a better version of the educational product.

The process of applying research results is not quite as straightforward as it might appear. The researcher interested in applying results of psychological research to the practical problems of children in the classroom will find it necessary constantly to alternate his attention between abstract or theoretical problems on the one hand, and concrete or practical issues on the other. The dichotomy between applied and basic research is never as clear in practice as it may seem to be in an abstract discussion. Sometimes initial work on a theoretical problem will lead to the later development of practical procedures for the use in the classroom, as will become apparent in Part III of this book. But even then, the relationship between the development of practical classroom materials and the discovery of new or "basic" knowledge is never entirely unidirectional; on the contrary, the relationship is more frequently one of symbiosis. It is clear that better applications will evolve from research on both basic and applied problems.

OVERVIEW OF THE BOOK

Given these remarks, the major chapter divisions of the present book reflect in a general way a reasonable progression from basic to applied research in education: First, a theory is proposed and basic research is conducted dealing with the psychology of children's learning and development; then, research is directed toward factors facilitating the learning process; finally, curricular materials and strategies for improving classroom instruction are devised. The content of the three major sections of this book illustrate these stages; an overview of the three sections will be presented briefly below.

In Part I, "Learning, Development, and Cognitive Abilities," the focus is on the presumed cognitive operations that are employed by children in various learning situations. These situations range from simply recognizing previous stimuli (Ghatala and Levin in Chapter 3) to the acquisition of complex concepts and principles (Klausmeier in Chapter 1). Moreover, in most cases the nature of the hypothesized cognitive operations may be expected to be influenced by age. In this sense, age is regarded as a potent "individual differences" variable which moderates what is learned and how it is learned. It will also become apparent that other individual differences apart from age, when considered in conjunction with different learning contexts, comprise useful ingredients in the process of theorizing and making predictions about various learning outcomes (Labouvie-Vief in Chapter 2).

Part II, "Strategies for Improving Cognitive Learning," is concerned with experimental manipulations and instructional training techniques that facilitate the learning process. Thus, strategies are developed to improve a child's memory (Levin in Chapter 4), to render printed materials more comprehensible (Davidson in Chapter 5), and to provide assistance in the mastery of rudimentary reading skills (Venezky in Chapter 6). Once again, the notion of individual differences arises— frequently in the form of prerequisite skills—and is discussed by the authors. At the same time, when investigators are devising appropriate learning strategies they attempt to capitalize on a number of research findings concerned with basic phenomena in human learning and development.

Finally, Part III, "Strategies for Improving Classroom Instruction," provides concrete examples of how educational researchers are able to take the penultimate step in the laboratory-to-the-classroom delivery system. Guided by theoretical and empirical work of the kind reported in Parts I and II, the investigators here (Klausmeier in Chapter 7, Davis in Chapter 8, and Allen in Chapter 9) seek to construct instructional materials and strategies for use in actual classroom settings. The goal of the efforts of authors in Part III is, of course, to discover the most effective means of facilitating the overall classroom performance of children.

PART I

Learning, Development, and Cognitive Abilities

At this point we shall examine in greater detail Part I of this book and present an overview of the content of the three chapters. Part I, "Learning, Development, and Cognitive Abilities," synthesizes empirical research directed toward understanding the psychological processes underlying children's cognitive learning and development. In some cases, the findings have been incorporated into existing learning and developmental theories; in other cases, alternative theoretical constructs have been proposed.

In Klausmeier's chapter, for example, a new model of conceptual learning and development is presented. According to the model, as children develop, they acquire various concepts at four progressively more complex levels. At the first (simplest), or **concrete** level, children are able to recognize a new object that is exactly the same as one previously experienced. At the second, **identity** level, children are able to recognize that a new object is the same as one previously experienced even when it is experienced in a different position or in a different sensory modality. At the third, or **classificatory** level, children are able to determine that two different instances of the same concept are equivalent. Finally, at the last (most complex), or **formal** level, persons are able to provide the technical, socially accepted definition of the concept in terms of its defining attributes, to engage in other symbolic activities associated with the concept, and to use the concept in understanding taxonomic and hierarchical relationships, in understanding principles, and in solving problems.

The reality of these levels, including their presumed hierarchical structure, has been validated by means of cross-sectional and longi-

1

tudinal research conducted by Klausmeier and his associates. As the author indicates, this research has resulted in the formulation of a number of fairly solid principles of conceptual learning and development. For example, it has now been well established that both the understanding of principles and problem solving involving particular concepts are most successful when the constituent concepts are attained at the formal level.

In the concluding part of his chapter, Klausmeier discusses Flavell's various conceptions of cognitive–developmental change, including both discontinuity–continuity and rate-of-change issues. The present model of conceptual learning and development is then related to existing theoretical notions, such as Bruner's modes of learning and representation and Gagné's learning hierarchies.

Just as Klausmeier considers concept acquisition in the context of age differences, Labouvie-Vief in her chapter considers learning and memory phenomena in the context of intellectual ability differences. Thus, to her it makes little sense to look for learning differences per se, as opposed to looking for them as they interact with selected intellec-tual abilities. Echoing the concerns of Cronbach, Jensen, and other psychologists, Labouvie-Vief argues that without considering the con-comitant influence of relevant individual differences variables, pre-dicted learning outcomes are liable to be masked by within-treatment variation.

She reviews a number of attempts to capitalize on a combined experimental–correlational methodology. This begins with a historical review of the literature and ends with a discussion of the successes and failures that she has experienced in her own research. For example, the initial finding that rote memory ability tends to predict performance early in a recall task, whereas intelligence tends to predict performance later in the same task, has not been replicated in subsequent research.

Although such outcomes pose interpretive dilemmas for researchers in this area, Labouvie-Vief concludes on a somewhat optimistic note. She believes that inconsistent patterns of results will force investigators to sharpen their psychological constructs, their measuring instruments, and their experimental treatments in order to obtain valid estimates of Ability X Learning interactions. A nice illustration of the potential educational significance of this attack is provided by Labouvie-Vief's study in which elderly persons were taught to employ effective problem-solving skills.

In the final chapter of Part I, Ghatala and Levin examine in some detail an ability that is assumed to comprise a central component of the Klausmeier model, namely the ability to discriminate previously seen stimuli from prevously unseen ones. In particular, these authors theo-rize about the functional cognitive processes underlying children's recognition memory. In so doing, they manipulate a number of stimulus and instructional variables which are known to influence recognition-memory performance.

With respect to stimulus manipulations, Ghatala and Levin conclude that with the incorporation of a mechanism somewhat akin to Weber's psychophysical law, recognition memory can be accounted for primarily in terms of Underwood's frequency attribute of memory. With respect to instructional manipulations, on the other hand, and based on results obtained using a combined experimental–correlational strategy similar to Labouvie-Vief's, these authors argue that memory attributes other than frequency are implicated.

In the final part of their chapter, Ghatala and Levin relate their findings directly to the Klausmeier conceptual learning model. Further, they specify important next steps to be taken in this area, which include the examination of recognition-memory phenomena in school-assessment situations such as those represented by multiple-choice testing.

The three chapters taken together emphasize the utility of theory-testing and theory-refining research in understanding children's cognitive performance. As will be seen in Parts II and III, this type of research is extremely useful in paving the way for experimental strategies and programs that are aimed at facilitating children's cognitive performance in the classroom.

CHAPTER 1

Conceptual Development during the School Years[1]

Herbert J. Klausmeier

American psychology is changing rapidly, most notably as regards the nature of experimentation and the substance of psychology itself. Piaget's (1970) genetic epistemology, Bruner's (Bruner, Olver, and Greenfield, 1966) instrumental conceptualism, the information theory of Newell and Simon (1972), Davis's (1973) creative problem solving (see also Davis, this volume), Gagné's (1970) cumulative learning, and Guilford's (1967) structure of intellect are representative of recent trends in developmental psychology, the psychology of learning, and psychological testing. The trends are clearly away from simplistic behaviorism toward the investigation of complex learning phenomena such as concept learning, problem solving, and the thinking process itself. Despite these changes, the contribution of psychology to educational theory and practice is less than might be expected (Klausmeier and Hooper, 1974; Rohwer, 1970). Moreover, compartmentalization among the branches of psychology persists; leaders of each branch appear to be unaware of the methods and knowledge of those in other branches (Neimark and Santa, 1975). An integration of the methods and knowledge of the various areas is in order if psychology is to contribute as it should to theory formulation and to understanding children's educational development during the school years.

A MODEL FOR THE ATTAINMENT OF CONCEPTS

An analytic, descriptive model of conceptual learning and development incorporating an integrative approach to theory building has been

[1] This chapter is based on a paper presented at the 1975 annual meeting of the American Educational Research Association, Washington, D.C. The author thanks Patricia S. Allen and Susan M. Markle for reading the chapter and providing helpful comments.

5

formulated (Klausmeier, 1971; Klausmeier, Ghatala, and Frayer, 1974). The model provides a theoretical framework for research on conceptual development and learning during the school years. According to this model, normally developing children and youth attain a given concept at four successively higher levels. As shown in Figure 1, these are *concrete, identity, classificatory,* and *formal.* The ability to learn a concept at each of the four successive levels is explained, first, in terms of the individual being capable of the prerequisite mental operations and, second, in terms of the external conditions that facilitate learning at a particular level. The initial manifestation of a particular mental operation at each level is presumed to be a product of both maturation and learning, or more broadly, of development. The external conditions for learning concepts include instruction designed specifically for particular students at their particular levels of conceptual development. Maturing individuals are able to progress from one level to the next as they become capable of the prerequisite mental operations of a particular level and as they have attained the concept at the prior level.

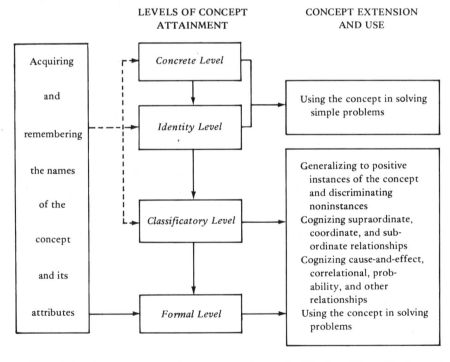

Figure 1. Levels of concept attainment, extension, and utilization. The solid lines and arrows indicate a prerequisite relationship. The broken lines indicate a possible but not prerequisite relationship.

Ability to use a concept in various ways is dependent on an individual's level of attainment. Concepts acquired at only the concrete and identity levels may be used in solving simple problems that require only the relating of sensory perceptions. However, concepts acquired at the more mature classificatory and formal levels may be used in identifying newly encountered instances as examples and nonexamples of the concept. They also may be used in understanding taxonomic and hierarchical relationships of which the particular concept is a part, in understanding principles involving the concept, and in solving problems.

Acquiring the name of the concept and the names of its defining attributes may come at any of the four levels; however, having the name of the concept and the names of its attributes is essential to attaining concepts at the formal level. Individuals may acquire the name about the same time they first attain the concept at lower levels, but this is not a prerequisite condition.

The proposition that a concept is attained at the four successive levels applies to concepts that: (a) have more than one example, (b) have observable examples or representations, and (c) are defined in terms of attributes. Not all concepts are of this kind. Some concepts have only one example, for example, the Earth's **moon.** Some do not have observable examples, for example, **atom, eternity, soul.** Still others are defined in terms of a single dimension, for example, **rough, thin,** or in terms of a relationship, for example, **south, between, above.** Not all levels are applicable to each of these kinds of concepts. The identity level is applicable to concepts that have only one example; the classificatory level is applicable to concepts of one dimension, or expressing a relationship; and the formal level is applicable to concepts that have no observable, classifiable examples. With this introduction to the four levels and the kinds of concepts under consideration, the mental operations pertaining to each level will be discussed.

Concrete Level

Attaining a concept at the concrete level is inferred by the individual's recognition of an object that has been encountered on a prior occasion. The operations involved in attaining this level, as shown in Figure 2, are attending to an object, discriminating it from other objects, representing it internally as an image or trace, and maintaining the representation (remembering). The infant, for example, attends to a large red ball, discriminates it from other objects in the environment, represents the image of the ball internally, maintains the image (remembers), and recognizes the red ball when experienced later in the identical form as initially experienced.

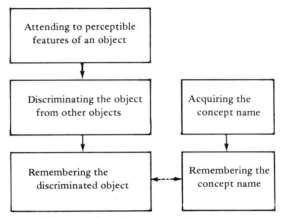

Figure 2. Cognitive operations in concept attainment at the concrete level.

Identity Level

Attainment of a concept at the identity level is inferred by the individual's recognition of an object as the same one previously encountered when the object is observed from a different spatio-temporal perspective or sensed in a different modality, such as hearing or seeing. For example, the child who makes the same response to the family poodle whether seen from straight ahead, from the side, or from various angles has attained the concept of the particular **poodle** at the identity level. As shown in Figure 3, the operations of attending, discriminating, and remembering are involved in attainment at the

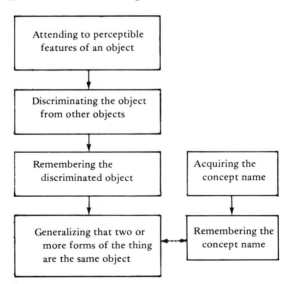

Figure 3. Cognitive operations in concept attainment at the identity level.

identity level as well as at the concrete level. However, concept attainment at the concrete level involves only the discrimination of an object from other objects, whereas attainment at the identity level involves not only discriminating various forms of the same object from other objects, but also generalizing the forms of the particular object as equivalent. Generalizing is the new operation postulated to emerge as a result of learning and maturation that makes attainment at the identity level possible.

Some psychologists (e.g., Gagné, 1970) treat concepts at the concrete and identity levels as multiple discriminations. Piaget (1970) does not differentiate the two levels but refers to them as object concepts. The critical matter is not what they are called, but to explain the internal and external conditions of concept learning at these two lowest levels.

Classificatory Level

As shown in Figure 4, the new mental operation that makes possible attainment of concepts at the classificatory level is generalizing that two or more things are alike in some way. The lowest level of attain-

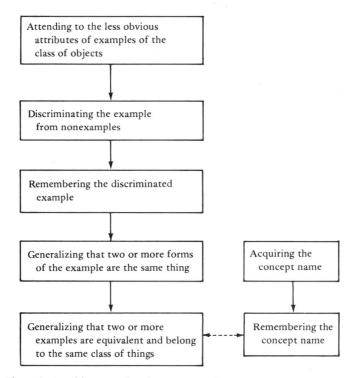

Figure 4. Cognitive operations in concept attainment at the classificatory level.

ment of a concept at a classificatory level is inferred when the individual responds to at least two different examples of the same class of objects, events, or actions as equivalent. For example, when the child treats the family's toy poodle and the neighbor's miniature poodle as poodles, the child has attained a concept of **poodle** at a beginning classificatory level. At this beginning level children seem to be able to classify, basing their classifications on some of the readily perceptible attributes of the concept; but they cannot give the basis of their classifications. It is not clear whether children use global properties or more discrete attributes to attain concepts at this lowest level. What the determinants are probably varies according to children's learning styles (Kagan and Kogan, 1970) and also according to the nature of the particular concepts (Klausmeier, Ghatala, and Frayer, 1974).

Individuals are still at the classificatory level when they can correctly classify a large number of instances as examples and others as nonexamples but cannot define the word that represents the concept nor explain the basis of their classification in terms of the defining attributes of the concept. At a higher phase in attaining concepts at the classificatory level, children seem to be able to discriminate some of the less obvious attributes of the concepts and to generalize correctly to a great variety of examples, some of which are very much like some nonexamples. Also they seem to be able to make the basis of their classification more explicit. In terms of Kofsky's (1966) analysis, the acquisition of a concept at the classificatory level as described here includes the following sequence proposed initially by Inhelder and Piaget (1964): consistent sorting, exhaustive sorting, conservation of classes, knowledge of multiple-class membership, and horizontal classification.

Formal Level

Attainment of a concept at the formal level is inferred when the individual can define the concept in terms of its defining attributes and can evaluate actual or verbally described examples and nonexamples of the particular concept in terms of the presence or absence of the defining attributes. To accomplish this the individual must be able to give the name of the concept and to discriminate and name its defining attributes. Thus, maturing children demonstrate a concept of **tree** at the formal level if when shown some examples of trees, shrubs, and herbs, they properly identify the trees and call them "trees"; discriminate and name the defining attributes of **tree**; give a societally accepted definition of **tree**; and evaluate how examples of trees differ from examples of shrubs and herbs in terms of the defining attritutes of **tree**. (Many college students cannot do all this without further study, but some high

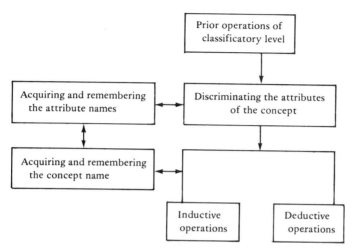

Figure 5. Kinds of operations and strategies of concept attainment at the formal level.

school students who have studied botany can.) When individuals can do these things which are readily tested, it is inferred that they are also capable of performing the cognitive operations at the formal level which are difficult to measure reliably.

As shown in Figure 5, persons may attain a concept at the formal level inductively or deductively if capable of the related operations. Whether persons use either of the two inductive strategies (to be described) or the deductive strategy, depends on the kind of formal and informal instruction they have experienced, the kind of concept instances they have experienced, their age, and other factors.

There are two patterns of inductive operations, as delineated in Figure 6. One pattern involves formulating and evaluating hypotheses regarding the attributes of the concept, and the other involves cognizing the attributes that are common to the positive instances. The operations involved in the inductive hypothesis-testing strategy characterize individuals who cognize the information available to them from both examples and nonexamples of the concept. These individuals apparently reason like this: "Instance 1 is land totally surrounded by water. It is a member of the class. Instance 2 is land that is only partially surrounded by water. It is not a member of the class. Therefore, lands totally surrounded by water belong to the class but lands only partially surrounded by water do not. Being totally surrounded by water is one of the defining attributes of the concept." This individual has attained a partial but accurate concept of **island** based on experience with only one positive and one negative instance. The individual has hypothesized a defining attribute, remembered and evaluated the hypothesis, and inferred the concept.

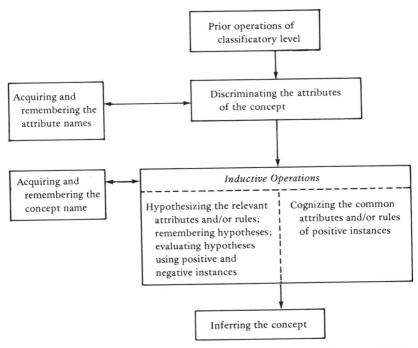

Figure 6. Cognitive operations and inductive strategies of concept attainment at the formal level.

A second way of inferring the concept inductively is by identifying the attributes that are common to the examples of the concept. Some hypothesizing and evaluating of hypotheses may be involved here, but if so, they are presumed to be more at a perceptual level than a conceptual level; also, available information from negative instances is not used. The commonality approach is used by students of elementary school age, apparently because they are either incapable of getting information from nonexamples or cannot carry out the hypothesizing and evaluation operations (Tagatz, 1967). Furthermore, the commonality strategy is the only one possible when only positive instances of the concept are available to the individual. (Many textbooks give only one example with a verbal definition.)

As shown in Figure 7, concepts may be learned through expository instruction. Learning a concept at the formal level deductively when given all the essential information[2] entails meaningful reception learning as described by Ausubel (1968). Information is thus assimilated, remembered, and used in evaluating examples and nonexamples pre-

[2] In our earlier writing (Klausmeier, Ghatala, and Frayer, 1974), the deductive operations of the formal level were subsumed under "cognizing the common attributes."

sented as part of the instruction. The concept thus learned can be used later in identifying examples and nonexamples. Much concept learning at the formal level by upper elementary, high school, and college students follows this pattern. In this kind of expository instruction, students are given the name of the concept, a verbal definition, verbal or pictorial examples and nonexamples, but usually no actual examples of the concepts.

Before leaving this section, a few words should be said about acquiring the names of concepts and their attributes. The importance of language in concept learning is widely acknowledged by American (Bruner, 1964) and Russian psychologists (Vygotsky, 1962). Having the labels of concepts enables the individual to think in symbols in addition to, or rather than, in images. It also permits individuals to attain some concepts, especially at the formal level, through language experiences in the absence of actual examples or pictorial representations. By the present definition of the formal level the individual must know the defining attributes of the concept and must be able to communicate this knowledge. Verbalizing is normally used in this kind of communication. However, deaf individuals and others who lack speech may

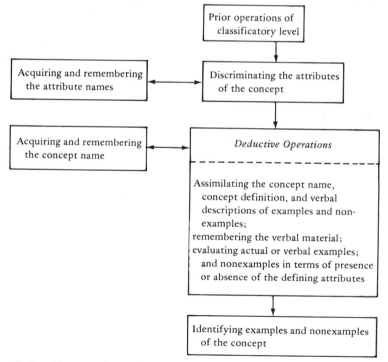

Figure 7. Cognitive operations and deductive strategies of concept attainment at the formal level.

attain concepts at the formal level. They use other types of symbolic communication (for example, sign language). Though speech, per se, is not necessary for the attainment of concepts at the formal level, some means for symbolizing and communicating the concept is essential.

METHODS FOR MEASURING AND DESCRIBING CONCEPTUAL DEVELOPMENT

The preceding description of conceptual learning and development has been formulated over a period of years and is based on behavioral analyses as described by Glaser and Resnick (1972), and on content analyses of many concepts used in learning experiments carried out in laboratories and schools. Until recently, however, certain implied predictions regarding conceptual development at the four levels, and the related uses, had not been verified through research with school-age children. For the purpose of testing certain of these predictions, we constructed scaled batteries to assess the level of conceptual development of children (kindergarten through high school), and began a cross-sectional—longitudinal study in 1972—1973.

Four batteries were used in the study, one battery for each of the following concepts: **equilateral triangle** (Klausmeier, Ingison, Sipple, and Katzenmeyer, 1973a), **noun** (Klausmeier, Ingison, Sipple, and Katzenmeyer, 1973b), **tree** (Klausmeier, Marliave, Katzenmeyer, and Sipple, 1974), and **cutting tool** (Klausmeier, Bernard, Katzenmeyer, and Sipple, 1973). Each battery had seven subtests, one for each of the four levels and one for each of three uses of concepts. The subtests were scored to determine whether an individual had attained each level and each use.

The design of the cross-sectional—longitudinal study as carried out in one school district is shown in Table 1. (A partial replication was completed in another school district.) As shown in the design, provisions were made to determine the effects of repeated testing and of cohort groups. Major testing took place at 1 year intervals at 4 points in time. At the start of the study (1972—1973) there were 50 boys and 50 girls of each grade group (kindergarten, third, sixth, and ninth). At the end of the study, the kindergarten children were third-graders, the third-grade children, sixth-graders, and so on. The fourth and final assessment was completed during 1975—1976.

Based on both the first and second year cross-sectional data analyses (Klausmeier, Allen, and Sipple, 1975; Klausmeier, Sipple, and Allen, 1974), five predictions regarding conceptual development were validated. The results appear so unequivocal that even before the longitudinal data are analyzed, the conclusions that follow are stated in the form of principles of conceptual development.

TABLE 1

Sampling Design for the Cross-Sectional–Longitudinal Descriptive Study[a]

Cohort	Time of Measurement			
	1972–1973	1973–1974	1974–1975	1975–1976
1967	6 (n=100) ⟶7		⟶ 8	⟶9
1968	[Kindergarten] ⟶6 (n=40)		⟶ 7	⟶8 (Cohort effect group)
1967		7 (n=40)		(Test effect group)
1969			6	7 (Cohort effect group)
1967			8	(Test effect group)
1970				6 (Cohort effect group)
1967				
1964	9 (n=100) ⟶10		⟶11	⟶12
1965	[Third Grade]	9 (n=40)	⟶10	⟶11
1964		10 (n=40)		
1966			9	10
1964			11	
1967				9
1964				
1961	12 (n=100) ⟶13		⟶ 14	⟶15
1962	[Sixth Grade]	12 (n=40)	⟶ 13	⟶14
1961		13 (n=40)		
1963			12	13
1961			14	
1964				12
1961				
1958	15 (n=100) ⟶16		⟶ 17	⟶18
1959	[Ninth Grade]	15 (n=40)	⟶ 16	⟶17
1958		16 (n=40)		
1960			15	⟶16
1958			17	
1961				15
1958				18

[a]The entries are approximate mean ages in years.

PRINCIPLES OF CONCEPTUAL DEVELOPMENT

Principle 1. Concepts Are Attained at Four Successively Higher Levels in an Invariant Sequence

Five patterns of passing or failing the tests of the four levels are consistent with the principle of an invariant sequence. The five patterns are as follows:

1. Fail the tests at all four levels (FFFF).
2. Pass the tests at the concrete level and fail the next three levels (PFFF).

3. Pass the tests at the concrete and identity levels but fail at the next two levels (PPFF).
4. Pass the tests at the first three levels but fail at the formal level (PPPF).
5. Pass the tests at all four levels (PPPP).

There are 11 patterns not in accord with the invariant sequence. In these 11 patterns, the student fails a test at an earlier level and then passes a test at a later one (for example, fails the concrete level but passes the identity level, or fails the identity level but passes the classificatory level). Supporting information for the three concepts for which validated assessment scales were available in the first year of the study indicated that 92% of all the children conformed to the five acceptable pass–fail patterns for **equilateral triangle**, 94% for **cutting tool**, and 98% for **noun**. Data on these same three concepts from 1973–1974 are presented in Table 2, and indicate slightly higher percentages conforming; data presented for a fourth concept, **tree**, also show high conformity to the predicted invariant sequence. These very high percentages conforming to the five pass–fail patterns provide the main support for the principle as stated.

Also related to this principle is the finding that the proportion of each successively higher grade group attaining each successive level increased. This conclusion applies to all three concepts, as may be inferred from Figures 8a–d. Information in Figure 8a shows that the percentage of children attaining the concrete level of each of the three concepts increased as a function of the grade group. For example, about 28% of kindergarten children, 96% of the third-graders, 98% of the sixth-graders, and 99% of the ninth-graders fully attained the

TABLE 2

Proportion of Total Subject Population Conforming to Predicted Pass–Fail Patterns of Attainment: Comparing the Four Concepts[a]

	Concept			
Pass–fail sequence	Equilateral triangle ($n=351$)	Cutting tool ($n=349$)	Noun ($n=362$)	Tree ($n=354$)
FFFF	.01	.00	.07	.00
PFFF	.01	.00	.12	.01
PPFF	.14	.06	.41	.15
PPPF	.56	.34	.32	.44
PPPP	.25	.57	.08	.37
Total	.97	.97	1.00	.98

[a]Klausmeier, Sipple, and Allen (1974).

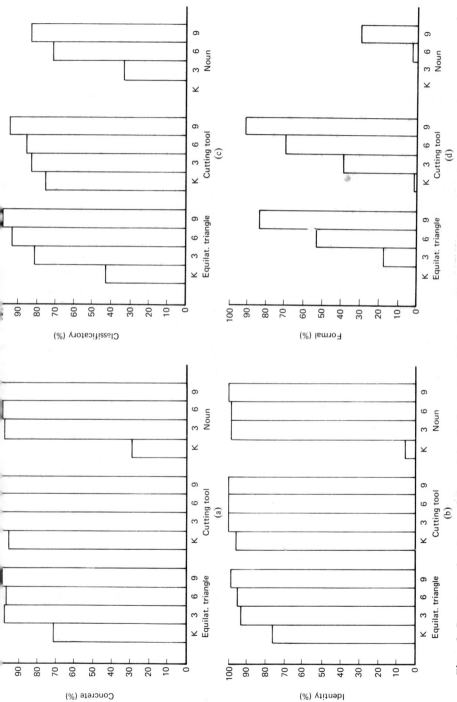

Figure 8. Percentage of each group fully attaining the four concept levels of *equilateral triangle, cutting tool,* and *noun* (Klausmeier, Sipple, and Allen, 1974).

17

concept **noun** at the concrete level. This was the most difficult of the three concepts at the concrete level, particularly for the kindergarten children. One minor exception to the trend is noted. Slightly fewer sixth-graders than third-graders attained the concrete level of **equilateral triangle**.

The same consistent developmental trend is shown in Figure 8b at the identity level of attainment, in Figure 8c at the classificatory level, and in Figure 8d at the formal level. The developmental trend is obvious at the formal level where no kindergarten children attained **equilateral triangle** or **noun**, and the spread among the successive grades was quite large and consistent for the three concepts.

The concepts under discussion are drawn from three different subject fields: English, mathematics, and science. At least 70% of the kindergarten children attained the concrete and identity levels of **equilateral triangle** and **cutting tool**, the two concepts for which there are actual or readily constructed instances in the immediate environment. This suggests that little instruction beyond kindergarten might be needed at these two levels for this kind of concept. On the other hand, attainment of **noun** at the formal level was very low by the sixth- and ninth-grade students. The form class, nominals, and the word for the class of things, **noun**, are human constructions. Although, early in life, the child says words that are classed as nouns, the words themselves stand for many different kinds of things, ideas, events, etc. This lack of observable examples is apparently responsible for the difficulty experienced by the children in identifying certain words as nouns and others as not-nouns. It is probable that the ninth-graders who did not attain **noun** at the classificatory or the formal level will never do so unless they receive further instruction. They will function throughout their adult lives at a low level of conceptualization with respect to **noun** (Nelson and Klausmeier, 1974).

Principle 2. The Attainment Level of Any Given Concept Varies Among Children of the Same Age

Variability in level of attainment among students of the same grade is large, as is visually represented in Figure 8d. About 17% of the third-grade children attained **equilateral triangle** at the formal level and 83% did not; similarly, about 93% of the ninth-grade students attained **cutting tool** at the formal level and about 7% did not. It is interesting, too, that some third-graders attained a higher level than did some ninth-graders.

Principle 3. Various Concepts Are Attained by the Same Children at Different Rates

The first year cross-sectional information indicates that attainment of **cutting tool** at the classificatory and formal levels precedes attainment of **equilateral triangle** and **noun**, as shown in Figures 8c and 8d. In fact, only 30% of the ninth-graders had attained **noun** at the formal level, whereas 90% had attained **cutting tool** at this level. It appears that concepts for which there are few or no perceptible instances (e.g., **noun**) are attained to a certain level (e.g., formal) much later than are concepts for which there are perceptible instances (e.g., **cutting tool**).

Principle 4. Concepts Learned at Successively Higher Levels Are Used More Effectively in Understanding Supraordinate–Subordinate Relationships, in Understanding Principles, and in Solving Problems

Table 3 shows the percentage of children who attained each of the four levels as their highest performance and who also passed tests of the three uses. Without exception, a higher percentage of the students who passed the test at the formal level, in comparison with those who passed only the classificatory-level test, performed each of the uses better. Furthermore, the difference in the actual size of the percentages is large. For example, the percentages of children who attained the formal level of **equilateral triangle**, in comparison with those who attained only the classificatory level, were as follows: 34% and 8% for understanding the supraordinate–subordinate relations, 43% and 5% for understanding the principles, and 34% and 3% for passing the problem-solving test. Only two instances were found of children who had attained a concept at no higher level than the concrete or identity level yet who were able to use the concept beyond solving simple perceptual problems.

In concurrence with this principle, the proportion of children of successively higher grade groups who mastered each concept use increased as is shown in Figures 9a, 9b, and 9c. There was only one exception to this finding. Fourteen percent of the third-graders passed the supraordinate–subordinate test for **equilateral triangle** and only 12% of the sixth-graders did. Despite this single exception, the increase across grade levels on the various uses for every concept is marked. For example, with respect to understanding supraordinate–subordinate relations involving **cutting tool** the increase was as follows: kindergarten— 8%, third grade—43%, sixth grade—66%, and ninth grade—82%.

TABLE 3

Relationship between Attainment Levels and Uses of
Equilateral Triangle, Cutting Tool, and Noun[a]

Concept uses	Concrete as highest			Identity as highest			Classificatory as highest			Formal as highest		
	S-S[b]	Pr[c]	P-S[d]	S-S	Pr	P-S	S-S	Pr	P-S	S-S	Pr	P-S
Equilateral triangle	.00	.00	.00	.07	.00	.00	.08	.05	.03	.34	.43	.34
Cutting tool	.00	.00	.00	.24	.03	.16	.27	.07	.20	.75	.48	.73
Noun	.00	.00	.00	.00	.01	.24	.02	.18	.55	.11	.86	.93

[a]Klausmeier, Sipple, and Allen (1974).
[b]S-S = Understanding supraordinate–subordinate relations.
[c]Pr = Understanding principles.
[d]P-S = Solving problems.

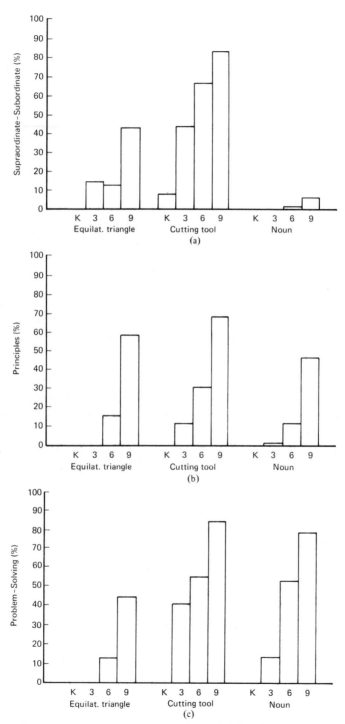

Figure 9. Percentage of each grade group fully attaining the three uses of **equilateral triangle, cutting tool** and **noun** (Klausmeier, Sipple, and Allen, 1974).

It is worth emphasizing that assisting students to attain concepts at the formal level is a worthy educational objective. Attainment at this level facilitates understanding relationships among concepts that comprise either a taxonomy or a hierarchy, understanding principles that involve the particular concept and other concepts, and solving problems involving the particular concept and/or principles.

Principle 5. Having the Names of the Concept and Its Attributes Facilitates Attainment of the Concept at the Various Levels and also the Three Uses of the Concept

Table 4 shows high positive correlations ranging from .43 to .79 between vocabulary score and the scores for the four levels, the three uses, and the combined levels and uses. Inasmuch as these positive relationships were found for concepts drawn from three different subject fields, similar results should be expected with other concepts. The correlations do not imply cause and effect. It seems clear, however, that acquiring the name of the concept and its defining attributes facilitates concept learning and also uses of the concept.

It should be noted that instructional conditions can facilitate conceptual development. Since the internal conditions of concept learning vary according to the four levels, instructional conditions must also vary if the instruction is designed to utilize the available capabilities of the learner. At the classificatory and formal levels, the following conditions have been identified as important in the design of instruction: the proper use of rational sets of examples and nonexamples (Klausmeier and Feldman, 1975; Markle and Tiemann, 1974; Tennyson, Woolley and Merrill, 1972), the proper matching of the examples and non-

TABLE 4

Correlations between Vocabulary Score and Scores on Levels of
Concept Attained, Uses of Attained Concepts, and Combined
Levels and Uses: Equilateral Triangle, Cutting Tool, and Noun [a]

Concept	Four concept levels	Three concept uses	Combined levels and uses
Equilateral triangle	.57	.56	.70
Cutting tool	.51	.43	.52
Noun	.67	.75	.79

[a]Klausmeier, Sipple, and Allen (1974).

examples (Tennyson, Woolley, and Merrill, 1972), the use of definitions (Feldman and Klausmeier, 1974), the use of cues (Frayer, 1970), and teaching a strategy (McMurray, Bernard and Klausmeier, 1974). It appears that knowledge about conceptual learning and instruction is sufficiently complete that instructional materials may be designed with precision to teach concepts (see Chapter 7 of this volume).

CONJECTURES REGARDING THE COURSE
OF CONCEPTUAL LEARNING AND DEVELOPMENT

If the longitudinal data support the cross-sectional data reported herein, what kind of view of conceptual development will be forthcoming? Will it correspond closely to Piagetian stage theory (1970), to Bruner's instrumental conceptualism (Bruner, Olver, and Greenfield, 1966), or to Gagné's cumulative learning theory (Gagné, 1968, 1970)? Before this question can be answered it is essential to examine the possible attributes of stages of cognitive development.

Flavell (1971) described three ways of viewing stages in cognitive development in terms of continuity–discontinuity between successive stages. A discontinuous stage is conceived as analogous to metamorphosis in insects, for example, the metomorphosis of the butterfly with its four distinct stages of egg, larva, pupa, and adult butterfly. This concept of stages is shown in Figure 10a. Let us think of all the mental operations, concepts, and classificatory skills as the cognitive items that comprise each stage. We may now relate these items to the metamorphosis analogy.

Four conclusions follow regarding the cognitive items. First, the items interact with one another in particular ways during each stage in the course of being utilized by the individual; they are not isolated and unrelated. The items of each stage and their relationships characterize the organized cognitive *structures* of the individual at each particular stage of development, just as a distinct and differentiated structure characterizes the butterfly in each particular stage of its development. Second, the structures are qualitatively different rather than just quantitatively different at each successive stage. The structures and their functions are new and different rather than merely being inproved versions of what had already been achieved. Third, within every stage each individual cognitive item—operation, concept, or skill—functions at its asymptotic, mature level of proficiency as soon as it functions at all. For example, children in the preoperational stage this week are incapable of conservation. Next week they will be in the concrete operations stage and will conserve as well as they ever will during the stage of concrete operations. Fourth, all the items that define any

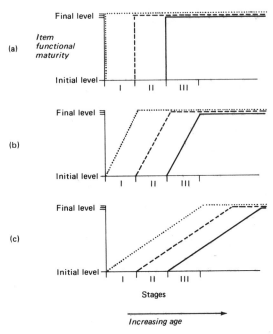

Figure 10. Possible patterns of stages of cognitive development (Based on Flavell, 1971, p. 426).

particular stage make this abrupt, fully mature transition simultaneously. Therefore, in line with these last two conslusions, the child abruptly enters the stage of concrete operations in full command of each operation, and is immediately capable of all the operations that define the stage.

Flavell (1971) does not accept the metamorphosis analogy to cognitive stages and presumes that Piaget does not. Flavell indicates that Piaget regards the structures and functions of each stage as reaching full maturity about the time the first structures and functions of the next stage emerge, as shown in Figure 10b. Flavell's own conception of stages is that shown schematically in Figure 10c. The curves in Figure 10c imply a qualitative change in the maturing individual's repertoire of classification skills, concepts, principles, etc., at the beginning of each stage. But the items that define each stage mature gradually rather than abruptly. The various items of any particular stage do not achieve their mature level until after the end of the stage that marked their initial appearance. It is probable that each of the three patterns just described is accepted by some American psychologists and educators.

In connection with the rate at which various items of a particular stage mature, Flavell depicts three possible patterns, as shown in Figures 11a, 11b, and 11c. Some items may emerge at approximately the same time, but mature at different rates and draw further apart (Figure 11a). Others may emerge at different points in time and reach their final level at the same time (Figure 11b). Still others may emerge at different points in time, mature at parallel rates, and, therefore, also reach full maturity at different times (Figure 11c). The previous information regarding differences in the age at which the concepts **noun** and **tree** are attained at the classificatory and formal levels supports the pattern depicted in Figure 11c, which also corresponds more closely to Bruner's views than to Piaget's.

Bruner's (1964) treatment of enactive, iconic, and symbolic representation indicates that these three means of representation emerge during the first years of life in the order given; however, rather than disappearing successively, each means of representation remains, and may improve, throughout much of the life span. Regarding classification, Bruner *et al.* (1966) identified the modes that persons of various ages (6 through 19) use in classifying things and events.

Figure 12 shows the percentages of groupings based on various modes. Six-year-olds classify according to perceptible properties of objects more than older children; but equally important, the oldest children still do some classifying on the basis of perceptible attributes, such as color, size, and shape. Also, all age groups classify on the basis of the functional attributes of concepts. The use of functional attributes increases as the use of perceptible attributes decreases. Although the use of perceptible attributes decreases relatively, this is not the

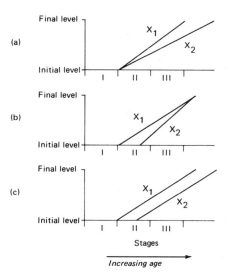

Figure 11. Possible patterns of relationships among dimensions of development (X_1 : Reading performance; X_2 : Mathematics performance) (Based on Flavell, 1971, p. 437).

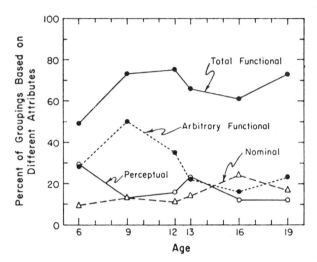

Figure 12. Percentage of students using different modes of classifying, or grouping (Bruner, Olver and Greenfield, 1966, p. 73).

same as indicating that with increasing age there is less effective use of the perceptible attributes. These and other developmental patterns identified by Bruner and his associates (Bruner *et al.*, 1966) do not give strong support to any of the possible stage patterns depicted by Flavell (Figure 10). At the same time, Bruner does recognize qualitative differences in performances, as proposed by Piaget, rather than quantitative and cumulative differences, as explained by Gagné.

Clearly rejecting a stage construct, as depicted in Figures 10a and 10b and possibly also in 10c, Gagné (1968) described both development and learning as changes in capabilities, and defined the difference between learning and development in terms of the amount of time required to bring about the changes. The capabilities resulting from learning and development accrue incrementally and cumulatively, and possibly additively, as successive capabilities are attained (Gagné, 1970, 1974). Gagné apparently presumes that there are no particular points in life, corresponding to stage endings and beginnings, that determine when a person is ready to learn or to develop any particular capability. Rather, the present capabilities of individuals are the determinants of what they can start to learn or develop next.

The various dimensions of conceptual learning and development throughout the school years are still not fully explained. Our data support many of Bruner's viewpoints, although there are some differences. Whereas Bruner specified three modes of acting upon the environment and representing experience as emerging sequentially prior to age 5, the new cognitive operations specified in our model of conceptual learning and development for each successive level of concept attainment appear to emerge with maturation and learning across a longer time interval. For example, discriminating among objects (concrete level) is present before age 2; whereas hypothesizing and evaluating the attributes of certain concepts, for example, **noun**, is not found is most students at age 16. Furthermore, as noted earlier, if the attributes of a concept are readily perceptible, the operations emerge earlier than if they are unobservable and must be inferred.

In summary, it appears that any cognitive theory which is helpful in understanding children's conceptual development during the school years must provide means for operationally defining and measuring cognitive development, explain the internal conditions prerequisite to learning any given level and the situational conditions that facilitate learning at each particular level, and account for the long-term emergence of the qualitatively different cognitive operations and the related cognitive structures that are essential for attaining concepts at each of the particular levels.

REFERENCES

Ausubel, D. P. *Educational psychology: A cognitive view.* New York: Holt, 1968.

Bruner, J. S. The course of cognitive growth. *American Psychologist,* 1964, *19,* 1–15.

Bruner, J. S., Olver, R. R., & Greenfield, P. M. *Studies in cognitive growth.* New York: Wiley, 1966.

Davis, G. A. *Psychology of problem solving: Theory and practice.* New York: Basic Books, 1973.

Feldman, K. V., & Klausmeier, H. J. The effects of two kinds of definition on the concept attainment of fourth and eighth graders. *Journal of Educational Research,* 1974, *67*(5), 219–223.

Flavell, J. H. Stage-related properties of cognitive development. *Cognitive Psychology,* 1971, *2,* 421–453.

Frayer, D. A. *Effects of number of instances and emphasis of relevant attribute values on mastery of geometric concepts by fourth- and sixth-grade children.* Technical Report No. 116. Madison, Wisc.: Wisconsin Research and Development Center for Cognitive Learning, 1970.

Gagné, R. M. Contributions of learning to human development. *Psychological Review,* 1968, *75,* 177–191.

Gagné, R. M. *The conditions of learning* (2nd ed.). New York: Holt, 1970.

Gagné, R. M. *Essentials of learning for instruction.* Hinsdale, Ill: Dryden, 1974.

Glaser, R., and & Resnick, L. B. Instructional psychology. In P. Mussen & M. Rosenzweig (Eds.), *Annual review of psychology.* Palo Alto, Ca.: Annual Reviews, Inc., 1972. Pp. 207–276.

Guilford, J. P. *The nature of human intelligence.* New York: McGraw-Hill, 1967.

Hooper, F. H., & Klausmeier, H. J. *Description and rationale for a longitudinal assessment of children's cognitive development and concept learning.* Working Paper No. 113. Madison, Wisc.: Wisconsin Research and Development Center for Cognitive Learning, 1973.

Inhelder, B., & Piaget, J. *The early growth of logic in the child: Classification and seriation.* New York: Harper & Row, 1964.

Kagan, J., & Kogan, N. Individual variation in cognitive processes. In P. H. Mussen (Ed.), *Carmichael's manual of child psychology.* New York: Wiley, 1970. Pp. 1273–1365.

Klausmeier, H. J. Cognitive operations in concept learning. *Educational Psychologist,* 1971, *9,* 1–8.

Klausmeier, H. J., Allen, P. S., & Sipple, T. S. *Second cross-sectional study of attainment of the concepts equilateral triangle, cutting tool, noun, and tree by children age 6 to 16 of city B.* Technical Report No. 347. Madison, Wisc.: Wisconsin Research and Development Center for Cognitive Learning, 1975.

Klausmeier, H. J., Bernard, M., Katzenmeyer, C., & Sipple, T. *Development of conceptual learning and development assessment series II: Cutting tool.* Working Paper No. 120. Madison, Wisc.: Wisconsin Research and Development Center for Cognitive Learning, 1973.

Klausmeier, H. J., & Feldman, K. V. The effects of a definition and a varying number of examples and nonexamples on concept attainment. *Journal of Educational Psychology,* 1975, *67,* 174–178.

Klausmeier, H. J., Ghatala, E. S., & Frayer, D. A. *Conceptual learning and development: A cognitive view.* New York: Academic Press, 1974.

Klausmeier, H. J., & Hooper, F. Conceptual development and instruction. In F. N. Kerlinger & J. B. Carroll (Eds.), *Review of research in education,* 2. Itasca, Ill.: F. E. Peacock, 1974. Pp. 3–54.

Klausmeier, H. J., Ingison, L. J., Sipple, T. S., & Katzenmeyer, C. G. *Development of conceptual learning and development assessment series I: Equilateral triangle.* Working Paper 119. Madison, Wisc.: Wisconsin Research and Development Center for Cognitive Learning, 1973(a).

Klausmeier, H. J., Ingison, L. J., Sipple, T. S., & Katzenmeyer, C. G. *Development of conceptual learning and development assessment series III: Noun.* Working Paper 121. Madison, Wisc.: Wisconsin Research and Development Center for Cognitive Learning, 1973(b).

Klausmeier, H. J., Marliave, R. S., Katzenmeyer, C. G., & Sipple, T. S. *Development of conceptual learning and development assessment series IV: Tree.* Working Paper No. 126. Madison, Wisc.: Wisconsin Research and Development Center for Cognitive Learning, 1974.

Klausmeier, H. J., Sipple, T. S., & Allen, P. S. *First cross-sectional study of attainment of the concepts equilateral triangle and cutting tool by children age 6 to 16 of city B.* Technical Report No. 288. Madison, Wisc.: Wisconsin Research and Development Center for Cognitive Learning, 1974.

Kofsky, E. A scalogram study of classificatory development. *Child Development,* 1966, *37,* 191–204.

Markle, S. M., & Tiemann, P. W. Some principles of instructional design at higher cognitive levels. In R. Ulrich, T. Stocknik, & J. Mabry, (Eds.) *Control of human behavior,* Vol. III. Glenview, Ill.: Scott, Foresman, 1974. Pp. 312–323.

McMurray, N. E., Bernard, M. E., & Klausmeier, H. J. *Lessons designed to teach fourth grade students the concept equilateral triangle at the formal level of attainment.* Practical Paper No. 14. Madison, Wisc.: Wisconsin Research and Development Center for Cognitive Learning, 1974.

Neimark, E. D., & Santa, J. L. Thinking and concept attainment. In M. R. Rosenzweig & L. W. Porter (Eds.) *Annual Review of psychology.* Palo Alto, Ca.: Annual Reviews, Inc., 1975. Pp. 173–205.

Nelson, G. K., & Klausmeier, H. J. Classificatory behaviors of low-socioeconomic-status children. *Journal of Educational Psychology,* 1974, *66,* 432–438.

Newell, A., & Simon, H. A. *Human problem solving.* Englewood Cliffs, N.J.: Prentice-Hall, 1972.

Piaget, J. Piaget's theory. In P. H. Mussen (Ed.), *Carmichael's manual of child psychology*. New York: Wiley, 1970. Pp. 703–732.

Rohwer, W. D., Jr., Cognitive development and education. In P. H. Mussen (Ed.), *Carmichael's manual of child psychology*. New York: Wiley, 1970. Pp. 1379–1454.

Tagatz, G. E. Effects of strategy, sex, and age on conceptual behavior of elementary school children. *Journal of Educational Psychology*, 1967, *58*, 103–109.

Tennyson, R. D., Woolley, F. R., & Merrill, M. D. Exemplar and nonexemplar variables which produce correct concept classification behavior and specified classification errors. *Journal of Educational Psychology*, 1972, *63*, 144–152.

Vygotsky, L. S. *Thought and language* (E. Hanfmann & G. Vakar, trans.). Cambridge, Mass.: M.I.T. Press, 1962.

CHAPTER 2

Intellectual Abilities and Learning: Retrospect and Prospect

Gisela Labouvie-Vief

During the first half of this century, research into individual differences in intelligence occupied a frontier position in promoting knowledge about the development of intelligence (Baltes and Labouvie, 1973; Carroll, 1974; Charles, 1970; Estes, 1974). But for some time there has been a growing feeling of uneasiness about the concept of intelligence among laymen and scientists alike. This dissatisfaction has its roots in the realization that knowledge about intelligence has thus far contributed little toward its potentially noble function—namely, the optimization of individual instruction. Rather, the primary emphasis has been on the assessment and the selection and deselection of individuals, and many writers (e.g., Baratz and Baratz, 1970; Ginsburg, 1972; Looft, 1973) now feel that research on individual differences in intelligence has tended to aggravate rather than alleviate major problems in our educational settings.

Much of the debate surrounding the intelligence concept has been of a highly emotional nature; but it has also been paralleled, not surprisingly, by a real danger of this area of research winding up in a theoretical blind alley. Historically, the methodology and research knowledge associated with the area of intelligence has been more closely linked to pragmatic than theoretical concerns. Indeed, as Mischel (1968, 1973) has pointed out for the domain of personality variables, the flourishing interest in assessing individual differences has not been paralleled by similarly vigorous efforts to address the question of the *source* of these individual differences. Instead there has often been a tendency to accept the fact that individuals differ in terms of their measured intelligence and to use this as an explanation per se. Thus, to label individuals as more or less intelligent came to be accepted as a *cause* for their behavior—as is quite explicitly implied in the use of such terms as "ability" or "endowment."

31

The tendency to go beyond the descriptive meaning of the existence of individual differences, and to attribute these to differences of qualities of a stable enduring disposition of a fixed, genetic basis has understandably "turned off" many researchers to the domain of intelligence in particular, and to individual differences in general. Thus individual differences research has tended to be separated from mainstream theoretical developments. And as a result, there are still few useful leads to guide process-oriented, hypothesis-testing research about individual differences in intelligence.

But to the educational psychologist, individual differences are a reality that cannot be denied. The problem, to the educational psychologist, becomes one of utilizing information about how individuals differ in order to target specific instructional programs or treatments, depending on individuals' entrance skills. This realization, in fact, underlies a tremendous body of research that has attempted to isolate (primarily on an empirical basis) ways in which individual differences in intelligence and scholastic aptitude might interact with different instructional treatments (for summaries see Berliner and Cahen, 1973; Cronbach and Snow, 1969; Gagné, 1967; Solomon, 1972).

However, the research attacking such Aptitude X Treatment interactions has not fulfilled its promise. Neither has it uncovered a means of assessing individual differences, nor has it successfully integrated them into a process theory to optimize instructional remedies. Due to the traditional separation of approaches dealing with individual differences on the one hand and task parameters on the other (Cronbach, 1957), no useful model to guide the research was available; accordingly, it had to proceed on the basis of trial and error (Solomon, 1972). As a result, research on Aptitude X Treatment interactions has overwhelmed us with a variety of results that are difficult if not impossible to render meaningful, or even to replicate. Many authors, therefore, have concluded that what we need is not so much a continued investigation of Aptitude X Treatment interactions per se, but concentrated efforts on trying to uncover a useful conceptual scheme which may serve on an a priori basis to generate research hypotheses.

While there is no *one* proven way to develop such conceptual models, my own approach reflects a conviction that one way to solve the dilemma may consist in examining "classical" notions of abilities and searching for anchor points in current formulations of learning processes. However, the opposite approach—attempting, from a knowledge of the learning literature, to identify important dimensions of individual differences—is viable as well, and reflected in Levin's (this volume) research on individual differences in picture and word learning. In fact, it is likely that both approaches may eventually converge on a useful theoretical analysis of the ability concept.

ABILITIES AND LEARNING:
SOME GENERAL CONSIDERATIONS

The success of interrelating learning processes and abilities depends on how abilities are defined. This seemingly trivial statement is of some importance as there are different criteria for isolating individual differences variables such as abilities. A considerable part of the difficulty of arriving at meaningful cross-linkages between learning processes and abilities may be based upon the fact that dissimilar criteria are being applied to learning tasks on the one hand and cognitive abilities on the other.

Thus, with regard to intellectual abilities, one is dealing with dimensions of considerable breadth. In fact, it is a popular assumption that intelligence refers to the individual's capacity to profit from experience and to adapt to new situations—as is readily demonstrated by a sampling of definitions of intelligence (e.g., Bayley, 1970; Reese and Lipsitt, 1970). It is easy to see that such definitions are rather elusive when a learning analysis is applied to the definition of an "ability." Indeed, trait and S—R theories traditionally have operated from rather opposite vantage points, the former emphasizing broad, intersituational, generalizable behavior classes, and the latter specific, intrasituational responses (Baltes and Labouvie, 1973; Whiteman, 1964). With the recent surge of interest in cognitive analyses of behavior and its development (Gagné, 1968; Goulet, 1973; Mischel, 1973; Staats, 1971), however, there have been a number of theoretical attempts at offering analyses of broad classes of skills which assume a status of generality similar to that of the ability concept (Labouvie-Vief, Levin, and Urberg, 1975).

The Ability Concept

It may be useful at this point to discuss the meaning of the ability concept, the key term used in psychometric approaches to the study of intelligence. In general, when referring to individual differences in a particular ability, several aspects need to be distinguished (see in particular, Mischel, 1968). The first, most obvious aspect, refers to an attribute (and, specifically, to an intellectual attribute) on which individuals display relatively stable differences. Beyond this rather unassuming and descriptive meaning, however, the ability notion is also used as an explanatory construct, namely, to offer an explanation for the existence of relatively enduring individual differences. Again, two facets may be distinguished here that differ in the extent to which the construct varies on an observed—inferred dimension. The former relates to the legitimacy with which a task can be said to index a particular ability, and the latter to the assumed causes for individual differences in an ability.

Turning to the more descriptive aspect first, we find general agreement among psychometric theorists with the statement that "the abstractions, concepts, or constructs, with which segments of behavioral science must ultimately deal, are not adequately indexed by single, observable responses [Nesselroade, 1970, p. 195]." Rather, a specific variable under study (e.g., a test of synonym identification) is assumed to be representative of a class or set of variables (e.g., verbal ability) that show some conceptual similarity and will, therefore, behave as a coherent unity across a set of conditions. Hence the concern with the interrelations among variables and constructs has taken the form of descriptively identifying classes of variables that show high patterns of intercorrelations.

As in any research effort, however, certain of the steps involved in this descriptive procedure involve implicit theoretical assumptions. For instance, the domain of behaviors thought to constitute "intelligence," the decision of how broad versus how specific an ability should be, or the substantive interpretation of an ability, are all matters that reflect theoretical preferences, and cannot be resolved unless many additional lines of evidence beyond the psychometric one converge to support the interpretation of an ability as more than a statistical unity.

An example from the domain of personality traits may be useful to illustrate this point. Based originally upon correlational information, Cattell and Scheier (1961) proposed to distinguish between two independent forms of anxiety: One is hypothesized to represent a fairly stable attribute of the individual, while the other supposedly is situation-dependent and reflects a response to threat-inducing stimuli. Clearly such a proposition suggests a number of corollary predictions that need to be examined in order to validate the distinction (Bartsch and Nesselroade, 1973; Hodges, 1968). For instance, do the two traits display differential short-term stability? Do they respond, as they should, as separate unities in experimental situations manipulating threat?

In the area of intelligence, however, similar process-oriented validation is sorely lacking. Rather, the identification of abilities has been primarily dependent on the analysis of correlational patterns. There is now agreement that early views of intelligence as a generalized learning ability are too simplistic, and some twenty traits or abilities have been distinguished since Thurstone's (1944) pioneer work in intelligence. A representative sample of these has been published by French, Ekstrom, and Price (1963) in their *Kit of Reference Tests for Cognitive Factors.*

On a more theoretical level, however, there has been considerable disagreement about issues which go beyond the statistical identification of ability factors. In particular, discussions have focused around the problem of how to conceptualize the interrelatedness of the various primaries (e.g., Eysenck, 1966; Humphreys, 1962; McNemar, 1964; Messick, 1973; Vernon, 1965). Guilford (1956, 1966, 1967; Guilford and Hoepfner, 1971), for instance, has proposed a *logical* model based upon a conceptual analysis of similarities among the primaries. He thus advances a three-way scheme, classifying factors according to the *operations* the intellect can perform (cognition, memory, divergent thinking, convergent thinking, evaluation), *contents* on which the operations are performed (figural, symbolic, semantic, behavioral), and *products* resulting from the operations on the content (units, classes, relations, systems, transformations, implications). Other theoreticians, in contrast, propose a structural model based upon psychological considerations—such as the lack of independence of abilities, and the developmental transformations of abilities. In Horn and Cattell's (1967; Horn, 1970) theory of fluid and crystallized intelligence, for instance, the former abilities are assumed to be tied to neurophysiological antecedents and mechanisms, while the latter presumably reflect individual variations in the exposure to a culture's systematic acculturation efforts.

The preceding interpretations are presented here to give a flavor of the multitude of theoretical issues that still are unresolved in psychometric theories of intellectual functioning. Indeed, it must be emphasized that a resolution of these questions cannot take place in the closed system of psychometric models per se, but will depend upon the interfacing of psychometric and process theories of intellectual functioning. Thus, we will next turn to the question of how such an interface has been visualized on a general level.

Process Analysis of Abilities

If stripped of its theoretical surplus meaning, the most essential aspects of the ability concept (such as the number of abilities and their psychological interpretation) cannot be explained within a psychometric framework. Rather, as Anastasi (1970) has cogently argued, such aspects need to be examined by relating the ability notion to current learning theories as well as to formulations about the developmental origin of abilities. In this section I will briefly examine a few propositions relevant to these problems.

Until only fairly recently, the assumption was often made

> ... that intellect is the ability to learn, and that our estimates of it are or should be estimates of ability to learn. To be able to learn harder things or to be able to learn the same things more quickly would then be the single basis of evaluation [Thurstone, 1926, in Estes, 1974, p. 740].

The first really important progress beyond this somewhat simplistic conceptualization was made by Ferguson (1954) in a significant but often neglected contribution. Aware of the fact that the structure of abilities in mature organisms is characterized by a considerable degree of differentiation, Ferguson rejected the idea of a generalized learning ability. He proposed that over the course of development, and as a function of training in specific problem areas and learning situations, a number of distinct classes of abilities would emerge. These, he assumed, did not essentially differ from the forms of learning examined in the laboratory. However, they represented relatively overlearned skills which have reached an asymptote, and thus were unlikely to show dramatic variations over brief time periods.

In the relatively mature organism, Ferguson assumed, these "abilities" constitute relatively broad classes of behavior. The aspect of breadth, or consistency, across situations was explained by pointing to the process of transfer, or the interactive (facilitative or interfering) effect of having learned one response upon the learning of other related responses. Equating the learning of a mature organism essentially with transfer learning, he proposed that abilities are those variables which exert transfer effects in any new learning situation. Hence, ability would refer to that class of behaviors across which learning transfers. Empirically, the behaviors representing this response class should be correlated and form the psychometrician's "ability."

Several of those who have since addressed themselves to the issue (Anastasi, 1970; Baltes & Nesselroade, 1973; Carroll, 1966; Fowler, 1969; Gagné, 1968; Jensen, 1971; Staats, 1971; Whiteman, 1964) have relied on the transfer notion as a potential bridge between abilities and learning processes. In addition, they have clarified some of the possible sources of transfer. Whiteman (1964) related the ability notion to any broadly applicable skill or strategy. He refers to Harlow's (1959) research on learning sets where, as a result of learning a sequence of simple two-choice discrimination problems, the organism eventually acquires a generalizable, effective strategy that permits the solution of such problems in one or two trials. Hence, if individuals differing in learning set experience were assessed across a range in problems, they would tend to perform consistently (poorly or well) across the problem set, and a factor would emerge. Similar considerations would hold for the concept of a Piagetian operation—as well as for a number of the cognitive strategies that now are proliferating with the "new look" cognitive orientation in learning research.

Ferguson himself was never specific in pinpointing the exact nature of the skills that could form a basis for transfer. However, his and similar viewpoints suggest that it would be necessary to attempt a systematic cross-mapping of those processes that play an important part in both ability test and learning performances. Jensen (1967) has used the genotype–phenotype distinction as an analogy to this conceptualization. Accordingly, *phenotypes* would be defined by variations in task characteristics, treatment parameters, stages of practice, etc., while *genotypes* would refer to those basic processes or skills that may be utilized across a range of tasks under varying phenotype conditions.

The first author to attempt such a cross-mapping was Thorndike (1926) who proposed an interpretation of intelligence in terms of the learning theory of his time:

> The standard orthodox view of the surface nature of intelligence has been that it is divided rather sharply into a lower half, mere connection-forming or the association of ideas, which acquires information and specialized habits of thinking; and a higher half characterized by abstraction, generalization, the perception and use of relations and the selection and control of habits in inference or reasoning, and ability to manage novel or original tasks. . . . The hypothesis which we represent and shall defend admits the distinction in respect of surface behavior, but asserts that in their deeper nature the higher forms of intellectual operation are identical with mere association or connection forming but requiring *many more of them* . . . [Thorndike, 1926, in Estes, 1974, p. 741].

According to Estes (1974), the number-of-connections hypothesis provded to be too meager conceptually to arouse much enthusiasm among psychologists. However, the assumption that intellectual skills may somehow be divided into two classes—"lower," associative skills (such as tests of memory, vocabulary, and information) and "higher," relational skills (such as abstraction and induction)—has subsequently been pursued along a number of different lines. On the one hand, the fluid–crystallized distinction of intellectual abilities mentioned in the previous section is clearly reminiscent of such a conceptualization. Similar propositions have been offered from the literature on learning processes as well (Goulet, 1973; Kendler and Kendler, 1962; White, 1965). And indeed, Jensen (1968, 1969, 1970, 1971) has proposed that the same classification may be applied toward a cross-mapping of *both* ability tests and learning performance. In Jensen's terminology, level I abilities (rote processes) refer to those mental processes that involve little elaboration of stimulus inputs. Level II (or conceptual) processes, in contrast, involve elaboration and transformation of stimulus inputs. Hence, diverse performance indices may be reduced to this rote–conceptual continuum. For instance, level I processes would be indicated by digit span tests, as well as serial recall and certain forms of free-recall and paired-associate learning (i.e., presented under conditions not conducive to elaboration). Level II processes, on the other hand, would be indicated by tests of abstract reasoning as well as learning performance in tasks that are highly conducive to elaborative activity.

A somewhat different duo-process conceptualization has recently been proposed by Das (1973). This author argued that Jensen's rote–conceptual classification may be of apparent rather than real validity, as various tests of "memory" often fail to intercorrelate and indeed may tap distinctly different processes. Das proposes that Jensen's distinction may be a rather superficial one based upon varying levels of complexities rather than distinct processes, and he argues that a more valid model could be based upon the consideration of whether information in a task is being processed in a successive or in a simultaneous fashion. We will return to Das's argument later; suffice it to state that his proposition ought to remind us that a truly successful linkage between learning processes and abilities must be able to go beyond merely apparent similarities to task format.

RELATIONSHIPS BETWEEN ABILITIES AND LEARNING: SOME REPRESENTATIVE RESEARCH

As indicated in the previous section, ideally the demonstration of a mutual interdependence of ability test and learning performance should be based upon an identification of proceses and/or basic mechanisms (Jensen, 1967) which produce patterns of intercorrelations among performance parameters. However, such unifying frameworks are rather meager, and much of the research has taken a descriptive and exploratory stance. Nevertheless, this research has produced some positive conclusions, both empirical and methodological in nature, that we will examine in this section.

Overview

Many of the earlier studies on Learning X Ability interactions were intended as a test of the conjecture that "intelligence" and "learning ability" are intimately related concepts. Not surprisingly, this assumption proved to be rather simplistic. First, intelligence itself does not constitute a unidimensional concept. Second, there is no unitary process permeating all learning—a conclusion derived from a number of key studies. In general, intercorrelations between different kinds of learning tasks proved very low (e.g., Husband, 1939, 1941; Roberts, 1968–1969; Stevenson et al., 1968; Stevenson and Odom, 1965), thus suggesting a number of separate interindividual differences dimensions in learning performance.

In a series of dissertations at Princeton University (Allison, 1960; Bunderson, 1965; Duncanson, 1964; Stake, 1961), an attempt was made to identify such individual differences dimensions in learning tasks in terms of known ability marker tests. These studies often involved some preliminary hypotheses about the formation of common factors among the samples of learning tasks and ability markers used. However, the outcomes of this research have tended to be rather pessimistic. In general, it was possible to demonstrate a number of factors confined either to the ability or the learning domain, but the cross-relationships proved to be rather few and poorly replicable.

Yet a few findings have been quite consistent and are worth noting in this context. In particular, it was repeatedly found that paired-associate tasks, originally assumed to tap rote processes, tended to correlate not only with memory abilities but with reasoning factors as well (Duncanson, 1964, 1966; Stake, 1961). This result has been substantiated, on a more global level, by Stevenson and his associates (Stevenson et al., 1968; Stevenson and Odom, 1965). In this research, a general IQ measure was found to be most consistently correlated with paired-associate tasks, as well as with verbal and figural rote memory tasks. We will take up this finding later, as it has some relevance to a redefinition of the nature of rote processes.

Concept learning has also been matched with ability markers, although the results are somewhat more equivocal. Neither Stake (1961) nor Duncanson (1964) were able to detect any substantial loadings of their concept learning tasks on any of the common ability factors. Stevenson et al. (1968) and Stevenson and Odom (1965) similarly reported low correlations between concept formation tasks and IQ. However, both Allison (1960) and Bunderson (1965) found meaningful cross-correlations. These involved, among others, a loading of concept tasks on reasoning tests. Lemke, Klausmeier, and Harris (1967) also found that the concept attainment and information processing tasks were consistently correlated with performance on tests of general and inductive reasoning (see also Dunham and Bunderson, 1969).

In general, however, this research has failed to offer a conclusive contribution to the clarification of processes basic to the various ability classifications. According to Jensen (1967), this inconclusiveness is the result of severe deficiencies of a conceptual nature: (a) the absence of models defining the structure of learning tasks, and (b) the lack of theories specifying the linkage between the structure of learning tasks and ability structure. Jensen's first point relates to the need for conceptualizing a universe of learning performances, or phenotypes—defined by variations in task characteristics, treatment parameters, stages of practice, etc.—and of attempting to structure this universe in terms of genotypes, or sets of pervasive processes and mechanisms. Such a unifying theory of learning is not presently available (see also Stevenson *et al.*, 1968). Rather, what is offered are structural analyses of individual tasks and the processes involved in their solution; The generalizability of such processes across tasks is rarely examined.

The absence of a structuring of genotypes has, according to Jensen (1967), resulted in a wide sampling of phenotypes from the learning domain and a very sparse sampling of tasks defining a particular genotype. As a result, hypothesized factors have tended to be "underdetermined," resulting in both a lack of common factors among learning tasks and a lack of interpretable learning–ability relationships.

Moreover, the lack of such models has resulted in a rather haphazard sampling of abilities (see also Dunham, Guilford and Hoepfner, 1968). One is overwhelmed by the sheer number of ability markers sampled more or less arbitrarily from the intelligence domain with little attempt to justify their relevance to the learning tasks included. This procedure has tended to produce a confusing multitude of relationships that are difficult to interpret in an ad hoc fashion. Thus, one must concur with the Dunham *et al.* (1968) assessment that research into learning–ability cross-linkages will profit from an orientation toward model building and hypothesis testing. This will require a concentration not merely on the description of learning–ability covariation patterns, but also attempts at manipulating such patterns by incorporating treatment parameters and hypotheses with regard to their effects on learning–ability interactions.

The criticims by Jensen (1967) and Dunham *et al.* (1968) of the prevalent mode of attempting to define cross-linkages between learning tasks and ability dimensions appear to carry an important message. In many ways, progress in this field of research would be more promising if it were less ambitious in attempting to answer all questions in a single study, but proceeded in the programmatic, step-by-step fashion of formulating hypotheses of how specific learning tasks align with a restricted set of abilities. Unlike many of the earlier efforts, such approaches would also have to center on a more careful consideration of tasks variations (as well as their interaction with age and/or practice) that would have modifying effect on learning–ability covariation patterns. As Ferguson (1954) postulated two decades ago, this would mean that the factors related to individual differences under a specified treatment condition or stage of learning may not be related, or may be related in a different way, to performance in another condition or stage of learning.

As an example, consider the notion (implicit in many of the pioneer studies on learning–ability covariations) that paired-associate learning should tap rote processes, and consequently tend to covary with psychometric tests of rote memory. Such a statement is meaningless unless the specific conditions (task- and subject-related) are pointed out under which paired-associate learning is assessed. Thus we know that in adult subject populations this task is one that involves a rich amount of abstract conceptual activity; at the same time, the ease with which such conceptual activity is induced varies considerably with such parameters as age, state of acquisition, mode of presentation, and instructional variations (Levin, this volume; Reese, 1970; Rohwer, 1970). Consequently, one would expect a *fluctuant* relationship between any task category and a selected set of abilities—yet a relationship that, at the same time, follows a lawful pattern.

It is important, then, to realize that of particular significance for the understanding of learning–ability covariation patterns are studies that attempt to modify such relationships experimentally. We will, in the following paragraphs, examine a few selected lines of research which have attempted to clarify the nature of ability concepts by the systematic introduction of experimental modifications.

Abilities and Psychomotor Learning

The most comprehensive and successful attempt thus far to come up with a process taxonomy that would spell out the linkage between abilities and learning performance has come, not from the area of verbal learning, but from that of learning complex psychomotor tasks. Since this work in many ways exemplifies the utility of such an attempt it will be summarized here.

The research program to be discussed originated from an attempt to develop psychomotor tests for the prediction of aircraft pilot success (Fleishman, 1967, 1972; Fleishman and Bartlett, 1969). The aim was to develop a taxonomy of basic processes that could describe a large number of perceptual–motor abilities. This taxonomy was, in turn, to be used as a system for predicting subjects' learning of a variety of psychomotor tasks under changing procedural conditions.

In the beginning—and characteristic of what was said earlier about the psychometrician's methodology—Fleishman and his co-workers did extensive factor-analytic work on a universe of psychomotor tests and tasks whose predictive validity for pilot success had been ascertained. As is true for ability research in general, many of the isolated ability factors suggested various interpretations as to the processes basic to performance. Although research in intelligence has usually halted at this step Fleishman, in a series of programmatic, interlocking studies, introduced a number of task variations to sharpen or limit the interpretations of the abilities.

One example (cf. Fleishman, 1972) is a rate control factor that was found to be common to a number of tracking tasks. To examine its generality, additional tasks were developed to test whether this factor extended to tasks where the subject was not following a target, but had to time a movement in relation to changing stimulus rates. After the interpretation of this factor was extended to such tasks, additional studies were performed to find whether the rate control factor emphasized an ability to judge stimulus rates as distinguished from an ability to actually time an adjustive movement (response) to a stimulus. Subjects were presented with a motion-picture task in which they were required to extrapolate the course of an airplane moving across a screen, but no adjustive movement was required and the response was simply indicated on an answer sheet. This task, however, was found to be unrelated to the other rate control tasks, and the factor interpretation therefore had to generalize to a situation where an adjustive response actually was asked for.

In similar sequences of studies, Fleishman eventually identified eleven perceptual–motor abilities and nine factors related to physical proficiency that accounted for subject variability in the universe of psychomotor tasks. How can such a taxonomy help in isolating a set of processes about Task X Ability interactions? In Fleishman's (1972) words, the method was

> . . . to develop tasks that can be varied along specified physical dimensions and to administer these tasks varied systematically along these dimensions to groups of subjects who also receive a series of "reference" tasks that are known to sample certain more general abilities (e.g., spatial orientation, control precision, etc.). Correlations between these reference tasks and scores on variations of the criterion task specify the ability requirements (and changes in these requirements) as a function of task variations [p. 1022].

In general, these studies not only suggested that ability requirements often change systematically with variations in task parameters, but also that the abilities "called for" at different stages of learning one task undergo shifts (Fleishman and Fruchter, 1960; Fleishman and Hempel, 1956; Parker and Fleishman, 1960, 1961). Typically, it was found that certain abilities discriminated between individuals high and low in performance on the learning task primarily at early stages of learning, while other abilities better discriminated at advanced stages. For instance, in a task requiring quick response to patterns of light signals, it was found that early in learning, spatial and verbal abilities predicted performance best, while the motor abilities measured appeared unimportant. At later states of learning, however, it was the motor abilities that best discriminated high and low learning proficiency. A similar result was also observed by Kohfeld (1966).

Fleishman (1972) himself elaborated on the broader significance of his results:

> Clearly, the possibility of different ability requirements for initial stages of learning in comparison with ability requirements of final stages of proficiency can have important implications for the prediction of ultimate task performance. Such shifts also have important implications regarding the nature of skill training and the emphasis that should be placed at various stages of practice. If the abilities required by a task change during the course of the learning period, a clear distinction between final proficiency and proficiency during training must be maintained in developing predictive instruments. Also, it may be possible to increase the efficiency of skill training by concentrating throughout the training period on those abilities required for final proficiency, rather than on those abilities required only in the early stages of skill acquisition [p. 1025].

This reasoning was applied in a study by Parker and Fleishman (1961), who developed a special training program for a highly complex flying simulation task, based upon their prior knowledge of those abilities that were important at different stages of learning this task. In this study, the special training group was found to learn at a faster rate, and to reach higher proficiency levels than groups of subjects learning under no special program.

Cognitive Abilities and Learning Strategies: From Correlation to Experiment

Fleishman's approach in many ways exemplifies the validity of the contention that research attempting to cross-map abilities and learning processes ought to proceed in a hypothesis-oriented, programmatic fashion in which the selection of individual differences measures and treatments is based upon specific hypotheses about their interactions, and that is predicated on the assumption that the relationship between abilities and learning is modified by changing task conditions. It might be noted, though, that Fleishman worked with a certain advantage if compared to a researcher starting a similar program with an already well structured domain of theory—and its associated measurement instruments—as is no doubt true if one were interested in cognitive abilities. The fact that he attempted to isolate meaningful individual differences dimensions for the same domain of psychomotor performances he eventually wanted to explicate and predict may have assured a degree of continuity that one may not necessarily be able to replicate when working in the areas of intellectual functioning. With this cautionary note in mind, let us then examine what substantive knowledge we have gained from similar research in the area of intellectual abilities.

In general, the studies to be cited were predicated on the assumption that the pattern of intercorrelations observed between abilities and learning performance reflects the operation of different strategies or mediational skills. In general, this assumption has been tested by manipulating those strategies that presumably play an important role, and by examining whether the resulting changes in learning–ability covariation followed the expected pattern.

On an empirical level, the research has uncovered a few differentiated relationships. Dunham and Bunderson (1969) administered a series of concept problems under two instructional conditions, decision-rule instruction and no-rule instruction. Unlike most of the research criticized earlier, this study is notable for its selection of very few markers for memory and reasoning abilities. Although results did not show any treatment-related differences in acquisition of concepts per se, clear-cut differences in learning–ability covariation were found between the two treatment groups. Associative memory and inductive reasoning were strongly related to performance under no-rule instruction, while induction and general reasoning were related to decision-rule instruction.

Several studies have not directly manipulated strategy choice, but rather examined practice-related changes in learning–ability interactions. Games (1962), relating a series of verbal learning tasks to rote and span memory factors, observed a shift in loading away from the span factor and towards the rote factor. Bunderson (1965) also found changes in factorial composition of concept formation tasks at different stages of practice. Specifically, perceptual speed and incidental memory contributed most strongly to early learning, while inductive and general reasoning were more predictive at later stages. Dunham et al. (1968) similarly examined performance in figural, symbolic, and semantic concept learning problems and their changing relationships to 15 reference factors. Again, systematic but quite complex changes in factorial composition were observed as learning proceeded.

A few studies have looked at the interaction of treatment and practice parameters with changes in learning–ability covariations. Roberts (1968–1969), administered a vocabulary learning task in which subjects learned word meaning either from synonyms or from dictionary definitions. Results showed that for the synonym group, the overall relationship of abilities and learning was initially positive and then declined; for the dictionary group, however, there was neither a significant overall relationship nor any notable trend. In a related vein, Frederiksen (1969) designed a study based on the hypothesis that choice of mediational strategies, if manipulated by treatment parameters, would produce diverging trial-to-trial changes in the covariation pattern between a set of ability tests on the one hand, and a set of factor-analytically derived response parameters on the other. A recall task was administered under three conditions: serial anticipation, free recall, and recall in clusters of five. Distinct patterns of covariation between learning and ability measures were demonstrated for each treatment group. Moreover, a significant overall relationship between abilities and learning existed for the free recall and clusters group, but not for the serial anticipation group.

From an empirical perspective the above studies are encouraging, since they suggest that it may be possible to differentiate the pattern of learning–ability interrelations. However, from a theoretical perspective, they are more difficult to interpret; Often the nature of the processes underlying practice- and treatment-related changes is far from clear. Hence, it would be advantageous to gear variations in task parameters specifically toward modifying processes that are well understood.

An attempt to specify those processes that may mediate changing covariation patterns between measures of learning and abilities was made by Labouvie-Vief and her associates (Labouvie, Frohring, Baltes, and Goulet, 1973; Labouvie-Vief, Levin, and Urberg, 1975) in a series of four experiments. This research was based on the associative–conceptual distinction inherent in many current formulations of developmental learning processes (Goulet, 1973; Jensen, 1971; Kendler and Kendler, 1970; Rohwer, 1973), and it was hypothesized that the pattern of intercorrelations between ability variables and learning effectiveness would reflect the extent to which subjects utilized (or did not utilize) a conceptual (as opposed to a rote) strategy. The task selected was free-recall learning, and an attempt was made to manipulate the degree to which subjects would rely on a conceptual strategy—namely, organizational chunking (Tulving, 1968).

In the first study (Labouvie et al.,973), the experimental parameters manipulated were practice and timing of recall (delayed versus immediate). It was hypothesized that conditions that facilitated organizational chunking would produce a high correlation between general reasoning abilities and free recall, while under more antagonists conditions, variables of the rote-memory type would be more predictive. Since both practice and a delay between stimulus presentation and recall are known to enhance organizational activity (e.g., Shuell, 1969) two main hypotheses were formulated. One involved differential recall–ability relationships between immediate and delayed timing of recall; and the other, changes in ability–recall covariation as a function of acquisition stage. Specifically, it was expected (a) that recall measures would show a strong relationship to general intelligence under delayed recall, while under immediate recall memory variables would show the strongest relationship to recall performance, and (b) that the overall contribution of memory variables to recall performance would be strongest during the early stages of learning, while at later stages the relationship with general intelligence variables would increase.

In terms of overall pattern, the results of this study confirmed the predictions with surprising clarity. Table 1 summarizes the multiple and canonical correlations that were computed to obtain a statistical assessment of these differences in correlational patterns. The overall relationship, as indicated by the canonical correlation coefficients (last column of Table 1) shows divergent results for the two treatment conditions. Although only the canonical correlation between primary mental abilities (PMA) variables and recall scores is statistically significant, the pattern suggests that intelligence variables relate most strongly to delayed recall, whereas memory variables are most predictive under immediate recall.

The multiple correlations between marker variables and trial scores at specific stages of acquisition (first four columns of Table 1) also

TABLE 1
Summary of Multiple and Canonical
Correlation Analyses[a]

Treatment group	Blocks of trials[b]				
	1–4	5–8	9–12	13–16	1–16
PMA					
Delay	.32	.29	.54*	.53*	.77**
no delay	.18	.30	.23	.23	.44
combined	.19	.26	.33	.32	—
Memory					
Delay	.42	.32	.37	.29	.45
no delay	.56**	.55**	.38	.32	.60
combined	.46**	.40*	.35	.28	—

[a]From Labouvie *et al.* (1973).

[b]Cell entries in first four columns are multiple correlation coefficients using Primary Mental Abilities (PMA) or memory variables as predictors and mean recall scores at a specified block of trials as criteria. Cell entries in last column are canonical correlations using PMA or memory variables as predictors and the four recall scores as criterion set.

*$p < .025$.

**$p < .01$.

support this notion of a differential relationship, in addition to verifying the hypothesized trial-to-trial pattern. On the one hand, considering delayed recall, there is an increase in the multiple correlation between recall and intelligence tests; the correlation between memory variables and recall performance (being nonsignificant to start with) shows a systematic decrease over trials. On the other hand, considering no-delay recall performance, it is the set of memory variables that shows a strong initial correlation to recall, followed by a systematic trial-related decrease, whereas the intelligence variables in this case do not exhibit a significant relationship to recall. Thus, intelligence variables are found to be good predictors for later stages of delayed recall, while memory variables are good predictors for early stages of immediate recall.

It appeared justified, then, to conclude that the particular hypothesis-testing framework adopted might be a powerful one in organizing interactions between abilities and learning. However, the picture became much more complex when we attempted to replicate and extend the findings of the first study. In a second experiment (Labouvie-Vief *et al.*, 1975, Experiment 1), we used both age and prelearning instructions to influence organizational processes in free recall. Thus, this study represents an attempt to extend the earlier research developmentally, since age has been found to be a potent variable affecting strategies in free-recall learning (e.g., Jensen and Frederiksen, 1973; Laurence, 1966; Rosner, 1971). It was predicted that older subjects would demonstrate a more strategic approach to free recall. Moreover, these age differences were expected to interact with the type of prelearning instructions presented. Specifically, it was predicted that if subjects were instructed to form mediational links or chunks between items, an increased emphasis on conceptual activity would result, which would in turn be reflected by an increased relationship between free recall and reasoning or general intelligence variables. Conversely, if subjects were provided with a strategy that interfered with chunking activity (thereby rendering the learning task more rote-like), a corresponding decrease in the contribution of reasoning and intelligence variables, and an increase in the contribution of rote memory variables would be observed.

Parallel predictions were derived for a third experiment (Labouvie-Vief *et al.*, 1975, Experiment 2). In this study we utilized timing of recall instead of instructional variations. The results of both experiments, however, were somewhat disappointing. First, Digit Span (a test of rote memory) failed to show any substantial relationship to recall performance. And second, there was little evidence for any differentiations with recall throughout all treatment conditions and stages of acquisition.

The interpretation of these findings, however, was somewhat obviated due to the fact that neither the prelearning instructions nor the timing of recall differentiated among subjects' performance, in terms of either overall recall or trial-related changes. Hence, although the hypotheses associated with these two studies may have been plausible, they may have been unsupported due to the fact that the task parameters were not potent enough. In a fourth study (Labouvie-Vief *et al.*, 1975, Experiment 3), therefore, we administered a paired-associate learning task which was employed under one of three variations designed to affect the degree of rote or conceptual activity engaged in by the children. In previous research (see Levin's chapter in this volume) this task has been found to produce dramatic performance differences as a function of instructional manipulations—as opposed to the usually smaller free-recall differences produced by similar parameters. Therefore, one group fourth-grade children was presented the learning task under a comfortable three-second rate condition; for a second group the rate was reduced from three seconds to one (in order to increase the reliance on rote activity); and in a third group, the comfortable rate was maintained but prior to the task subjects were instructed to imagine an interaction between the items to be associated (in order to provide subjects with a potentially helpful learning strategy).

The markers employed in this study were a digit span test ("rote" memory) and Raven's Progressive Matrices (a test of reasoning). When we computed partial correlations between paired-associate performance (summed over three trials) and each of these two markers (the other markers partialed out), we indeed found some support for the hypotheses. These partial correlations are presented in Table 2.

Two aspects of the data in Table 2 are worth pointing out: first, a stronger relationship between associative learning and Raven performance than between associative learning and digit span in the standard condition; and second, a difference in patterns between the strategy and speeded conditions. With regard to the former, this finding underscores previous agruments that so-called "rote-learning" tasks are anything but that (see Rohwer and Levin, 1971). If they were, then the short-term memory processes called upon in reproducing a series of digits should similarly be called upon in associating pairs of words, but the correlational data suggest that they are not. Rather, it appears that paired-associate learning may call upon some of the reasoning and conceptual processes involved in Raven performance. With regard to the latter, when subjects are required to employ a cognitive strategy in the learning task the relationship with Raven performance is similarly

TABLE 2
Summary of Partial Correlation Analyses[a]

	Condition		
Ability	Standard (n=17)	Strategy (n=17)	Speeded (n=18)
Raven	467*,[b]	514*	−060
Digit Span	130	367	356

[a]From Labouvie-Vief et al. (1975, Experiment 3).
[b]Decimals are omitted throughout.
*p <.05, one-tailed.

strong; whereas, when the learning task is speeded to the point where such cognitive processes cannot be effectively utilized the relationship disappears.

This interpretation was further supported when the data were subjected to further analysis. For both markers separately, we divided the subjects into high and low scorers based upon their being above or below the median of the respective test. Using these high–low classifications and the three experimental conditions as factors, we then performed analyses of variance on the paired-associate data.

Mean paired-associate performance across trials, according to ability classifications and experimental conditions may be found in Table 3. Based on the analysis of variance it may be concluded that treatment-related variation was indeed produced ($p < .001$)—unlike the results of the previous two experiments—with the performance of strategy sub-

TABLE 3
Mean Paired-Associate Performance, as a Function of Ability
Classifications and Experimental Conditions[a]

	Standard		Strategy		Speeded	
Ability	High	Low	High	Low	High	Low
Raven	13.50	11.09	23.12	17.67	8.86	7.36
Digit span	10.83	12.54	22.75	18.00	6.54	10.14

[a]From Labouvie-Vief et al. (1975, Experiment 3).

jects being highest (mean = 20.24), that of standard subjects intermediate (11.94), and that of speeded subjects lowest (7.94).

Concerning the major hypothesis, when high and low Raven classifications were compared within each treatment condition it was found, according to predictions, that the largest different occurred in the strategy condition ($p < .05$, one-tailed), a difference of about 5.5 items (see Table 3). This difference is reduced to about 2.5 and 1.5 items in the standard and speeded conditions, respectively, with neither resulting in a significant classification effect.

Consistent with the correlational data, no significant differences due to digit span classifications were detected. Just as in the previous studies, this test failed to show any reliable correlations with learning effectiveness.

Concluding Commentary on Cognitive Abilities and Learning Strategies

What may we conclude, at this point, about the success of attempting to relate learning strategies to a variety of measures of intelligence? In general, the overall pattern of successes and failures in the research cited suggests some optimism for approaches aimed at cross-linking learning processes and intellectual abilities, since a number of studies indeed report differentiated patterns that appear to be meaningful. Yet there are also sufficient negative results to temper an overly enthusiastic position. And it is of importance to speculate on the reason for a lack of success, as well, if we wish to derive some constructive guidelines for further research.

Recall in this context the basic rationale underlying the approach adopted here: A successful linkage between abilities and learning processes, in this view, ultimately requires the conceptualization of a universe of learning performances or phenotypes, and the structuring of this universe in terms of genotypes or sets of basic processes. In line with this reasoning, most of the cited research utilized a number of task variations that were hypothesized to tap differential processes and, thereby, to produce predictable changes in the covariation pattern with selected abilities. And hence, such an analysis suggests that the reason for a lack of success may be sought in two factors which may have been less than optimally attended to: (a) the particular selection and/or traditional interpretation of ability factors, and (b) the treatment conditions utilized.

With regard to the treatment conditions, two of the Labouvie-Vief et al. (1975) studies observed that the manipulations did not affect the amount recalled. It was concluded in this research that the failure to isolate interpretable differentiations in covariation pattern was not necessarily due to flaws in the approach per se, but rather to the lack of potency of treatment conditions. And it would appear that the same reasoning applies to a number of other studies (Dunham and Bunderson, 1969; Frederiksen, 1969; Labouvie et al., 1973) which, although producing changes in ability–learning covariation, did not observe corresponding changes in learning performance itself. Thus the explanation in terms of underlying common processes is often based on shaky grounds. And hence, one important conclusion to be derived from this review is that we should expect to be able to detect and understand differentiated learning–ability relationships only as long as the underlying processes are well understood—as they are more likely to be if experimental conditions are utilized which induce reliable differences on whatever index is utilized to indicate the "causative" process.

A second major set of conclusions to be derived from the present research relates to the adequacy and/or interpretation of the markers included in some of the research. For instance, take the findings—consistently emerging in the Labouvie-Vief et al. (1975) research—that digit span performance systematically fails to correlate with learning, under whatever condition learning is assessed. This certainly is not in accordance with the assumption that rote processes are such a pervasive set of processes that they comprise a major classification, or that most learning that does not involve elaboration (Rohwer, 1970) is essentially rote in nature. Rather, if one takes the digit span test as an indicator of rote processes—or the ability to reproduce items in a tape-recorder-like fashion—it may well be a factor much more limited in nature than has been assumed thus far.

Somewhat similar speculations may also be advanced with regard to the findings of learning–ability covariations that involve tests of reasoning. On the one hand, these results are somewhat encouraging and substantiate the earlier argument. That is, since many of the studies report high correlations between reasoning tests and learning efficiency, this research similarly argues against the generality of rote processes, and for the assumption that most learning involves skills and strategies that are more complex. Taking this argument further, we might then offer a partial explanation for the failure of reasoning tests to often yield remarkable differential correlations with learning under changing task conditions. That is, due to their complex and general nature, tests of reasoning may well distinguish among individuals if they happen to be differentiated along a fairly broad class of processes. However, if treatment manipulations primarily affect one or more of the subclasses, they may well fail to show up in reasoning–learning covariations unless the relevant subcomponents or subprocesses are identified and separately subjected to experimental analysis.

A LOOK INTO THE FUTURE

Variety of Individual Differences in Intellectual Abilities

In general, the preceding review leaves us with a set of conclusions that in many ways argues against an uncritical acceptance of the claims usually raised by psychometric theory as to the "meaning" of its factors. Some of them, like the digit span test, may well tap a much narrower set of functions than is typically assumed; while others, like tests of reasoning, seem to tap a whole gamut of different, as yet to be specified, processes or skills. Given this, what are some of the next steps that research in this area might take?

In a recent review, Estes (1974) has called attention to the fact that most psychometric tests of ability, even presumably "pure" ones, do not represent measures of any unitary source of individual variance. Rather, he argues, there are diverse ways in which individual differences may arise with respect to performance in many tests of this kind. This argument is, in fact, not new and has been similarly advanced in the literature on human development—both that of children (e.g., Ginsburg, 1972) and of adults (e.g., Baltes and Labouvie, 1973; Labouvie-Vief, Hoyer, Baltes, and Baltes, 1974).

Consider, for example, performance on a test like Raven's progressive matrices. This test presents the subject with a matrix-like arrangement of figural symbols, and a missing symbol is presumed to be substitutable if the subject discovers the rules that guide transformations of the symbols both along the rows and columns of the matrix. However, Hunt (1974) has recently pointed out that many of the problems can be solved by the application of a simpler set of rules, or algorithms, and hence two algorithms may be distinguished that can lead to successful solution. In Hunt's (1974) terminology,

> . . . one algorithm represents a Progressive Matrix problem as a plane figure in which certain figures can be detected, and applies physically defined transformations to that representation. The other algorithm represents a problem as an ordered collection of sets of features, and applies logical and arithmetical transformations to these features. In a more traditional language, the first algorithm will be called the Gestalt algorithm, as it deals with a problem by using the operations of visual perception, such as the continuation of lines through blank areas and the superimposition of visual images upon each other. The second algorithm will be called the analytic algorithm, as it applies logical operations to features contained within elements of the problem matrix [p. 133].

If this hypothesis were true, the failure of Raven—or similar tests of reasoning—to produce differentiated patterns of correlations is not surprising. Were we able to isolate that component which is more directly *visual* we would expect to obtain substantial correlations with a learning task that requires a *visual* imagery strategy. This hypothesis is currently being pursued in two studies. In the first, we are utilizing a free-recall task similar to the one used in the second study described in the previous section—however, with modifications that are likely to produce a more pronounced effect of prelearning instructions. The reasoning markers in this study were selected to represent more adequately a concrete—abstract differentiation: One (figure grouping) relies primarily on a detection of similarities and differences in geometric patterns, while a second (word grouping) consists in more abstract class relationships between words. We expect that free-recall performance in an imagery-chunking condition will show an increasing relationship to the former test (spatial visualization ability) rather than the more abstract test.

In a second ongoing study, we are exploiting a similar rationale. Here, however, we are attempting an even more direct differentiation of concrete—abstract processing functions. The "reasoning" markers are word grouping tests. However, they are divided into two different types. The first contains highly concrete words which appear to be easily amenable to an "imaginal" comprehension of class relationships. The second, in contrast, is composed of less concrete words, and the class membership here is based on more abstract relationships. Similarly, two groups of subjects learn a paired-associate task under two different conditions. In one condition, subjects learn a list of highly concrete words, employing a visual imagery strategy involving the formation of an interactive image. In the second condition, subjects learn a list of abstract nouns by forming a sentence linking the two nouns together. In line with a hypothesis of two differentiated components, we expect that learning of the first paired-associate task will relate to "concrete" reasoning, while learning of the second will relate to more "abstract" reasoning.

These experiments, then, are designed as a test of the assumption that psychometric abilities may not—as often assumed—represent tests of "pure," unidimensional sources of individual differences. If this assumption turns out to be tenable, studies of this kind will indeed suggest a degree of reservation in accepting some of the traditional interpretations about the nature of intellectual functioning. This is likely since the present analysis has merely focused on *two* potential components that might create individual differences in *one* simple class of tests. However, it is also likely that *many more* components will eventually serve as candidates for similar analyses. As an example, various authors have raised criticisms of the usual practice of excluding *motivational* components at the expense of a purely *cognitive* interpretation of intellectual performance (e.g., Atkinson, 1974; Baltes and

Labouvie, 1973; Katz, 1970; Labouvie-Vief, Hoyer, Baltes, and Baltes, 1974; Zigler, Abelson, and Seitz, 1973)—such as subjective expectancy of success, test anxiety, and achievement motivation. Hence, it will no longer be necessary to treat cognitive abilities as "functional unities." Rather, a systematic exploration into the sources of individual variation by means of controlled research will be needed.

Certainly, such experiments are but a first step in a new direction. No doubt, however, they are a step in the right direction. In Estes's (1974) words, "Present instruments for measuring intelligence . . . operate primarily by sampling performance, and in every type of intellectual task any given level of performance can arise in many different ways [p. 749]." If indeed the primary aim of research into intellectual functioning is not merely to predict and to classify, but rather to indicate possible steps for training and remediation, then research of this kind should without doubt receive primary attention in the future.

Educational Implications: An Illustrative Example

But how, to be more specific, might we attempt to translate some of the conclusions of this chapter into workable steps for educational research? As an illustration, let me cite an example from my research with older people. Although most of the earlier discussion has centered on age groups younger than adults, the problems that research with elderly people is dealing with are similar and their solution may suggest implications of a much broader nature.

Indeed, the domain of adult intellectual development has been afflicted until very recently with the same conceptual malaise that is likely to spread wherever individual differences in intelligence have been examined from a solely psychometric perspective: that of over-loading ability constructs with untested surplus meaning connoting the existence of enduring, largely biologically based characteristics. Hence those age (or cultural and subcultural) groups that show below standard performance have come to be branded as being deficient in a way that is highly resistant to change.

On a purely descriptive level, there is a large body of literature to suggest that older people perform less well on intelligence tests than younger ones—even if age groups are equated in terms of education, health, and similar characteristics (for a review, see Baltes and Labouvie, 1973). This tends to be particularly true for tests of complex abstract functions such as inductive reasoning or, in Cattell's and Horn's language (Horn and Cattell, 1967; Horn, 1970), for tests of fluid abilities. And hence it became a widely accepted explanation that these tests were indicative of a "normal" and universal developmental process which was caused by the onset of gradual biological breakdown starting after adolescence.

Reasonable as it sounds on an intuitive level, this conceptualization is coming more and more to be challenged. First, one line of research (see Schaie and Labouvie-Vief, 1974; Schaie, Labouvie and Buesch, 1973) has recently demonstrated that performance differences between young and old may have little to do with intraindividual development, per se. While today's younger adult does indeed score higher on most tests than his/her middle-aged or elderly contemporary, these differences are indicative of generational change. Much the same argument, indeed, would be applicable if adult age differences in height were plotted. The taller height of young adults is with them to stay, except for very minor alterations, and it is a phenomenon to be attributed to generational rather than developmental change. And in a similar vein, for older adult's lower intellectual performance appears to be accounted for, not by biological decrement, but by the fact that he/she has grown up (and still is living) in an altogether different cultural milieu.

This leads us to the second major evidence discrediting the biological deficit view—namely that thus far it has been impossible to isolate biological–physiological correlates of differences in intellectual functioning *unless* one is dealing with samples afflicted with pathology, living in instutions, or within close proximity of their natural death (Baltes and Labouvie, 1973; Jarvik, 1975). No such relationship exists, however, in healthy, community-living older people.

From this and similar evidence we concluded that it might be worthwhile to search for experiential sources of variation that might be related to the elderly individual's poorer facility in complex problem-solving tasks. We hypothesized that if the older person's poor performance constitutes an experience-related deficit, then it should be possible to enhance his or her performance by supplying a set of strategies that might be helpful to problem solution.

But what set of strategies were we to focus on? As emphasized throughout this chapter, there is little in psychometric theory that informs us about the processes people do, or should, utilize, to reach high levels of performance. Here, however, some of our earlier considerations proved helpful. In accord with the research cited earlier, we conjectured that the skills necessary in the tests of complex reasoning could be represented by a number of strategies of abstraction, organization, and verbal and nonverbal elaboration as they have been summarized by Jensen (1971) under the label of level II skills.

Hence, we (Labouvie-Vief and Gonda, 1975) designed a training program geared at enhancing and strengthening the use of such organizational and elaborative skills in our subjects (elderly women of a mean age of 76 years). We started out modeling the use of such strategies by verbalizing them to experimental subjects while working on a set of problems, and then gradually had the elderly join in, and eventually take over, as a means of establishing cognitive self-control.

The results of this training procedure were quite encouraging, although the program itself was very brief, lasting only about one hour. Nevertheless, our experimental groups improved their inductive reasoning performance as compared to that of a control group. Moreover, this facilitative effect was maintained over a 2-week period, and it generalized to a test of inductive reasoning that had not specifically been trained—and was indeed quite different in format from the training material.

Inspired by this initial success, we are now planning to launch a 3-year longitudinal study in which elderly people will receive training in a number of skills that we assume are facilitative for problem-solving performance. Clearly, such research may demonstrate that many of the core contentions of this chapter may prove helpful in advancing our understanding about the nature and development of intellectual processes. Namely, once we take descriptive research for what it is—a simple preliminary demonstration of the existence of individual differences—and then are ready to carefully test and revise hypotheses about the sources of individual differences, the potential payoffs for an educational psychology and an optimization of individual development are likely to be rewarding.

REFERENCES

Allison, R. A., Jr. *Learning parameters and human abilities.* Educational Testing Service Technical Report. Princeton, N.J.: Educational Testing Service, 1960.

Anastasi, A. On the formation of psychological traits. *American Psychologist,* 1970, *25,* 899–910.

Atkinson, J. W. *Motivation and achievement.* New York: Wiley, 1974.

Baltes, P. B., & Labouvie, G. V. Adult development of intellectual performance: Description, explanation, and modification. In C. Eisdorfer & M. P. Lawton (Eds.), *The psychology of adult development and aging.* Washington, D.C.: American Psychological Association, 1973.

Baltes, P. B., & Nesselroade, J. R. The development analysis of individual differences on multiple measures. In J. R. Nesselroade & H. W. Reese (Eds.), *Life-span developmental psychology: Methodological issues.* New York: Academic Press, 1973.

Baratz, S. S., & Baratz, J. S. Early childhood intervention: The social science base of institutional racism. *Harvard Educational Review,* 1970, *40,* 29–50.

Bartsch, T. W. & Nesselroade, J. R. Test of trait-state anxiety distinction using a manipulative factor-analytic design. *Journal of Personality and Social Psychology,* 1973, *27,* 58–64.

Bayley, N. Development of mental abilities. In P. H. Mussen (Ed.), *Carmichael's manual of child psychology* (Vol. 1). New York: Wiley, 1970.

Berliner, D. C., & Cahen, L. S. Trait-treatment interaction and learning. In F. N. Kerlinger (Ed.), *Review of research in education.* Itasca, Ill.: Peacock, 1973.

Bunderson, V. C. *Transfer of mental abilities at different stages of practice in the solution of concept problems.* Unpublished doctoral dissertation, Princeton University, 1965.

Carroll, J. B. Factors of verbal achievement. In A. Anastasi (Ed.), *Testing problems in perspective.* Washington, D. C.: American Council on Education, 1966.

Carroll, J. B. Psychometric tests as cognitive tasks: A new "structure of intellect." Technical Report No. 4 (RB 74-16). Princeton, N.J.: Educational Testing Service, 1974.

Cattell, R. B., & Scheier, I. H. *The meaning and measurement of neuroticism and anxiety.* New York: Ronald Press, 1961.

Charles, D. C. Historical antecedents of life-span developmental psychology. In L. R. Goulet & P. B. Baltes (Eds.), *Life-span developmental psychology.* New York: Academic Press, 1970.

Cronbach, L. J. The two disciplines of scientific psychology. *American Psychologist,* 1957, *12,* 671–679.

Cronbach, L. J. & Snow, R. E. *Individual differences in learning-ability as a function of instructional variables.* Stanford: Stanford University, 1969.

Das, J. P. Structure of cognitive abilities: Evidence for simultaneous and successive processing. *Journal of Educational Psychology,* 1973, *65,* 103–108.

Duncanson, J. P. *Intelligence and the ability to learn.* Research Bulletin, 64–29. Princeton, N.J.: Educational Testing Service, 1964.

Duncanson, J. P. Learning and measured abilities. *Journal of Educational Psychology,* 1966, *57,* 220–229.

Dunham, J. L., & Bunderson, V. C. Effect of decision-rule instruction upon the relationship of cognitive abilities to performance in multiple-category concept problems. *Journal of Educational Psychology,* 1969, *60,* 121–125.

Dunham, J. L., Guilford, J. P., & Hoepfner, R. Multivariate approaches to discovering the intellectual components of concept learning. *Psychology Review,* 1968, *75,* 206–221.

Estes, W. K. Learning theory and intelligence. *American Psychologist,* 1974, *29,* 740–749.

Eysenck, H. J. Intelligence assessment: A theoretical and experimental approach. *British Journal of Educational Psychology,* 1966, *36,* 81–98.

Ferguson, G. A. On learning and human ability. *Canadian Journal of Psychology,* 1954, *8,* 95–112.

Fleishman, E. A. Individual differences and motor learning. In R. M. Gagné (Ed.), *Learning and individual differences.* Columbus, Ohio: Merrill Books, 1967, 165–191.

Fleishman, E. A. On the relation between abilities, learning, and human performance. *American Psychologist,* 1972, *27,* 1017–1032.

Fleishman, E. A. & Bartlett, C. J. Human abilities. *Annual Review of Psychology,* 1969, *20,* 349–380.

Fleishman, E. A., & Fruchter, B. Factor structure and predictability of successive stages of learning Morse code. *Journal of Applied Psychology,* 1960, *44,* 96–101.

Fleishman, E. A., & Hempel, W. E. Factorial analysis of complex psychomotor performance and related skills. *Journal of Applied Psychology,* 1956, *40,* 96–104.

Fowler, W. The effect of early stimulation: The problem of focus in developmental stimulation. *Merrill-Palmer Quarterly,* 1969, *15,* 157–170.

Frederiksen, C. H. *Abilities, transfer, and information retrieval in verbal learning.* Multivariate Behavioral Research Monographs, 1969, No. 2.

French, J. W., Ekstrom, R. B., & Price, L. A. *Manual for the Kit of Reference Tests for Cognitive Factors.* Princeton, N.J.: Educational Testing Service, 1963.

Gagné, R. M. Contributions of learning to human development. *Psychological Review,* 1968, *75,* 177–191.

Gagné, R. M. *Essentials of learning for instruction.* Hinsdale, Ill.: Dryden, 1974.

Gagné, R. M. *Learning and individual differences.* Columbus, Ohio: Merrill Books, 1967.

Games, P. A. A factorial analysis of verbal learning tasks. *Journal of Experimental Psychology,* 1962, *63,* 1–11.

Ginsburg, H. *The myth of the deprived child.* Englewood Cliffs, N.J.: Prentice-Hall, 1972.

Glasman, L. D. *A social-class comparison of conceptual processes in children's free recall.* Unpublished doctoral dissertation, University of California, Berkeley, 1968.

Goulet, L. R. The interfaces of acquisition: Models and methods for studying the active, developing organism. In J. R. Nesselroade & H. W. Reese (Eds.), *Life-span developmental psychology: Methodological issues.* New York: Academic Press, 1973.

Guilford, J. P. Intelligence: 1965 model. *American Psychologist, 1966, 21,* 20–26.

Guilford, J. P. *The nature of human intelligence.* New York: McGraw-Hill, 1967.

Guilford, J. P. The structure of intellect. *Psychological Bulletin,* 1956, *53,* 267–293.

Guilford, J. P., & Hoepfner, R. *The analysis of intelligence.* New York: McGraw-Hill, 1971.

Harlow, H. F. Learning set and error factor theory. In S. Koch (Ed.), *Psychology: A study of a science* (Vol. 2). New York: McGraw-Hill, 1959.

Hodges, W. The effects of ego threat and threat of pain on state anxiety. *Journal of Personality and Social Psychology,* 1968, *8,* 364–372.

Horn, J. L. Organization of data on life-span development of human abilities, In L. R. Goulet & P. B. Baltes (Eds.), *Life-span developmental psychology.* New York: Academic Press, 1970.

Horn, J. L., & Cattell, R. B. Age differences in fluid and crystallized intelligence. *Acta Psychologica,* 1967, *26,* 107–129.

Humphreys, L. G. The organization of human abilities. *American Psychologist,* 1962, *17,* 475–483.

Hunt, E. Quote the Raven? Nevermore! In L. W. Gregg (Ed.), *Knowledge and Cognition.* New York: J. Wiley & Sons, 1974.

Husband, R. W. Intercorrelations among learning abilities, I. *Journal of Genetic Psychology,* 1939, *55,* 353–364.

Husband, R. W. Interrelations among learning abilities, IV. *Journal of Genetic Psychology,* 1941, *58,* 432–434.

Jarvik, L. F. Thoughts on the psychobiology of aging. *American Psychologist,* 1975, *30,* 576–583.

Jensen, A. R. How much can we boost IQ and scholastic achievement? *Harvard Educational Review,* 1969, *39,* 1–123.

Jensen, A. R. The role of verbal mediation in mental development. *Journal of Genetic Psychology,* 1971(b), *118,* 39–70.

Jensen, A. R. Social class and verbal learning. In M. Deutsch, I. Katz, & A. R. Jensen (eds.), *Social class, race, and psychological development.* New York: Holt, 1968.

Jensen, A. R. A two-level theory of mental abilities. In A. R. Jensen & W. D. Rohwer (Eds.), *An experimental analysis of learning abilities in culturally disadvantaged children.* Final Report, Office of Economic Opportunity, Contract No. OEO 2404, 1970.

Jensen, A. R. Varieties of individual differences in learning. In R. M. Gagné (Ed.), *Learning and individual differences.* Columbus, Ohio: Merrill Books, 1967.

Jensen, A. R. & Frederiksen, J. Free recall of categorized and uncategorized lists: A test of the Jensen hypothesis. *Journal of Educational Psychology,* 1973, *65,* 304–312.

Katz, I. Negro performance in interracial situations. In P. Watson (Ed.), *Psychology and race.* Baltimore: Penguin, 1973(a).

Kendler, H. H., & Kendler, T. S. Developmental processes in discrimination learning. *Human Development,* 1970, *13,* 65–89.

Kendler, H. H., & Kendler, T. S. Vertical and horizontal processes in human concept formation. *Psychological Review,* 1962, *69,* 1–18.

Kohfeld, D. L. The prediction of perceptual-motor learning from independent verbal and motor measures. *Psychonomic Science,* 1966, *4,* 413–414.

Labouvie, G. V., Frohring, W. R., Baltes, P. B., & Goulet, L. R. Changing relationship between recall performance and abilities as a function of stage of learning and timing of recall. *Journal of Educational Psychology,* 1973, *64,* 191–198.

Labouvie-Vief, G. *Intelligence and learning: A review of empirical and theoretical issues.* Theoretical Paper No. 47. Madison, Wisc.: Wisconsin Research and Development Center for Cognitive Learning, 1973.

Labouvie-Vief, G., & Gonda, J. N. *Cognitive strategy training and intellectual performance in the elderly.* Unpublished manuscript, University of Wisconsin, 1975.

Labouvie-Vief, G., Hoyer, W. J., Baltes, M. M., & Baltes, P. B. Operant analysis of intellectual behavior in old age. *Human Development,* 1974, *17,* 259–272.

Labouvie-Vief, G., Levin, J. R., & Urberg, K. A. The relationship between selected cognitive abilities and learning: A second look. *Journal of Educational Psychology,* 1975, *67,* 558–569.

Laurence, M. W. Age differences in performance and subjective organization in the free-recall of pictorial material. *Canadian Journal of Psychology,* 1966, *20,* 388–399.

Lemke, E. A., Klausmeier, H. J., & Harris, C. W. Relationship of selected cognitive abilities to concept formation and information processing. *Journal of Educational Psychology,* 1967, *58,* 27–35.

Looft, W. R. Conceptions of human nature, educational practice, and individual development. *Human Development,* 1973, *16,* 21–32.

McNemar, Q. Lost: Our intelligence. Why? *American Psychologist,* 1964, *19,* 871–882.

Messick, S. *Multivariate models of cognition and personality: The need for both process and structure in psychological theory and measurement.* Research Bulletin RB-73-50. Princeton, N.J.: Educational Testing Service, 1973.

Mischel, W. *Personality and assessment.* New York: Wiley, 1968.

Mischel, W. Toward a cognitive social learning reconceptualization of personality. *Psychological Review,* 1973, *80,* 252–283.

Nesselroade, J. R. Application of multivariate strategies to problems of measuring and structuring long-term change. In L. R. Goulet & P. B. Baltes (ed.), *Life-span developmental psychology.* New York: Academic Press, 1970.

Parker, J. F., Jr. & Fleishman, E. A. Ability factors and component performance measures as predictors of complex tracking behavior. *Psychological Monographs,* 1960, *74* (16, Whole No. 503).

Parker, J. F., Jr., & Fleishman, E. A. Use of analytical information concerning task requirements to increase the effectiveness of skill training. *Journal of Applied Psychology,* 1961, *45,* 295–302.

Reese, H. W. (Ed.). Imagery in children's learning. *Psychological Bulletin,* 1970, *73,* 383–421.

Reese, H. W., & Lipsitt, L. P. *Experimental child psychology.* New York: Academic Press, 1970.

Roberts, D. M. Abilities and learning: A brief review and discussion of empirical studies. *Journal of School Psychology,* 1968–69, *7,* 12–21.

Rohwer, W. D., Jr. Elaboration and learning in childhood and adolescence. In H. W. Reese (Ed.), *Advances in child development and behavior.* New York: Academic Press, 1973.

Rohwer, W. D., Jr. Mental elaboration and proficient learning. *Minnesota Symposia on Child Psychology,* 1970, *4,* 220–260.

Rohwer, W. D., Jr., and Levin, J. R. Elaboration preferences and differences in learning proficiency. In J. Hellmuth (Ed.), *Cognitive studies* (Vol. 2). New York: Brunnu/Mazel, 1971.

Rosner, S. R. The effect of rehearsal and chunking instructions on children's multi-trial free recall. *Journal of Experimental Child Psychology,* 1971, *11,* 93–105.

Schaie, K. W., Labouvie, G. V., & Buech, B. U. Generational vs. cohort-specific differences in adult cognitive functioning: A fourteen-year study of independent samples. *Developmental Psychology,* 1973, *9,* 151–166.

Schaie, K. W., & Labouvie-Vief, G. Generational versus ontogenetic components of change in adult cognitive behavior: A fourteen-year cross-sequential study. *Developmental Psychology,* 1974, *10,* 305–320.

Shuell, T. J. Clustering and organization in free recall. *Psychological Bulletin,* 1969, *72,* 353–374.

Solomon, G. Heuristic models for the generation of aptitude-treatment interaction hypotheses. *Review of Educational Research,* 1972, *42,* 327–343.

Staats, A. W. *Child learning, intelligence, and personality: Principles of a behavioral interaction approach.* New York: Harper & Row, 1971.

Stake, R. E. Learning parameters, aptitudes, and achievements. *Psychometric Monographs,* 1961, No. 9.

Stevenson, H. W., Hale, G. A., Klein, R. E., & Miller, L. K. Interrelations and correlates in children's learning and problem solving. *Monographs of the Society for Research in Child Development,* 1968, *33,* No. 7.

Stevenson, H. W., & Odom, R. D. Interrelationships in children's learning. *Child Development,* 1965, *36,* 7–19.

Thurstone, L. L. A factorial study of perception. *Psychometric Monographs,* No. 4. Chicago: University of Chicago Press, 1944.

Thurstone, L. L. *The nature of intelligence.* New York: Harcourt, 1926.

Tulving, E. Theoretical issues in free recall. In T. R. Dixon & D. L. Horton (Eds.), *Verbal behavior and general behavior theory.* Englewood Cliffs, N.J.: Prentice-Hall, 1968.

Vernon, P. E. Ability factors and environmental influences. *American Psychologist,* 1965, *20,* 723–733.

White, S. H. Evidence for a hierarchical arrangement of learning processes. In L. P. Lippsitt & C. C. Spiker (Eds.), *Advances in child development and behavior* (Vol. 2). New York: Academic Press, 1965.

Whiteman, M. Intelligence and learning. *Merrill-Palmer Quarterly,* 1964, *10,* 298–309.

Zigler, E., Abelson, W. D., & Seitz, V. Motivational factors in the performance of economically disadvantaged children on the Peabody picture vocabulary test. *Child Development,* 1973, *44,* 294–303.

CHAPTER 3

Children's Recognition Memory Processes

Elizabeth S. Ghatala
Joel R. Levin

Over the past few years we have been conducting research in an area which may be loosely described as "children's recognition memory." In this chapter we report one aspect of our research, namely that concerned with *understanding why certain variables affect children's recognition memory in the way they do.* At the outset, it should be mentioned that we intend to be selective in our approach. That is to say, since our intent here is to discuss our research in the context of the theoretical perspective within which it was conceived and has since developed, we shall not include others' work in the area of children's recognition memory except as it relates to central issues in our own work. For the same reason we shall not explore in any depth alternative theoretical positions for viewing the issues raised.

Before we go on to consider the research per se and its implications, we must first provide a necessary framework and rationale. Accordingly, in Section I:

1. We outline our reasons for investigating children's recognition memory.
2. We examine the nature of the particular recognition memory task that we have utilized.
3. We describe in some detail tenets of the major theory that has been advanced to account for performance on this task.
4. We place the current theory into a broader perspective in order to deal with the many variables affecting children's recognition memory.

REASONS FOR STUDYING CHILDREN'S RECOGNITION MEMORY

First, a general description of procedures for measuring recognition memory may be helpful. Typically the subject is initially shown a group

61

of target items and then on a test trial is asked to select the target items from among a group of items which includes distractor items (i.e., items which were not presented on the study trial). Note that what the subject is required to do is to discriminate the target items from the distractor items. There are numerous ways of structuring the recognition memory situation, one of which we shall describe in detail later in this section. However, Wallace (1972) has pointed out two key characteristics of tests of recognition memory. The first is that recall of specific items (in a reproductive sense) is not required. The second is that distractor items are presented along with target items during the test.

Historically there has always existed the operational distinction between memory tasks involving *recognition* as described above and those involving *recall*. In the latter task, the subject is required to reproduce specific items to which he has previously been exposed on a learning trial. For a long while psychologists considered recall and recognition tasks as different ways of measuring the same thing. That is, although subjects score much higher when given a recognition test than when given a recall test on the same material, this quantitative difference has been assumed to reflect merely the difficulty of the two tasks and not any qualitative differences in the processes underlying recognition and recall. Recently, however, this assumption has been called into question, and the possibility has been raised that the processes and/or types of stored information utilized in recognition decisions differ from those utilized in recall (see primarily Underwood, 1972, but also Kintsch, 1970, and McCormack, 1972).

To date, much of the research on learning and memory has been concerned with how subjects retrieve or reproduce items from memory, and has employed either the free-recall or the paired-associate paradigm. In contrast, much less work has been done on investigating processes in recognition memory per se, although some research has been undertaken to identify recognition as a subprocess in recall (cf. Kintsch, 1970). As Underwood (1972) has pointed out, a clear understanding of the processes involved in both types of memory tasks and how they differ may be one of the most important techniques for understanding the workings of memory in general.

Aside from the above reason for studying recognition memory, we must not overlook its probable role in supporting performance in many higher-order conceptual learning tasks. This has been emphasized by Gagné (1970), Klausmeier, Ghatala, Frayer (1974), and others, who view stimulus discrimination and recognition as fundamental abilities at the base of a set of hierarchically-ordered abilities. In their model of concept attainment, for example, Klausmeier *et al.* view the recognition of previously discriminated objects and events, and abstracted attributes of objects and events, as an important operation involved in attaining concepts.

The major reason for utilizing children in our investigation of recognition memory stems from our commitment to relate psychological principles to educational practice. Consistent with this commitment, we stress the importance of recognition memory in concept attainment and other types of school-related performance. Thus, any understanding of how recognition memory can be facilitated by an appropriate choice of learning materials and instructional strategies may have important implications for school learning. The description which follows of the actual task employed in our research indicates how closely it resembles recognition tasks encountered in school, such as so-called "objective" examinations (i.e., those containing multiple-choice, true-false, and matching items).

NATURE OF THE TASK

The task which we have utilized in studying recognition memory is referred to in the literature as a verbal-discrimination learning task. While the name of the task includes the words "verbal discrimination," the stimulus materials utilized in the task need not be verbal; and, as will become apparent, the paradigm is a procedure for studying recognition memory and is only tangentially related to the study of discrimination learning in the classic psychological sense, that is, where perceptual discriminations related to threshold determinations and stimulus transpositions are of interest (see, for example, Osgood, 1953).

In general, the task procedure involves the presentation of several pairs of items. One member of each pair is arbitrarily designated the "correct" item or the item which the subjects must learn to choose whenever that pair appears. The items within a pair may appear side by side or one above the other. The position of the correct items within the pairs on any given trial is random, and the position of the correct member of a pair is nonsystematically varied over trials with the restriction that over the several trials each item occurs in each position about equally often (in order to eliminate position biases associated with the correct items). The subject's task is quite simple. As each pair of items is presented, the subject indicates which member of the pair he/she thinks is correct, followed by feedback provided by the experimenter. Learning is demonstrated by a gain in the number of correct responses over trials.

It is apparent from this brief description that the task embodies the characteristics of a test of recognition mentioned earlier (i.e., no reproduction is required and distractor items are present during test). If the correct member of each pair is considered as the target item and the incorrect member as the distractor, then the task can be conceived as a unique type of recognition memory paradigm in which a given target and distractor consistently appear together during both inspection (study) and test phases of the experiment (Wallace, 1972). Our choice of this task as a research tool for investigating variables influencing children's recognition memory was governed by the following considerations.

First, many studies employing this paradigm have included manipulations of procedural variables. Thus, from the literature we can gain a fairly good notion of how particular task variations might affect performance (see Wallace, 1972, or Eckert & Kanak, 1974, for a review of these variations). A second consideration which led us to utilize this particular recognition memory task is the fact that it can be easily administered even to very young children. Finally, a theoretical analysis of the processes involved in performing the task has been developed and submitted to extensive testing. Thus, we have at hand an established framework for generating our hypotheses and guiding interpretations of our data.

FREQUENCY THEORY

Frequency theory was first developed to account for learning in the verbal-discrimination paradigm (Ekstrand, Wallace, and Underwood, 1966) and has subsequently been extended to other recognition memory paradigms (Underwood and Freund, 1970; Underwood, Zimmerman, and Freund, 1971). The theory emphasizes the discriminative properties of "frequency," the basic notion being that subjects have the ability to discriminate differences in the frequency with which items have been previously exposed. In this sense, the frequency of an item may be regarded as its acquired familiarity.

The fundamental postulate of the theory is that the correct alternative in each pair acquires more frequency "units" on each exposure of the pair than does the incorrect item. Thus, the subject can utilize the "rule":

> *Choose the more frequent (i.e., the more familiar) member of each pair in performing the task.*

The postulated buildup of a frequency differential favoring the correct item in each pair was derived from considerations of the typical task procedure. First, the procedure involves the presentation of both members of the pair during the anticipation interval. This exposure provides one frequency unit to each member of the pair since the subject is presumed to perceive (or make a representational response to) each item. Second, the correct member of each pair receives at least one additional frequency unit, since during feedback the experimenter indicates which member of the pair is correct (so the subject will attend to the correct item again and possibly rehearse it). The net result is that frequency accrues faster to correct alternatives than to incorrect alternatives, and the theory asserts that subjects perform successfully in this task by selecting the members of pairs which they perceive as having higher frequency values. (The theory also postulates that frequency which accrues to an item may also accrue to associates of that item via an "implicit associative response" mechanism, although this aspect of the theory will not receive attention here.)

Wallace (1972), in his review of the literature, points out that the theory has been tested in a variety of ways. The results of some tests are favorable while others point up inadequacies of certain aspects of the theory (which he then attempts to rectify). However, despite any difficulties which the theory may have, it currently provides the most complete interpretation of how successful verbal discriminations are achieved.

Frequency theory is easily extended to more traditional types of recognition memory tasks in which subjects are presented target items which they must then select from among nonpresented distractor items. Again, it is postulated that target items acquire frequency during the study trial, and on the test trial the subject utilizes his/her ability to discriminate frequency differences in order to select the old items and reject the new. Thus, Underwood and his associates have asserted that the frequency "attribute of memory" (Underwood, 1969) dominates in recognition tasks. That is, while other attributes of memory may be used to support, check, or even displace the frequency attribute, frequency is believed to be the dominant attribute in the usual recognition situation (Underwood et al., 1971).

Frequency as a Memory Attribute

It may be helpful to the reader if at this point we place frequency theory in a broader perspective. Underwood (1969) has defined a memory for an event as consisting of a collection of "attributes" (an attribute being a type of encoded information about an event) which serve to discriminate one memory from another and to act as retrieval mechanisms for a target memory. Some attributes, such as the frequency, temporal, and spatial attributes, appear to be responsible primarily for discriminations among memories, and as such are responsible primarily for recognition performance. However, returning to the process distinction mentioned earlier between recognition and recall, it is doubtful whether a discriminative attribute such as frequency is, by itself, sufficient to *retrieve* memories. Other so-called retrieval attributes (e.g., verbal associations) must also be involved in recall (Underwood, 1969).

We make use of "memory attribute" notions in interpreting the results of our own research in children's recognition memory. Consistent with the theory of Ekstrand *et al.* (1966), we believe that the frequency attribute plays an important role in accounting for many discrimination learning phenomena. At the same time, we have found that frequency per se cannot account for everything, and where it cannot we have had to seek out other candidate memory attributes.

Before continuing, it makes sense to agree on what it is we mean when we say that frequency "accounts for" discrimination learning (or more broadly, for recognition memory). As Underwood (1975, p. 129) points out in his discussion of this issue, the term *model* used strictly means that a set of empirical laws developed in one discipline is applied to another area of research as a possible explanatory system. However, this borrowing of one area from another need not be across disciplines; it can be within a discipline. In this sense, frequency theory is a within-discipline model since it states that the laws and relationships which hold for frequency discriminations per se will also hold for performance on discrimination learning or other recognition memory tasks.

There are several types of evidence which can lend credence to frequency theory as a model for discrimination learning. The first level of evidence is essentially *correlative* in nature. Thus, one might observe that under naturally occurring circumstances, subjects' competencies in the two behavioral domains are correlated. That is, subjects who are good at discriminating frequency per se (i.e., those with a well functioning frequency attribute) might also be good verbal-discrimination learners, or at least better than those who are poor at discriminating frequency. (Note that this relationship might also be of a threshold, or of a necessary-but-not-sufficient, variety.) To provide a different illustration of a *correlative* level of evidence, one might observe that particular variables exert similar influences in both domains; for example, it might be noted that certain stimulus variables and/or rehearsal strategies positively (or negatively) affect both frequency discriminations and verbal-discrimination learning in the same manner.

At the *causative* level of evidence, one might be able to anticipate outcomes in one domain by directly manipulating aspects of the other. That is, if frequency per se accounts for verbal-discrimination learning, then manipulating the former experimentally should have predictable consequences on the latter. In our research we have sought both types of evidence for the frequency theory as a model for children's discrimination learning.[1]

However, our research has involved more than the mere search for empirical evidence to test the veracity of the frequency theory model. For, as Underwood (1975) also noted, frequency theory is an unusual kind of model in that when the theory was formulated there was no body of laws and relationships concerning frequency discriminations to transfer to the recognition memory situation. Accordingly, some of our research has been directed toward developing the theory as a model by incorporating a psychophysical construct that synthesizes the laws governing frequency discrimination performance.

One might state the goals of our research as follows:

1. Determine the effects of various stimulus materials and rehearsal strategies on children's discrimination learning.
2. Ascertain whether or not our results can be accounted for (in either sense of the term, as just described) in terms of frequency theory.
3. Expand frequency theory as a model by incorporating constructs from another domain (psychophysics) to explain frequency discrimination behavior.

At the risk of belaboring the obvious, at one level we have a conglomeration of facts concerning children's discrimination learning which we have attempted to "account for" by describing in terms of the operation of the frequency attribute as stipulated by frequency theory. At another level, we have attempted to explain the operation of the frequency attribute by creating an analogy with psychophysical phenomena.

REVIEW AND PREVIEW

We have sketched the outlines of a theory which postulates frequency as an independent attribute of memory, one which provides the predominant information utilized by subjects in making recognition decisions. As mentioned earlier, this analysis of the role of frequency in recognition memory was developed on the basis of experiments with verbal materials (primarily in the verbal-discrimination paradigm) and adult subjects.

---

[1] Refer to Howell (1973) for an account of frequency discriminations at still another level, namely in terms of posited internal processes and mechanisms.

In what follows we:

1. Review some of our research with children, indicating the variables we have manipulated.
2. Attempt to provide a theoretical account of the results.

A major focus of this discussion is whether or not the empirical evidence supports a frequency theory account of differences in children's recognition memory with respect to variations in stimulus materials and rehearsal strategies employed in the discrimination task. At the same time, we attempt to strengthen frequency theory as a model for recognition memory by introducing certain constructs which we have found relevant to subjects' frequency discrimination behavior.

Finally, we consider some of the educational implications (and obvious next steps) flowing from our research to date. As will be seen, in order to suggest useful educational implications, we are forced to consider carefully the limitations of frequency theory as a general model for children's recognition memory. Most of the boundary conditions for frequency theory can be derived directly or indirectly from the research reported in the following section. Once these boundary conditions are established, we are able to suggest manipulations of instructional materials and strategies which relate to conceptual learning and to existing learning and assessment procedures within educational settings.

VARIABLES INFLUENCING CHILDREN'S RECOGNITION MEMORY

The purpose of this section is to review some of our research concerned with children's recognition memory, as manifested through performance on discrimination learning tasks. (For extensive reviews of related research with adults, see Wallace, 1972, and Eckert & Kanak, 1974.) As will become apparent shortly, in the experiments wherein properties of *stimulus materials* have been manipulated, we have been able to account reasonably well for various discrimination learning phenomena in terms of Ekstrand *et al.*'s (1966) frequency theory. In contrast, this is not the case when it comes to a consideration of experiments wherein the nature of subjects' *rehearsal strategies* has been manipulated. Indeed, some recently collected data have been influential in convincing us that simple frequency discriminations do not appear to enter into discrimination learning performance when certain rehearsal strategies are incorporated into the task. As a result, when we deal with these findings a different explanatory route will be taken.

Components of the Frequency Theory Assumption

Before we present data which permit a frequency-attribute account of discrimination learning outcomes, let us first examine the basic assumption of the frequency theory vis-à-vis the discrimination learning paradigm. Recall that it is assumed that subjects master the discrimination task by learning to choose the more "frequent" member of each pair, with the increased frequency resulting from the additional exposure received by (i.e., attention paid to) the correct item during feedback. There are two obvious components of this assumption: (*a*) subjects do indeed focus more on the correct item than on the incorrect item during feedback, thereby increasing its (the correct item's) frequency; and that having done so: (*b*) subjects are capable of discriminating frequency differences. Each of these assumption components has received empirical support in the most straightforward tests of them possible.

For example, it has been demonstrated that following a single study trial of a discrimination list, subjects are able to recognize previously correct items better than previously incorrect items from a list containing each of these, as well as some distractors (e.g., Wilder, Levin, Kuskowski, and Ghatala, 1974). While the *incorrect* items clearly have greater subjective frequency than previously unseen distractors (since the two are easily recognized as "old" or "new," respectively), the finding that *correct* items are recognized better than *incorrect* items attests to the plausibility of component *a* above.

Similarly, the reasonableness of component *b* has been substantiated in what are called "frequency judgment" tasks. In such tasks, a long list of items is presented, with some items presented only once and others presented more than once (i.e., two, three, four, or more times). The subject's subsequent task is to discriminate these presentation frequencies by indicating either how many times each item previously appeared upon its re-presentation (absolute frequency judgments), or which of two items in a pair previously appeared more often (relative frequency judgments). Subjects are very good at such tasks, inasmuch as their performances are far above what would be expected on the basis of chance or haphazard guessing (e.g., see Underwood and Freund, 1970). This is true even for young children (e.g., Ghatala and Levin, 1973). Data of this sort are clearly compatible with Underwood's (1969) claim that "frequency" is a well functioning memory attribute.

How can we be sure, however, that even though subjects are *capable* of making frequency discriminations, that they utilize this ability in the discrimination learning task? In other words, how can we be sure that the frequency attribute is materially involved in subjects' discrimination performance? Although we cannot be sure, we are able to provide evidence which indicates that this speculation is plausible. Thus, it has been substantiated that frequency judgment ability and discrimination learning performance are respectably correlated (see, for example, Underwood and Freund, 1970). Certainly no causal ties relating frequency judgment ability and discrimination learning may be imputed on the basis of such evidence; but at the same time, the available evidence suggests that similar processes seem to be at work in both tasks, and that these processes are quite separable from subjects' general cognitive ability and other memory attribute variables (Ghatala, Levin, and Subkoviak, 1975; Levin and Ghatala, in press). Returning to our earlier discussion, this constitutes evidence of the *correlative* variety which suggests that discrimination learning can be accounted for in terms of the frequency theory model.

Now that we have reviewed the components of the frequency theory assumption, let us examine the data bearing on the question of discrimination learning differences as a function of variations in stimulus materials.

Stimulus Materials Differences

Pictures versus Words

For some time now Allan Paivio and his associates (see Paivio, 1971) have reported that pictures are learned more easily than words in a variety of learning tasks (see also Levin, this volume). With respect to present emphases, such "picture superiority" has been noted even in tasks which demand no verbal productions on the part of the subject, as in discrimination learning; and also when the subjects have consisted of children rather than adults (e.g., Ghatala, Levin, and Makoid, 1975, Experiment 2; Rowe, 1972; Wilder and Levin, 1973). To account for this result in terms of *correlative* evidence, the frequency theory would have to predict that presentations of pictures result in apparent (or subjective) frequencies which differ in certain ways from apparent frequencies produced by presentations of words.

And, indeed, this is precisely what we have discovered. In one experiment, for example, using an absolute frequency judgment task we (Ghatala, Levin, and Wilder, 1973) found that pictures were judged to have been presented more frequently than words (even though the two in reality had been presented equally often). Moreover, the variability of subjects' judgments was much smaller with pictures than with words. Both results (greater apparent frequency and lesser variability for pictures than for words) are consistent with a frequency-theory notion concerning why pictures should comprise superior learning materials in the discrimination task. Put simply, larger and less variable apparent frequency units should be easier to discriminate.[2] (A figural representation of these situations has been provided by Fozard, 1970, to deal with picture—word differences in *recency*, or temporal discriminations.)

Even stronger (i.e., *causative*) evidence may be provided to trace picture—word differences in discrimination learning to a simple apparent frequency mechanism. Specifically, if discrimination learning differences have their causal basis in apparent frequency differences, then, if the latter are in some way made to disappear, so should the former. To use an analogy, if vehicle A runs faster than vehicle B *solely because* it has a larger engine, if we provide equal-sized engines for the two vehicles they should run equally fast.

Utilizing the frequency judgment data of Ghatala *et al.* (1973), we conducted a second experiment (Levin, Ghatala, and Wilder, 1974) in which we included pictures and words that were either closely matched or greatly separated in terms of the previously described measures of apparent frequency (means and variances). If apparent frequency is responsible for the discrimination learning differences associated with the two types of material, performance differences should be largest when the apparent frequency measures associated with pictures are widely discrepant from those associated with words and smallest when these measures are close together for the two types of material. Not only were the theoretical predictions upheld, but under the closely matched conditions picture—word differences on the discrimination learning task disappeared completely. For example, as may be seen in Figure 1, with materials where the picture apparent frequency variances were much smaller than the word variances, pictures improved performance relative to words; however, with materials where the picture and word variances were closely matched, the advantage of pictures was greatly reduced and, in fact, statistically nonsignificant. Since plausible alternative hypotheses concerning other stimulus attributes (perhaps correlated with apparent frequency) that might account for the pattern of our results were ruled out on empirical grounds (cf. Levin *et al.,* 1974) there remained little doubt that apparent frequency is the primary mechanism responsible for picture—word discrimination learning differences.

---

[2] In subsequent research we have found that subjects' frequency judgment *variability* and a somewhat related measure, *accuracy* (or the number of correct judgments made), as associated with different types of stimulus materials, are measures which consistently have counterparts in discrimination learning differences, whereas *mean* frequency differences do not (see, for example, Ghatala and Levin, 1973, 1974).

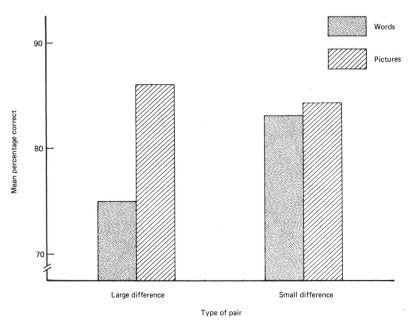

Figure 1. Discrimination learning performance with pictures and words either widely separated or closely matched with respect to a measure of apparent frequency.

Rare versus Common Words

Just as we have capitalized on frequency theory notions to account for picture-over-word effects in the discrimination task, we can similarly do so in accounting for the finding that words that are relatively rare in occurrence in the English language are often easier to learn in the discrimination task in comparison to commonly occurring words (see Wallace, 1972). What is more, by incorporating (in expanded form) a speculation offered by Ekstrand *et al.* (1966) in their initial formulation of the theory, we believe that the frequency theory model is greatly strengthened in its ability to account for the rare versus common word effect.

Frequency Accrual and Weber's Law. Specifically, Ekstrand *et al.* (1966) posited, almost as an aside that:

> . . . (according to Weber's law) . . . adding one unit to an item already high in frequency should be less noticeable than adding one frequency unit to an item low in frequency . . . Other things being equal . . . an extra frequency unit added to a member of a high-frequency pair should not be "worth as much" in terms of cue value as a frequency unit added to a member of a low frequency pair [pp. 575–576].

Thus, Ekstrand *et al.* (1966) suggested that like various sensory discriminations—where stimuli of very high intensities (e.g., two different tones well above perception thresholds) are more difficult to discriminate between than stimuli of lower intensities (e.g., two different tones just above perception thresholds)—frequency discrimination is perhaps characterized by a function analogous to Weber's psychophysical law. It should be noted, however, that we will be treating the Weber's law analogy (as applied to frequency discriminations) as just that, namely, an analogy. That is, although we can provide evidence that there is a *tendency* for discriminations between items of low "base" frequencies to be superior to those between items of high "base" frequencies, we certainly do not pretend to be attributing a precise mathematical *function* to this relationship. (The reader is cautioned that henceforth when we refer to "Weber's law" in the context of frequency discriminations we have in mind the analogy just described.)

As we shall see, Weber's law seems to hold in the case of direct *experimental* manipulation of frequency inputs. Subsequently, the law has been invoked to explain the effects of *extraexperimental* sources of frequency inputs. Let us first consider some data which are directly interpretable in terms of Weber's law as applied to frequency discrimination.

Experimental Manipulations of Frequency. Recall the frequency judgment task that was described earlier in this section. There it was stated that such a task may be used to determine the extent to which subjects are capable of making accurate frequency discriminations. We further pointed out that the existing data suggest that subjects are very good at discriminating among frequency inputs. Hereafter, we shall refer to such discriminations as *intrasituational* frequency discriminations, in that subjects are required to discriminate among frequencies induced within the same experimental situation.

In this context, the data of Ghatala and Levin (1973) may be used to illustrate the topic of present concern, namely the operation of Weber's law in frequency discrimination. Elementary school children were administered an orally presented list of words (common nouns) each occurring with varying frequencies (from one to eight times) throughout the list. Following the presentation list, subjects were presented with pairs of words and were required to indicate which word in each pair had been previously presented more often (relative frequency judgments). In addition, the test list included items which had not been presented previously. The complete design of the test list is presented in Table 1, where each cell may be regarded as a discrimination between two items containing different base frequencies. For example, the

TABLE 1
Relative Frequency Judgment Performance as a Function of
Base and Difference Frequencies: Mean Percentage Correct[a]

0 versus 1	0 versus 2	0 versus 3
86	92	94
1 versus 2	1 versus 3	1 versus 4
83	83	75
3 versus 4	3 versus 5	3 versus 6
64	89	86
5 versus 6	5 versus 7	5 versus 8
67	72	80

[a]After Ghatala and Levin (1973).

upper left cell pitted an item that had initially been presented once against one that had never been presented before (a "zero" item); whereas the lower left cell pitted an item that had initially been presented six times against one that had been presented five times. If Weber's law applies here, even though the absolute frequency difference between two items is the same, subjects should be better at discriminating between items with low base frequencies than between items with high base frequencies. That this prediction was confirmed may be readily seen by the percentage accuracy scores in Table 1. Holding the frequency difference constant (i.e., within each column), it is apparent that performance is generally better in the upper portion of the table (where base frequencies are low) than in the lower portion (where base frequencies are high).[3] Underwood and Freund's (1970) and Hintzman's (1969) data based on adult subjects confirm these findings.

An additional source of support for Weber's law comes from the manipulation of items' frequencies in *different* experimental situations (i.e., *intersituational*). In such studies, items' base frequencies may be built up in a context apart from the discrimination task of interest. In one paradigm, for example, subjects are given "prefamiliarization" with the stimuli that are to be used in a subsequent discrimination learning task. The idea here is that prefamiliarization with the to-be-

---

[3] Note, however, that the decreasing accuracy trend is not perfect, which may be a function of item peculiarities.

discriminated stimuli should serve to increase their base frequencies and thereby decrease their subsequent discriminability à la Weber's law.

Levin, Ghatala, and DeRose (1974) conducted just this experiment with fourth-grade children. In the first phase of the study, subjects performed identification and matching tasks with a collection of stimuli. In the experimental conditions, these stimuli consisted of printed words that comprised a discrimination list administered in the second phase of the study. Subjects in the control condition performed the initial tasks with stimuli unrelated to those used subsequently. As anticipated from the base frequency differences induced in the two conditions, the discrimination learning performance of control subjects by far surpassed that of experimental subjects. Thus, the results of this study (as well as those based on adult subjects, e.g., Berkowitz, 1968; Lovelace, 1969) are entirely consistent with predictions derived from Weber's law.

Extra-experimental Sources of Frequency Inputs: Background Frequency. Thus far we have been operating under the assumption that exposures of a stimulus, either within or between experimental stations, induce frequency into the stimulus which has an effect on its subsequent discriminability. In general as the amount of induced frequency applied to two or more stimuli increases, it becomes more difficult for subjects to discriminate interitem frequency differences. Vis-à-vis the present paradigm, the higher the experimentally induced base frequency of stimuli, the more difficult it is for a subject to choose the correct item in a verbal-discrimination task.

It is unreasonable to suppose, however, that all verbal stimuli—at least, meaningful English words of the kind we have considered—enter into the typical experimental situation with the same pre-experimental frequency. Obviously, in our daily lives we come into contact (through oral and written communications) with some words more frequently than others. How many times, for example, has the price of *rutabagas* entered into your conversation as opposed, say, to the price of *sugar*? Clearly, the word *sugar* has a much higher preexperimental base frequency than does the word *rutabaga* (unless, by chance, you happen to be a rutabaga freak). In this chapter, we will sometimes refer to the extra-experimental base frequency of a stimulus as its "background" frequency. But how does such a notion help us to account for our initiating phenomenon, namely the usual superiority of rare over common words in a discrimination task?

There is good reason to believe that the base frequency—discriminability relationship (as characterized by our Weber's law analogy) is not restricted to "artificial" situations such as those in which base frequencies are selectively built up by an experimenter. Rather, it could be assumed that the same relationship obtains when nature is allowed to take its course, that is, when stimuli which differ in their background frequencies are selected for the discrimination task. This can be accomplished by referring to published norms which reflect the frequency of occurrence (in print or in speech) of various words.

For example, the Carroll, Davies, and Richman (1971) norms provide us with a fairly good idea of words which are and which are not common in the experiences of elementary school children. In one experiment (Ghatala, Levin, and Makoid, 1975, Experiment 2) we selected words which the norms indicated were quite common to fourth graders and compared the verbal-discrimination learning of such words with that produced by words which the norms indicated were less common. If Weber's law operates on pre-experimentally induced frequency inputs in a manner similar to how it operates in the laboratory (see our previous discussion), then it would be expected that the less common words (i.e., those with lower background frequencies) would be more easily discriminated than the more common words (i.e., those with higher background frequencies). This was precisely the case, with the children correctly discriminating an average of 80% of the less common words, as opposed to an average of 70% of the more common words.

But could our sample of low-frequency words have differed from the high-frequency words with regard to some other characteristic(s) which may have been responsible for these results, rather than background frequency per se? Possibly, but great care was taken to equate the two types of stimuli in as many ways as possible. For instance, only nouns were included, all of which were highly concrete (in the sense of having tangible referents). Moreover, wherever possible an attempt was made to match the high- and low-frequency materials both with respect to semantic characteristics (e.g., the class of objects they represented—thus, the high-frequency item *window* had its low-frequency counterpart in *chimney*) and orthographic characteristics (e.g., word length).

There is one additional datum that is of interest. It cannot be argued that the low-frequency words selected happened to be "special," in the sense that they were (in general terms) just more "learnable" than the high-frequency materials. Note that Weber's law has been applied to tasks which require item *recognitions* and *discriminations,* namely the kind that we have considered exclusively until now. A different outcome would be expected on a task which requires item *recall* since familiarity (as reflected by background frequency) and probability of retrieval (as reflected by successful recall) are positively correlated. Indeed, the opposite relationship between frequency and recognition, on the one hand, and frequency and recall, on the other, has been firmly established with adult subjects (see Kintsch, 1970). This proved to be the case in our experiment as well. When the same stimuli (which produced discrimination learning differences in favor of the low-frequency materials) were presented to additional fourth-grade subjects who were instructed to remember as many of them as they could in a free-recall task, the high-frequency materials were recalled somewhat *better* than the low-frequency materials. Thus, an "item peculiarity" explanation of the negative background frequency–discriminability relationship reported earlier will not suffice. If the low-frequency materials were just plain easier for one or more reasons, why then were they not recalled better than the high-frequency materials?

Meaningfulness as a Moderating Variable. But not all of the story has been told regarding the negative relationship between background frequency and verbal-discrimination learning performance. In the Ghatala, Levin, and Makoid (1975) study, it was pointed out that the literature contains obvious across-experiment discrepancies with respect to finding or not finding the relationship. One interesting hypothesis seemed to us worth pursuing. Quite simply, we hypothesized that a stimulus must first be meaningfully encoded before frequency begins to accrue to it.[4] This hypothesis was suggested by the abundant evidence in learning and retention studies that the meaningfulness of stimulus materials is an important determinant of performance. Contrast, introspectively, the different degrees of success you would likely encounter in memorizing a list of familiar names or places on the one hand, and a list of esoteric scientific terms (from a field in which you are a functional layman) on the other. So too might the applicability of Weber's law depend on similar meaningfulness considerations. And, indeed, our review of the literature revealed that in several experiments where the negative background frequency effect was *not* obtained, the low-frequency materials employed were of *such low frequency* that many may have been functionally meaningless to the subjects (but see Lovelace and Bansal, 1973). In the absence of a meaningful encoding of such stimuli, frequency might not accrue to them in the same manner as it would with more meaningful stimuli.

Our materials consisted of high- and low-frequency nouns taken from the Thorndike and Lorge (1944) adult norms. The low-frequency words could be further divided into those for which our subjects (sixth-graders) either could or could not provide definitions (according to very flexible criteria). Low-frequency, high-meaningfulness (Lo-F/Hi-M) items consisted of those low-frequency words which most of these

---

[4] Ekstrand *et al.* (1966) speculated that apparent frequency may not be built up effectively until "... the item is integrated sufficiently for its representation to be reliable. . . [p. 576]." Our hypothesis goes even further by asserting that in addition to a word being *stably* encoded (i.e., consistently perceived in the same way) it must be *meaningfully* encoded (i.e., semantically interpreted in a reasonable fashion). Some data recently provided by Rowe (1974) suggest that even the particular semantic interpretation may have to be stable.

children could define (e.g., *hatchet*), whereas low-frequency, low-meaningfulness (Lo-F/Lo-M) items consisted of those low-frequency words which most of the children could not define (e.g., *dory*). It should be pointed out that despite these differences in meaningfulness, the two types of materials were virtually identical in terms of normed frequency (both averaging about six occurrences per million). Moreover, most subjects could pronounce the Lo-M and Hi-M words equally well, thereby suggesting that both types of items were stably encoded (see Footnote 4).

In two experiments, subjects performed an absolute frequency judgment task (Ghatala and Levin, 1974, Experiment 2; Ghatala, Levin, and Wilder, 1975) and in another, they performed a discrimination learning task (Ghatala, Levin, and Makoid, 1975, Experiment 1). In both cases it was found that the predictions stemming from Weber's law (i.e., discriminations between Lo-F words easier than those between Hi-F words) were confirmed only for the Lo-F/Hi-M materials (and not for the Lo-F/Lo-M materials), thereby supporting the hypothesis that the meaningfulness of the stimuli may be a crucial moderator of the background frequency–discrimination learning relationship. The poorest frequency judgment performance of all in the Ghatala and Levin (1974) experiment was obtained in a condition which utilized materials with even lower meaningfulness to subjects than Lo-F/Lo-M words; namely, with materials which were quasi-words (e.g., *vaplasf*, which represents a systematic transformation of the Lo-F/Lo-M word, *tankard*). Consistent with Ekstrand *et al.*'s (1966) speculations, such quasi-words are likely to be less well integrated by subjects, that is, less stably encoded, thereby reducing their subsequent discriminability.

In concluding our treatment of background frequency and verbal-discrimination learning, we should make explicit what has thus far been implicit in our discussion. Note that background frequency (moderated by meaningfulness) produced results in accord with Weber's law in *both* the frequency judgment task and in the verbal-discrimination task. That is, the situational frequencies of meaningful low-frequency words were easier to discriminate than the situational frequencies of high-frequency words; and, meaningful low-frequency words were better learned in the verbal-discrimination task than were high frequency words. These two results taken in combination support the following:

1. Background frequency influences situational frequency discriminations in such a way that its effect on performance in the verbal-discrimination task can be accounted for in terms of frequency theory.

2. Weber's law (as demonstrated in the laboratory with experimentally-induced frequency) can be extended to account for why background frequency influences situational frequency discriminations.

Thus, we know a little more about the laws and relationships governing frequency discrimination performance which (because they also hold in the discrimination learning situation) in turn strengthens the frequency theory model.

Other Stimulus Materials Findings

Abstract versus Concrete Nouns. Attention to the assumed role of frequency assists us in accounting for other discrimination learning phenomena as well. For example, for some time Paivio and his associates (see Paivio, 1971) have documented that stimuli which are concrete and image-evoking are learned more easily in a variety of tasks than those which are not. The superiority of concrete nouns (such as *water* and *barber,* which subjects rate high in visual imagery evocativeness) over abstract nouns (such as *thought* and *sobriety,* which subjects rate low) has been noted in verbal-discrimination tasks (e.g., Rowe and Paivio, 1971b, 1972).

In order to determine whether it is possible to reconcile frequency theory with the concreteness or imagery effect, Wallace, Murphy, and Sawyer (1973, Experiment 7) contrasted high-imagery and low-imagery nouns in a relative frequency judgment task. They found that the high-imagery (concrete) words yielded more accurate frequency discriminations than did the low-imagery (abstract) words—a result which provides correlative evidence for a frequency-theory account of the imagery effect. Wallace *et al.* did not speculate as to the reason for the effect of imagery upon frequency discriminations.[5]

Following our previous discussion of Weber's law, a plausible explanation is suggested when the findings of Galbraith and Underwood (1973) are considered. These authors investigated other properties which might be differentially associated with abstract and concrete words. Subjects were presented with both abstract and concrete words, such as those above, and simply asked to indicate how common each was perceived to be in printed discourse. Interestingly, the abstract words were judged to occur *more frequently* than the concrete words *even when their actual normative* (according to either the Thorndike and Lorge, 1944, or Kucera and Francis, 1967, count) *frequencies were the same.*

Galbraith and Underwood concluded that since concreteness and phenomenal frequency are confounded, learning outcomes attributed to the influence of the former may instead reflect the influence of the latter. Indeed, one could make use of Weber's law to explain the

[5] It should be noted that Rowe (in press) has been unable to replicate some of the Wallace *et al.* (1973) findings. However, this does not include the result mentioned here.

difference favoring concrete over abstract words in a frequency discrimination task. Since abstract words are *perceived* to have higher background frequencies than concrete words, situational frequency inputs should not be "worth as much" for them, which would in turn explain why abstract words are more poorly discriminated (consistent with the previously discussed high- versus low-frequency stimulus results).

This explanation has been supported by a recent experiment (Ghatala and Levin, in press) in which we systematically separated the effects of the concreteness–imagery and phenomenal frequency variables in verbal-discrimination learning. First, we had a sample of college students rate a large number of abstract and concrete nouns on a 5-point frequency scale. As expected, the abstract (low-imagery) words were rated significantly higher than were the concrete (high-imagery) words even though the two sets of words were equated on Thorndike–Lorge frequency and on meaningfulness. This result replicates that of Galbraith and Underwood (1973, Experiment 3). Then, utilizing these phenomenal frequency values, we were able to form one verbal-discrimination list in which pairs varied widely in concreteness and imagery but were equated on phenomenal background frequency and meaningfulness (small-difference list). A second list consisted of pairs which varied on concreteness and imagery *and* on phenomenal frequency (large-difference list), with items comprising abstract pairs having higher frequency than those comprising concrete pairs.

The results are summarized in Figure 2, and they may be seen to parallel those associated with picture–word manipulations in Figure 1. In particular, the usual significant concrete-over-abstract effect was obtained in the large-difference condition (where phenomenal frequency was allowed to vary), but not in the small-difference condition (where it was controlled). We conclude from these results that background frequency underlies the concreteness–imagery effect in verbal-discrimination learning. Thus, like most of the other stimulus variables that we have investigated, the concreteness–imagery effect in verbal-discrimination learning is amenable to explanation in terms of laws governing frequency discriminations.

Age as a Moderator of Stimulus Materials Effects. In our research concerning the effect of stimulus materials variations on discrimination learning performance, we have had occasion to focus on age differences within the elementary school grades. For example, in one study we found that the ability to judge frequency improves throughout this age range, and with it the previously noted picture–word differences increase (Ghatala and Levin, 1973). Moreover, the results of two recently completed studies in our laboratory suggest that both perceived background frequency effects and discrimination learning differ-

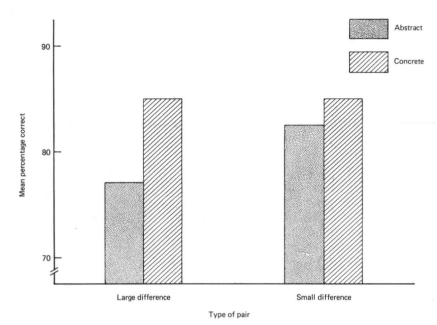

Figure 2. Discrimination learning performance with abstract and concrete nouns either widely separated or closely matched with respect to a measure of perceived background frequency.

ences, in favor of concrete over abstract materials, similarly increase with age.

Although it is possible to offer theoretical explanations to account for each of these results, we consider it premature to do so here, since what evidence there is concerning developmental effects is still sparse, existing in bits and pieces. Because of this, we will withhold our interpretations until more evidence has been assembled.

Frequency Theory and Stimulus Materials: A Recapitulation

In summarizing the information presented so far, we will reiterate a view that was espoused early on: Frequency theory accounts nicely for the results of our discrimination learning studies involving stimulus materials variations. Thus, in those situations where we have discovered apparent frequency differences associated with different stimulus materials, we have discovered concomitant discrimination learning differences associated with them (see also Bourne, Levin, Konewko,

Yaroush, and Ghatala, in press; and Levin, Bourne, Yaroush, Ghatala, DeRose, and Hanson, in press). Moreover, in the studies where we empirically equated stimuli on the basis of various frequency measures, discrimination learning differences were obliterated (Ghatala and Levin, in press; Levin, Ghatala, and Wilder, 1974). Therefore, for at least two classes of variables (abstract versus concrete nouns and pictures versus words), we have fairly compelling *causative* evidence supporting the conclusion that different stimulus materials influence discrimination learning *because* they are associated with corresponding frequency differences.

Our experiments (as well as those of others) concerning the effects of experimental manipulations of actual frequency on frequency judgment performance indicate the appropriateness of incorporating a Weber's law-like process into the theory. Furthermore, the extension of a Weber's law construct to account for the effects of extraexperimental sources of frequency (background frequency) on frequency discrimination performance strengthens the theory as a model for recognition memory. That is, the same construct can be utilized to describe the relationship between the background frequency of materials (moderated by meaningfulness) and performance in both frequency discrimination and verbal-discrimination learning studies.

The background frequency notion has been of still further interest to us. In our earlier writings we sought a single unifying explanation of all stimulus materials differences (including picture—word differences) in discrimination learning by attempting to stretch the background-frequency—Weber's law interpretation as far as possible. The argument was simply that pictures, like meaningful, low-frequency words, are low in background frequency, in that the *particular* pictorial materials used in experiments are not likely ever to have been viewed before by the subjects (indeed, they could be assumed to possess "zero" background frequency). Although we considered the explanation reasonable and parsimonious at first (see, for example, Ghatala and Levin, 1973), we are currently uncomfortable about its veracity since not all of our data are consistent with predictions following from a strict application of the explanation (e.g., Ghatala, Levin, and Makoid, 1975, Experiment 2; Levin, Ghatala, and DeRose, 1974). Thus, at the present time, the background frequency—Weber's law hypothesis taken alone does not appear to provide an unambiguous explanation for picture—word differences (see, for example, Levin, Bourne, Yaroush, Ghatala, DeRose, and Hanson, in press). However, we have not given up completely on this hypothesis—there still remain several experiments to be conducted which may help to resolve these difficulties. At the same time, we are considering other interpretations of our picture—word data (e.g., Paivio's "dual-coding" hypothesis—cf. Paivio, 1971). It should be noted, however, that any such explanation will have to deal with our finding that apparent frequency differences associated with pictures and words appear to be causally related to differences associated with the two types of materials in discrimination learning tasks.

Rehearsal Strategy Differences

In the final part of this section we continue to consider the verbal-discrimination learning paradigm, but in so doing, we focus on instructional variations that have been employed to influence performance. Such variations generally consist of rehearsal strategies adopted by the subject and, in particular, involve some activity or response by the subject directed toward the correct item in each pair. In addition to assessing the comparative facilitation associated with various rehearsal strategies (including their interactions with characteristics of the stimulus materials), we have also attempted to account for the empirical results in frequency—theoretic terms. We note at the outset (as we did at the beginning of this section) that such attempts have failed. As we proceed we hope to indicate why.

Facilitative Rehearsal Strategies in Children's Discrimination Learning

Vocalization and Imagery. Two rehearsal strategies which have been examined extensively require that the subject either *vocalize* or *image* the correct response during feedback. For example, it has been observed for some time now that when adults are confronted with a verbal-discrimination task of sufficient difficulty, their performance is enhanced by verbally rehearsing the correct response during feedback (e.g., Carmean, 1971; Underwood and Freund, 1968; Wilder, 1971). Moreover, the same result has been obtained in our research with children (Ghatala, Levin, and Subkoviak, 1975; Levin, Ghatala, DeRose, Wilder, and Norton, 1975; Levin, Ghatala, Wilder, and Inzer, 1973), with the effect being especially noticeable when the discrimination materials consist of pictures (Levin *et al.*, 1973; Wilder and Levin, 1973) or low-frequency materials of potentially high meaningfulness as described earlier in this chapter (Ghatala, Levin, and Wilder, 1975).

Similarly, when adult subjects are instructed to generate a visual image of the correct item's referent, their discrimination performance is facilitated (e.g., Rowe and Cake, 1974; Rowe and Paivio, 1971a)—a result that has also been established with children in our laboratory (Ghatala, Levin, and Subkoviak, 1975; Levin *et al.*, 1975, Experiment 1; Levin *et al.*, 1973).

A Distinction between Overt and Covert Rehearsal Strategies. Both imagery and vocalization strategies have been utilized in forms which may be referred to as *overt* or *covert*. The vocalization results discussed so far have been based on an overt manifestation of the strategy, inasmuch as the subject performs the rehearsal aloud. It may be argued that such overt vocalization activity results in articulatory and/or acoustic feedback from which the subject may benefit when later discriminating correct and incorrect items. On the other hand, the imagery results discussed so far have been based on a covert manifestation of the strategy, in that the strategy has been implicitly executed by the subject and without benefit of external feedback.

This is not to say that covert vocalization and overt imagery strategies cannot be devised. Indeed, we have been studying the effect of having children vocalize the correct response *to themselves*, and have externalized the imagery strategy by having children actually trace with their finger the imagined outline of the correct item's referent (Levin, Ghatala, DeRose, and Makoid, in press; Levin *et al.*, 1975). The important thing to mention here is that (at least for elementary school children) the overt version of each strategy is clearly superior to the covert version. Thus, children benefit substantially more from overtly verbalizing than from covertly verbalizing, and more from overtly imaging than from covertly imaging.

Because of the circumscribed focus of this chapter, we have elected to exclude data pertaining solely to comparisons of imagery and vocalization strategies (see, for example, Levin, Ghatala, DeRose, and Makoid, in press, Experiment 2; Levin *et al.*, 1975, Experiments 1 and 3; Levin *et al.*, 1973; Rowe and Paivio, 1971a). For similar reasons, and as we did in the case of stimulus materials, we will not pursue any of the potentially interesting developmental issues which come out of such comparisons (see, for example, the Levin, Ghatala, DeRose, and Makoid, in press, discussion of Experiment 2).

What we *will* do, however, is to review in some detail the outcomes that would be expected if the frequency theory were sufficient to account for the facilitative effects of imagery and vocalization strategies. Then, discovering that the empirical data do not match these theoretical expectations, we will consider an alternative hypothesis to account for the findings.

Frequency Theory and Rehearsal Strategy Effects
(Correlative Evidence)

Evidence Based on Similar Effects in Different Tasks. As we argued earlier, in order to maintain a frequency-theory perspective in the discrimination learning paradigm, a correspondence must be found between frequency discriminations per se and performance on a discrimination learning task. Thus, if frequency discrimination is indeed the primary mechanism underlying discrimination learning, then variables shown to influence the latter should similarly influence the former. This was generally found to be the case with stimulus materials, inasmuch as whenever a stimulus materials manipulation was shown to exert an influence on discrimination learning, the manipulation was traced to its exertion of a similar influence in frequency judgment performance. For example, pictures are better discriminated than words, and their situational frequencies are judged more accurately; the same is true with meaningful, low-frequency words as compared to high-frequency words. Can the same statements be made with respect to effective discrimination learning rehearsal strategies such as imagery and vocalization?

Apparently not. In their work with adults, Hopkins, Boylan and Lincoln (1972, Experiment 1) found that the mean judgments of subjects who pronounced all items in a list did not differ from those of subjects who remained silent. (More will be said shortly about Experiment 2 of Hopkins *et al.*) Our own analysis of the Hopkins *et al.* data—which were graciously shared with us by Professor Ronald Hopkins—revealed that neither were the pronunciation subjects more accurate in judging frequencies than subjects who did not pronounce.

We have reached the same conclusion in a number of experiments with children. In the Ghatala *et al.* (1973) absolute frequency judgment task, there were no significant differences between pronunciation and control subjects with either verbal or pictorial stimuli—a result that we have since corroborated using both an absolute and a relative frequency judgment task. At the same time, it would be misleading to state that we have *never* observed an effect of pronunciation on subjective frequency, for in fact we have (Wilder, Levin, Ghatala, and McNabb, 1974). In that experiment subjects who pronounced each stimulus were more accurate and less variable in judging frequency than subjects who remained silent. However, the words used in the experiment were relatively rare, and the effect of pronouncing them may simply have been to enhance their meaningfulness, which would in turn improve frequency discriminations (see our earlier discussion of meaningfulness and frequency accuracy). This interpretation has received some support from a subsequent experiment in which the issue was addressed directly (Ghatala, Levin, and Wilder, 1975).

Our discussion extends to the consideration of frequency differences associated with the use of visual imagery as a rehearsal strategy. In particular, Ghatala *et al.* (1973) found that subjects instructed to image each item as it appeared judged frequency no differently than subjects not so instructed—a result that has since been replicated in a relative frequency judgment task.

Evidence Based on Subject Consistencies in Different Tasks. Since, in the case of stimulus materials variations, frequency theory expectations were confirmed through their exerting similar effects on different tasks (verbal-discrimination learning and frequency judgment) there was no need to seek additional *correlative* evidence. However, because of the initial disconfirmed expectancies using the same approach to account for rehearsal strategy effects, an alternative attack on the problem was instigated. Specifically, if frequency discrimination ability is an important ingredient of discrimination learning, then (consistent with our earlier discussion concerning the nature of *correlative* evidence) there should be a substantial correlation between frequency judgment and discrimination learning ability. And, indeed (as was mentioned at the beginning of this section), such a correlation has been reported in the case of adult subjects performing frequency judgments and the usual verbal-discrimination learning task, that is, without the benefit of a rehearsal strategy (see Underwood and Freund, 1970).

To determine whether we could duplicate this result with children, we (Ghatala, Levin, and Subkoviak, 1975) administered to two groups of sixth-graders both a relative frequency judgment task and a verbal-discrimination learning task, using different sets of verbal items. For these subjects, the correlation between the two tasks was quite respectable ($r = .40$ for each group), and was certainly anticipated under the assumption that the frequency attribute is involved in discrimination learning. But two other groups of subjects were also included in the experiment, namely those who performed the discrimination learning task using a rehearsal strategy (either vocalization or imagery). For these subjects, the correlation between the two tasks was negligible (r's = .04 and −.08 for vocalization and imagery respectively). Thus, the implication of these results seems clear: The usual discrimination learning task appears to involve processes similar to those called upon in judging situational frequency. However, when the same discrimination task is administered in the company of efficient rehearsal strategies, the just mentioned frequency-judgment processes do not appear to be involved. To put this another way, Underwood's (1969) frequency attribute does not appear to be reflected in children's discrimination learning when either a vocalization or an imagery rehearsal strategy is employed.

But if frequency cannot be implicated (in either a task- or a subject-consistency sense) to account for rehearsal strategy effects in children's discrimination learning, what can? Let us consider an alternative possibility.

Subjects' Rehearsal Activity as a Memory Attribute

We have adopted the point of view that frequency is a dominant memory attribute in the usual discrimination learning task. However, frequency may not be the *only* attribute involved, especially when the task is not "usual." For example, Wallace (1972) reviews studies where frequency as a cue has been effectively removed from the discrimination task (e.g., in so-called "double function" lists, where the correct item in one pair is the incorrect item in another pair). If frequency were the only discriminative attribute relied on in such tasks, subjects would be unable to succeed in mastering them (in the double function list, for example, correct and incorrect alternatives have the same frequency across pairs). Yet subjects do succeed in mastering such tasks. Similarly, Wallace (1972) cites as "special cases" those studies in which "obvious" discriminative cues are provided within the verbal-discrimination list. For example, each correct item may occupy the right-hand position in each pair. In such cases, differential frequency may be eliminated as a cue at the item level (cf. Wallace, 1972, p. 296).

One could analogously argue that when an imagery or vocalization strategy is executed by a subject in a discrimination learning task, the task is not "usual" any more. That is to say, under such conditions the nature of the task changes from one which implicates frequency as the functional discriminative cue to one which implicates some other discriminative cue instead. In the Ghatala, Levin, and Subkoviak (1975) study we tested this notion. It will be recalled that in the usual version of the discrimination task (i.e., with no strategy), frequency judgment ability was correlated with performance, whereas in the strategy versions of the task it was not.

However, a third task was included in the study—one that we have not yet described—which was expected to be related to discrimination learning when a rehearsal strategy was present. The task, termed a "strategy identification" task following Zechmeister and Gude (1974), consisted simply of presenting subjects with a long list of words and having them employ a strategy for some words but not others. In one version of the task, subjects pronounced some words but not others; in the second version of the task, they imaged some but not others. Following the study list, subjects were presented each of the words again (in a different random order than initially) and were required to indicate which they had previously rehearsed and which they had not.

Interestingly, performance on both versions of the strategy identification task was completely unrelated to either frequency judgment ability or to discrimination learning in the absence of rehearsal instructions (in no case was the correlation significantly different from zero), thereby suggesting that the specific abilities tapped by the strategy identification task seemed to be separable from those tapped by the other tasks. Of primary importance for present purposes, however, was the finding that when the discrimination task was administered in the company of a rehearsal strategy, performance was substantially related to strategy identification ability ($r = .64$ for both imagery and vocalization strategies).

Thus, the interpretation is clear. In the usual discrimination learning task, performance seems to involve simple frequency discriminations. When the same task is accompanied by effective strategy instructions, however, it does not. Rather it seems to involve discriminations based on "activity" decisions, that is, decisions of the form, "For which of these two items did I previously engage in the specified rehearsal activity?" In the latter situations it may be reasonably concluded (based on the empirical evidence cited above) that frequency discriminations have been supplanted by activity discriminations, with the accuracy of these discriminations being predictive of discrimination learning performance.

Indeed, we are inclined to incorporate activity discriminations into Underwood's (1969) memory attribute framework, inasmuch as these seem closely akin to the kind of discriminations stemming from his "modality" attribute (e.g., discriminating whether a particular stimulus was initially presented in a visual or in an acoustic form). Relying on an "activity" attribute representation, we can better understand certain previously difficult-to-interpret findings. For example, it has been found that vocalization rehearsal generally influences subsequent frequency discriminations in situations where subjects pronounce some but not other items in a list, but not in situations where they pronounce all of them (cf. Ghatala *et al.*, 1973; Hopkins *et al.*, 1972; Hopkins and Edwards, 1972; Wilder, Levin, Kuskowski, and Ghatala, 1974). Clearly, when subjects have rehearsed *every* item in a list they are unable to utilize the activity attribute as a basis for discrimination; however, they can when only *some* of the items have been rehearsed.

On the other hand, it is possible to stretch the frequency-theory position and assume that the activity attribute is based primarily on a frequency decision. That is, discriminating one's rehearsal activity involves an apparent frequency judgment associated with each item, in the same manner as in a simple recognition memory task (see Underwood and Freund, 1970). However this assumption is not easily reconciled with our previously reported finding that activity and frequency decisions are uncorrelated. To fit the assumption to the empirical data requires a reformulation of the present unidimensional conception of the frequency attribute, which certainly detracts from its appeal to parsimony.

Frequency Theory and Rehearsal Strategies: A Recapitulation

We have been led to conclude on the basis of empirical evidence that frequency theory cannot account for rehearsal strategy effects in children's discrimination learning. In fact, the evidence indicates that when strategies are introduced into the task, the frequency cue is supplanted by what we have called the activity attribute (for followup research and discussion, see Levin and Ghatala, in press). Thus, our work on strategies has uncovered one set of circumstances in which the frequency attribute is not utilized by children. In the next section we attempt to provide a more comprehensive analysis of the circumstances under which frequency will and will not be utilized by children as a dominant cue in more complex (and more educationally relevant) recognition memory tasks.

DIRECTIONS FOR FURTHER RESEARCH AND IMPLICATIONS FOR EDUCATION

The focus of our research, as recounted in the preceding section, has been concerned with whether children can and do utilize their ability to assimilate and discriminate situational frequencies in performing recognition memory tasks. On the basis of the evidence assembled, the answer would appear to be a qualified "yes," with the qualifications (as we see them) related to *the extent to which the recognition memory situation makes available to the learner discriminative cues other than frequency.* First we will provide illustrations of two general classes of cues (implicit and explicit) that may supplement or supplant frequency under certain conditions; and having done this, we will make apparent the limitations of a strict frequency-theory perspective of recognition memory.[6] Then we will assess what we need to know in order to present a more comprehensive view of recognition memory, one which has serious implications for education.

What We Know and What We Need to Know

We know that elementary school children as young as kindergarten age are capable of very accurate frequency discriminations (cf. Ghatala

---

[6] The implicit–explicit distinction may be related to Rowher's (1973) identification of various types of learning "prompts." The discussion which follows is somewhat reminiscent of Tulving's (1972) distinction between "episodic" and "semantic" memory as well as of Brown's (in press) elaboration of the distinction.

and Levin, 1973). Thus, frequency is a well-functioning memory attribute in children as well as adults. We also know that children appear to
utilize the frequency attribute as a basis for performing recognition
memory tasks (Ghatala, Levin, and Subkoviak, 1975; Levin and
Ghatala, in press) and, moreover, that recognition memory differences
associated with different types of materials may be traced to their
differing influence on subjective frequency (Bourne *et al.*, in press;
Ghatala and Levin, in press; Ghatala, Levin, and Makoid, 1975; Levin,
Ghatala, and Wilder, 1974).

Consider, however, the procedure by which one typically studies the
recognition memory process. The classical verbal-discrimination paradigm used in our and others' experiments is one which might be
characterized as affording a relatively impoverished stimulus environment. That is, correct and incorrect items within and across pairs are
systematically chosen to be undifferentiable with respect to every
dimension that the experimenter can imagine (e.g., concreteness, meaningfulness, association value, normative frequency). There is, therefore,
nothing in the stimulus situation per se (excepting unknown idiosyncratic factors) which can plausibly be perceived by subjects as a useful
discriminative cue for mastering each of the pairs in the list. In other
words, frequency is about the only reliable cue available.

We know, however, that verbal-discrimination lists can be constructed in such a way that discriminations on the basis of apparent
frequency alone become difficult, if not impossible (e.g., Kausler and
Boka, 1968). At the same time, one can construct lists containing
implicit discriminative cues, which, if recognized by the learner, enable
him/her to approach the task as more than a simple item-frequency
encoder. Wallace (1972), p. 296), for example, cites evidence showing
that when alternative cues become available (e.g., all correct items
occupy the same spatial position in each pair), adults can capitalize on
these and, as a result, effectively abandon item apparent frequency as
the functional discriminative cue. It should be noted that the "if
recognized" proviso above is important. Thus, it is not sufficient that
alternative discriminative cues are simply made available. In order to
become functional, such cues must be perceived by subjects; and it
appears that cues are more likely to be recognized (and hence utilized)
if they are congruent with the learner's cognitive makeup (as defined by
such characteristics as age, cognitive ability, and the like). As an
illustration, Ingison and Levin (1975, Experiment 2) demonstrated that
whereas both younger (kindergarten) and older (sixth-grade) children
could take advantage of cognitively lower-level cues embedded in a
pictorial discrimination list (i.e., all the correct items were of the same
size and shape), only the older children benefited from the provision of

cognitively more demanding cues (i.e., all the correct items were from the same taxonomic category).

Let us now consider what we mean by an *explicit* enrichment of the recognition memory situation. We know that when subjects are explicitly instructed to employ an imagery or a vocalization rehearsal strategy in a discrimination learning task, performance generally improves (e.g., Ghatala, Levin, and Subkoviak, 1975). If one interprets such strategy effects in terms of the provision of alternative discriminative cues for the learner, then the previous comments relating to the role of frequency in this situation are again relevant. In particular, under strategy instructions, subjects seem to abandon apparent frequency as the dominant discriminative cue in favor of their own rehearsal activity (Ghatala, Levin, and Subkoviak, 1975).

As with the implicit cue results, however, probable interactions with subject characteristics should be noted. The conclusion in the preceding paragraph applies to a group of fifth- and sixth-grade children quite homogeneous in general ability (average or slightly below average in IQ). Adopting the argument that subjects of this age and/or ability are unlikely to perform *spontaneous* effective rehearsals in an uninstructed condition (cf. Rohwer, 1973), it would be of interest to determine whether frequency continues to be the predominant discriminative cue among cognitively more mature subjects. On the one hand, there is evidence (cf. Rowe and Paivio, 1971b) that under certain conditions college students report spontaneously employing an imagery strategy in the verbal-discrimination task. On the other, even such subjects seem to benefit from the explicit instruction to employ an imagery rehearsal strategy (e.g., Rowe and Paivio, 1971a); and moreover, in the uninstructed version of the task Underwood and Freund (1970) have noted a frequency judgment ability–verbal-discrimination learning correlation comparable to what we have found with children. The Ghatala, Levin, and Subkoviak (1975) paradigm might provide a convenient way of distinguishing between what learners actually do and what they report doing in this task.[7]

Although additional basic research questions have been generated by our investigations, we will not include them here. Rather let us sum up the information in the preceding paragraphs:

1. Fifth- and sixth-graders of average ability (and most certainly younger children) appear to utilize the frequency attribute in recognition memory tasks unless the stimulus environment is enriched.

[7] A study with college students, completed after this chapter was prepared, fully corroborates our conclusions based on children.

2. The enrichment can be accomplished if potentially useful discriminative cues are embedded in the materials themselves. Whether or
   not these cues are perceived by subjects, however, likely depends
   on the subjects' cognitive maturity.
3. In addition, enrichment can be accomplished by instructing children to employ rehearsal strategies that will furnish useful discriminative cues.

Once again it may be assumed that there are subject differences in the
extent to which such strategies are necessary and/or supplant apparent
frequency as the predominant discriminative attribute.

Now, having considered the circumstances under which frequency
apparently governs children's performance in recognition memory
tasks, as well as the circumstances under which other memory attributes likely predominate, we can begin to speculate about the implications of our research in educationally relevant contexts. Research
alluded to previously (and some not alluded to here) is currently being
conducted with these contexts in mind.

Implications for Education

Recognition as a Component in Higher Order Learning Tasks

We noted earlier that one reason we are interested in studying
children's recognition memory is that it is an important component of
more complex forms of learning. Concept learning, for example, is a
primary focus of education. And based on what we have found out
about the mental processes which are involved in recognition memory
under various circumstances (e.g., frequency and other attributes) we
can perhaps specify more analytically how such processes might be
involved in concept learning.

Klausmeier, elsewhere in this volume, describes a model of conceptual learning and development (Klausmeier, Ghatala, and Frayer, 1974)
which asserts that many concepts are learned at each of four successive
levels. The sequence of concept learning through these levels is postulated to be invariant, with each higher level dependent on attainment
at the next lower level. The logical analysis of concept learning provided by the model has received empirical support (Klausmeier, Sipple,
and Allen, 1974).

The first level of concept learning is the *concrete* level which,
according to the model, involves the operations of discriminating
among stimuli and remembering (i.e., recognizing) the stimulus when it
reoccurs. Presumably, for many concepts whose instances are readily

available in the environment, this stage is achieved by individuals at a very young age, and frequency may well be the mechanism underlying recognition at this level. At the next higher level, the *identity* level, the operation of generalizing that two or more forms of the same thing are equivalent may also proceed on the basis of a frequency mechanism. That is, those aspects of an object which remain the same across transformations will acquire greater frequency than those which are radically altered. Young children may base their identity responses on features with stably encoded frequency.

The *classificatory* level of concept attainment can also be achieved by young children and involves the additional operation of generalizing that two or more different instances are equivalent in some way. Again, this generalization could, in the absence of instruction which explicitly points out the rules for classifying, rest on the discrimination of a frequency differential which builds up between relevant and irrelevant attributes of the class members. Thus, relevant features which are always present in exemplars receive greater frequency than do irrelevant features which change from instance to instance (see Bourne, Ekstrand, Lovallo, Hiew, and Yaroush, 1974, for a similar analysis). Recall that earlier we emphasized that frequency will probably be utilized in recognition memory tasks (as at the concrete level) by very young children who may be incapable of utilizing other potential cues in the environment. Moreover, simple classifying behavior (as at the identity and classificatory levels) by young children who lack logical reasoning ability may also be based on simple frequency mechanisms. In line with our earlier conclusions, older children may also utilize frequency for classifying, unless provided with instruction which essentially teaches them a logical strategy for inducing concepts.

Klausmeier and his associates are conducting a combined cross-sectional–longitudinal study of concept attainment which is aimed primarily at charting the natural development of conceptual learning vis-à-vis the levels in the model. Initial cross-sectional data (Klausmeier, Sipple and Allen, 1974) indicate that not all kindergartners have achieved the concrete and identity levels of concepts such as **equilateral triangle** and **cutting tool**, and that large proportions of kindergartners and third-graders have not mastered these concepts at the classificatory level. It is within this age range, then, that research on frequency and other discriminative attributes of memory could be carried out within the context of tasks assessing these levels of concept learning. For example, studies utilizing the Ghatala, Levin and Subkoviak (1975) paradigm could be conducted to assess the extent of involvement of the frequency attribute in learning concepts at each of these levels for each age group.

Taking a different approach, manipulations could be carried out within the identity and classificatory level tasks which would make performance based on frequency discriminations either relatively easy or relatively difficult. One could then assess the effects of such manipulations on acquisition at these levels and on later acquisition of the same concept at the *formal* level. For example, acquisition at the classificatory level on the basis of frequency discrimination could be made quite difficult by presenting exemplars which do not display much variability with respect to irrelevant features and nonexemplars which share many of the same relevant and irrelevant features of the exemplars. This is an intrasituational manipulation of frequency which assures that the base frequencies of both relevant and irrelevant features of instances are quite high and therefore difficult to discriminate between, à la Weber's law. The reverse of this manipulation could be done to make classification on the basis of frequency discriminations among relevant and irrelevant features quite easy. If in fact these manipulations produce results in accord with frequency predictions, one would have *correlative* evidence that frequency discriminations are involved in concept learning at these levels with these age groups. One might then attempt to ameliorate the negative effects of such frequency manipulations by inducing subjects to employ strategies which would provide them with alternative cues upon which to base their recognition of class membership. Such strategies might involve the use of simple logical rules for distinguishing between relevant and irrelevant features. An interesting question involves the lower age limit at which such strategies can be utilized by children.

Such direct investigation of the role and nature of recognition memory processes in concept attainment would help to provide an analytical understanding of the operations specified by the Klausmeier, Ghatala and Frayer (1974) model to be involved in concept attainment at lower levels. Such increased understanding of the concept learning process could also eventuate in improved concept instruction. However, with respect to finding out more about children's recognition memory per se and its relevance to learning and instruction in educational settings, the following research avenue appears promising.

Encoding Styles, Strategies, and the Assessment of Instructional Outcomes: An Individual Differences Approach

From first-grade through graduate level education in this country, the most pervasive instrument for assessing learning is the so-called fixed-response objective test exemplified by multiple-choice, true–false, and matching items. This type of test differs from free-response objective tests in that the former requires students to *select* a response from among supplied alternatives while the latter requires the student to *supply* a response such as in short-answer or fill-in-the blank items. We shall concentrate here on the multiple-choice test because of its resemblance to the paradigm of verbal-discrimination learning which we have utilized in our research on recognition memory.

The typical multiple-choice item consists of a lead-in or stem followed by several options (usually four or five). The student must select the one option which correctly answers the question stated or, implied in the stem.[8] Usually only one option is correct—the other options which are designed to detect the uninformed student are called distractors. In "good" items such distractors are plausible and more likely to be selected by the less knowledgeable than by the more knowledgeable student. We shall further restrict our attention to those multiple-choice tests designed to test *acquisition* of knowledge. It is quite possible to utilize the multiple-choice format to test students' mastery of reasoning skills, problem-solving skills and other forms of *application* of knowledge.

Our earlier discussion of what we know about children's recognition memory and what we need to know suggests some interesting and important questions which can be answered in the following typical school situation: Students read (study) material concerning some topic. They are then given a standardized or, more usually, a teacher-made multiple-choice test to assess what they have learned, followed by some type of feedback concerning their performance. A later retest on the same material may be given to assess long-term retention.

One question concerns the relationship between individual differences in encoding processes and performance on multiple-choice tests under various circumstances. We concluded earlier that the frequency attribute would dominate recognition memory performance in the absence of experimenter-provided or subject-generated alternative discriminative cues. In comparison to the situation in which we have studied recognition memory, the learning situation described above is relatively rich with respect to cues available in the stimulus situation. However, it is probable that children differ in the ways in which they process information for subsequent retention and, therefore, the cues upon which recognition is based in the multiple-choice test will vary among children. For example, some children may engage in rote processing which involves little or no encoding of semantic properties of the

---

[8] Note that the multiple-choice item, because it contains a *context* (provided by the stem) in which one of the alternatives is correct, involves more than a simple frequency discrimination as in the verbal-discrimination task. Rather, a decision (if based on frequency at all) must involve discriminating the alternative with the highest *contingent frequency* (cf. Underwood, Patterson and Freund, 1972) associated with the stem proposition. For further discussion and encouraging empirical results, refer to Levin, Ghatala, Guttmann, Subkoviak, McCabe, and Bender, in press.

material.[9] We would expect performance of these children on a multiple-choice test covering the material to be governed by frequency processes. Thus, variables known to influence frequency discriminations should have strong effects on these students' performance on multiple-choice tests. Such variables could be manipulated in the learning material, on the test itself, or in feedback. On the other hand, many children may process the material they are attempting to learn at a "deeper" semantic level (cf. Craik and Lockhart, 1972). Since it appears that semantic cues provide a more effective basis than frequency on which to make decisions on a recognition test (discussed by Levin and Ghatala, in press), we would not expect much influence on semantic processors of variables designed to influence frequency discrimination. (For some initial support of this contention, see Gugliemella & Phye, 1975.)

The above research hypothesis is couched in terms of differentiating children in terms of an intrinsic individual-differences variable (cf. Jensen, 1967), namely level of encoding. However, because of the effort which would have to be invested in order to identify and reliably assess such encoding styles (see Ghatala, 1970b), less expensive preliminary research might be undertaken to ascertain the reasonableness of the hypothesis. Such preliminary research would involve "manipulating" those extrinsic individual-differences variables which one would logically presume to be related to the intrinsic difference of interest. Thus, low achievers might be more likely to process materials in a rote fashion than high achievers. Age might also be an extrinsic subject variable related to encoding styles, with young children more likely to engage in nonsemantic encoding than older children (Ghatala, 1970a). If encouraging results in favor of our hypothesis are found in preliminary research with extrinsic subject variables, then work can begin on direct assessment of encoding skills. (A conceptual framework for this assessment has been provided by Ghatala, 1970b.)

The second research question in this area is really complementary to the first. That is, assuming that we can reliably assess semantic encoding

---

[9] Within the framework of an attribute theory of memory (Underwood, 1969), we interpret semantic processing as involving encoding of associational and conceptual relationships embodied in the material. Nonsemantic processing involves encoding features of the material not related to *meaning*. Nonsemantic features of the material may include its acoustic, spatial, temporal, orthographic, frequency and other such characteristics. We assume that these latter types of information can be encoded along with semantic features and can serve useful purposes (e.g., providing a basis for discriminating between, and thus reducing interference between, different memories). We also assume that passing performance on multiple-choice tests in school settings can be achieved by discriminating the correct alternatives from distractors on the basis of nonsemantic features (most notably frequency differentials). However, we rather doubt that performance based on such attributes is the objective of teachers or developers of instructional materials (see, for example, Anderson, 1972).

skill deficits in children, can we remediate such deficits? Levin and Ghatala (in press) report data which indicate that instructing children to utilize strategies relating to the semantic features of items in the verbal-discrimination task greatly facilitate their performance in comparison to both control (no strategy) children and children instructed to employ strategies relating to the nonsemantic features of items. We need to know more about the effects of different types of strategies in school-learning tasks where the unit of learning is greater than a single verbal or pictorial item. In addition, we need to know more about the relationship of subjects' learning styles (in terms of the encoding skills they manifest) and the types of semantic processing strategies they can be taught to utilize.

Instructing children to employ various types of learning strategies may be one way to induce semantic encoding. However, there may be other, more effective methods of remediating semantic encoding deficits which will become apparent once we know more about encoding skills per se. Our current research has taught us much about children's encoding of one type of information—frequency—a type of non-semantic information which plays a prominent role in recognition memory under certain circumstances. Now we need to assess children's ability to encode and utilize other types of information (particularly semantic information) so that we may understand and be able to optimize children's performance on a wide variety of educationally relevant learning tasks.

ACKNOWLEDGMENTS

Part of this chapter was prepared while the second author was a Visiting Fellow at the National Institute of Education. We are grateful to our students and colleagues—especially to Dr. Larry Wilder—who collaborated on experiments cited in the chapter. Both authors contributed equally to the work represented here.

REFERENCES

Anderson, R. C. How to construct achievement tests to assess comprehension. *Review of Educational Research*, 1972, *42*, 145–170.

Berkowitz, J. Verbal discrimination learning as a function of experimental frequency. *Psychonomic Science*, 1968, *13*, 87–98.

Bourne, L. E., Jr., Ekstrand, B. R., Lovallo, W. R., Hiew, C. C., & Yaroush, R. A. *A frequency analysis of attribute identification.* Report No. 22. Boulder, Col.: Institute for the Study of Intellectual Behavior, 1974.

Bourne, L. E., Jr., Levin, J. R., Konewko, M., Yaroush, R. A., & Ghatala, E. S. Picture–word differences in discrimination learning: II. Effects of conceptual categories. *American Journal of Psychology,* in press.

Brown, A. L. The development of memory: Knowing, knowing about knowing and knowing how to know. In H. W. Reese (Ed.), *Advances in child development and behavior* (Vol. 10). New York: Academic Press, in press.

Carmean, S. L. *Overt verbalization and discrimination learning.* Paper presented at the annual meeting of the Speech Communication Association, San Francisco, 1971.

Carroll, J. B., Davies, P., & Richman, B. *The American heritage word frequency book.* New York: Houghton Mifflin, 1971.

Craik, F. I. M., & Lockhart, R. S. Levels of processing: A framework for memory research. *Journal of Verbal Learning and Verbal Behavior,* 1972, *11,* 671–684.

Eckert, E., & Kanak, N. J. Verbal discrimination learning: A review of the acquisition, transfer, and retention literature through 1972. *Psychological Bulletin,* 1974, *81,* 582–607.

Ekstrand, B. R., Wallace, W. P., and Underwood, B. J. A frequency theory of verbal-discrimination learning. *Psychological Review,* 1966, *73,* 566–578.

Fozard, J. L. Apparent recency of unrelated pictures and nouns presented in the same sequence. *Journal of Experimental Psychology,* 1970, *86,* 137–143.

Gagné, R. M. *The conditions of learning.* New York: Holt, 1970.

Galbraith, R. C., & Underwood, B. J. Perceived frequency of concrete and abstract words. *Memory & Cognition,* 1973, *1,* 56–60.

Ghatala, E. S. *Encoding verbal units in memory: Changes in memory attributes as a function of age, instructions, and retention interval.* Technical Report No. 134. Madison, Wisc.: Wisconsin Research and Development Center for Cognitive Learning, 1970(a).

Ghatala, E. S. *Memory attributes: Some directions for further research and implications for education.* Theoretical Paper No. 27. Madison, Wisc.: Wisconsin Research and Development Center for Cognitive Learning, 1970(b).

Ghatala, E. S., & Levin, J. R. Developmental differences in frequency judgments of words and pictures. *Journal of Experimental Child Psychology,* 1973, *16,* 495–507.

Ghatala, E. S., & Levin, J. R. Discrimination learning as a function of differences in materials: A proposed explanation. *Memory & Cognition,* 1974, *2,* 395–400.

Ghatala, E. S., & Levin, J. R. Phenomenal background frequency and the concreteness/imagery effect in verbal discrimination learning. *Memory & Cognition,* in press.

Ghatala, E. S., Levin, J. R., & Makoid, L. A. A clarification of frequency effects in children's discrimination learning. *Memory & Cognition,* 1975, *3,* 1–6.

Ghatala, E. S., Levin, J. R., & Subkoviak, M. J. Rehearsal strategy effects in children's discrimination learning: Confronting the crucible. *Journal of Verbal Learning and Verbal Behavior,* 1975, *14,* 398–407.

Ghatala, E. S., Levin, J. R., & Wilder, L. Apparent frequency of words and pictures as a function of pronunciation and imagery. *Journal of Verbal Learning and Verbal Behavior,* 1973, *12,* 85–90.

Ghatala, E. S., Levin, J. R., & Wilder, L. Pronunciation and the frequency-meaningfulness effect in children's frequency discrimination. *Journal of Experimental Psychology: Human Learning and Memory,* 1975, *1,* 655–659.

Gugliemella, J., & Phye, G. *Semantic and frequency differential processing in immediate and delayed retention on a multiple-choice test following delayed feedback.* Paper presented at the annual meeting of the American Educational Research Association, Washington, D.C., March/April, 1975.

Hintzman, D. L. Apparent frequency as a function of frequency and the spacing of repetitions. *Journal of Experimental Psychology,* 1969, *80,* 139–145.

Hopkins, R. H., Boylan, R. J., and Lincoln, G. L. Pronunciation and apparent frequency. *Journal of Verbal Learning and Verbal Behavior.* 1972, *11,* 105–113.

Hopkins, R. H., and Edwards, R. E. Pronunciation effects in recognition memory. *Journal of Verbal Learning and Verbal Behavior,* 1972, *11,* 534–537.

Howell, W. C. Representation of frequency in memory. *Psychological Bulletin*, 1973, *80*, 44–53.

Ingison, L. J., & Levin, J. R. The effect of children's spontaneous cognitive sets on discrimination learning. *Journal of Experimental Child Psychology*, 1975, *20*, 59–65.

Jensen, A. R. Varieties of individual differences in learning. In R. M. Gagné (Ed.), *Learning and individual differences*. Columbus, Ohio: Merrill, 1967.

Kausler, D. H., & Boka, J. A. Effects of double functioning on verbal discrimination learning. *Journal of Experimental Psychology*, 1968, *76*, 558–567.

Kintsch, W. Models for free recall and recognition. In D. A. Norman (Ed.), *Models of human memory*. New York: Academic Press, 1970.

Klausmeier, H. J., Ghatala, E. S., & Frayer, D. A. *Conceptual learning and development: A cognitive view*. New York: Academic Press, 1974.

Klausmeier, H. J., Sipple, T. S., & Allen, P. S. *First cross-sectional study of attainment of concepts* equilateral triangle, cutting tool, *and* noun *by children age 5 to 16 of City A*. Technical Report No. 287. Madison, Wisc.: Wisconsin Research and Development Center for Cognitive Learning, 1974.

Kucera, H. & Francis, W. N. *Computational analyses of present-day American English*. Providence: Brown University Press, 1967.

Levin, J. R. What have we learned about maximizing what children learn? In J. R. Levin & V. L. Allen (Eds.), *Cognitive learning in children: Theories and strategies*. New York: Academic Press, 1976.

Levin, J. R., Bourne, L. E., Jr., Yaroush, R. A., Ghatala, E. S., DeRose, T. M., & Hanson, V. Picture-word differences and conceptual frequency judgments. *Memory & Cognition*, in press.

Levin, J. R., & Ghatala, E. S. More about rehearsal strategy effects in children's discrimination learning. *Journal of Experimental Psychology: Human Learning and Memory*, in press.

Levin, J. R., Ghatala, E. S., & DeRose, T. M. *The effect of stimulus prefamiliarization on children's discrimination learning*. Technical Report No. 285. Madison, Wisc.: Wisconsin Research and Development Center for Cognitive Learning, 1974.

Levin, J. R., Ghatala, E. S., DeRose, T. M., & Makoid, L. A. *Image tracing: An analysis of its effectiveness in children's pictorial discrimination learning*. Technical Report No. 352. Madison, Wisc.: Wisconsin Research and Development Center for Cognitive Learning, in press.

Levin, J. R., Ghatala, E. S., DeRose, T. M., Wilder, L., & Norton, R. W. A further comparison of imagery and vocalization strategies in children's discrimination learning. *Journal of Educational Psychology*, 1975, *67*, 141–145.

Levin, J. R., Ghatala, E. S., Guttmann, J., Subkoviak, M. J., McCabe, A. E., & Bender, B. G. *Processes affecting children's learning from sentences*. Working Paper No. 144. Madison, Wisc.: Wisconsin Research and Development Center for Cognitive Learning, in press.

Levin, J. R., Ghatala, E. S., & Wilder, L. Picture-word differences in discrimination learning: I. Apparent frequency manipulations. *Journal of Experimental Psychology*, 1974, *102*, 691–695.

Levin, J. R., Ghatala, E. S., Wilder, L., & Inzer, E. Imagery and vocalization strategies in children's verbal discrimination learning. *Journal of Educational Psychology*, 1973, *64*, 360–365.

Lovelace, E. A. Verbal-discrimination learning: Varied familiarization on correct and incorrect items. *Canadian Journal of Psychology*, 1969, *23*, 227–232.

Lovelace, E. A. & Bansal, K. Verbal discrimination: Re-pairing, language frequency, and associative properties of the stimuli. *American Journal of Psychology*, 1973, *86*, 491–506.

McCormack, P. D. Recognition memory: How complex a retrieval system? *Canadian Journal of Psychology*, 1972, *26*, 19–41.

Osgood, C. E. *Method and theory in experimental psychology*. New York: Oxford University Press, 1953.

Paivio, A. *Imagery and verbal processes*. New York: Holt & Co., 1971.

Rohwer, W. D., Jr. Elaboration and learning in childhood and adolescence. In H. W. Reese (Ed.), *Advances in Child Development and Behavior*. New York: Academic Press, 1973.

Rowe, E. J. Discrimination learning of pictures and words: A replication of picture superiority. *Journal of Experimental Child Psychology*, 1972, *14*, 303–312.

Rowe, E. J. Depth of processing in a frequency judgment task. *Journal of Verbal Learning and Verbal Behavior*, 1974, *13*, 638–643.

Rowe, E. J. Measurement of rehearsal strategies in verbal discrimination learning as a function of noun imagery. *American Journal of Psychology*, in press.

Rowe, E. J., & Cake, L. J. Imagery and sentence mediators in verbal discrimination learning. *Memory & Cognition*, 1974, *2*, 169–175.

Rowe, E. J., & Paivio, A. Imagery and repetition instructions in verbal discrimination and incidental paired-associate learning. *Journal of Verbal Learning and Verbal Behavior*, 1971(a), *10*, 668–672.

Rowe, E. J., & Paivio, A. Word frequency and imagery effects in verbal discrimination learning. *Journal of Experimental Psychology*, 1971(b), *88*, 319–326.

Rowe, E. J., & Paivio, A. Effects of noun imagery, pronunciation, method of presentation, and intrapair order of items in verbal discrimination. *Journal of Experimental Psychology*, 1972, *93*, 427–429.

Thorndike, E. L., & Lorge, I. *The teacher's word book of 30,000 words*. New York: Bureau of Publications, Teachers College, 1944.

Tulving, E. Episodic and semantic memory. In E. Tulving & W. Donaldson (Eds.), *Organization of memory*. New York: Academic Press, 1972.

Underwood, B. J. Attributes of memory. *Psychological Review*, 1969, *76*, 559–573.

Underwood, B. J. Are we overloading memory? In A. W. Melton & E. Martin (Eds.), *Coding processes in human memory*. New York: Wiley & Sons, 1972.

Underwood, B. J. Individual differences as a crucible in theory construction. *American Psychologist*, 1975, *30*, 128–134.

Underwood, B. J., and Freund, J. S. Two tests of a theory of verbal-discrimination learning. *Canadian Journal of Psychology*, 1968, *22*, 96–104.

Underwood, B. J., and Freund, J. S. Relative frequency judgments and verbal discrimination learning. *Journal of Experimental Psychology*, 1970, *83*, 279–285.

Underwood, B. J., Patterson, M., & Freund, J. S. Recognition and number of incorrect alternatives presented during learning. *Journal of Educational Psychology*, 1972, *63*, 1–7.

Underwood, B. J., Zimmerman, J., and Freund, J. S. Retention of frequency information with observations on recognition and recall. *Journal of Experimental Psychology*, 1971, *87*, 149–162.

Wallace, W. P. Verbal discrimination. In C. P. Duncan, L. Sechrest, & A. W. Melton (Eds.), *Human memory: Festschrift for Benton J. Underwood*. New York: Appleton-Century-Crofts, 1972.

Wallace, W. P., Murphy, M. D., and Sawyer, T. J. Imagery and frequency in verbal discrimination learning. *Journal of Experimental Psychology Monograph*, 1973, *101*, 201–219.

Wilder, L. Spoken rehearsal and verbal discrimination learning. *Speech Monographs*, 1971, *38*, 113–120.

Wilder, L., & Levin, J. R. A developmental study of pronouncing responses in the discrimination learning of words and pictures. *Journal of Experimental Child Psychology*, 1973, *15*, 278–286.

Wilder, L., Levin, J. R., Ghatala, E. S., & McNabb, S. Pronunciation and apparent frequency in a between-subjects design. *Journal of Experimental Psychology*, 1974, *102*, 321–323.

Wilder, L., Levin, J. R., Kuskowski, M., & Ghatala, E. S. Pronunciation effects in verbal discrimination learning. *Journal of Experimental Psychology*, 1974, *103*, 366–367.

Zechmeister, E. B., and Gude, C. Instruction effects in recognition memory. *Bulletin of the Psychonomic Society*, 1974, *3*, 13–15.

PART II

Strategies for Improving Cognitive Learning

The second major section in this book, "Strategies for Improving Cognitive Learning," consists of three chapters that describe research directed toward improving the cognitive learning of children. The studies and theories reported in the three chapters of Part II illustrate some of the strategies offered by researchers in this area over the past several years.

In the first chapter of this section, Levin discusses experiments investigating the effectiveness of pictures and visual images as a way of improving children's learning and memory. On the basis of a review of the research conducted by himself and others, Levin concludes that the research findings do indeed confirm the old maxim that "A picture is worth a thousand words." It is clear from a large body of empirical research that many kinds of learning are substantially improved through the use of pictures.

In his research, Levin has discovered fairly stable individual differences in the degree to which children profit from the use of pictures in learning. Three basic types of learners are typically found: children who learn well from both pictures and words; children who learn poorly from both pictures and words, and children who learn well from pictures but poorly from words. Given that a substantial proportion of children comprise the latter category—Levin has suggested as much as 20%—the importance of carefully matching instructional materials with individual learners becomes evident.

An ability-by-instructional-strategy stance, along the lines of Labouvie-Vief's in Part I, is also adopted by Levin in his discussion of visual imagery as an effective learning strategy. In this regard, it has been noted that visual imagery is successfully utilized by only certain kinds of learners and under certain conditions. For example, unlike older children and adults, children under 6 or 7 years of age do not seem to profit from simple instructions to generate visual imagery even though they do profit from various other learning strategies. In the concluding part of his chapter, Levin demonstrates how researchers can capitalize on interactions between individual differences and experimental conditions to argue for the "psychological reality" of an inferred cognitive strategy such as visual imagery.

In the second chapter of this section, Davidson marshals a wide range of data in support of his contention that "hypostatization" processes play an important role in the facilitation of learning, comprehension, and memory. By the term *hypostatization,* Davidson refers to cognitive activity that is basically metaphorical or analogical in nature. Thus, hypostatization involves the transformation of complex or abstract information into more familiar forms, thereby making it easier to learn or understand. The principal forms of hypostatization processes discussed by Davidson are metaphors of the verbal–symbolic and visual-imagery type, and verbal–pictorial analogies.

Davidson relates several anecdotes from the history of science which attest to the importance of hypostatization processes in problem solving and in the comprehension of abstract concepts. Although the strategies discussed in Davidson's chapter should be helpful in learning and understanding abstract concepts, he points out that these strategies have their limitations as well. For example, employing these strategies may sometimes produce "cognitive distortions," as when an abstract concept such as intelligence is reified.

Davidson discusses several experiments in which hypostatization processes were employed in connection with two general types of psychological tasks. One type of task requires a person to learn or understand an abstract concept; another kind of task requires a person to learn or comprehend inferential information—that is, to go beyond the information immediately available. As the reader will see, these general strategies discussed by Davidson are very closely related to several topics discussed in other chapters in this book, for example, creative problem solving (Davis), concept formation (Klausmeier), visual imagery (Levin), and intellectual ability (Labouvie-Vief).

The third chapter in Part II is more directly concerned with the cognitive performance of children in a specific content area than was the case with the preceding two chapters. In Chapter 6 Venezky discusses the cognitive skills that are necessary for a child's learning to read; then he describes a curricular program developed for the express purpose of providing training for children on specific prereading skills.

After having made a thorough review of the relevant research literature, Venezky argues that many of the cognitive and perceptual skills formerly assumed to be important determinants of a child's ability to learn to read are simply not essential skills at all. On the contrary, it is maintained that the skills required for a child to learn to read are quite specific and limited in number. Therefore, the author of this chapter does not accept the theory that a set of general and nonspecific "readiness" skills are requisite to reading ability.

Venezky reports results of several experiments from his program of empirical research, which has as its goal the delineation of the specific cognitive and performance skills that a child must possess in order to learn to read. For example, one essential skill involves the ability to recognize that specific spatial arrangements of letters convey different meanings (e.g., *b* versus *d*). In this example, confusion easily arises for young children because much of their everyday experience has taught them to ignore positional differences in space (e.g., a cup is called a cup regardless of whether the handle is pointed in the left or right direction)—in Klausmeier's terminology, the child has not yet acquired an identity concept in this context.

Based on the results of his empirical research studies, Venezky and his colleagues embarked upon the task of developing a prereading program that would provide kindergarten children with training in the skills they need in learning to read. The several stages in the development of this prereading skills program is described in the present chapter. Summative evaluation research was conducted after the program had been tested, revised, and retested in several kindergarten schools. The program is now available in commercial form for use with preschool children.

CHAPTER 4

What Have We Learned about Maximizing What Children Learn?

Joel R. Levin

As a concerned year-in, year-out consumer of educational research, you are entitled to ask what we have learned about maximizing what children learn. As a concerned year-in, year-out conductor of educational research, I am compelled to answer. If what we have learned about maximizing what children learn were "little" or "nothing," I would not have chosen to initiate this venture. Happily, however, in recent years queries into the realm of children's learning have proven extremely fruitful, in terms of both currently accessible knowledge and promises of things to come.

This chapter does not pretend to encompass a complete summarization of the children's learning literature (for earlier reviews, see Goulet, 1968, and Keppel, 1964). Nor does it pretend to bear directly on educational policy or curricular decision making (see Glaser, 1972, and Rohwer, 1972). Rather, in this chapter I shall provide an up-to-date account of our research program at the Wisconsin Research and Development Center for Cognitive Learning. Where appropriate, I will incorporate our findings into the larger body of children's learning literature, was was done in an initial report of our research (Levin, 1972b).

In the evolution of our research program, we—as others before us—have come to realize that the task of maximizing what children learn can generally be accomplished through the use of techniques which *concretize* what is to be learned. That is, we have opted for methods and materials which capitalize on children's previous encounters with their environments and which provide a closer approximation to those environments than can be provided through more abstract representations. Specifically, our efforts toward concretization have involved *pictures*, both as learning materials and as the principal ingredient in learner-initiated cognitive strategies. What follows, then, is essentially a case for pictures in children's learning, with occasional caveats where necessary.

PICTURES AS LEARNING MATERIALS

One of the more ubiquitous findings in the literature is that pictorially represented objects are more memorable than their associated verbal labels. This, of course, comes as no surprise to the visual shapers of our culture and commercial society who are well aware of the potential benefits of pictures as a mode of communication. Yet despite the obvious contributions of the entrepreneurs of Madison Avenue (and more recently, of our children's friends on *Sesame Street*), the puzzle of pictures continues to fascinate educational researchers at various levels of scientific investigation. Let us begin by considering some of the empirical studies in which pictures and words have been compared.

Evidence for Picture Superiority

In 1967, Roger Shepard discovered that while adults have an unusually large capacity for storing verbal material, it is substantially smaller than their capacity for storing pictures. Shepard examined performance on three recognition memory tasks (see Ghatala & Levin, this volume, for a description of such tasks), each consisting of approximately 600 stimuli, and found that while previously exposed words and sentences were recognized with about 89% accuracy, pictures were recognized with about 97% accuracy; the pictorial level decreased to the verbal level only after a one-week interval between presentation and testing. An even more impressive demonstration of pictorial recognition memory capacity has been provided by Standing, Conezio, and Haber (1970), who reported over 90% accuracy for more than 2500 pictures, even with delays of three days between presentation and testing.

Although such evidence of apparent "unlimited memory" for pictures may capture one's imagination, it does not address itself to the issue of concern here, namely, memory differences between pictures and words. Across-materials comparisons in the Shepard (1967) data may be made only in an offhand way since (a) the data were obtained from different subject populations in sequentially conducted experiments and (b) the word and picture lists were not identical either in length or in content (the former consisting of English nouns and adjectives and the latter consisting of pictures taken primarily from magazine advertisements). However, subsequent research with adults (e.g., Paivio and Csapo, 1969) in which recognition memory for line drawings of familiar objects (e.g., a clock, a house, a piano) was better than that for the verbal labels of the same objects permits a more direct inference.

Precisely the same conclusions are reached when the children's learning literature is examined. That is to say, recognition memory for pictures is extremely high, even for preschoolers (e.g., Brown and Scott, 1971), and direct picture–word comparisons reveal the superiority of pictures (e.g., Corsini, Jacobus, and Leonard, 1969; see also Ghatala and Levin, this volume). Similarly, picture superiority has been documented in a number of studies where children are required to *recall* (rather than simply *recognize*) previously exposed stimuli (e.g., Reese, 1970)—an outcome also substantiated by the adult research (cf. Paivio, 1971).

Pictures and the Comprehension of Prose

In addition to the picture-word comparisons in studies using unconnected materials, several recent experiments have focused on children's recall of narrative prose passages, with and without pictorial supplements (e.g., Bender and Levin, 1976; Guttmann, 1976; Lesgold, Levin, Shimron, and Guttmann, 1975; Peeck, 1974; Shimron, 1974). In each of these studies it was found that providing pictures along with the orally presented passage substantially improved the children's performance (see also Rohwer and Harris, 1975; and Rohwer and Matz, 1975). We will see fit to consider some additional prose-learning/"picture" findings in more detail in a later section.

The Role of Individual Differences:
An Empirically Derived Representation

Although the picture-over-word effect has been found to generalize across a wide variety of populations as represented by such subject variables as age, sex, IQ, and SES–race (cf. Rowher and Levin, 1971), we have noted in a number of studies that the *magnitude* of the effect varies reliably with certain of these variables. For example, we have observed several instances in which the relative superiority of pictures to words has increased with age from childhood through adolescence (see also Ghatala and Levin, 1973, and Reese, 1970). As an illustration, in one of our studies (Levin, Davidson, Wolff, and Citron, 1973) across two different methods of assessing associative learning (recognition and recall), we found that younger children (second graders) correctly associated an average of 14% of the pictorial items and 12% of the verbal items—a difference of 2%. For older children (fifth-graders), however, this difference increased to 15%; these children correctly associated 28% of the pictures and 13% of the words. While the age populations and experimental tasks sampled across studies are not sufficiently comparable to provide a strict confirmation of an age by picture–word interaction (specifically, an increasing difference between picture and word learning with increasing age), the trends abstracted from a composite of several studies are consistent with this suggestion.

Picture–word differences appear to interact with other subject characteristics as well, much in the manner that I have described elsewhere (Levin, 1972a, in press), and which will be expanded upon here. Figure 1 depicts an admittedly oversimplified conceptualization of individual differences in learning as a function of variations in methods or materials.

As will be seen, both the "population" and "method–materials" labels in Figure 1 can be adapted to characterize a number of learning outcomes that have been noted in our own research and in that of others. For now, in order to concretize the intent of Figure 1, let us assume that the population variable represents a gross breakdown of the academic accomplishments of students in a particular classroom; that is, students from Population I are "good" learners, students from Population II are "average" learners, and students from Population III are "poor" learners, and individual students are loosely allocated to one of the three populations, let us say, on the basis of a teacher's long-term assessment of in-class achievement. Let us assume further that we wish to determine each student's mastery of a particular instructional lesson.

This is where the method–materials variable comes in. Suppose that the students were taught the lesson in a mildly disorganized, uninspiring fashion (due either to a fault of the teacher or the textbook or to some combination). If we assess mastery following such "impoverished" instruction, which might be Method A in Figure 1, we will note that only the good learners (from Population I) succeed—in a sense, they will have learned *despite* the instruction. In contrast, the average and poor learners (from populations II and III) will fail; at least some of them will not have learned *because of* the instruction.

On the other hand, suppose that the lesson were presented to the students in a highly organized, effective manner (Method B). The good learners will still succeed, probably to an even greater degree than before. However, the clarity of the instruction will now enable those students (from Population II) who would otherwise fail (under Method A) also to succeed. At the same time, some of the nonlearners under Method A (those from Population III) will continue to fail even with optimal instruction—they will fail *despite* the improved instruction. (This is not to say that Population III students can never be taught the lesson successfully, but rather that the variable considered here,

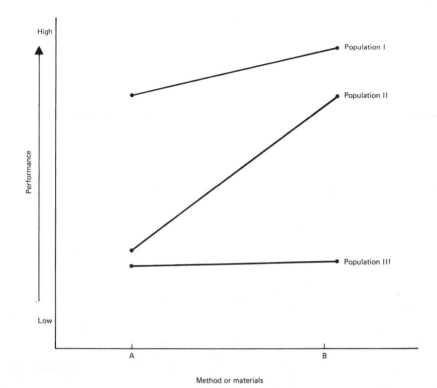

Method or materials

Figure 1. A conceptualization of individual differences as related to the potential effectiveness of a cognitive strategy. (A connected line graph is utilized here simply to emphasize the interaction of interest that is discussed throughout the text.)

namely, a poor versus a good presentation to a group of students, may not be sufficient to effect mastery for them.)

What is important in this example is that for a large number of students the probability of mastery is closely related to the quality of instruction received. With poor instruction many children who would otherwise succeed will fail. It would, therefore, appear to be a worthwhile endeavor to identify instructional techniques which maximize the success ratio for a given group of students. Following my (Levin, 1972a) distinction between external and internal variables which affect learning, we will be concerned with identifying student-initiated cognitive strategies which enable learning to occur despite a lack of optimal instructional methods and materials.

But first let us look at a few experiments dealing with picture– word differences in learning from which the representation in Figure 1 was itself modeled. In an earlier study, conducted by Rohwer, Ammon, Suzuki, and Levin (1971), and concerned with learning differences among certain age, sex, and socioeconomic groups, we (Levin, Rohwer, and Cleary, 1971) noted that even within these demographically defined groups there appeared to be reliable individual differences in learning from pictures and words. In particular, subjects who were classified as exhibiting either relatively large or relatively small picture-word differences tended to be similarly reclassified on a parallel form of the task administered two days later. This was found to be true in 10 of the 12 samples studied; the effect was statistically significant in 6 of them.

Following up this notion, Levin, Divine-Hawkins, Kerst, and Gutt-mann (1974) discovered that with such a task, the vast majority of subjects—in this case, fourth-graders—could be classified into three learner types: subjects who learn relatively well from both pictures and words (Hi P, Hi W), subjects who learn relatively poorly from both pictures and words (Lo P, Lo W), and subjects who learn relatively well from pictures but relatively poorly from words (Hi P, Lo W). It is interesting to point out that, in accordance with the research findings reported thus far, virtually all subjects learned picture items better than word items. The evidence for this was (a) consistently superior picture recall within the Hi-P, Hi-W and Lo-P, Lo-W groups and (b) a very small number of subjects classified as Lo-P, Hi-W subjects (a result which led to our eventual decision that the Lo-P, Hi-W category is not a learner-type classification of practical importance).

To investigate the stability of the three learner types identified, a parallel form of the learning task was administered to the subjects on the day following their initial classification. These tasks, unlike those of our earlier study, were group administered. The results of the study are summarized in Table 1; it may be seen that 30 out of 41 initial classifications (nearly 75%) were confirmed by the second assessment. While such data do not speak to the long-term stability of learner types nor to their concomitant characteristics, they should encourage future investigations into an area which has been beset by serious method-ological and substantive difficulties (cf. Levin, Rohwer, and Cleary, 1971). A preliminary effort in this direction was made in a second experiment by Levin et al. (1974), which will be described in a later section.

For now, it is worth noting that in the two experiments reported by Levin et al. (1974), 36 Hi-P, Hi-W subjects, 40 Lo-P, Lo-W subjects, and 22 Hi-P, Lo-W subjects were identified by initial classification proce-dures. On the basis of these data it certainly appears that the ability to learn from pictures and the ability to learn from words are highly correlated in our task (since most of the classifications are of the Hi-P, Hi-W type, or the Lo-P, Lo-W type). However, it is also apparent that for a good 20% of the children, the ability to learn is related to the type of materials presented. That is, the Hi P, Lo W children function like

TABLE 1
Correspondence between Initial and Subsequent
Learner-Type Classifications[a]

| | | Day 1 | | |
		Hi P, Hi W	Lo P, Lo W	Hi P, Lo W
Day 2	Hi P, Hi W	9	1	1
	Lo P, Lo W	2	14	1
	Hi P, Lo W	1	2	7

[a]There were 3 additional subjects initially classified as Lo P, Lo W who would have been classified subsequently as Lo P, Hi W. From Levin et al. (1974).

poor learners (Lo-P, Lo-W children) when words are presented but like good learners (Hi-P, Hi-W children) when pictures are presented. This situation is represented in Figure 1 by the seeming inability of subjects from Population II (here, Hi-P, Lo-W children) to perform successfully when materials of one kind (words) are presented and their startlingly different performance when materials of another kind (pictures) are presented. In the experiment just reported, for example, when word pairs were presented, the Hi-P, Lo-W subjects correctly recalled an average of 16%, as compared to 14% by Lo-P, Lo-W (Population III) subjects and 50% by Hi-P, Hi-W (Population I) subjects. On the other hand, when picture pairs were presented, the mean performance of Hi-P, Lo-W subjects (61% correct) clearly surpassed that of Lo-P, Lo-W subjects (33% correct) and rivaled that of Hi-P, Hi-W subjects (66% correct). Since Figure 1 was derived from a composite of several experiments, it does not portray this result exactly, but it closely approximates it.

A Footnote to the Benefits of Pictures in Learning

Before concluding this section it must be noted that in a number of experiments that have focussed on the acquisition and use of concepts by subjects, pictures have been found to be not only nonfacilitative in comparison to words (e.g., Katz and Paivio, 1975) but frequently inferior. For example, Runquist and Hutt (1961) found that concepts selected to represent a series of stimulus instances (e.g., the concept soft for the instances *bed, fur, pillow,* and *moccasin*) were acquired more rapidly when the stimuli were words than when they were pictures. Just how is this curious reversal of picture–word differences—based on what we have learned till now—explained? Runquist and Hutt suggest (as does Hollenberg, 1970, in another context discussed later) that the vast number of unique perceptual details associated with pictures may impede the formation or retrieval of broader, more abstractly defined concepts. Support for the notion that irrelevant perceptual details may contribute to such "conceptual blindness" was obtained in the Runquist and Hutt study, where the word-over-picture effect was diminished when pictures were used which perceptually highlighted the intended concept (e.g., for the concept **soft**, the bed was made to appear "soft and billowy").[1]

Additional support for this view may be extracted from an experiment by Deno (1968), in which subjects were presented an associative-learning task consisting of either familiar picture or word stimuli paired with 12 unfamiliar Japanese words. In one version of the task the stimuli were 3 different instances from each of 4 conceptual categories (buildings, clothing, furniture, and animals), and in the other they were 12 unrelated items. According to verbal-learning theory, performance in the conceptually related list should suffer relative to that in the unrelated list, since the conceptually similar items should produce intralist interference. The result of concern here is that while this was indeed the case when the stimuli were presented as words, there was little interference when the stimuli were presented as pictures. This result is consistent with the notion that the conceptual categories were not elicited as readily in the picture condition where the perceptual details of the pictures dominated the subjects' attention (although other interpretations are possible). We have recently obtained a similar result in two studies dealing with item recognition rather than item recall (Bourne, Levin, Konewko, Yaroush, and Ghatala, in press; Levin, Bourne, Yaroush, Ghatala, DeRose, and Hanson, in press).

It is worth noting that the "distraction" explanation also fits a large number of studies in which it has been found that children's initial word decoding is retarded by the inclusion of pictures (cf. Samuels, 1970). That is, the addition of a picture to represent a to-be-decoded word is thought to pull subjects' attention toward the picture and away from the critical letter configurations. This notion has received some support by Lippman and Shanahan (1973), who observed that when

[1] Further evidence comes from Wohlwill's (1968) research utilizing Piagetian class-inclusion tasks, where mastery is assumed to be synchronous with the emergence of concrete operations in the child. Wohlwill has found that verbally presented class-inclusion problems are answered more accurately than pictorially presented problems, but that the difference can be reduced by presenting the pictures in ways that help to break down their perceptually biasing features.

pictures were physically integrated with the letters themselves (e.g., striped letters resembling candy canes to represent the word *candy*), word learning was facilitated.

By way of summary, let me reiterate that in the vast number of learning studies that I have come across in the psychological literature, there is precious little evidence to refute the claim that pictures are learned better than words.[2] One notable exception to this statement consists of a class of experiments, some of which were noted above, dealing with the acquisition and utilization of concepts and/or semantic categories. This class of experiments should not be confused, however, with situations in which pictures are used *in conjunction with* (or as "adjuncts" to) verbal descriptions, as in the prose studies mentioned earlier and in contexts where the addition of a picture increases the comprehensibility of an obscure passage (Bransford and Johnson, 1972) or of an abstract concept (Davidson, this volume).

VISUAL IMAGERY
AS AN ORGANIZATIONAL STRATEGY

Although one way to maximize what children learn is to use pictures, another is to embed the materials in a meaningful context or organization in which learning can occur. For example, it will take most children several trials to recall a 14-item list of words such as *cat, log, street, bowl, milk, chair,* . . . in their correct serial order. However, this becomes virtually a one-trial proposition when the items are presented as "The grey *cat* jumped over the *log* and crossed the *street* to find the *bowl* of cold *milk* under the *chair* . . ." (Levin and Rohwer, 1968). As Rohwer (1967) has aptly noted, in such situations performance is greatly enhanced by *adding* to the to-be-remembered stimuli, a finding which prompts the seemingly paradoxical inference that the more there is to learn, the better the learning. Thus, in this example the number of words to be processed in the first case (14) is substantially less than when the sentence context is added (52); yet the learning in the first case is substantially worse. Of course, this finding poses no paradox at all for students of organizational processes in memory who view the difficulty of a task in terms of associational and contextual factors rather than in terms of individual items per se (cf. Anderson and Bower, 1973).

One can also apply the notion of organization to the data considered in the previous section. Recall, a consistent finding is that pictures are

[2] However, this statement may be restricted to normal rates of stimulus presentation, since Paivio and Csapo (1969, 1971) have found that pictures are serially recalled more poorly than words when they are presented too rapidly for verbal labeling to occur.

more easily associated than words. However, the magnitude of this effect is typically not nearly as great as that produced when the experimenter provides an organizational context for the paired items. Thus, the sentence context, "The *cat* jumped over the *log*," has a marked facilitative effect on the learning of the pair, *cat–log*, as does a pictorial context in which a cat is depicted jumping over a log. Examples of the potency of such context effects in associative learning for both younger and older subjects, as well as for subjects from different social class and ability strata, may be found in Rohwer (1967).

While others have embraced strategies in which the experimenter provides a sentence or pictorial context to facilitate learning, our preference has been to provide learners with a strategy for generating their own organizations. This distinction between *imposing* an organization on learners and *inducing* an organization in learners has been discussed elsewhere (Levin, 1972b), as has our rationale for opting for the latter approach (Levin, 1972a).

Essentially, our argument is that most "real world" learning situations are less than optimally structured in that they require active mental transformations and elaborations on the part of learners in order for them to process the to-be-learned material effectively. Accordingly, efficient learning will occur only if learners are equipped with organizational strategies that will free them from the typically impoverished quality of incoming stimuli. By hypothesizing about the nature of such strategies and then by testing these hypotheses in samples of presumed effective and ineffective learners (e.g., older versus younger subjects), we should be able both to document their (the strategies') psychological reality and to determine whether or not it is plausible to instruct others in their usage.[3]

We have begun to launch an attack in this direction. For instance, in an associative-learning task, rather than "spoon organizing" the pairs for subjects by providing them with an effective sentence or pictorial context, we have instructed subjects to generate appropriate sentences— and especially, dynamic visual images—for themselves. Thus, when the items *cat–log* appear, subjects are instructed to think up a sentence or to make up a vivid picture in their minds which relates the pair members to one another in some meaningful way. The results of such instructions have been astounding in that learning gains have been observed which rival—and in some cases surpass—those obtained from supposedly optimally defined (i.e., experimenter-imposed) organiza-

---

[3] This is not to say that an equally convincing case cannot be made for the "imposed" approach, where variations in stimulus materials (e.g., semantic and syntactic properties) may be precisely defined and carefully controlled and their effect on subsequent learning noted.

tions. In the following sections, then, I will discuss certain of our investigations into visual imagery as an organizational strategy.

The Development of a Visual Imagery Strategy

One of the more intriguing findings that we have uncovered is that the ability to benefit from an experimenter-*induced* organizational strategy is, in large part, a function of the cognitive maturity of the learner. Thus, it has been noted that while children younger than six or seven years of age have little difficulty in using an experimenter-*imposed* strategy effectively, they are typically unsuccessful when requested to generate such a strategy on their own. And the developmental disparity between "using" and "generating" appears greater for visual imagery than for sentence production, as indicated by some recent evidence refuting Jensen and Rohwer's (1965) claim that young children are unable to generate appropriate mediating sentences in an associative-learning task (McCabe, 1973; McCabe, Levin, and Wolff, 1974).

But let us concentrate exclusively on the development of visual imagery. In their most recent work on the topic, Piaget and Inhelder (1971) distinguish between two general classes of visual imagery in the child. The first, *reproductive* imagery, is ontogenetically more primitive in that it emerges in the child's preoperational years. Being static in nature, it is typified by internalized copies or imitations of external events. The second, *anticipatory* imagery, does not emerge until a later stage of development—in particular, the onset of operations at about age 7 or 8. This type of imagery is dynamic in nature in that with it the child is capable of employing unique mental operations (e.g., spatial rotations and transformations) to static or physically removed events.

We may distinguish between reproductive and anticipatory imagery in terms of our associative-learning paradigm. The preoperational child is capable of imagining only a perceptual copy of the to-be-associated items, whereas the operational child is capable of manipulating these images in novel ways (e.g., conjuring up an imaginal interaction between the paired items). If a thematic interaction is the basis for optimal associative-learning performance, then it would not be surprising to find that an operational child who is successfully employing an imagery strategy learns more quickly than either a preoperational child who is unsuccessfully employing one or an operational child who is not employing one. This prediction was tested and further elaborated in a series of studies conducted by Peter Wolff, myself, and others.

In one experiment we found that both second- and fifth-graders benefited from an induced visual imagery strategy (i.e., "make up a picture in your head of the two things in each pair doing something together") in an associative-learning task (Levin, Davidson, Wolff, and Citron, 1973). On the other hand, Montague (1970) had previously reported that her sample of first-grade, inner-city children did not benefit from such a strategy. Thus, indirect support for the proposed anticipatory imagery deficit in younger children might be inferred.

However, in order to make a direct test of this proposition (i.e., by utilizing the same task and materials with subjects from a geographically and demographically similar location), Wolff and Levin (1972) compared the performance of third-graders and kindergartners, assuming that the former possessed well-developed anticipatory imagery while the latter did not. The outcome was precisely as anticipated: In the third-grade sample, instructions to employ an imagery strategy facilitated performance relative to a nonimagery control condition (77% correct versus 32% correct, respectively); however, in the kindergarten sample a nonsignificant difference (41% versus 30%) was observed. Apart from these performance data, the children's attitudes during imagery generation (i.e., holding their heads motionless, keeping their eyes closed or gazing upward, and obviously concentrating) and their subsequent verbal reports, lent credence to the conclusion that third-graders did indeed comply with the imagery request while kindergartners did not.

But this is not the whole story. One fundamental assumption of Piagetian theory is that operational thought grows out of the early sensorimotor activity of the child. In the present context, visual imagery is regarded as internalized motor activity in that it originates in the child's early play and imitation, which later become internalized. If the child's overt motor activity does in fact provide the basis from which covert imagery evolves, then it is not unreasonable to assume that children approaching the operational stage (i.e., our kindergartners) could produce an external motoric representation which in turn might mediate the formation of an internalized imaginal representation.

In the Wolff and Levin (1972) study just reported, the stimulus materials consisted of children's toys. While in one of the conditions already described, the child was instructed to generate a visual interaction between the paired toys internally, in a third experimental condition he or she was permitted to generate the visual interaction externally by actually manipulating the toys. Clearly this was no problem even for the kindergartners, and it was clear that the interactions they produced had memorial consequences as evidenced by the increased learning in this condition (64% correct), surpassing by far the kindergarten control situation (30%) and approaching the imagery condition performance of third-graders (77%).

While it is tempting to interpret these results in terms of the overt motor activity eliciting covert visual imagery, a more straightforward interpretation is that subjects in the manipulation condition actually were provided with an *imposed* interaction in that not only were they generating an interaction (a process), but they were able to view the result of this activity (a product) as well. Since it is well known that imposed visual interactions facilitate associative learning (as also found in the Wolff—Levin study when the experimenter actually created the interaction), it could be argued that these interactions—and not the motor activity preceding them—were the proximate causes for performance differences between the manipulation and the imagery conditions in the kindergarten sample.

To resolve this problem, Wolff and Levin (1972) conducted a second experiment in which some children were permitted to manipulate the object pairs but were not permitted to see the resultant interactions, since the manipulations took place behind a curtain which shielded the toys from the children's view. The learning of the manipulation-instructed subjects was 58% better than that of the imagery-instructed subjects who were permitted to hold onto the toys through the curtain but not allowed to manipulate them. This finding compares favorably with the 55% facilitation figure in the first experiment where visual inspection of the interaction was allowed. As further evidence of the nonessentiality of visual feedback to the motor effect, in a subsequent study Wolff, Levin, and Longobardi (1972) independently varied the visual and tactual components of the motor activity. It was found that relative to appropriate control conditions, the quality of the subject-produced interactions and subsequent learning were not related to the presence or absence of visual feedback.

These experiments suggest that anticipatory visual imagery constitutes a useful organizational strategy in associative-learning tasks. Although older children can benefit directly from simple imagery instructions, younger children appear unable to do so. For them, however, it is possible to induce covert visual imagery through overt motor activity; when this is done, the learning of younger children approximates that of older children given simple imagery instructions.[4] (Note that these induced imagery findings can be easily incorporated into the representation in Figure 1, which will be done in a later section.)

---

[4] The notions of "mediational," "production," and "control" deficiencies (Flavell, 1970; Kendler, 1972) are applicable and differentially evident throughout this research, although they will not be pursued here.

Furthermore, a study by Varley, Levin, Severson, and Wolff (1974) indicates that even though young children do not appear to benefit from simple imagery instructions per se (i.e., in the absence of concurrent motor involvement), they can be trained to do so. Essentially, it was found that after prolonged practice involving motor manipulations kindergartners successfully accommodated imagery instructions (with no concurrent motor activity) on a subsequent task, in comparison to children who were given covert imagery practice without accompanying motor activity. Thus, the possibility of eliciting anticipatory imagery in young children via motor training is promising. Two additional comments seem appropriate here. First, it looks as though it is possible (by employing appropriately worded instructions) to "trick" young children into generating visual imagery, even in the absence of either concurrent motor activity or prior motor-imagery training (see Bender and Levin, in press). And second, just as there appears to be a lower age limit—of about 7 years—in the ability to benefit from a simple imagery instruction, we have discovered that motor inducement of visual imagery may also have a lower age limit—of about 5 years (Levin, McCabe, & Bender, 1975). Clearly, the long-term benefits of such efforts, as well as their breadth of transfer, deserve careful study.

Some Further Evidence for the Age-Imagery Relationship

In the preceding section we proposed that the ability to benefit from simple visual imagery instructions in associative learning develops in children beyond the age of 6 or 7. In this section, however, we examine evidence that suggests that the ability does not become fully realized until a later stage of development—something once again interpreted in terms of Piagetian theory.

Let us begin with the empirical observation that while imagery instructions have been found to facilitate the learning of adults (cf. Bower, 1972), this has not been true as consistently for children—even for those well into the concrete-operational stage. Although it is difficult to compare results across studies (where subject and task characteristics vary considerably), Levin (1972b) has observed that in experiments where imagery instructions have failed to improve children's associative learning, the stimuli have typically consisted of verbal materials (i.e., printed or aural noun pairs). To pursue this observation further, we conducted two experiments with 11- and 12-year olds and found that although the children benefited from an imagery strategy when the stimuli consisted of line drawings, they did not when the stimuli consisted of printed words (Levin and Kaplan, 1972). And in a follow-up to this study, Eoff and Rohwer (1972) detected a developmental shift within the elementary school grades: Initially subjects could not employ an imagery strategy with either pictures or words; at a later age, they could employ the strategy with pictures but not with words; finally, at still a later age, they could employ it with both.

On the basis of these results, it may be tentatively concluded that the effectiveness of an imagery strategy (especially for children at the elementary school age) depends on the concreteness of the materials to be organized. That is, just as Paivio (1971) has reported that imagery generation proceeds more slowly with abstract nouns (e.g., truth, democracy) in adults, it is reasonable to suppose that children find imagery generation from words a relatively difficult task. Levin (1972b) has presented a flow chart depicting the hypothesized steps required when transforming either picture or word pairs into an interactive image; with words (less concrete) the number of transformations involved in the encoding and decoding phases is seen to be greatei than with pictures (more concrete).

Thus, it may be presumed that even though children benefit from an organizational imagery strategy under certain conditions (e.g., when objects or pictures are the stimulus materials), they may not under others (e.g., when the stimuli are words). However, as was stated previously vis-à-vis the differing task and subject characteristics of the studies investigated, this generalization should be interpreted loosely at present, for although Horvitz and Levin (1972) found that third-graders could not effectively utilize imagery instructions with verbal materials, Levin, Davidson, Wolff, and Citron (1973) found that second-graders could when these materials were embedded in a single list containing both word and picture pairs. It is clear that a more systematic investigation of the "stimulus concreteness" phenomenon needs to be conducted and its limiting parameters specified.

The same type of systematic documentation needs to be assembled for a finding that we have repeatedly noted in our research, exemplified here by the data of Kerst and Levin (1973). In that experiment, fourth- and fifth-graders were instructed to generate visual imagery to facilitate their learning of a list of paired pictures. As would be anticipated on the basis of the research reviewed so far, the performance of the induced imagery subjects was by far superior to that of control subjects and, in fact, equalled that of subjects who were shown experimenter-imposed pictorial interactions. But what is of particular interest here is that the distribution of the induced imagery group was considerably more variable than the distributions of the other two groups.

On the basis of the Kerst and Levin (1973) data it was concluded that (a) some but not all children benefit from a self-generated imagery strategy (as evidenced by the greater variability of the induced imagery distribution), but (b) for those who do, performance surpasses that of subjects given experimenter-generated organizations (as evidenced by the slightly greater number of extremely high scores in the induced imagery distribution than in the imposed imagery distribution). We have interpreted this latter result as being consistent with the plethora of American, Genevan, and Soviet data demonstrating the importance of the organism's active role in the learning process. That is, we believe that optimal learning occurs when the subject interacts with the environment in a meaningful way, and clearly our own research with induced organizational strategies supports this position. Moreover, in accordance with "active participation" theorists, there are associative-learning data to suggest that given a well-organized event, the memorial consequences are superior when the event has been constructed by the subject himself than when it has merely been presented to him (e.g., Bobrow and Bower, 1969; Bower and Winzenz, 1970; Wolff, Levin, and Longobardi, 1974).

Let us now attempt to account for the finding that imagery instructions seem to produce a variable effect with children, as reflected by performance both within a task as in the Kerst and Levin (1973) study and from one type of materials to another (e.g., from pictures to words), as in the Levin and Kaplan (1972) study. To do this, we will capitalize on the Piagetian belief that the concrete-operational thought of elementary school children evolves to the formal-operational thought of adolescents (at about 11 to 13 years of age). It is only at this later stage of development that children become completely free from the stimulus-boundedness of their earlier concrete-operational thought in the sense of being able to exploit symbolic representations more fully and to deal with abstractions more proficiently.

The elementary school grades encompass children representing a wide range of cognitive-developmental levels: from transitional pre-operational/concrete-operational children to transitional concrete-operational/formal-operational children. And, based on our own observations and those of others, within any particular grade level at a given school (especially in the middle elementary grades, grades 3 to 5) virtually this entire developmental spectrum is represented. Given that certain task demands (e.g., imagery generation) seem to be related to the cognitive-developmental maturity of the learner (see, for example, Labouvie-Vief, Levin, and Urberg, 1975, Experiment III), it is therefore not surprising that increased performance variability would result because some subjects are able to comply successfully and others are not. On the other hand, when the task demands are sufficiently obscure (as in a control condition) or sufficiently easy (as in an imposed organization condition), performance tends to be less variable (even when ceiling and floor effects are ruled out). It should also be noted here that the same variability argument may be applied to Rohwer's (1972) model where subjects exhibit, during the adolescent years, an increasing propensity for employing organizational strategies spontaneously (i.e., as they would have to do to succeed in a control condition).

Finally, the Kerst and Levin (1973) data have implications for the "active participation" hypothesis mentioned earlier. That induced imagery led to performance which was comparable in mean level to, yet considerably more variable than, that of performance in the imposed imagery condition is clearly compatible with the hypothesis, as long as individual differences are considered. That is to say, if the poor performance of certain induced imagery subjects stems mainly from their being at a stage of cognitive development which precludes their benefiting from the strategy, it would be expected that had the task been administered a year or two later, their performance would have increased dramatically, thereby creating a mean increase and variance reduction relative to the performance of imposed imagery subjects. Unfortunately, such a "wait till next year" hypothesis has yet to receive empirical verification, as does the simpler cross-sectional hypothesis that an imagery strategy will produce increasingly less variable performance from the elementary school years into adolescence.

Visual Imagery and the Comprehension of Prose

Just as we have found that experimenter-imposed pictures can serve as adjunct aids to facilitate prose learning, we have also found experimenter-induced visual imagery to be facilitative. Thus, the effects of a visual imagery strategy that were discussed in the context of associative-learning tasks seem to generalize to more complex forms of information-processing as well. For example, our imagery–comprehension research has been conducted with children in the upper elementary grades where, as noted in the previous section, visual imagery has been found to be a process accessible to many children. For children at this stage of development, simple examples and instructions to "think up pictures in your head while you are reading (or listening to) the story about what the people are doing, what they look like . . ." seem to improve performance on a subsequent test of factual recall.[5]

Some of the individual difference variables (apart from age) which were identified earlier have also proven to be worth studying using prose materials. Recall the experiment in which we classified children on the basis of how well they learned from pictures (Hi P versus Lo P). Given the validity of these classifications, it is not unreasonable to

[5] In studies recently reported by others, more extensive training procedures have been examined (e.g., Lesgold, McCormick, and Golinkoff, 1975; Pressley, in press); moreover, the age/imagery relationship discussed previously is receiving support in prose-learning contents (e.g., Guttmann, 1976; Shimron, 1974).

assume that the Lo-P subject, like the child who has not yet acquired anticipatory imagery, probably experiences some difficulty in pictorially representing stimulus materials and/or mentally manipulating them to enhance learning. Whatever causes Lo-P subjects to have difficulty in learning from externally presented pictures should also operate to reduce the effectiveness of an internalized pictorial strategy.

In a second experiment of the Levin *et al.* (1974) study, we presented Hi-P and Lo-P subjects a prose passage to be read either in the presence or in the absence of visual imagery instructions. As may be seen in Figure 2, while the performance of the Hi-P subjects (including that of both Hi-P, Hi-W and Hi-P, Lo-W subjects) increased under imagery instructions, the performance of Lo-P subjects did not, and in fact, decreased. (Perhaps the addition of an unfamiliar strategy complicated a task on which Lo-P subjects have learned to succeed through the use of other cognitive processes.) At any rate, even though there was an overall increase in performance when visual imagery was induced, the important point here is that not all subjects appeared to benefit from such a strategy.

Precisely the same conclusion is reached when we examine the results of a reading study conducted by Levin (1973). In an earlier article by Wiener and Cromer (1967), it was argued that although certain children

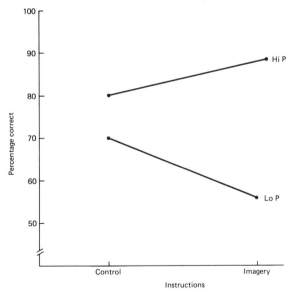

Figure 2. Reading comprehension of two types of learners under different instructional conditions. (A connected line graph is utilized here simply to emphasize the interaction of interest that is discussed throughout the text.)

fail to comprehend what they read because they are unable to derive meaning from *individual words* (due to decoding or vocabulary problems), other so-called "poor readers" possess adequate word reading skills but are unable to derive meaning from *combined words and phrases* (due to organizational-synthesis problems). These authors have referred to poor readers of the first type (i.e., those with vocabulary and/or decoding problems) as *deficit poor* readers and to those of the second type (those with organizational problems) as *difference poor* readers. Under normal reading conditions, difference poor readers are assumed to behave differently from good readers in that they do not spontaneously summon up effective organizational strategies to help them comprehend what they are reading.

Accordingly, we speculated that inducing difference poor readers to employ an imagery organizational strategy while reading would improve their comprehension of the passage. On the other hand, inducing such a strategy in deficit poor readers should not prove helpful since they are lacking the vocabulary–decoding skills which are prerequisite to receiving assistance through organization. Good and poor readers were identified through standardized reading achievement scores, teachers' ratings, and reading-track placement within the school. Within the poor reader category, difference and deficit subjects were identified in terms of their respective standardized reading vocabulary and comprehension subtest scores. That is, the comprehension scores of both types of poor readers were low, but the vocabulary scores of deficit poor readers were substantially lower than those of difference poor readers.

As in the Levin *et al.* (1974) study, half the subjects received imagery instructions before reading a passage and half read it under normal conditions. Although imagery instructions were facilitative overall (84% correct versus 72% correct), the predicted interaction emerged. When the difference poor readers were given imagery instructions, they correctly answered more questions than their nonimagery counterparts (a difference of 26%); deficit poor readers given imagery instructions exhibited no improvement (actually a difference of 2% in favor of the nonimagery group). And, in accordance with the comparative performances of Population I and Population II subjects in Figure 1, although under normal reading conditions the good readers by far surpassed the difference poor readers (81% versus 60% correct), when the difference poor readers were provided with an organizational strategy their performance (86% correct) approximated (in this case, slightly exceeded) that of good readers reading under normal conditions.

The results of these investigations accord well with predictions, in that they (*a*) document the possibility of improving comprehension through the implementation of a self-generated organizational strategy and (*b*) suggest that the potential benefits from such a strategy are closely tied to the prerequisite skills of the user. With regard to the second point, this is not to say that we should give up on children who do not seem to profit from simple imagery instructions and regard them as doomed to failure. Quite to the contrary, it is of especial importance to determine whether deficit poor readers will benefit from imagery instructions if vocabulary and decoding demands are eliminated and whether Hi P, Lo W children will benefit from alternative types of organizational strategies (e.g., verbal paraphrase) or from subject-generated supplements to an imagery strategy (e.g., relevant motor activity) in much the same way that the learning of "pre-imagery" children has been facilitated by sentence production (Levin, McCabe, and Bender, 1975; McCabe *et al.*, 1974) and motor involvement (Varley *et al.*, 1974; Wolff and Levin, 1972).

A Footnote to the Benefits of Visual Imagery in Learning

Thus far we have presented evidence compatible with the assertion that a visual imagery strategy facilitates learning and comprehension. But, as with our earlier discussion of pictorial facilitation, we must ask how universal this assertion is. We have already argued that the success of an imagery strategy depends on the capabilities of the user, and we have identified the individual's cognitive-developmental level as a particularly relevant subject variable. Similarly, we will now show that the unique features of a particular task may also moderate the strategy's effectiveness.

For example, Bower (1970) has demonstrated that imagery per se does not facilitate associative learning. To do this, he instructed subjects to form an image of the pair members one next to the other (i.e., not interacting). He found that performance was no better than that of subjects given rote-rehearsal instructions and appreciably worse than that of subjects given interactive imagery instructions. Thus, it may be safely concluded on the basis of these and other data that if the imagery is devoid of an organizational component, associative learning is not enhanced. Similar conclusions have been reached about strategies which would and would not be expected to facilitate other types of learning (cf. Levin and Rohwer, 1968; Rowe and Paivio, 1971).

Unfortunately, knowledge of these nominal task characteristics is not sufficient to permit speculation as to whether or not a particular strategy will be effective. Rather, procedural factors and the nature of the stimulus materials provided in the task also need to be considered. With regard to procedural factors, we mentioned previously that the usual picture-over-word effect in serial learning vanishes when the presentation rate is too rapid for the pictures to be implicitly labeled, even though they are perceived (see Footnote 2). The same may be assumed to be true of the imagery strategy effect in learning and comprehension tasks when a fast rate of presentation is employed (cf. Levin and Divine-Hawkins, 1974; Paivio, 1971). Now let us show how the effectiveness of an imagery strategy may depend on the stimulus materials provided.

Earlier it was stated that it may be easier for children to utilize an interactive imagery strategy in associative learning when the stimulus materials are pictures than when they are words. This was assumed to be related to the differing transformational complexities associated with each. For different reasons, imaging the referent of individual words for subsequent recall should be more effective than simply pronouncing the word (Paivio and Csapo, 1973), whereas pronouncing the label of a picture or object should be more effective than imaging it (Davies, 1972; Paivio and Csapo, 1973). Aspects of this interaction have recently been discussed by Levin, Ghatala, DeRose, Wilder, and Norton (1975) in the context of a discrimination learning task where recall is not required.

Such observations clearly limit the potential benefits accruing to visual imagery as a cognitive strategy. So do observations that indicate that the magnitude and direction of imagery effects vary across tasks which ostensibly require different cognitive processes. A case in point is a study by Hollenberg (1970). Recall the earlier suggestion that while experimenter-provided pictures facilitate certain types of learning, they may interfere with others. In particular, they may be assumed to be a deterrent to concept acquisition–utilization if the perceptual character- istics of particular exemplars prevent the learner from retrieving the more abstract conceptual information required. Hollenberg reached the same conclusions when comparing the learning skills of children identi- fied as high and low imagers on the basis of selected tests for imagery ability. Her finding of major concern here is that even though high- imagery children out-performed low-imagery children on an associative- learning task, they were subsequently less able to transfer this knowl- edge to a conceptual-learning task involving the same items.

Considering Hollenberg's (1970) data alongside the comparable results produced from picture–word comparisons discussed previously suggests that what is true of "pictures" when defined as externally provided (imposed) representations may also hold for "pictures" when defined as internally generated (induced) representations. With refer- ence to our own research, the finding that children who learn well from pictures can benefit from an imagery strategy on a comprehension task while children who do not learn well from pictures cannot (cf. Figure 2) certainly serves to corroborate this notion. The finding also serves as a basis for inferring that similar cognitive processes are evoked when pictures are perceived and images are generated (Levin and Divine-Hawkins, 1974; Paivio, 1971; and Peterson, 1975; but see Anderson and Bower, 1973; Katz and Paivio, 1975; and Pylyshyn, 1973). This paper will be concluded with a discussion of that inference.

INFERRED COGNITIVE STRATEGIES: A PROPOSED APPROACH AND SOME ILLUSTRATIONS

Throughout this chapter I have distinguished between imposed and induced cognitive strategies; a desired mental process is presumably evoked directly in the case of the former (via experimenter-provided materials) and indirectly in the case of the latter (via experimenter-suggested strategies). However, when investigating a covert process such as visual imagery, one of the questions that must be addressed is whether such procedures evoke covert mental processes and, if so, whether these are in fact the processes desired. Although some investigators have taken advantage of subject reports, typically answers to the first part of the question are inferred on the basis of performance differences between subjects presented with a strategy and those not presented with one (e.g., imagery-instructed versus control subjects); answers to the second part are inferred on the basis of performance differences between subjects presented with one strategy and those presented with another, or on the basis of performance differences obtained with different tasks or different sets of materials.

It should be noted that such indirect measures of a cognitive process are abhorrent to some who believe that only through direct, visible methods (like "peeking into the brain" by means of electrode implantations and associated EEG readouts) are inferences about cognitive processes warranted. However, in the absence of refinements of such techniques (where "noise" and variability are the order of the day), others consider indirect measures of a cognitive process to be acceptable, if not preferable, at present. It should also be mentioned that questions dealing with the psychological reality of a cognitive process like visual imagery encompass far-reaching theoretical issues. Because of the essentially applied focus of this paper, only scant attention will be paid to them here. However, the reader is referred elsewhere for a discussion of some of these issues (cf. Bower, 1972; Neisser, 1967; Paivio, 1971; Pylyshyn, 1973; Sheehan, 1972).

To illustrate the matter of inferring that a cognitive process such as visual imagery is operating, I have presented a prototypic paradigm and idealized data set (Figure 3). In Figure 3, two "tasks" are represented; in this discussion, "task" refers loosely to procedural or stimulus-materials variations within a task, as well as to the literal meaning of

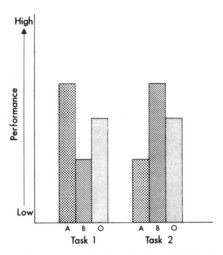

Figure 3. A proposed approach to the investigation of inferred cognitive processes.

nominally different tasks. Various imposed or induced strategies are labeled A, B, and O in the figure; A and B represent experimental strategies and O denotes a control strategy.[6] With reference to our question about the existence and nature of covert mental processes, differences between experimental (A or B) and control (O) performance may be taken as evidence that subjects presented with a strategy have done something differently from subjects not presented with a strategy, while performance differences between Strategy A and Strategy B within tasks (or, preferably, in interaction with tasks) may be taken as evidence that the two strategies have evoked different cognitive processes.

A recently reported sentence-learning study by Levin, Ghatala, Guttmann, Subkoviak, McCabe, and Bender (in press, Experiment 1) illustrates a within-task manipulation, while a discrimination-learning study by Levin, Ghatala, Wilder, and Inzer (1973) illustrates a differential strategy effect from one task to the next. In the sentence-learning study, sixth-graders were required to remember the content of 20 aurally presented sentences under basically three types of rehearsal strategies: *imagery,* in which subjects were instructed to image the content of each sentence as it was presented; *repetition,* in which subjects were instructed to repeat each sentence three times as it was presented; and *control,* in which no rehearsal strategy was suggested. The mean prompted recall of subjects in the respective conditions is adequately

---

[6] As will be seen shortly, however, this variable can also incorporate strategy differences as inferred from identifiable differences among learners.

represented by the Task 1 profile in Figure 3. That is, imagery organization (A) was superior to (either overt or covert) repetition (B), with control (O) intermediate to the two. This pattern suggests that subjects in conditions A and B were doing something different from the control subjects (or possibly that some control subjects were spontaneously employing Strategy A and others Strategy B?), but more importantly, it shows that the two strategies resulted in different levels of performance. The result is consistent with the data of Bower (1972) and Rohwer (1972) which show that filling the study interval with an irrelevant or ineffectual rote-rehearsal strategy is interfering, relative to both a semantic-organizational strategy such as the imagery instruction here and a no-strategy control where at least some (and especially older) subjects are presumably adopting an effective semantic-organizational strategy. What is of additional interest here, however, is that the performance of subjects instructed to repeat the sentences *silently to themselves* was substantially depressed relative to imagery subjects, suggesting that the children's covert rehearsals associated with the two strategy instructions were quite differentiated.

Now let us incorporate Task 2 of Figure 3 in order to approximate the results of the Levin, Ghatala, Wilder, and Inzer (1973) discrimination-learning study. Before doing so, however, a word about the discrimination-learning paradigm is in order (see also Ghatala and Levin, this volume). In it, the subject must learn which item in each of several pairs has been arbitrarily designated "correct" by the experimenter. Rowe and Paivio (1971) have demonstrated that an effective rehearsal strategy in this paradigm is one that provides rehearsal of the "correct" item, thereby increasing its familiarity (Ekstrand, Wallace, and Underwood, 1966). In the Levin, Ghatala, Wilder and Inzer (1973) study, the stimulus materials consisted of printed nouns and the subjects were requested to employ one of three rehearsal strategies during the informative feedback interval: *imagery,* in which subjects were instructed to form an image in their mind of each "correct" item's referent; *verbal,* in which subjects were instructed to pronounce aloud each "correct" item; and *control,* in which subjects were left to their own devices. Included in the stimulus materials were pairs of homonyms, for example, sun–son (Task 1 in Figure 3), and pairs of synonyms, for example, boy–lad (Task 2); it was predicted that if subjects were actually adopting the specified strategies, a different pattern of strategy effectiveness would emerge on each task. In particular, imagery (A) should constitute a relatively more effective strategy than verbal (B) when the subject is discriminating between homonyms (similar-sounding items), whereas the reverse should be true for synonyms (similar-looking items). This is because the lack of a relevant discriminative cue might retard increased familiarity with the "correct" item. The results of two experiments essentially confirmed the predictions—depicted by the idealized representation in Figure 3.

Experiments such as these are important in that when the same strategy can be shown to produce different effects with different materials, inferences are strengthened about the psychological reality of the processes assumed to be operating. Other studies in which we have attempted (not always successfully) to produce differential effects by manipulating procedures and materials are those of Davidson and Levin (1973), Horvitz and Levin (1972), Levin and Divine-Hawkins (1974), and Levin and Horvitz (1971).

An alternative inferential approach would incorporate subjects who are assumed to employ (or benefit from) different strategies into the ABO distinction of Figure 3. Hollenberg's (1970) study and our study in which Hi P and Lo P subjects responded differently to visual imagery instructions are illustrative of this approach. However, one of the most clever illustrations is by Paivio and Okovita (1971), who found that subjects deficient in visual imagery (blind subjects) did not benefit from materials rich in visual imagery-arousal as sighted subjects do. On the other hand, they did benefit from materials rich in *auditory* imagery-arousal whereas sighted subjects did not. This utterly fascinating and fertile research area dealing with cognitive processes deserves continued investigative efforts, as the wealth of information contained therein promises to be of value to both the psychologist and the educator.

SUMMARY

What have we learned about maximizing what children learn? Let us attempt to summarize the highlights.

1. In a large number of learning tasks children seem to learn better when the materials are pictures than when the materials are words. This has been noted not merely for simple item-learning tasks but also for more complex prose-learning tasks.

2. There appear to be limitations to the effectiveness of pictures in terms of both learner and task differences. With regard to the learner, we have found that certain children learn appreciably better from pictures than from words and, for these children, the type of materials presented during learning largely determines whether they will resemble good or poor learners. With regard to task differences, in tasks demanding the formation or utilization of conceptual categories, pictures tend not to be facilitative and may even impede performance.

3. Subject-generated organizational strategies (visual imagery in particular) greatly facilitate associative learning. The ability to generate

effective imaginal organizations appears to be closely related to the cognitive-developmental level of the learner. However, even children below the necessary level may be induced to generate imagery by means of appropriate auxiliary activity, training, or instructions. The ability to generate effective verbal organizations appears, developmentally, to be an earlier process than the ability to generate effective imaginal organizations. This is interesting in that it suggests that (a) even young children can benefit from an induced organizational strategy if it is an appropriate one and (b) covert verbal and imaginal processes may be differentiated in the young child.

4. Benefits from an imagery strategy have also been obtained on tasks requiring comprehension of a prose passage, but once again there are identifiable learner and task characteristics that are useful in predicting the effectiveness of the strategy. With regard to the former, subjects lacking prerequisite word-decoding skills and those who do not learn well from pictures do not seem to generate effective imaginal organizations. With regard to the latter, throughout this research we are constantly reminded that the potential effectiveness of a strategy is dependent on the nature of the task and materials. What constitutes an appropriate strategy in one context may be completely inappropriate in another, and it is up to the experimenter (and, more practically, the "cognitively mature" learner) to recognize which strategy will be helpful when.

5. We have also learned that a great deal remains to be understood about the external and internal mechanisms responsible for the phenomena that have been observed. For example: Why are pictures generally easier to learn than words? What is accomplished by imaginal or verbal organizations that make them effective learning strategies? What other individual differences variables are related to the ability to profit from a particular strategy? While the picture is far from complete at present, one cannot help but imagine the glittering psychological treasures buried just beyond the next horizon.

ACKNOWLEDGMENTS

I am grateful to my colleagues and students who collaborated on the research reviewed here, and to Sharon Stevens for her thoughtful editorial suggestions.

REFERENCES

Anderson, J. R., & Bower, G. H. *Human associative memory.* Washington, D. C.: V. H. Winston & Sons, 1973.

Bender, B. G., & Levin, J. R. Motor activity, anticipated motor activity, and young children's associative learning. *Child Development,* in press.

Bender, B. G., & Levin, J. R. *Why do pictures facilitate young children's learning of oral prose?* Paper presented at the annual meeting of the American Educational Research Association, San Francisco, April 1976.

Bobrow, S. A., & Bower, G. H. Comprehension and recall of sentences. *Journal of Experimental Psychology*, 1969, *80*, 455–461.

Bourne, L. E., Jr., Levin, J. R., Konewko, M., Yaroush, R. A., and Ghatala, E. S. Picture-word differences in discrimination learning: II. Effects of conceptual categories. *American Journal of Psychology*, in press.

Bower, G. H. Imagery as a relational organizer in associative learning. *Journal of Verbal Learning and Verbal Behavior*, 1970, *9*, 529–533.

Bower, G. H. Mental imagery and associative learning. In L. Gregg (Ed.), *Cognition in learning and memory*. New York: John Wiley & Sons, 1972.

Bower, G. H., & Winzenz, D. Comparison of associative learning strategies. *Psychonomic Science*, 1970, *20*, 119–120.

Bransford, J. D., & Johnson, M. K. Contextual prerequisites for understanding: Some investigations of comprehension and recall. *Journal of Verbal Learning and Verbal Behavior*, 1972, *11*, 717–726.

Brown, A. L., & Scott, M. S. Recognition memory for pictures in preschool children. *Journal of Experimental Child Psychology*, 1971, *11*, 401–412.

Corsini, D. A., Jacobus, K. A., & Leonard, D. Recognition memory of preschool children for pictures and words. *Psychonomic Science*, 1969, *16*, 192–193.

Davidson, R. E. The role of metaphor and analogy in learning. In J. R. Levin & V. L. Allen (Eds.), *Cognitive learning in children: Theories and strategies*. New York: Academic Press, 1976.

Davidson, R. E., & Levin, J. R. *Imagery in transfer*. Technical Report No. 249. Madison, Wisc.: Wisconsin Research and Development Center for Cognitive Learning, 1973.

Davies, G. M. Quantitative and qualitative aspects of memory for picture stimuli. *Journal of Experimental Child Psychology*, 1972, *13*, 382–393.

Deno, S. L. Effects of words and pictures as stimuli in learning language equivalents. *Journal of Educational Psychology*, 1968, *59*, 202–206.

Ekstrand, B. R., Wallace, W. P., & Underwood, B. J. A frequency theory of verbal-discrimination learning. *Psychological Review*, 1966, *73*, 566–578.

Eoff, J. E., & Rohwer, W. D., Jr. *A developmental study of imagery instructions in noun-pair learning*. Paper presented at the annual meeting of the American Educational Research Association, Chicago, April 1972.

Flavell, J. H. Developmental studies of mediated memory. In L. Lipsitt & H. Reese (Eds.), *Advances in child development and behavior* (Vol. 5). New York: Academic Press, 1970.

Ghatala, E. S., & Levin, J. R. Developmental differences in frequency judgments of words and pictures. *Journal of Experimental Child Psychology*, 1973, *16*, 495–507.

Ghatala, E. S., & Levin, J. R. Children's recognition memory processes. In J. R. Levin & V. L. Allen (Eds.), *Cognitive learning in children: Theories and strategies*. New York: Academic Press, 1976.

Glaser, R. Individuals and learning: The new aptitudes. *Educational Researcher*, 1972, *1*(6), 5–12.

Goulet, L. R. Verbal learning in children: Implications for developmental research. *Psychological Bulletin*, 1968, *69*, 359–376.

Guttmann, J. *The effects of pictures and partial pictures on children's oral prose learning*. Paper presented at the annual meeting of the American Educational Research Association, San Francisco, April 1976.

Hollenberg, C. K. Functions of visual imagery in the learning and concept formation of children. *Child Development*, 1970, *41*, 1003–1015.

Horvitz, J. M., & Levin, J. R. Semantic and imaginal factors in learning as related to age. *Journal of Experimental Child Psychology*, 1972, *14*, 11–20.

Jensen, A. R., & Rohwer, W. D., Jr. Syntactical mediation of serial and paired-associate learning as a function of age. *Child Development*, 1965, *36*, 601–608.

Katz, A. N., & Paivio, A. Imagery variables in concept identification. *Journal of Verbal Learning and Verbal Behavior*, 1975, *14*, 284–293.

Kendler, T. S. An ontogeny of mediational deficiency. *Child Development*, 1972, *43*, 1–17.

Keppel, G. Verbal learning in children. *Psychological Bulletin*, 1964, *61*, 63–80.

Kerst, S., & Levin, J. R. A comparison of experimenter-provided and subject-generated strategies in children's paired-associate learning. *Journal of Educational Psychology*, 1973, *65*, 300–303.

Labouvie-Vief, G., Levin, J. R., & Urberg, K. A. The relationship between selected cognitive abilities and learning. *Journal of Educational Psychology*, 1975, *67*, 558–569.

Lesgold, A. M., Levin, J. R., Shimron, J., & Guttmann, J. Pictures and young children's learning from oral prose. *Journal of Educational Psychology*, 1975, *67*, 636–642.

Lesgold, A. M., McCormick, C., & Golinkoff, R. M. Imagery training and children's prose learning. *Journal of Educational Psychology*, 1975, *67*, 663–667.

Levin, J. R. Comprehending what we read: An outsider looks in. *Journal of Reading Behavior*, 1972(a), *4*, 18–28.

Levin, J. R. When is a picture worth a thousand words? In *Issues in imagery and learning: Four papers*. Theoretical Paper No. 36. Madison, Wisc.: Wisconsin Research and Development Center for Cognitive Learning, 1972(b).

Levin, J. R. Inducing comprehension in poor readers: A test of a recent model. *Journal of Educational Psychology*, 1973, *65*, 19–24.

Levin, J. R. *Learner differences: Diagnosis and prescription*. New York: Holt & Co., in press.

Levin, J. R., Bourne, L. E., Jr., Yaroush, R. A., Ghatala, E. S., DeRose, T. M., & Hanson, V. Picture-word differences and conceptual frequency judgments. *Memory & Cognition*, in press.

Levin, J. R., Davidson, R. E., Wolff, P., & Citron, M. A comparison of induced imagery and sentence strategies in children's paired-associate learning. *Journal of Educational Psychology*, 1973, *64*, 306–309.

Levin, J. R., & Divine-Hawkins, P. Visual imagery as a prose-learning process. *Journal of Reading Behavior*, 1974, *6*, 23–30.

Levin, J. R., Divine-Hawkins, P., Kerst, S., & Guttmann, J. Individual differences in learning from pictures and words: The development and application of an instrument. *Journal of Educational Psychology*, 1974, *66*, 296–303.

Levin, J. R., Ghatala, E. S., DeRose, T. M., Wilder, L., & Norton, R. W. A further comparison of imagery and vocalization strategies in children's discrimination learning. *Journal of Educational Psychology*, 1975, *67*, 141–145.

Levin, J. R., Ghatala, E. S., Guttmann, J., Subkoviak, M. J., McCabe, A. E., & Bender, B. G. *Processes affecting children's learning from sentences*. Working Paper No. 144. Madison, Wisc.: Wisconsin Research and Development Center for Cognitive Learning, in press.

Levin, J. R., Ghatala, E. S., Wilder, L., & Inzer, E. Imagery and vocalization strategies in children's verbal discrimination learning. *Journal of Educational Psychology*, 1973, *64*, 360–365.

Levin, J. R., & Horvitz, J. M. The meaning of paired associates. *Journal of Educational Psychology*, 1971, *62*, 209–214.

Levin, J. R., & Kaplan, S. A. Imaginal facilitation of paired-associate learning: A limited generalization? *Journal of Educational Psychology*, 1972, *63*, 429–432.

Levin, J. R., McCabe, A. E., & Bender, B. G. A note on imagery-inducing motor activity in young children. *Child Development*, 1975, *46*, 263–266.

Levin, J. R., & Rohwer, W. D., Jr. Verbal organization and the facilitation of serial learning. *Journal of Educational Psychology*, 1968, *59*, 186–190.

Levin, J. R., Rohwer, W. D., Jr., & Cleary, T. A. Individual differences in the learning of verbally and pictorially presented paired associates. *American Educational Research Journal*, 1971, *8*, 11–26.

Lippman, M. Z., & Shanahan, M. W. Pictorial facilitation of paired-associate learning: Implications for vocabulary training. *Journal of Educational Psychology*, 1973, *64*, 216–222.

McCabe, A. E. *An investigation of the interaction of motor activity and sentence production in young children*. Technical Report No. 207. Madison, Wisc.: Wisconsin Research and Development Center for Cognitive Learning, 1973.

McCabe, A. E., Levin, J. R., & Wolff, P. The role of overt activity in children's sentence production. *Journal of Experimental Child Psychology*, 1974, *17*, 107–114.

Montague, R. B. *The effect of mediational instructions on associative skills of first grade innercity children*. Paper presented at the annual meeting of the American Educational Research Association, Minneapolis, March 1970.

Neisser, U. *Cognitive psychology*. New York: Appleton-Century-Crofts, 1967.

Paivio, A. *Imagery and verbal processes*. New York: Holt, Rinehart and Winston, 1971.

Paivio, A., & Csapo, K. Concrete-image and verbal memory codes. *Journal of Experimental Psychology*, 1969, *80*, 279–285.

Paivio, A., & Csapo, K. Short-term sequential memory for pictures and words. *Psychonomic Science*, 1971, *24*, 50–51.

Paivio, A., & Csapo, K. Picture superiority in free recall: Imagery or dual coding? *Cognitive Psychology*, 1973, *5*, 176–206.

Paivio, A., & Okovita, H. W. Word imagery modalities and associative learning in blind and sighted subjects. *Journal of Verbal Learning and Verbal Behavior*, 1971, *10*, 506–510.

Peeck, J. Retention of pictorial and verbal content of a text with illustrations. *Journal of Educational Psychology*, 1974, *66*, 880–888.

Peterson, M. J. The retention of imagined and seen spatial matrices. *Cognitive Psychology*, 1975, *7*, 181–193.

Piaget, J., & Inhelder, B. *Mental imagery in the child*. New York: Basic Books, 1971.

Pressley, G. M. Mental images help eight-year-olds remember what they read. *Journal of Educational Psychology*, in press.

Pylyshyn, Z. W. What the mind's eye tells the mind's brain: A critique of mental imagery. *Psychological Bulletin*, 1973, *80*, 1–24.

Reese, H. W., (Chm.). Imagery in children's learning: A symposium. *Psychological Bulletin*, 1970, *73*, 383–421.

Rohwer, W. D., Jr. *Social class differences in the role of linguistic structures in paired-associate learning: Elaboration and learning proficiency*. Final report on basic research Project No. 5-0605, U. S. Office of Education, 1967.

Rohwer, W. D., Jr. Decisive research: A means for answering fundamental questions about instruction. *Educational Researcher*, 1972, *1*(7), 5–11.

Rohwer, W. D., Jr., Ammon, M. S., Suzuki, N., & Levin, J. R. Population differences and learning proficiency. *Journal of Educational Psychology*, 1971, *62*, 1–14.

Rohwer, W. D., Jr., & Harris, W. J. Media effects on prose learning in two populations of children. *Journal of Educational Psychology*, 1975, *67*, 651–657.

Rohwer, W. D., Jr., & Levin, J. R. Elaboration preferences and differences in learning proficiency. In J. Hellmuth (Ed.), *Cognitive Studies* (Vol. 2). New York: Brunner/Mazel, 1971.

Rohwer, W. D., Jr., & Matz, R. Improving aural comprehension in white and in black children: Pictures versus print. *Journal of Experimental Child Psychology*, 1975, *19*, 23–36.

Rowe, E. J., & Paivio, A. Imagery and repetition instructions in verbal discrimination and incidental paired-associate learning. *Journal of Verbal Learning and Verbal Behavior*, 1971, *10*, 668–672.

Runquist, W. N., & Hutt, V. H. Verbal concept learning in high school students with pictorial and verbal representation of stimuli. *Journal of Educational Psychology*, 1961, *52*, 108–111.

Samuels, S. J. Effects of pictures on learning to read, comprehension and attitudes. *Review of Educational Research*, 1970, *40*, 397–407.

Sheehan, P. W. (Ed.), *The function and nature of imagery*. New York: Academic Press, 1972.

Shepard, R. N. Recognition memory for words, sentences, and pictures. *Journal of Verbal Learning and Verbal Behavior*, 1967, *6*, 156–163.

Shimron, J. *Imagery and the comprehension of prose by elementary school children*. Unpublished doctoral dissertation, University of Pittsburgh, 1974.

Standing, L., Conezio, J., & Haber, R. N. Perception and memory for pictures: Single-trial learning of 2500 visual stimuli. *Psychonomic Science*, 1970, *19*, 73–74.

Varley, W. H., Levin, J. R., Severson, R. A., & Wolff, P. Training imagery production in young children through motor involvement. *Journal of Educational Psychology*, 1974, *66*, 262–266.

Wiener, M., & Cromer, W. Reading and reading difficulty: A conceptual analysis. *Harvard Educational Review*, 1967, *37*, 620–643.

Wilder, L., & Levin, J. R. A developmental study of pronouncing responses in the discrimination learning of words and pictures. *Journal of Experimental Child Psychology*, 1973, *15*, 278–286.

Wohlwill, J. F. Responses to class-inclusion questions for verbally and pictorially presented items. *Child Development*, 1968, *39*, 449–465.

Wolff, P., & Levin, J. R. The role of overt activity in children's imagery production. *Child Development*, 1972, *43*, 537–547.

Wolff, P., Levin, J. R., & Longobardi, E. T. Motoric mediation in children's paired-associate learning: Effects of visual and tactual contact. *Journal of Experimental Child Psychology*, 1972, *14*, 176–183.

Wolff, P., Levin, J. R., & Longobardi, E. T. Activity and children's learning. *Child Development*, 1974, *45*, 221–223.

CHAPTER 5

The Role of Metaphor
and Analogy in Learning

Robert E. Davidson

The research that will be discussed in this chapter is concerned with the ways in which a subset of "higher mental processes" can facilitate or distort learning, comprehension, and memory. Despite the fact that most of this research has been conducted with comparatively older subject populations (i.e., adolescents and adults), in the latter part of this chapter I will review a few studies that have been conducted with younger children. In fact, Davis's chapter in this volume includes instructional training procedures for young children that capitalize on some of the present notions.

The particular higher mental activity that we have investigated will be referred to as the *hypostatization*[1] processes (Davidson, 1971). Hypostatizations refer to cognitive transformation processes that may be called into play when the learner is faced with complex or abstract learning tasks. The goal of such processes is to transform the complex or abstract information into forms that make the information more comprehensible or easier to learn. For example, a learner might try to "understand" an abstract concept in terms of a concrete concept that is familiar. Essentially, hypostatization is cognitive activity that is metaphorical–analogical in character. Examples of present interest include verbal-symbolic and visual-imagery metaphor; and verbal and pictorial analogy.

Unfortunately, injecting hypostatization into a learning task can produce unwanted side effects or cognitive distortions. Cognitive distortions take different forms. For example, the tendency to imbue an abstraction with substance (e.g., the reification of "intelligence" or "id"), is a particularly virulent form of cognitive distortion. Laymen

---

[1] Hypostatize \ hiɔ́pästə, tiz \ [GK Hypostatos (ὑποστατός) substantially existing?; (a) to transform a conceptual entity into or construe as a self-subsistent substance, (b) to assume as concrete (From Webster's *Third New International Dictionary*).

and scientists alike are infected by it. Many years ago, A. N. Whitehead (1929) warned of the "fallacy of misplaced concreteness." That warning has been taken seriously in my own program of research, and ways must be found to assess cognitive distortions and prevent their occurrence.

The central objective of the program has been an experimental attack on the hypostatization processes, but an understanding of the operation of these processes presumes interests in two other aspects as well. The first concerns the characteristics of the learning tasks; the second deals with characteristics of the subject populations. Three characteristics of the learning tasks can be distinguished:

1. The information within the task may vary in terms of degree of complexity or abstractness.
2. The task itself may vary along a "simple-difficult" continuum (e.g., paired-associates learning or comprehension of text).
3. The manipulation of the task may vary so that the learning materials are hypostatized for the learner or the materials await learner-generated hypostatization (see Levin's "imposed—induced" distinction in this volume).

Population characteristics of principal interest are age, sex, socioeconomic status, and IQ. Experimental variations among the process, task, and populations characteristics will help to establish the boundary conditions for hypostatization.

In his book, *Cognitive Psychology,* Ulric Neisser (1966) says: "There is relatively little to say about [the higher mental processes], even after 100 years of psychological research [p. 11]." Despite such pessimism, there are several lines of inquiry into the higher mental processes that bear on our research topic. Some of these lines of inquiry are represented by experimental investigations—but only some. These investigations, including experiments carried out by the author, will be reported at the end of this section. First, however, it might be instructive to provide a small sample of anecdotes that show hypostatization at work. Subsequently, the theories that form the conceptual bases for the processes will be delineated. Included are aspects from psychological and rhetorical inquiries. (A linguistic basis for our research program also has relevance, but it will not be considered here.)

ANECDOTES FROM THE HISTORY OF SCIENCE

In an invited address to the American Psychological Association, J. Robert Oppenheimer (1956) chose as his topic "Analogy in Science":

> Analogy is inevitable in human thought. We come to new things with what (psychological) equipment we have, which is how we have learned to think, and above all how we have learned to think about the relatedness of things (p. 129).

The history of science is replete with examples of hypostatized thinking.

Item (analogical imagery). Kekulé on the discovery of the benzene ring:

> I turned the chair to the fireplace and sank into a half sleep. The atoms flitted before my eyes. Long rows, variously, more closely, united; all in the movement wriggling and turning like snakes. And see, what was that? One of the snakes seized its own tail and the image whirled scornfully before my eyes. As though from a flash of lightning I awoke; I occupied the rest of the night in working out the consequences of the hypothesis [Baker, 1942].

Item (analogical imagery). Einstein in a letter to M. Hadamard:

> The physical entities which seem to serve as elements in thought are certain signs and more or less clear images which can be "voluntarily" reproduced and combined. There is, of course, a certain connection between these elements and relevant logical concepts. . . . According to what has been said, *the play with the mentioned elements is aimed to be analogous to certain logical connections one is searching for* [italics mine; Ghiselin, 1952].

Item (personification). T. A. Rich, award winner in electronics

> . . . describes how he puts himself in the middle of a problem, trying as he says, to "think" like an electron whose course is being plotted or imagine himself [to be] a light beam whose reflection is being measured [The Minneapolis Star, February 18, 1965].

Item (pictorial analogy). Richard Jones cites an example from a sixth-grade boy who was asked

> . . . to say what infinity was. He replied, "It's like a box of Cream of Wheat." (The Cream of Wheat label formerly pictured a chef holding a box of Cream of Wheat, which pictured a chef holding a box of Cream of Wheat, etc.) He was censured for his silliness [Jones, 1967].

Anecdotes do not constitute "hard" data, but they do serve to point up the pervasiveness and varieties of hypostatization. The kind of psychological research that extends the anecdotal account is represented by the interview method. For example, in the course of a study on the personality characteristics of 64 "eminent research scientists," Roe (1951) "gradually became aware" of the frequency with which mental imagery was reported. Often the imagery was of a "manipulable" kind. Unfortuantely, she did not follow up the mental processes involved. She noted, however, that biologists and experimental physicists predominated in the use of visual imagery while theoretical physicists, psychologists, and anthropologists reported little or no use of imagery. Similarly, Walkup (1965) reported imagery and personification among inventors. However interesting they may be, anecdotal accounts and interview data provide little help for a detailed analysis of how the hypostatization processes operate.

TWO CONCEPTUAL BASES FOR HYPOSTATIZATION

Psychological Aspects

The framework for hypostatization is built upon the observations by Bartlett (1932) that ". . . every human cognitive reaction—perceiving, imaging, remembering, thinking, and reasoning—is an *effort after meaning* [italics in original, p. 44]." "Speaking very broadly, such effort is simply *the attempt to connect something that is given with something other than itself* [italics mine, p. 227]." Efforts after meaning are grounded in biological utility. They are "construction or reconstruction" processes that "turn around on their own schematic organizations [p. 312]."

Bartlett's observations were the result of his research on remembering (also the title of his book). But, clearly, the observations apply beyond memory. Constructive, transformational "schemata" allow flexibility, adaptability, and economy in learning and thinking. But these advantages may be achieved only at some cost. The cost may be forms of cognitive distortion—forms that include simplification, overgeneralization, reification, and importation of information.

Modern equivalants of Bartlett's "schemata" are to be found in the "cognitive theories," where they go by various names: "plans" (Miller, Galanter, and Pribram 1960), "strategies" (Bruner, Goodnow, and Austin, 1956), "conscious constructions" (Posner, 1972), "rules" (Rumelhart, Lindsay, and Norman, 1972), and "organizational factors" (Bower, 1970). However, it is the work of Bruner (1957a, b, c; 1962) and Berlyne (1960, 1965) that provide the principal extensions and refinements for that subset of "schemata" called hypostatizations. Bruner's work represents the cognitive aspects; Berlyne, the motivational aspects.

Bruner (1957a) assumes that the basic cognitive task is to cope with "the surprise value of the environment." Prior habits and contingencies are often inadequate for new and complex problems. To deal with these, "working models" are constructed that enable a person to go beyond the confines of the data from which the model was derived (Bruner, 1957c). Going beyond the information given is described as having a "metaphoric idea" or a "combinatorial idea" (Bruner, 1957b). Berlyne (1960; 1965) has convincingly demonstrated that certain stimulus variables (novelty, surprisingness, incongruity, ambiguity, uncertainty, and complexity) activate an "orientation reaction" which is a correlate of arousal. And arousal, in turn, is identified with the motivational state called "drive." He offers the following observations:

> Human beings will take action to lower arousal once it has been raised by environmental events. . . When drive or arousal is driven upward by an encounter with an exceptionally novel, complex or puzzling stimulus, cognitive activity is likely to supervene and the accrual of information that results serves to bring the drive or arousal down again. This reduction in drive may provide reinforcement facilitating the retention of information in question and strengthening the subject's inclination to engage in such activity in comparable situations. . . The symbolic capacities with which human beings are so well endowed makes the expedient of seeking to relieve arousal by acquisition of information by far the most effective as a rule [1965, p. 253].

Note should be taken that Berlyne's observations implicate "extrinsic sources" for arousal motivation. But the motivation has its "intrinsic sources" as well. Hebb (1955) and Platt (1961) review evidence to show that human beings will seek activities which provide, in Berlyne's (1960) terms, "arousal jags." Such activities are sought only insofar as the arousal-increase is moderate and has a high probability of being followed by arousal-decrease.

A linkup of the cognitive and motivational aspects provides a formulation for the hypostatization processes that speaks to their utility in behavior. Hypostatizations are viewed as constructive, transformational 'schemata' (operationally, metaphorical–analogical devices—cf. "Rhetorical Aspects," the following section) that serve as efforts after information and meaning. They are motivated by the arousal capacity of novel, abstract, and complex tasks, with the aim of arousal-reduction. Both the nature of these 'schemata' and their aim at arousal-reduction can act to facilitate and distort cognition.

Rhetorical Aspects

Two definitions of rhetoric are pivotal with respect to our program of research. The first is the succinct statement by Bryant (1965): "Rhetoric is the fitting of people to ideas or ideas to people." The second is from I. A. Richards (1936): "Rhetoric, I shall urge, should be a study of misunderstanding and its remedies." Bryant's definition points up a persisting dichotomy in rhetoric—that between argumentation and comprehension. Only comprehension—the fitting of ideas to people—has been of interest in our research. Richards's definition of rhetoric is interpreted to be an expression of concern about cognitive distortion.

The facilitation of comprehension and the assessment (and prevention) of cognitive distortion are, for the purposes of our research, placed in the context of hypostatization. That context provides further limits to the perspective from rhetorical inquiry. That is, hypostatizations are identified with the so-called "rhetorical figures." But rhetorical figures abound. Perleman (1969), for example, indexes no fewer than 62 of them, and he and other rhetoricians associate certain kinds of cognitive processes with figures. Consider the following:

> Hyperboles using concrete expressions create images. Their role is to provide a reference which draws the mind in a certain direction only to force it later to retreat a little to the extreme limit of what seems compatible with the idea of the human, the possible, the probable.

It isn't necessary to comment on the quote because, while hyperbole and other rhetorical figures may qualify as hypostatization, this proposal singles out a limited set for theory and experiment, namely, metaphor and the related forms:

> A memorable metaphor has the power to bring two separate domains into cognitive and emotional relation by using language directly appropriate to one as a lens for seeing the other [Black, 1962].

Modern rhetoricians view metaphor as a "transmutive" (usually verbal-symbolic) process which involves a semantic interaction or semantic transfer between two concepts (Black, 1962; Perleman, 1969; Richards, 1936; Wheelwright, 1962). The two concepts, one of which may be an abstraction, are termed "tenor" and "vehicle" by Richards (1936). The vehicle is better known than the tenor and can be used to deliver meaning to the tenor. Often the meaning transfer in the metaphor is represented as a "commanding visual image" (Wheelwright, 1962). For example, Vigotsky (1962) has described thought as "cloud showers of words."

For Perleman (1969) metaphor is, in fact, a condensed, four-term, direct analogy which "strives after a resemblance of structures," the most typical of which is: A is to B as C is to D. These structures are viewed as informal, quasi-logical expressions of similarity. For example, white blood cells (A) are to the body (B) as soldiers (C) are to the country (D). The component terms A and B constitute the tenor, C and D the vehicle. Thus, the compressed metaphor, "soldier-cells," in the context of health, can be analyzed as a four-term, direct analogy which contains a latent structure and a transfer of meaning among the components of the structure. White blood cells take on some of the features of soldiers: Soldiers are good for the country, of great necessity, and are active in times of attack. And the body, like the country, becomes an area to be defended. (An experimental investigation patterned after the four-term, direct analogy will be described subsequently.) Upton (1961) is in substantial agreement with Perleman, but suggests in addition that "some analogies are expressions of similarity between ratios of proportions." That is, Upton detects latent mathematical forms in some analogies.

Although many other rhetorical analyses of the metaphorical forms could be detailed, this section will conclude with an analogical form that "elucidates by double hierarchy" (Perleman, 1969). The double hierarchy expresses a point-by-point isomorphism between the features (or terms) of two "ideas." The assumption behind writing text that is cast in a double hierarchy is that the reader already knows the hierarchical relationship among the terms of one of the hierarchies (idea 1); and the second hierarchy (idea 2) is "elucidated" as the isomorphism between the terms unfolds in the text.

EXPERIMENTAL INVESTIGATIONS

The studies to be reported are all, properly speaking, psychological experiments. But for present purposes the studies will be organized on the basis of the two conceptual aspects that prompted them: psychological and rhetorical.

Psychological Investigations

A variety of phenomena, for example, synesthesia (Osgood, 1953), hypnagogic imagery (McKellar, 1957; Oswald, 1962), phonetic symbolism, and other sensory qualities of words (Brown, 1958), are considered to be instances of hypostatization. For example, Kekule's imagery of a snake swallowing its tail (Baker, 1942) would be an instance of hypnagogic imagery. Nevertheless, the above variety of phenomena would seem to be more "primitive" or "primary process" (Hilgard, 1962) manifestations of hypostatization processes which, while interesting in their own right, are not of direct interest here. In any event, adequate reviews of such phenomena are to be found in the works cited above, and only a few of the studies need be reviewed. It is interesting to note, however, that some aspects of primary process "thinking" have given rise to systematic theory and method in psychology. For example, the semantic differential method for the measurement of meaning had its origin in research on synesthesia (Osgood, 1952).

Subjects with synesthetic capacity report "seeing" colors and forms as responses to music (Karwaski, Odbert, and Osgood, 1942; Simpson, Quinn, and Ausubel, 1956). Neisser (1966) reports an instance of hypnogogic imagery in which an abstract idea like "I am unable to obtain the necessary information" is transformed by "the primary process" into the concrete image of a "morose secretary." Brown, Leiter, and Hildum (1957) have shown that nonauditory sense terms (cold, dry, brittle, bright, etc.) are applied reliably to voice qualities.

Word-Learning Studies

Of greater interest to our research program has been studies that employ experimental methods designed to reveal the operation of "secondary process" (Hilgard, 1962) forms of hypostatization. For example, one of our claims for hypostatization is that the concretization of abstractions will facilitate learning. In that regard, Marshall (1965) reports a paired-associate study in which abstract word pairs were mediated by concretizing the items. By way of example, the pair **formula–innocence** was mediated by the concrete word "baby" or by the picture of a baby. Over trials of learning, concrete picture mediators facilitated learning differentially better than concrete words (i.e., an interaction was reported). Further, the picture mediators produced fewer intrusion errors, suggesting that pictorial concretizations limit the subjects' responses to a smaller or more discriminable pool of items. A similar study was reported by Wollen (1968) using high and low imagery items. For example, the pair **horse–tree** (high imagery) was shown in conjunction with a unified picture depicting a horse and tree; the pair **lubricant–strength** (low imagery) was shown with a picture depicting an oil-applicator and a dumbbell. This relevant picture condition was contrasted with an irrelevant picture condition (pictures randomized to pairs), and a no-picture condition (word pairs alone). The subjects in the relevant picture condition recalled almost twice as many responses as did subjects in the other two conditions. This was true for both low and high imagery pairs. Concretization of the more abstract, low imagery pairs (e.g., dumbbell for "strength") in this experiment did not lead to greater numbers of importations or intrusions.

In one of the experiments from our own program (Davidson, 1971), we used a 7-point scale adapted from Paivio, Yuille, and Madigan (1968), and asked independent groups of college subjects to rate single words and compressed metaphors for their imagery value. The pools of stimulus items consisted of single abstract nouns (e.g., "opportunity"), single concrete nouns ("soup"), compressed metaphors composed of some of the abstract nouns plus a modifier ("golden opportunity"), and metaphors composed of some of the concrete nouns plus a modifier ("duck soup"). Each of the metaphors constituted a cliche in English, while many of the single words were definitional equivilants of the metaphors (e.g., "easy" = "duck soup"). Mean imagery value for the modified abstractions (e.g., "golden opportunity") exceeded the mean imagery value of their single word counterparts (e.g., "opportunity"). Imagery value for the hypostatized abstractions was 3.7; for single word abstractions, 2.6. Exactly the opposite effects were found for the concrete items: Single concrete words exceeded modified concrete words (imagery value = 6.1 versus 4.7). This latter result was not surprising; indeed, it followed directly the prediction for such pairs. That is, if the argument is turned back on itself, the abstract word "easy" can be represented by the cliche "duck soup," and when the mean imagery value for the three interrelated stimulus items are calculated they are, respectively, "soup" = 6.44, "duck soup" = 3.08, and "easy" = 3.21.

In a subsequent experiment, we (Davidson, 1971) used similar sets of modified abstract words, and modified concrete words in a paired-associates task patterned after Paivio (1965). The mixed list contained 16 pairs—four AA item-types (abstract stimulus—abstract response), four AC item-types (abstract stimulus—concrete response), four CA item-types, and four CC item-types. Nineteen college-age subjects were randomly assigned to each of three independent groups. A control group learned unmodified pairs. This condition was an attempt to replicate Piavio's (1965) results. Two experimental conditions manipulated the pairs in "literal appropriate" and hypostatization contexts. In the former condition, the stimulus terms (abstract or concrete nouns) were modified in a way that produced a phrase that had little "surprise" value to it (e.g., "hairy head" or "excellent opportunity"). In the latter condition, the stimulus terms were hypostatized (e.g., "egg head" or "golden opportunity"). The phrases served as the stimulus terms, and were paired with single nouns (abstract or concrete) as responses— i.e., the pair **excellent opportunity—soul** was an AA item-type in the literal appropriate condition, and the pair **egg head—window** was a hypostatized CC item-type. The results, measured as the mean number correct in four trials of learning, are presented in Figure 1.

The important result for this discussion is that the experimental conditions by item-type interaction was statistically significant. This interaction follows directly the predictions made for the experiment. By way of interpretation, the interaction indicates that the hypostatized AA item-types **(golden opportunity—soul)** were superior to their literal appropriate counterparts **(excellent opportunity—soul)**. At the

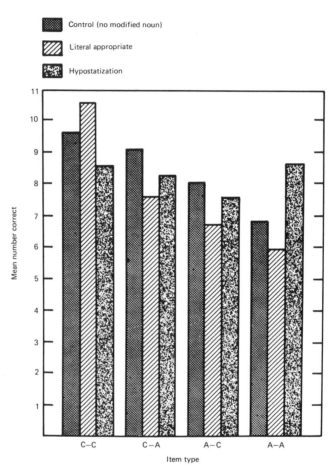

Figure 1. Mean number of correct responses as a function of experimental conditions and item-types.

same time, hypostatized CC item-types (**egg head–window**) were inferior to the literal appropriate item-types (**hairy head–window**). That is, hypostatized concrete nouns move in the direction of an abstraction (e.g., egg head = intellectual), and hypostatized abstractions are concretized. Thus, the same hypostatizing operation for different kinds of learning materials shows itself capable of impeding and facilitating learning. Both of these effects are of interest to our research effort—the facilitation and distortion of cognition and learning.

The argument might be made that the novelty of the hypostatized forms is alone responsible for the effects produced in the experiment just described—that is, the forms have arousal and attention value. This possibility cannot be ruled out, although it doesn't explain why the hypostatized concrete terms depress performance. On the other hand, the argument might be made that cliches are hardly novel, and that familiarity explains the results. Again, the nature of the interaction (simultaneously facilitating and depressing performance) does not make familiarity particularly appealing as an explanation. In any event, issues that turn on novelty, familiarity and the constructive nature of the hypostatization process themselves require further investigation. For example, what would be the effects in learning for noncliche, adjective—noun compound phrases (e.g., **black idea**)? Would sensory compounds (e.g., **blue mood; sweet disposition**) be more, or less, facilitating and distorting than category compounds (e.g., **monkey business; puppy love**)? Furthermore, what effects in learning might result from a contrast between experimenter-constructed versus subject-generated compounds?

Prose-Learning Studies

The concretization of abstractions in more difficult tasks such as the processing of information contained in text is not represented in recent psychological literature. This is true despite the fact that psychologists themselves often resort to abstract—concrete comparisons when discussing psychological constructs or systems of relations among constructs. For example, Bower (1970) used one of science's root metaphors—the machine metaphor—to increase his own, and (consequently) his reader's, understanding of a reallocation theory of grouping operations. Abstract theoretical constructs were placed in the context of a machine complete with "activated storage locations," "match and mismatch signals," and various "shunting operations."

Bartlett (1932) describes several experiments on the recall of folk tales and other verbal passages. Most of the information in the passages was concrete to begin with, but wherever there was abstract information, a common simplification transformation would occur which Bartlett termed "the bias toward the concrete."

Werner and Kaplan (1963) inquired into the imagery associated with a related series of "abstract" sentences. For example, the sentences might relate to the concept of time—past, present, and future. Under hypnosis, subjects were asked to transform the sentences into imagery. In the series, "He fought," "He fights," "He is fighting," "He will fight," subjects reported a variety of (idiosyncratic) concretizing imagery. "He fought" might become "a soldier lying dead"; "He will fight" might be represented as the soldier cleaning his gun, etc. Werner and Kaplan (1963) suggest that subjects have difficulty with the "representation of relatively abstract concepts or abstract conceptual relations; the only way such a task can be meaningfully executed is by concretizing the referent [p. 49]."

A set of studies by Huttenlocher (1968) indicated that subjects use spatial imagery to solve three-term comparison problems such as "Tom is taller than Sam and John is shorter than Sam—who is tallest?" Huttenlocher's experiments suggest that subjects apply a spatial imagery strategy regardless of the abstractness of the categories being compared.

We performed an experiment in which abstract concepts and abstract relations among the concepts were embedded in a concretizing, extended metaphor (Davidson, 1971). Actually, the metaphor used has existed in literature for 124 years. It was "The Mat Maker" chapter from Melville's *Moby Dick*. In the passage, the abstract concepts and the interrelationships among them (i.e., time, fate, chance, freewill, and necessity), are compared to the parts and the interworkings of a sword-mat loom. Warp and woof, for example, are necessity and free will; the sword represents chance, etc. The sword-mat loom is an archiac root metaphor, but it was reasoned that if subjects were brought up to date by means of a picture and a description of the loom's operation, it could be used as an appropriate hypostatizing device for understanding Melville's concept of the abstractions and their relationships. It seems safe to say that such was Melville's intent.

Three independent conditions were formed. Equal numbers of college freshman (from English courses) were assigned randomly to separate conditions and tested in small groups. All subjects admitted knowing "about" *Moby Dick*, but none of them claimed to have read it. Under one of the conditions, *relevant picture*, subjects were shown a picture of a sword-mat loom accompanied by a 158-word description of the operation of its parts. In a second group, *irrelevant picture*, subjects saw a picture and read a 159-word description of a "Portable Power and Resistor Unit" constructed by the author and designed to be equal in complexity to the loom in terms of the number and operation of its parts. A third condition (no picture) served as a control.

Instructions to read the passage for "understanding" followed a 4-minute paraphrase and question-and-answer session concerning the apparatus shown (immediate reading of the passage in the case of the control). The subjects were given 5 minutes to read and process the passage. The passages were removed, and three dependent observations, counterbalanced over subject groups, were obtained:

1. Free recall of "main ideas."
2. Word associations [production method, (Noble, 1952)] to 20 critical and filler words.

3. Yes—no responses to assertions based on the text—for example, "The sword is like chance" (yes), "The sea is like necessity" (no).

The following paragraphs present the results in detail.

To be brief, the author could make little sense out of the free recall data. Such experiences are not unheard of in the comprehension-of-text literature, and elaborate schemes for systematizing such data are undergoing development (Carroll and Freedle, 1972).

The word association data were analyzed by the statistic called the *relatedness coefficient* (Garskof and Houston, 1963; Johnson, 1967; Moss and Pucel, 1967). The relatedness coefficient measures the extent to which two response distributions overlap—that is, the number of word associates that the distributions share in common. The relatedness coefficient is therefore a measure of the associative relatedness of two concepts. The size of the relatedness coefficient measure is said to be inversely proportional to the psychological distance between two concepts (Moss and Pucel, 1967). A relatedness coefficient of 1.00 indicates that the response distributions for two concepts are exactly identical; a relatedness coefficient of .00 indicates no overlap.

Median relatedness coefficients for critical words (picture groups only) are presented in Table 1. Two complementary ways of interpreting the matrix of numbers are possible: (*a*) the quadrant method, (*b*) the line—column method (an example of the line—column method is outlined on the table showing the relatedness of the word "sword" to the other word concepts).

TABLE 1

Median Relatedness Coefficients for Relevant (Loom) and Irrelevant (Resistor Unit) Picture Groups

Word	Sw	Lo	Sh	Wa	Wo	Ch	Ti	Fr	Ne	Fa
Sword (Sw)		58	17	17	26	14	06	04	00	05
Loom (Lo)	18		43[a,c]	31	40	13	08	10	00	29
Shuttle (Sh)	00	65[b,c]		21	43	06	04	06	00	00
Warp (Wa)	00	16	12		18	10	06	03	00	05
Woof (Wo)	24	23	09	05		09	06	35	00	05
Chance (Ch)	00	00	00	00	00		08	14	00	15
Time (Ti)	00	00	00	00	00	00		14	15	15
Freewill (Fr)	00	00	00	00	00	50	00		13	34
Necessity (Ne)	00	00	00	00	00	40	00	28		09
Fate (Fa)	00	00	00	00	00	49	00	40	09	

[a]Relevant picture group above the diagonal.
[b]Irrelevant picture group below the diagonal.
[c]Decimals omitted throughout.

For interpretation under the quadrant method, note that the words are arranged so that five concrete (loom) words are followed by five abstract words. Note also that the lower left quadrant (5 × 5 entries of coefficients) contains nothing but zeros. That is, the five concrete words show no overlap with the five abstract words in the irrelevant picture group. On the other hand, the upper-right quadrant (relevant picture group) contains a number of nonzero entries indicating that different numbers of associates were shared in common among the abstract and the concrete words. Specifically, for the relevant picture group (outlined within the matrix) word associates were shared in common between sword and warp (.17); between sword and chance (.14); between sword and free will (.04), etc. Similar comparisons for the irrelevant picture group (outlined column) reveal nothing but zeros. The relatedness coefficient matrix for the control condition indicated that the control was similar to the irrelevant picture group.

The third dependent measure of the Mat Maker study was the subject's number of correctly circled "yes" and "no" assertions (similes) based on the text. There were 36 assertions—18 yes, 18 no. A second classification of the assertions was in terms of the nature of the comparison that was asserted. Eighteen of the assertions (9 yes, 9 no) were concrete to abstract comparisons (e.g., "The sword is like chance"). The remaining 18 assertions (9 yes, 9 no) were abstract to concrete comparisons (e.g., "Free will is like the warp").

The results indicated that the subjects in the relevant picture condition made significantly fewer errors than irrelevant picture and control subjects—mean numbers of correct circlings were, respectively, 25.91, 16.80, and 18.37. Furthermore, the pattern of responses for the three conditions differed with respect to the concrete to abstract or abstract to concrete comparisons. The subjects in the relevant picture group made equal numbers of errors in both classes, while irrelevant picture and control subjects committed more abstract to concrete comparison errors than concrete to abstract comparison errors. This latter finding is intriguing. It indicates that when the subject of the sentence (simile assertion) is concrete, the comparison is more easily evaluated in terms of its truth value as based on the text. It is not entirely clear why this should be the case. On the other hand, the subjects in the relevant picture condition were not similarly affected. In any event, the finding is worthy of further investigation.

The concretization of abstract information by imagery and metaphor is one aspect of hypostatization. Another aspect of the processes concerns their use in the comprehension and learning of complex information that may not involve abstract concepts or relationships. Of particular interest here are those processes that allow the subject "to go beyond the information given" in nonabstract, complex tasks.

A representative study is that of Rohwer and Matz (1975). High- and low-SES children heard a 168-word passage called "Some Monkeys." Patterned after the work of Frase (1969, 1970), the passage was built on a precisely controlled structural characteristic. A series of sentences embedded in nonrelevant filler material asserted that A's are B's, B's are C's, C's are D's, and D's are E's. For example, banana tree monkeys (A) have curly tails (B); curly tail monkeys (B) watch their children (C); watchful monkeys (C) fear humans (D); fearful monkeys (D) gather sticks (E). Following a reading of the passage, subjects were asked to agree or not agree with two kinds of assertions. The first kind of assertion was stated explicitly in the text—i.e., A's are B's, D's are E's, etc. The second kind of assertion required implicit inferences to be made at various levels of complexity—i.e., A's are C's represented an assertion at one level of complexity, while A's are E's was an assertion at a more difficult level of complexity. That is, for the subject to be able to confirm that A's are E's (i.e., Banana tree monkeys gather sticks) he would have had to process information contained in four sentences. Rohwer and Matz (1973) argued that the presence of pictorial contexts depicting the various sentences would aid their subjects in processing the needed information. An interesting aspect of the pictorial contexts was their cumulative nature. Thus, as the sentences were read one-by-one, successive picture parts were added to a scene. Results for the picture contexts condition was contrasted to a passage-only condition.

Results showed that picture contexts facilitated the overall performance of low-SES learners; but pictures had little effect on the overall performance of high-SES learners. (For possible implications of these results, see Levin's chapter in this volume.) However, the data hinted at a possible interaction between pictorial contexts and assertion complexity for high-SES children. Under pictorialization, high-SES children performed slightly better on complex assertions. Thus, the data suggest that high-SES children may read dynamic (movement) qualities into the static pictorial scene—manipulating components that allows them to answer correctly the complex assertions.

The manner in which the pictorial contexts were manipulated provides an interesting set of speculations. The speculations touch issues such as imagery as a substitute for pictorialization or vice-versa; the spontaneity of imagery in populations of various age, SES, sex, and other characteristics; the manipulability of imagery or pictorialization on a static–dynamic dimension. Experiments directed at these issues should provide the information necessary to identify and specify the population and task variables that interact to produce learning that goes beyond the information given.

Special note should be taken of the text materials that Frase (1969,

1970), and Rohwer and Matz (1975) have used. The passages have known characteristics that provide rigorous experimental control. Obviously, such passages are very desirable stimulus materials for a program of research on the higher mental processes. The controlled structural characteristics of the passages, combined with their approximation to "natural" reading materials found in schools, make such materials doubly desirable.

Learning of Set Relations

The studies of Dawes (1964, 1966) also represent an attempt to understand the comprehension processes that occur when subjects read text materials. But Dawes has examined more complex relational concepts, which hold among key elements in text. For Dawes (1966), "The measurement method (of the reading comprehension process) is based on the fact that *meaningful declarative statements assert set relations* . . . The central thesis is that memory and distortion of meaningful material may be measured by the memory and distortion of the set relations asserted in the material. Set relations embody 'what is said' in the passage [p. 77]."

Dawes developed three of the five Gergonne set relations for use in his experimental passages

1. *Exclusion* relations (sets X and Y have no elements in common).
2. *Inclusion* relations (all elements of set X are in set Y, but not all elements of set Y are in set X).
3. *Disjunction* relations (sets X and Y share some elements in common, but neither set is included in the other).

Without developing the argument completely here, it can be said that 1 and 2 are nested relations. Using these set relations and some simplifying assumptions to guide his measurement method, Dawes (1964) asked his subjects to read "newspaper-like stories" about political or economic groups (sets). By means of a test the subjects were asked direct questions about the set relations between any two of the groups—for example, "No farmers were senators" (nested exclusion), "All of the senators were ranchers" (nested inclusion), "Not all, but some ranchers voted for construction of the canal" (disjunction). The test construction was such that subjects' errors could be classified as either overgeneralizations (beliefs that disjunctive relations are nested) or "pseudo-discriminations" (beliefs that nested relations are disjunctive). Subtracting pseudo-discrimination errors (disjunctive relations) from overgeneralization errors (nested relations) produced what Dawes called a simplification score. In a second experiment (Dawes, 1964) subjects were asked to index their confidence in their answers. Results of the studies indicated that overgeneralization errors (i.e., simplifications) were more common and that they engendered greater confidence.

Dawes's (1964) concluding statement can be paraphrased to show its implications for our own program of research. Dawes emphasizes that overgeneralization may produce unrealistic simplifications of the information that is processed in text. Since information reduction is desirable in some contexts but not in others, "cognitive distortion can be viewed as the result of a normal cognitive process run amok."

Current attempts to develop the work of Dawes, especially in terms of more extensive and subtle scoring systems, have found success in the research of Frederiksen (1972), Freedle (1972), and Keesey (1969). Various aspects of this current research speak to the issue of subjects' ability to go beyond the information given. Thus, Frederiksen (1972) demonstrated that "task induced cognitive operations" (i.e., incidental or intentional problem-solving orientations to guide subjects' information processing) had little effect on explicitly stated set relations, but they had a dramatic effect on improving performance for inferred set relations. Freedle (1972) found that the adequacy of inferential information processing increased as a function of the adequacy of explicit information processing. Keesey (1969) showed that the more rapid the rate of presentation of the passages, the poorer the information processing of both explicit and inferred set relations.

Combining the results of the three studies suggests that an adequate processing of explicit information is a necessary but insufficient condition for going beyond the information given. Furthermore, the research to date indicates that subjects continue to distort some of the information that is contained in the text. For example, Freedle (1972) reports that his subjects showed a tendency toward simplification of information (replicating Dawes, 1964, 1966); they make contradiction errors, and they import identity set relations that were not represented in the text.

Using the materials of Dawes (1964), we performed an experiment that attempted to facilitate subjects' information processing without concomitant cognitive distortions. The experiment used three independent groups of college-age subjects. The first two groups performed under conditions that exactly replicated Dawes's original experiment. The first group served as a control; they responded to a test on the passages without having read them. The second group read the passages. The third group was put through a short training program in the use of Venn diagrams as representations for set relations asserted in sentences and short paragraphs. The training materials were unrelated to the passages.

Following training, subjects in the third group were encouraged to "imagine" Venn diagram representations of the passages while reading them. Subsequently, the original Dawes test was administered, although it does contain some obvious flaws (Freedle, 1972). The major reason for proceeding with the original test was to make certain that Dawes's results could be replicated and to contrast a new treatment with the replication. As a final task, the subjects were given a reconstruction task that required them to complete complex Venn diagrams of the stories they had read by inserting names of the groups (sets) on lines provided in the diagrams.

Three dependent measures were obtained from the Dawes test (although Dawes reported only one):

1. The total number of correct (c) answers.
2. The proportion of correct transformation (t) responses (explicit set relation responses minus inferred set relation responses).
3. The number of simplification(s) errors—Dawes's original dependent variable.

The Dawes test contains equal numbers of nested and disjunctive set relation questions. Thus, if the subject produces equal numbers of errors on the two types of questions, the s-score is zero. Therefore, the s-score has the interesting characteristic of indexing two kinds of distortions. If a subject responds with more disjunction errors than nested errors, the s-score will be marked negative $(-)$ which suggests that he–she is complicating information.

Dawes (1964) reported a mean s-score of -3.90 for his control group; the mean s-score for the control in the present experiment was -3.72. These results indicate that control subjects have a tendency to choose more disjunctive alternatives than nested alternatives. Interpretively, the scores indicate that control subjects do not simplify their guessing responses; indeed, they respond as though they read greater complexity into the test than is necessary. On the other hand, the task confronting the control subjects is, to use Dawes' word, "bizarre" since they do not read the passages. Therefore, knowing what to make of the control group's bias toward complicating the test is a difficult task that would require additional study. Subsequent discussion of the results excludes the control group.

A consideration of the c-score and the t-score provides information about cognitive facilitation. That is to say, in relation to a passage-only group (Dawes's original experimental group) we may ask whether the Venn-diagram training allows subjects to increase their total number of correct answers and increase their proportion of correct inferential responses. The answer is equivocal despite the results reported here. The mean c-score for passage-only subjects was 8.50 items correct, and

8.80 for Venn-diagram subjects. Statistically, the means were not different. A Venn-diagram training program did not facilitate information processing when measured as total number correct.

The t-scores for the Dawes test are represented as proportions because there are unequal numbers of questions representing inferred and explicit set relations. The t-scores marked positive (+) indicate that more explicit set relation information has been obtained than inferred set relation information. Negative t-scores (−) indicate that more inferential information has been obtained than explicit information. The mean t-score for passage-only subjects was +.156; for Venn-diagram subjects, +.215. The means did not differ statistically, and both indicate that more explicit set relation information was obtained. Incidentally, it was observed that only 4 subjects out of 20 in the passage-only group and 3 subjects out of 20 in the Venn-diagram group had negative t-scores. Very few of the subjects were able to transform the text information to produce correct inferential responses.

To summarize with respect to cognitive facilitation, it can be concluded that there is little evidence in the present experiment to indicate that Venn-diagram training facilitated the subjects' ability to process information compared to the passage-only group.

As assessment of the s-score (simplification score) provides information concerning cognitive distortion. The mean s-score for the passage-only group was +1.25. Dawes (1964) reports +1.02 for this group. The mean s-score for Venn-diagram subjects was +.500. A statistical test showed this difference to be marginally significant. The s-score data *within* each group were analyzed by a sign test, on the assumption that positive and negative s-scores are equally likely. The result was statistically significant for passage-only subjects, but not for Venn-diagram subjects. Combining these various results for s-score data suggests that Venn-diagram training did prevent some degree of cognitive distortion. The subjects in the Venn-diagram group did not simplify the information to the extent that passage-only subjects did.

Two dependent measures were obtained from the reconstruction task. The first was simply the number of exactly correct insertions (out of a possible 11) of the group (set) names into the diagrams. Mean correct insertions for passage-only and Venn-diagram subjects were 4.64 and 6.16 respectively. The means did not differ statistically. The second dependent variable was a proportional measure based upon combinations of the set relations that had been asserted in the story. That is, the subject inserted group (set) names into the diagrams; although an insertion might be incorrect in an exact sense, in combination with another of his insertions, it could form a set relation that was correct. With 11 set-name insertions taken two at a time, the total number of set relations is 55. This total includes unequal numbers of inclusion, exclusion and disjunction set relations—thus the need for a proportion measure. Before proceeding further, it should be pointed out that a knowledge of the relations that hold among all two-set combinations will not necessarily determine a unique Venn diagram. A "proof" of that assertion by way of example need not be offered here. Suffice to say that the Venn diagrams constructed to represent the Dawes stories were the same for both the passage-only and Venn-diagram groups.

The mean proportions of correct set relations are presented in Figure 2. Statistical analyses confirmed some of the differences displayed. The Venn-diagram performance was superior to that of passage-only subjects. Inclusion relations were inferior to exclusion and disjunction relations, while the last two did not differ. Finally, the Experimental-condition by X Set-relation interaction was not significant.

Interpretively, Figure 2 indicates that subjects in both groups had less trouble with the disjunction relations than was expected. That is, the disjunction asserts a complicated set relation which, as the s-score indicates, subjects tend to distort into a less complicated nested relation. The unexpected result may be somewhat misleading, however, because the type of set relation is confounded with inferred and

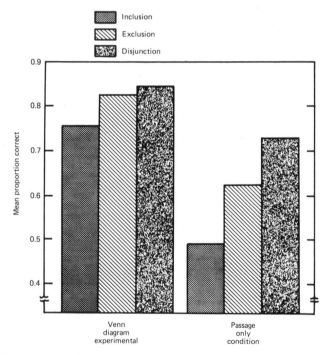

Figure 2. Mean proportion of correct set relations as a function of experimental conditions and type of set relation.

explicit information in the Dawes passages. Rather than attempt post-hoc analyses for such complicated interactions in the Dawes materials, it would be advisable to construct new materials that provide better control over the variables of interest.

Nevertheless, the Dawes (1964, 1966) and the Frase (1969, 1970) approaches are very adequate guides to the construction of structurally controlled passages. Extensions of their work with respect to new scoring methods for cognitive facilitation and distortion (e.g., Frederiksen, 1972; Freedle, 1972) provide the necessary indices for the measurement of learning and comprehension. When those approaches and scoring methods are combined with experimental treatments that encourage in the learner—or display for the learner—imaginal or analogical representations for the passage content, satisfactory experimental conditions and experimental control are created. All of these factors are necessary ingredients for a research program aimed at understanding the conditions that lead to cognitive facilitation and distortion.

In summary, certain forms of the hypostatization processes have been revealed in a number of experimental psychological tasks. In general, the tasks lend themselves to classification into two kinds: (a) tasks that require subjects to learn or comprehend abstract word concepts or abstract conceptual relations, and (b) tasks that require subjects to go beyond the information given by learning or comprehending inferential information at various levels of complexity. The hypostatizing processes revealed in the psychological tasks are, in the main, forms of imaginal representation—concretizing imagery, spatial imagery, and imaginal analogy. But a larger variety of potential hypostatization processes exist and are available for study. Many of these processes, little studied by psychologists under controlled experimental conditions, are suggested by rhetorical and linguistic investigations.

Rhetorical Investigations

In an earlier section reference was made to a dichotomy in rhetorical study—that between argumentation and comprehension. Although only the latter is relevant to our research program, it is interesting to note that most experimental investigations have been addressed to the former. Many social psychological studies of persuasion and attitude change (e.g., use of the syllogism) represent experimental investigations of argumentation. But experimental—rhetorical studies have been contributed as well. For example, Bowers (1964) used an experimental design to investigate the potency of a concluding sexual metaphor to persuade subjects in favor of an argument for reducing national tariffs. He concluded that the argumentative use of metaphor was capable of changing attitudes. Aspects of rhetoric that bear on the comprehension processes have been little studied under controlled experimental procedures despite the call for such studies by Carroll (1968) and Freedle and Carroll (1972). Furthermore, the metaphorical–analogical forms of rhetoric have been studied almost not at all.

In a nonexperimental study, we (Davidson, 1971) sampled at random 100 words in a simile dictionary (Wilstach, 1924). Sixty of the words selected were concrete; 40 were abstract—words like money, clothes, dawn, love, kindness, memory, etc. The words had different numbers of entries—for example, "love" had 92 entries. The median number of entries was about 6 for both abstract and concrete words. Of the entries for abstract words, 87% were hypostatizations (i.e., comparing the abstract word to something that is concrete). For concrete words, 88% were concrete-to-concrete comparisons.

Gordon (1971) reports nonexperimental observations of elementary-age pupils "increasing their understanding" of "strange new concepts" by means of a variety of metaphorical–analogical forms, including direct analogy, personal analogy, and "compressed conflict" (in rhetoric, oxymoron). Rosenshine (1968) studied how well high-school students learned from being told. He identified 21 categories that differentiated "good" from "poor" lectures. One of the most potent categories was what the author termed "explaining links." Often the links took the form of verbal analogy.

Under the direction of the present author, Divine-Hawkins (1971) examined the potential facilitating effects of one rhetorical form—analogy by double hierarchy. Rhetoricians suggest that an unfamiliar, hierarchically arranged conceptual structure may be set against a familiar structure such that the terms in each structure exhibit a term-by-term isomorphism. The familiar hierarchy and the relations among its elements may thus "elucidate" the unfamiliar structure by analogy.

The familiar hierarchy chosen for the study involved the human activity of work, with "job" as the central conceptual element. The unfamiliar hierarchy contained ecological concepts with "niche" as the central concept. The double hierarchy is displayed in Figure 3. Each hierarchy was embedded in a separate passage as follows:

Occupational passage
   Human beings have many kinds of activity including eating, playing, and working. The term "work" includes such large groups of jobs as unskilled, skilled and professional occupations. Each of these large groups contains smaller groups of jobs. "Professional Occupations," for instance, include lawyers, scientists, and doctors. Each individual profession has its own type of work to do: a doctor does not do a lawyer's job and a lawyer does not do a doctor's job. Within the doctor's profession, however, there are many specific jobs which are filled by different kinds of doctors. These individual jobs may be general such as that of the general practitioner or specialized such as that of the brain surgeon. Each doctor's job

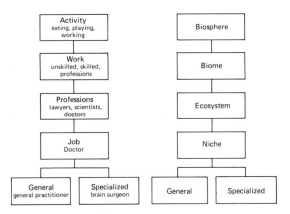

Figure 3. Structural organization of the occupational and ecological hierarchies.

includes what he does, where he does it and the other people (such as nurses, other doctors and patients) with whom he works.

Ecological passage
   All organisms live in a part of the biosphere. The biosphere contains a number of large areas known as biomes. Each biome includes many different ecosystems. The ecosystem includes individual niches which are filled by separate species. These niches may be broad and general or narrow and specialized. Each organism's niche includes its activities, its habitat and the other inhabitants of the ecosystem with whom it interacts.

The subjects in the experiment were 96 sixth-grade students. They were assigned randomly by sex to three experimental conditions. The study was conducted in two stages, using groups of students. At the first stage the three treatments were randomized among subjects. The first treatment (hypostatization) required subjects to "study" the occupational passage silently. The second treatment (story) required subjects to "study" a hospital story equal in length and difficulty to the occupational passage. The story included all of the critical words (e.g., work, job, etc.) of the occupational hierarchy. The third treatment (blank page) asked subjects to draw or write anything of their choice while others were studying. Five minutes were allowed for study. At stage two the ecology passage, mounted as a 2″ × 2″ slide, was projected onto a screen at the front of the experimental room. The subjects were encouraged to read silently while the experimenter read aloud. A 2.5-minute, free recall period followed the slide presentation. The slide-recall sequence was presented for a second trial. Following the second recall, two additional tasks were administered, word association and similarity ratings.

Word associations to the 10 critical words of the hierarchies, arranged in two random orders, were obtained by the production method (Noble, 1952). Similarity ratings along a 7-point scale were obtained for pairs of words existing in various vertical and horizontal relationships within the ecological and occupational hierarchies. Because of time limitations, not all combinations of word pairs in the matrix could be rated. The 13 word pairs retained thus represent those relationships judged most crucial to the hierarchical structures. These stimulus items included 4 pairs representing vertically adjacent relationships (biosphere–biome, activity–work, specialist–surgeon, niche–specialist); four horizontally adjacent relationships (ecosystem–profession, niche–job, biosphere–activity, biome–work); four vertically distant relationships (activity–surgeon, biome–niche, work–job, job–surgeon); and one horizontally distant relationship (biosphere–specialist).

Overall, the results of this experiment were disappointing. The free recall protocols were scored for three measures:

1. Absolute number of critical words recalled.
2. Proportion of critical words to total recall.
3. Set-relation assertions among the critical words.

There were no significant differences among main effects or interaction for any of the recall measures. The amount of recall for all groups was quite low. Similarity ratings revealed no significant differences, and the extreme portions of the scales were little used. The word association data, transformed into relatedness coefficients (Garskof and Huston, 1963), are presented in Table 2. Except for the nexus of coefficients

TABLE 2

Median Relatedness Coefficients for Two Experimental Groups: Occupational Passage (Above Diagonal) and Story Passage (Below Diagonal)

Word	1	2	3	4	5	6	7	8	9	10
1. Biosphere		98[a]	94	89	00	00	00	00	00	00
2. Biome	99[a]		96	88	00	00	00	00	00	00
3. Ecosystem	74	73		84	00	00	00	00	00	00
4. Niche	74	72	71		04	06	03	08	07	10
5. General	00	00	00	00		13	07	17	12	20
6. Specialized	00	00	00	00	00		16	30	47	38
7. Activity	00	00	00	00	00	00		31	19	30
8. Work	00	00	00	00	00	00	46		42	67
9. Profession	00	00	00	00	00	24	19	56		63
10. Job	00	00	00	00	00	02	19	67	65	

[a]Decimals omitted throughout.

produced by the niche–job relationship under the occupational passage condition, the matrix is unremarkable.

Obviously, any of a number of factors can contribute to nonsignificant results. Not the least of such factors that must be entertained is the possibility that analogy by double hierarchy simply is not a viable hypostatizing process. But it would seem premature to draw that conclusion. On a number of grounds the experiment was a severe test for the double hierarchy. First, the hierarchies were embedded in temporally discrete passages. An extended analogy usually draws explicit one-to-one comparisons within a single passage (as in "The Mat Maker" passage discussed previously). Second, hypostatization by double hierarchy *or by any other hypostatization process* may require the cognitive capacities of older subjects. The work of Piaget and Bruner (e.g., Bruner, Olver, Greenfield, *et al.*, 1966) would suggest as much. Though the cognitive development issue poses a significant problem in terms of self-generated hypostatization, it may be less of a problem in terms of experimenter constructed hypostatization if materials and training procedures are developed properly.

Inzer (1972) facilitated the learning and comprehension of sixth-grade subjects by four-term direct analogies in a learning-to-learn study that manipulated three treatments. Each day of a 4-day period, subjects in one treatment (hypostatization) studied four different analogies embedded in text materials. All analogies were elaborations of the form A is to B as C is to D. The terms A and B constituted a familiar "vehicle", while C and D made up an unfamiliar "tenor" (Richards, 1936). For example, "follow the leader" (A) is to children's games (B) as fugue (C) is to music (D). Inzer provided three passages for study on each day. The first passage described the vehicle, the second the tenor, and the third integrated vehicle and tenor by making explicit the relationships that existed among the component terms. Analogies were counterbalanced across days. Each day's achievement was measured by a 15-item test following the integrated passage. Some items tested for knowledge of the analogy, and other items tested for knowledge of the unfamiliar tenor. A second treatment group read the vehicle and tenor passages, but an unrelated story was substituted for the integrative passage. A third treatment studied the unfamiliar tenor only.

The results indicated that the hypostatization treatment became differentially more effective over days when compared to the interpolated story group, which also showed some improvement in achievement scores over days. Both of the above treatments were superior to a control which showed no improvement from day 1 to day 4. Thus, it appears that signaling explicit relationships, although not required, provides more efficient learning and better comprehension in young children. Perhaps explicit pictorial analogies for even younger children may do work for them that they cannot do for themselves. In any event, future steps in our research program will try to establish the boundary conditions for the hypostatization process of direct analogy.

CONCLUDING REMARKS

In one sense, my intentions for this chapter were quite limited in scope. I simply wanted to provide the framework for and the preliminary results from a program of research on cognition.

In another sense, however, my intentions were wider in scope. They encompass a particular orientation for education. These intentions are, I think, implicit in the framework of the program. The key phrases for that framework are "effort after meaning" (Bartlett, 1932) and "click of comprehension" (Brown, 1958). For both education and cognition, the stress is on the attempt, either on the part of the learner or teacher, to construct contexts, in the present case analogical—metaphorical contexts, that render abstract or complex information *comprehensible.*

There are other orientations for education and cognition that play down meaning and comprehension. The emphasis is almost exclusively on observable behaviors, and when attention is focused on observable behavior with little consideration to what is behind the behavior, meaning and comprehension are diminished in importance. In short, the contrast is "knowing" versus "knowing how to." Or, to play off of a current hypostatization for the higher mental processes, if the mind is like a computer, then all it can do is compute, it cannot comprehend.

REFERENCES

Baker, J. R. *The scientific life.* London: George Allen & Unwin Ltd., 1942.
Bartlett, F. C. *Remembering.* Cambridge, England: Cambridge University Press, 1932.
Berlyne, D. E. *Conflict, arousal, and curiousity.* New York: McGraw-Hill, 1960.
Berlyne, D. E. *Structure and direction in thinking.* New York: Wiley, 1965.
Black, M. *Models and metaphors.* Ithaca, New York: Cornell University Press, 1962.
Bower, G. H. Organizational factors in memory. *Cognitive Psychology,* 1970, *1,* 18–46.
Bowers, J. W. Some correlates of language intensity. *Quarterly Journal of Speech,* 1964, *50,* 415–420.
Brown, R. *Words and things.* New York: The Free Press, 1958.
Brown, R. W., Leiter, R. A. & Hildum, D. C. Metaphors from music criticism. *Journal of Abnormal and Social Psychology,* 1957, *54,* 347–352.
Bruner, J. S. On perceptual readiness. *Psychological Review,* 1957(a), *64,* 123–152.
Bruner, J. S. Going beyond the information given. In H. E. Gruber *et. al.* (Eds.), *Contemporary approaches to cognition.* Cambridge: Harvard University Press, 1957(b).
Bruner, J. W. What social scientists say about having an idea. *Printers Ink,* 1957(c), *260,* 48–52.
Bruner, J. S. *On knowing: Essays for the left hand.* Cambridge: Harvard University Press, 1962.

Bruner, J. S., Goodnow, J. J. & Austin, G. A. *A study of thinking.* New York: Wiley, 1956.

Bruner, J. S., Olver, R. R. & Greenfield, P. M. *Studies in cognitive growth.* New York: Wiley, 1966.

Bryant, D. C. Rhetoric: Its functions and its scope. In M. Natanson & H. W. Johnstone (Eds.), *Philosophy, rhetoric and argumentation.* University Park, Pa: The Pennsylvania State University Press, 1965.

Carroll, J. B. On learning from being told. *Educational Psychologist,* 1968, *5,* 1–10.

Carroll, J. B. & Freedle, R. D. *Language comprehension and the acquisition of knowledge.* Washington, D. C.: V. H. Winston & Sons, 1972.

Davidson, R. E. *Hypostatization processes.* Paper presented at the annual meeting of the American Educational Research Association, New York, 1971.

Dawes, R. M. Cognitive distortion. *Psychological Reports,* 1964, *14,* 443–459.

Dawes, R. M. Memory and distortion of meaningful written material. *British Journal of Psychology,* 1966, *57,* 77–86.

Devine-Hawkins, P. *Hypostatization of selected environmental concepts in elementary school children.* Unpublished masters thesis, University of Wisconsin, 1971.

Frase, L. T. Structural analysis of knowledge that results from thinking about text. *Journal of Educational Psychology,* 1969, *60* (Monograph Supp. 6).

Frase, L. T. Influence of sentence order and amount of higher level text processing upon productive and reproductive memory. *American Educational Research Journal,* 1970, *7,* 307–319.

Frederiksen, C. H. Task-induced cognitive operations. In J. B. Carroll & R. O. Freedle (Eds.), *Language comprehension and the acquisition of knowledge.* Washington, D. C.: V. H. Winston & Sons, 1972.

Freedle, R. O. Language users as fallible information-processors. In J. B. Carroll & R. O. Freedle (Eds.), *Language comprehension and the acquisition of knowledge.* Washington, D. C.: V. H. Winston & Sons, 1972.

Freedle, R. O. & Carroll, J. B. Language comprehension and the acquisition of knowledge: reflections. In J. B. Carroll & R. O. Freedle (Eds.), *Language comprehension and the acquisition of knowledge.* Washington, D. C.: V. H. Winston & Sons, 1972.

Garskof, B. D. & Houston, J. P. Measurement of verbal relatedness: An ideographic approach. *Psychological Review,* 1963, *70,* 377–388.

Ghiselin, B. *The creative process: A symposium.* Berkeley: University of California Press, 1952.

Gordon, W. J. J. *The metaphorical way of learning & knowing.* Cambridge, Mass.: Porpoise Books, 1971.

Hebb, D. O. Drive and the C. N. S. (conceptual nervous system). *Psychological Review,* 1955, *62,* 243–254.

Hilgard, E. R. Impulsive versus realistic thinking: An examination of the distiontion between primary and secondary process in thought. *Psychological Bulletin,* 1962, *59,* 477–488.

Huttenlocher, J. Constructing spatial images: A strategy in reasoning. *Psychological Review,* 1968, *75,* 550–560.

Inzer, E. *Learning to learn by analogy.* Unpublished masters thesis, University of Wisconsin, 1972.

Johnson, P. E. Some psychological aspects of subject-matter structure. *Journal of Educational Psychology,* 1967, *58,* 75–83.

Jones, R. M. *Contemporary educational psychology.* New York: Harper Torchbooks, 1967.

Karwaski, T. F., Odbert, H. S., & Osgood, C. E. Studies in synesthetic thinking: II. The roles of form in visual responses to music. *Journal of Genetic Psychology,* 1942, *26,* 199–222.

Keesey, J. C. *Memory for logical structure and verbal units in prose material at increased rates of presentation.* Unpublished doctoral dissertation, University of Oregon, 1969.

Marshall, G. R. *The effect of concrete noun and picture mediation on the paired-associate learning of abstract nouns.* Paper presented at the meeting of the Eastern Psychological Association, Atlantic City, 1965.

McKellar, P. *Imagination and thinking.* New York: Basic Books, 1957.

Miller, G. A., Galanter, E., & Pribram K. H. *Plans and the structure of behavior.* New York: Holt, 1960.

Moss, J. & Pucel, D. J. *Using the free association methodology to determine the conceptual structure of radio and television repairmen.* Minneapolis: Minnesota Research Coordinating Unit for Vocational Education, 1967.

Neisser, U. *Cognitive psychology.* New York: Appleton, 1966.

Noble, C. E. An analysis of meaning. *Psychological Review,* 1952, *59,* 521–430.

Osgood, C. E. The nature and measurement of meaning. *Psychological Bulletin,* 1952, *49,* 197–237.

Osgood, C. E. *Method and theory in experimental psychology.* New York: Oxford, 1953.

Oppenheimer, J. R. Analogy in science. *American Psychologist,* 1956, *11,* 127–135.

Oswald, I. *Sleeping and waking.* New York: Elsenier, 1962.

Paivio, A. Abstractness, imagery, and meaningfulness in paired-associate learning. *Journal of Verbal Learning and Verbal Behavior,* 1965, *4,* 32–38.

Paivio, A., Yuille, J. C., & Madigan, S. Concreteness, imagery, and meaningfulness values for 925 nouns. *Journal of Experimental Psychology Monograph Supplement,* 1968, *76*(1, Pt. 2).

Perleman, C. H. and Olbrechts-Tyteca. *The new rhetoric: a treatise on argumentation.* London: University of Notre Dame Press, 1969.

Platt, J. R. Beauty: Pattern and change. In D. W. Fisk & S. R. Maddi (Eds.), *Functions of varied experience.* Homewood, Ill.: Dorsey Press, 1961.

Posner, M. I. & Warren, R. E. Traces, concepts and conscious constructions. In A. W. Melton & E. Martin (Eds.), *Coding processes in human memory.* Washington, D. C.: V. H. Winston & Sons, 1972.

Richards, I. A. *The philosophy of rhetoric.* New York: Oxford University Press, 1936.

Roe, A. A study of imagery in research scientists. *Journal of Personality,* 1951, *19,* 459–470.

Rohwer, W. D. Jr., & Matz, R. D. Improving aural comprehension in white & in black children: pictures versus print. *Journal of Experimental Child Psychology,* 1975, *19,* 23–36.

Rosenshine, B. *Behavior correlates of effectiveness in explaining social studies material.* Unpublished doctoral dissertation, Stanford University, 1968.

Rumelhart, D. E., Lindsay, P. H., & Norman, D. A. A process model for long-term memory. In E. Tulving & W. Donaldson (Eds.), *Organization of memory.* New York: Academic Press, 1972.

Simpson, R. H., Owinn, M. & Ausubel, D. Synesthesia in children: Association of colors with pure tone frequencies. *Journal of Genetic Psychology,* 1956, *89,* 95–103.

Upton, A. *Design for thinking.* Stanford: Stanford University Press, 1961.

Vigotsky, L. S. *Thought and language.* Cambridge: M. I. T. Press; and New York: Wiley, 1962.

Walkup, L. E. Creativity in science through visualization. *Perceptual and Motor Skills,* 1965, *21,* 35–41.

Werner, H., & Kaplan, B. *Symbol formation: An organismic-developmental approach to the psychology of language and the expression of thought.* New York: Wiley, 1963.

Wheelwright, P. *Metaphor and reality.* Bloomington, Ind.: University Press, 1962.

Whitehead, A. N. *Process and reality: An essay in cosmology.* New York: Macmillan, 1929.

Wilstach, F. J. *A dictionary of similes.* New York: Bonanza Books, 1924.

Wollen, K. A. *Effects of relevant or irrelevant pictorial mediators upon forward and backward recall.* Paper presented at the annual meeting of the Psychonomic Society, St. Louis, November, 1968.

CHAPTER 6

Prerequisites for Learning to Read

Richard L. Venezky

Several thousand years ago, reading was considered to be an uncomplicated task that centered primarily upon letters and their various combinations. Consequently, neither reading readiness nor prereading skills were considered issues among the Greeks, the Romans, the Minoans, the Etruscans, or any of the other ancient populations that exhibited the slightest traces of literacy. Plato, who recommended that instruction in reading and writing commence only at the age of 10, quotes Socrates as saying:

> Just as in learning to read, I said, we were satisfied when we knew the letters of the alphabet, which are very few, in all their recurring sizes and combinations; not slighting them as unimportant whether they occupy a space large or small, but everywhere eager to make them out; and not thinking ourselves perfect in the art of reading until we recognize them wherever they are found [The Republic, III, 402A].

THE EVOLUTION OF READING READINESS

Huey (1908), writing more than 2200 years after the death of Plato, was among the first to convince educators that learning to read required more than a knowledge of the letters. Nevertheless, nearly 20 years passed before concern for the proper preparation of children for reading instruction was shown. "Reading readiness," a phrase that was first given widespread exposure in the 1925 *Yearbook of the National Society for the Study of Education,* gave purpose to a kindergarten movement whose rationale at that time was neither understood nor accepted by school administrators (Weber, 1969, pp. 198f). But by the late 1920s teaching children to read was seen as a serious and complex business, and the enlistment of the kindergarten for readiness or even formal reading instruction was readily welcomed.

163

Reading readiness developed first as an attempt, as recommended by Thorndike (1913), to produce the appropriate predisposition for reading and to purge those conditions that might interfere with this "proper mental set." This concept was tempered by the maturational concepts of the 1930s, particularly those of Gesell (1933) which emphasized the necessity for certain structural developments to occur before functional changes could take place. The ready acceptance of maturational prerequisites was especially reflected in the overgeneralization of a study by Morphett and Washburne (1931). This study concluded, on the basis of a single instructional technique and a sample of upper middle-class suburban children, that:

> By postponing the teaching of reading until children reach a mental level of six and a half years [on the Detroit First-Grade Intelligence Test], teachers can greatly decrease the chances of failure and discouragement and can correspondingly increase their efficiency [p. 503].

In spite of overwhelming evidence to the contrary, this belief lingers on in the reading rituals of some school systems, and was probably not unknown to the late Paul Goodman, who claimed that if left on their own, children would mature into reading by the age of 9 or 10 just as they grow into speaking at the age of 2 or 3.

Two other readiness developments of the 1930s which are more important for our current concerns were the increased concern for experiential readiness and the introduction of skill-oriented, prereading activities. These developments eventually merged into the composite programs which were used during the 1950s and 1960s by most readiness-oriented kindergartens.

In the current decade, reading readiness has noticeably shifted away from experiential readiness and toward an emphasis of prereading skills; that is, toward those skills which are believed to relate most directly to the specific processes involved in initial reading instruction. In this regard, it is difficult to argue with the editor of the *New Encyclopaedia of Child Care and Guidance*:

> Reading readiness has come to mean something different than it did in the past [Gruenberg, 1958, p. 452].

The prereading skill approach is not, however, the only available approach to reading readiness, nor is it a single approach within itself. Both the selection of prereading skills and the instructional procedures chosen for them vary widely from program to program; but the general approach is sufficiently widespread to merit careful inspection, especially of its theoretical foundations and its relationship to instruction.

Since prereading skills programs are relatively new and few formal attempts have been made to explain or justify them, much of the analysis presented here will be drawn from unpublished work, particularly from research and development centers and regional laboratories and, in particular, from my own research program at the Wisconsin Research and Development Center for Cognitive Learning. My primary goal is to present for inspection an approach to reading readiness which I feel is both interesting and productive, but has yet to have its most basic assumptions subjected to thorough and critical analysis.

At the same time, I would like to discuss the complexities and pitfalls that result from attempting to relate the theoretical and experimental conclusions presented here to curriculum design, in particular in an 8-year project that has struggled, with some success, to produce an experimentally-based prereading skills program.

In spite of the negative connotations which the phrase *reading readiness* has acquired from certain ill-conceived and unconscionable practices, it is still an adequate general term for activities carried out as prerequisites to formal reading instruction. In other words, "reading readiness" is defined by intent, and includes any activities that are intended to prepare children for reading. Whether these activities engage the ears, eyes, toes, or cerebral cortex of the child, and whether they involve letters, numbers, geometric forms, or pictures is immaterial. Just as rational and irrational numbers are still numbers, and rational and irrational psychologists are still psychologists, so are rational and irrational readiness programs still readiness programs.

Prereading skills are defined more qualitatively as those skills that relate most closely either to the reading process or to the procedures that are employed in teaching reading. In this sense, teaching prereading skills is one approach to reading readiness. Other approaches might concentrate on motor behavior, socialization, or oral language, for example, but none of these qualifies as a prereading skill. What prereading skills are, how they are discovered, and what value they have in reading readiness are the primary concerns of the following sections of this chapter.

PREREADING AND READING

Prereading skills are derived by logical analysis of the reading task and by instructional conventions (which, admittedly, are somewhat arbitrary). If we select those tasks that characterize the first year or so of reading instruction and then ask which skills are prerequisities to the tasks that have been selected, the result will be a list of prereading skills. Obviously, not everyone agrees on what should occur in the first year or so of reading instruction, and not everyone is in agreement about the prerequisites for any complex reading task; but this simply yields competing skill sets, not competing approaches. For example, if we select sight-word recognition as one initial reading task, then certain prerequisite skills are immediately indentifiable, including visual matching of letters and of letter strings. We might extend this analysis to more primitive levels and thereby include ability to direct and focus the eyes, concepts of same and different for visual forms, ability to attend to a visual pattern, etc. Where this analysis is terminated must be based on a knowledge of the age level for which the skills are being defined; that is, upon observation of those skills that have already been mastered by the target population. However, at the point where the skills defined are so basic as to be prerequisites for almost all learning, we have clearly gone beyond prereading.

In other words, we arrive at prereading skills by identifying a complete set of initial reading tasks and then by defining all of the prerequisite skills for this set of tasks. Then, for a given population of prereaders, those skills which all or almost all members of the population have mastered are eliminated. Those that remain are labeled "prereading skills" for purposes of instruction.

By this process we are forced to the conclusion that the intermodal integration task investigated by Birch and Belmont (1964) is not a prereading task because it is not a prerequisite for any known instructional task or reading skill. At the same time we can eliminate most of the Frostig motor control tasks (Frostig, 1963) because they have already been mastered by almost all children at the level at which they are typically introduced. The same considerations lead to abandoning phonemic discrimination tasks for almost all native speakers of English, primarily because careful testing reveals that almost all children enter kindergarten with well-developed discrimination ability. Claims to the contrary are based on testing paradigms that are generally not valid for one-pass testing of young children (Rudegeair and Kamil, 1970).

One might become highly skeptical of the procedure advocated here, due to the apparent diversity in instructional methods. However, the real differences in classroom tasks among the various so-called teaching methods—phonics, whole-word, linguistic, and so on—are, as I have argued elsewhere (Venezky, 1974), more apparent than real. All rational approaches to reading instruction include both sight-word learning and letter–sound learning, with its concomitant reliance on sound blending. Methods differ in the sequencing and presentation of these tasks, but in little else. The language-experience approach might appear as an exception, but many classrooms that use language experience also use some other approach (such as phonics) to introduce basic decoding skills. Even where no overt instruction in decoding is given, our task in defining prerequisite skills remains the same: to define which reading skills were acquired and then to determine prerequisites for them.

It is assumed that eventually an empirical test will be made of the relationship between the skills that have been chosen and reading. Further discussion of this will be presented in a later section of this chapter which discusses the problems of developing and evaluating prereading instruction.

Identification of Specific Skills

The two most important tasks in initial reading are sight-word recognition and decoding. These form the basis for reading connected text and for comprehension and, as such, are the objects of our search for prerequisite skills.

Sight-word recognition involves visual discrimination of letter strings, association and retention of labels for these strings, and the ability to retrieve and articulate the labels when shown the appropriate stimuli. That children at the kindergarten level can generate novel sentences from previously learned words (that is, that they can communicate via oral language) is an indication that words can be stored and retrieved. (For the remainder of this chapter I will assume a kindergarten level target population.)

Furthermore, nearly 75 years of paired-associate learning studies have shown that 5-year-olds can acquire verbal responses to visual stimuli, although the limitations on this capability have barely been explored. Kindergarten norms for the Peabody Picture Vocabulary Test, for example, clearly demonstrate that children can retain and produce verbal labels and associate them with visual stimuli.

This leaves the visual discrimination component of word recognition as a candidate for prereading skill definition. If we knew with any certainty the processes through which adults recognize words, we could identify quite rapidly the prerequisite abilities for this task. However, there is probably no area of reading so torn by controversy as word recognition (Gibson and Levin, 1975; Smith and Spoehr, 1974). The more tenable models for recognition center on unmediated recognition of letters or letter groups, with some degree of parallel processing of subunits. However, even with an inchoate model for the recognition process, a number of prerequisite skills can be identified, especially from studies of recognition errors. Letter matching is one candidate, but for kindergarten level children the only consistent problem found in matching single letters is in attending to letter orientation, particularly the lower case pairs, *p-q*, *b-d*, *n-u*, and to a lesser degree, *m-w* and *s-z* (Calfee, Chapman, and Venezky, 1972). A second visual matching problem results from failure to attend to the order of letters in words, that is, the classic *was-saw, no-on* confusions. Hill (1936) identified order reversals as a major source of word-matching errors made by children just prior to formal reading instruction, and also after 10 to 14 weeks of reading instruction. Similar results are reported by Calfee, *et al.* (1972) and Robinson and Higgins (1967).

The only other failure reported consistently in word-matching studies is the failure to attend to the entire visual array—that is, in basing a judgment on an insufficient number of visual features. Hill (1936) reported from her studies of word-matching errors that training "apparently tended to pull the attention of children more and more to the beginning of the word [p. 497]." Analyses of word substitution errors in oral reading show the identical effect (Bennett, 1942; Weber, 1970).

The tendency in some children to base word identity primarily upon initial letters often leads to successful word recognition strategies in the early stages of reading when vocabulary is severely limited. For example, we have noticed from the primary-level vocabulary list published by Durr (1973), that more than 75% of the words occurring in children's readers in the first through third grades can be discriminated on the basis of their initial two letters plus length. At some point, however, an initial-letter strategy collapses, with diastrous effects for the child.

These three skills (attending to letter orientation, attending to letter order, and attending to word detail) comprise the most important skills related to word recognition. They are not independent, as shown by Chapman (1971), but they are sufficiently distinct to merit separate attention (correlations ranged from .39 for detail and orientation to .67 for detail and order).

Different prereading skills result from a task analysis of decoding, primarily because of the acoustical component. At a minimum, decoding involves the following subtasks:

1. Letter differentiation.
2. Association of a sound with a letter.
3. Blending of sounds to produce a word.

Observation of children attempting to decode words reveals, however, that several other processes can also operate. Typically, beginning readers sound out a word to themselves and then decide whether it is acceptable. If so, they pronounce it aloud; if not, they usually alter a single sound and repeat the testing procedure. But to alter a single sound in this context implies an ability to attend to individual speech sounds within the continuous speech stream—an ability that many children have difficulty developing. It is further observed that the acquisition of letter–sound generalizations presupposes the ability to recognize similarities and differences between sounds in different words. For example, for a second-grade child to give a long pronunciation to the *a* in *nabe* and short pronunciation to this same letter in *nab* requires that he–she notice the similarity of the sounds for *a* in words like *cab, tab,* and *lab,* and that they differ from the *a* sound in *race, cape,* and *lake.* The alternative hypothesis, that the child generalizes from a verbalization of a rule, is inconsistent with experimental data reported by Venezky and Johnson (1973) for English letter–sound patterns.

In summary, the skills that may be adduced from an analysis of decoding are:

1. Letter differentiation.
2. Association of a sound with a symbol (letter).
3. Blending.
4. Identification of a sound within a word.
5. Sound matching within words.

Of these skills, letter differentiation has already been discussed, and most children have already mastered part of the ability to associate sounds with letters prior to their entry into kindergarten. Marsh and Sherman (1971) have demonstrated that contrary to the dicta of Bloomfield (1942) and Fries (1963), kindergarten children have little difficulty in pronouncing individual speech sounds in isolation. (The percentage errors for consonants was 13.29, and for vowels 5.96; the corresponding figures for phonemes in words were significantly lower.) Venezky, Chapman, Seegal, Kamm, and Leslie (1971) demonstrated that when an individual speech sound response is paired with a picture of an object that ostensibly makes the sound involved (e.g., a snake that says /s/), learning by kindergarteners for series of such correspondences is extremely rapid, and retention is exceedingly high. This is precisely what is expected from the observation that preschoolers have little difficulty in acquiring single speech sound responses in meaningful contexts, as for example, in learning the sounds that certain animals make.

The question of whether to include symbol–sound learning as a prereading skill is moot. Certainly it should be included in preparation for reading instruction which is heavily weighted towards letter–sound associations, perhaps not otherwise. The remaining three skills listed previously qualified as prereading skills, although the fourth and fifth skills might profitably be collapsed into a single sound-matching skill.

This analysis completes the identification of prereading skills that are the immediate prerequisites to initial reading. Conspicuously missing, among others, are letter–name knowledge, fine-motor performance, and

visual discrimination of objects and shapes—all skills that are promi-
nently featured in popular readiness programs and are assessed on
standardized reading-readiness tests (e.g., Metropolitan, Clymer-
Barrett). There is strong evidence showing that training in these skills
yields little gain in reading scores. Gates, Bond, and Russell (1939)
found that at the primarly level the correlation of geometric form
perception with reading achievement was significantly lower than the
correlation of word perception with reading. Paradis (1974) reports a
series of studies concluding that reading achievement at the primary
level was little affected by discrimination training with nonverbal stimuli, and Muehl (1960) found that kindergarten children who received
pretraining in visual discrimination of words performed better in a
"reading" task involving these same words than children who received
pretraining on different words or on geometric forms.

Letter naming is central to the popular conception of reading instruction, but a logical justification for such prominence has never been
made. According to Durrell (1956), letter names are effective mediators
for the letter sounds—a position which a cursory glance at the alphabet
renders indefensible. Three letters —*h, w, y*—have names that do not
contain their sounds, and seven others—*a, e, i, o, u, c, g*—do not contain
the sound that is typically taught first in reading programs. Of the
remaining 16, nine are composed of a consonant—vowel structure while
seven are vowel—consonant (e.g., *f, l, m, n*). This means that 40% of the
letter names are not useable as sound mediators and the remaining 60%
must be differentiated according to where the mediated sound occurs.
As most reading teachers know, there are more effective approaches to
teaching letter sounds. It should also be pointed out that there is no
evidence showing that instruction in letter naming improves reading
achievement. (In all fairness to *Sesame Street* and other programs which
emphasize letter naming, it should be noted that there is some redeem-
ing value to letter names. They are convenient labels for talking about
the letters, and their vocal declaration by the child, especially in an
approximation of the approved ordering, is often sufficient proof to
parents of the efficacy and good intentions of the school system.)

Fine-motor training is in the same position as letter naming: It
possesses neither a strong logical connection to reading nor an experimental justification. On the contrary, attempts to affect initial reading
skills through fine-motor training have failed, both with alphabetic
materials (Pryzwansky, 1972) and nonalphabetic materials (Cohen,
1967; Rosen, 1966).

That some of these skills (or ones rejected earlier, such as ocular-
motor control) show high correlations with reading achievement is not
a sufficient condition for their classification as prereading skills. The

cost of the automobile which a child's parents drives also correlates highly with reading achievement, but it would be absurd to claim that giving expensive cars to parents will improve their children's reading scores. The identification of prereading skills is based upon logical analysis and upon the effect which skill instruction has on later reading achievement. This measure must be applied with caution, however, in that what is taught is often more than a single skill, no matter how carefully designed the instructional materials might be.

The Necessity for Prereading Instruction

One response to the preceding skill derivation discussion could be to accept the relationship between the prereading skills just defined and reading, but to deny that instruction in them, especially at the kindergarten level, can have a major effect. Strict maturational theories (e.g., Benda, 1954) hold that development is primarily biological and cannot be interfered with through instruction. Another response might be to claim that all of the skills just named can be derived from universally innate potentialities which can be developed only through guided discovery. Neither argument can or should be totally refuted. There is evidence for both maturational and higher level cognitive factors in learning to read, but the more important evidence related to prereading and initial reading points away from these variables.

In a study which my colleagues and I recently completed (Venezky, 1974), 104 kindergarten children were tested at the beginning and end of the school year on four prereading skills: (a) attending to letter order, (b) attending to letter orientation, (c) attending to word detail, and (d) sound matching. Fifty-eight of these children received specific instruction for the skills they lacked while the remaining 46 received general types of readiness activities (control subjects). When these children entered kindergarten, the number (across the two groups) who showed mastery of the skills varied from 5.6% (sound matching) to 31.2% (orientation). These entry data demonstrate that, within the limitations of the instruments and subject population used, these particular skills are generally lacking in children when they enter kindergarten.

By the end of the school year, 77.5% of the skill failures in the skill-program group had changed to skill mastery. For the control group, only 38.1% of the failures had been changed to mastery. The significance of these figures is not suggested in the efficacy of the skill-oriented instruction, but in the low level of mastery in the control group (i.e. in the lack of any appreciable effect from maturation or general readiness instruction).

The argument advanced here is that initial reading requires a low cognitive load when compared to advanced reading for which comprehension is a major factor, or to logical–mathematical abilities, and that prereading skills are basically attentional–informational. Data in support of this position can be found in studies of IQ and reading (e.g., Gates, 1921) which show that the relationship between IQ and reading increases with increased reading level. Furthermore, teachers will usually include a child with an IQ of 80 to 85 in a regular initial reading class, but will not include this same child in a regular class at a higher grade level.

The second type of support for this position is found in attempts to induce children to discover prereading or early reading skills. Silberman (1964), Gibson, Farber, and Shipela (1967), and Jeffreys and Samuels (1967) report unsuccessful results with 5- and 6-year-old children in inducing discovery of specific visual–acoustical relationships; but they were considerably more successful when the relationships were made explicit. Silverman (1964), and Jeffreys and Samuels (1967) tested transfer of letter–sound associations; Gibson, Farber, and Shipela (1967) were concerned with letter order as a variable in the abstraction of spelling patterns. Similarly, Caldwell and Hall (1969), and Hall and Caldwell (1970) found that attention alone was not sufficient for teaching young children to discriminate between rotations and reversals of geometric forms. The essential element in these studies was making explicit the appropriate concept of "same" and "different."

Similar conclusions can be drawn from word recognition studies by Otto and Pizillo (1970), and McCutcheon and McDowell (1969). In summarizing these studies, Koehler (1971, p. 2) reports that kindergarten and first-grade children "will attend to and encode only the cues required to minimally distinguish words during word acquisition." In other words, the strategies adopted for word recognition derive directly from the visual differences among the words on which the child is initially trained—a result which, in part, accounts for the initial letter strategy mentioned earlier.

Another approach to evaluating the maturational and innate potential theories is to inspect the patterns of prereading skills deficits. If prereading skills were simply different surface manifestations of a single underlying factor, we would tend to find an all-or-nothing distribution of skill deficits, but data reported by Chapman (1971) for mastery of five prereading skills by 138 kindergarteners show a wide dispersion of mastery–nonmastery patterns.

Finally, a logical analysis of the prereading skills isolated in the previous section shows that many of them are based upon arbitrary relationships. Attending to letter order and letter orientation are skills that are unique to reading. The objects in the child's environment, prior to the first encounter with the alphabet, retain their identity under order and orientation reversal. The letters of the alphabet (and numbers) are the first objects for which the child must attend to orientation in labeling, and words (and numbers) are the first objects for which order is significant (see also Klausmeier's discussion of an identity concept in Part I of this volume.) There is no reason, therefore, to expect the child to induce these conclusions from his encounters with the environment.

Similar arguments, although perhaps not as strong, can be made for the sound skills, especially for sound matching where certain features, such as intensity and duration, must be ignored while others, such as voicing, must be discerned. In short, the weight of the evidence points in the direction of direct instruction.

Validation

Whatever may be the logical basis for our selection of prereading skills, and eventually of the methods selected for teaching them, we are still responsible for an empirical validation of our choices. Guidelines can be developed for evaluating instructional methods, based on the mastery levels assumed for the skills involved, but ascertaining the necessity of each skill for learning to read is a far more complex matter.

First, since no one skill listed above is a sine qua non for learning to read, gross comparisons of skill deficits to later reading achievement, although perhaps suggestive of trends, are not accurate measures of skill necessity. Second, a skill which is lacking just prior to formal reading instruction might be acquired as a result of reading instruction itself. For example, a child who does not attend to orientation in letter identification might learn to do so in learning to read, because of the instruction received on such sight word pairs as *bad–dad* and *rib–rid*. The need for instruction in prereading skills is not based on an all-or-none concept of learning; instead, it is based on efficiency: the child who comes to beginning reading instruction with mastery of all prereading skills should have considerably less difficulty in learning to read than the child who does not. Furthermore, the difficulties that we expect a child to have in learning to read should be predictable from prereading skill deficits.

This assertion is the basis for empirical validation of prereading skills, and its implication is that while the child is learning to read we search for particular types of errors (or the absence thereof) according to the prereading skills which the child lacked upon entry to initial reading instruction. Exactly how to do this is not immediately evident, however, since a teacher who finds a child struggling to acquire a particular skill may provide sufficient personal help to overcome earlier deficits, and thereby alter the child's error patterns. Nevertheless, the direction that validation must take is clear; only the procedure needs to be resolved.

In summary, the prereading skills approach, which emphasizes direct and explicit instruction in skills directly tied to learning to read, is based upon: first, a logical analysis of the initial reading task; second, experimental data derived from different attempts to teach particular prereading skills; and, finally, data showing that many children do not acquire prereading skills without explicit instruction in them. Skills that are logical prerequisites for initial reading skills are candidates for prereading instruction; but they are not selected until it is shown that a sufficient number of prereaders lack them, which justifies their inclusion in an instructional program. It should be noticed that the processes just mentioned make minimal use of statistical correlation and of instruction per se for the identification of specific skills. Predictive studies, which are of questionable value for any classroom application, may suggest skills needing further analysis, but by themselves are often incomplete and misleading, due to their penchant for numerical potency over logical relationships. As Edmund Gordon (1965) noted, correlational studies offer no guidelines for instruction, and may lead to spurious statistical bases for popular mythology. Similarly, to champion a particular skill because instruction in it produces an increase in some reading ability, such as, for example, word recognition, is also unacceptable unless the process of instruction is carefully decomposed so as to show precisely what was taught.

The conclusions reached here contrast noticeably with the preschool models derived from the work of Piaget, and potentially with those of the language remediation school. Furth and Wach (1974), for example, who represent one of many differing attempts to translate Piaget's generalizations into instruction, insist that children should discover auditory skills themselves:

> Group instructors should allow the children's auditory thinking skills to develop naturally in response to games; they should never give the "right" answer—when the games involve a nonsense language, the children are expected to discover the code themselves [174f].

While the interpretations of "discovery" might vary, the implication of this statement is directly opposed to the results of the studies cited earlier which failed to induce mastery of related skills through discovery techniques. To my knowledge, no experimental evidence has been produced to justify the discovery approach to prereading skills at the kindergarten level.

Language remediation approaches to reading readiness (Bereiter and Engelmann, 1966; Stern, 1968) are compatible with the approach discussed here, to the extent that language deficits can be shown to interfere with the acquisition of prereading skills themselves. But some language skills included in language remediation programs—including especially phonemic discrimination—have not been shown by valid experimental means to be lacking in the subject populations for which these programs were designed.

There is an obvious limitation to the prereading skill approach as a total model for child development—but this it does not pretend to be. Instead, it concentrates only on those skills that relate directly to learning to read, and leaves such skills as motor development and socialization to other programs and other approaches.

A more serious limitation to the evidence in favor of the prereading skill approach is due to a dependence upon short-term studies and paradigms which produce immediately observable effects. Piaget's concern, in contrast, is with continual, long-term development, and this approach may not receive fair evaluation when assessed on the basis of ability to show quick results (see the Preface of this volume). To address this issue, we will need to wait until some of the more recently developed programs for teaching prereading skills have been in use long enough to assess their contribution to reading instruction.

DESIGN OF PREREADING SKILLS INSTRUCTION

To propose that certain skills are necessary prerequisities for learning to read and to establish a need for instruction in such skills is for the most part a matter of composition and salesmanship. Some of the supporting data for these notions have been available for the last decade, and the ideas themselves have been around since the 1930s. Gates *et al.* (1939) were headed in this direction when they wrote: "The most useful reading readiness tests are tests of ability clearly involved in learning to read [p. 29]." Nevertheless, a proper respect for the complexity of child development, learning, instruction, and the reading task itself leads us to require sufficiently greater evidence for the efficacy of prereading skills instruction than has been presented or implied in this chapter so far.

Instructional procedures need to be designed, tested, and shown to produce better results than other approaches to reading readiness. The first requirement is the concern of this section. Some of the problems encountered in implementing the second requirement—program evaluation—are discussed in the final section. In particular, this section will present the results of almost five years of experience in developing and testing a kindergarten level prereading skills program. The purpose in discussing this endeavor is not to justify or promote the program itself, but to exemplify the enormous chasm between idea and object and between research and development.

Background

The prereading skills instruction (PRS)[1] program described here was developed at the Wisconsin Research and Development Center for Cognitive Learning between 1970 and 1974, and was based initially on prereading and early reading studies done by Calfee *et al.*, 1972; and Venezky and Chapman 1970). Our initial goals were to develop instructional procedures based on the Individually Guided Education (IGE) model (Klausmeier, in press) for a limited group of prereading skills. Over the development and testing period, however, several other goals or constraints were adopted, based upon classroom experiences. These required decisions which in most cases could not be drawn from the prereading approach or from experimental data and are outlined as follows:

Attention to Individual Needs

As specified by the IGE model, children should receive instruction only where they need it. This implies that the teacher be provided with diagnostic techniques for determining skill needs and with a scheduling and management scheme that allows the teacher to plan and implement instruction according to individual needs.

Variation in Instruction Grouping

The traditional classroom uses whole-class grouping for most instruction; programmed instruction relies almost exclusively upon individual instruction. As a steady diet neither extreme is healthy for children or efficient for individualization. (It should be noted, also, that programmed instruction, although doled out in individual portions, is not necessarily individualized instruction. In general, all children, regardless

---

[1] The lead authors of PRS are Susan Pittelman and Marga Kamm. Ron Leslie was responsible for the diagnostic tests contained in the program while Jane Seegal and Susan Chicone were contributing authors. The present writer was program director.

of their needs, follow the main course of the program. Branching for further help on particular questions is in no way equivalent to tailoring instruction to specific skill deficits.) In preparation for reading instruction, a variety of instructional groupings are required, ranging from whole class (or unit) to individual. Emphasis on small groups, however, seems appropriate for the kindergarten level where socialization remains a major goal.

Compatibility with a Kindergarten Philosophy

The kindergarten philosophy that we find most agreeable is one emphasizing development of the whole child within an open and accommodating environment. We do not view the kindergarten as an appropriate level for hard-core instruction in academic matters, at least not for most children. It is important, therefore, that instruction in prereading skills not use a major portion of the kindergarten day, and that instruction be based on songs, games, stories, and other kindergarten-level activities which allow a learning-by-doing approach. Where possible, the children should be led to discover relationships on their own. However, this approach must be tempered according to the arbitrariness and complexity of the task (as discussed above) and by the capabilities and learning styles of the child.

Development of a Positive Attitude toward Reading

As a complement to our skill-mastery goals, we also wanted to create a positive attitude for learning to read. Learning the prereading skills, therefore, has to be enjoyable for the children; in addition, they should experience success as often as possible so that they feel that they can learn to read. (There is an obvious danger to this as pointed out by Entwisle, 1974. The child who receives continual positive reinforcement even though he or she is operating far below the class average must eventually be confronted with the fact that he or she has failed.) Associated with the goal of positive attitude is the desire to provide continual exposure to the vocabulary, processes, and paraphernalia of reading instruction—including worksheets, tests, letters, and words.

Minimal Teacher Preparation

Individualizing instruction, especially for a teacher who has 35 children in a class and no aide, is difficult. To require this teacher to participate in extensive preservice—inservice training and to do extensive preparation for each lesson would doom any program to failure. Therefore, the program had to be designed for use without an inservice session and with at most a half-day preservice session. It had to contain all of the materials required for instruction: schedules, teacher guides, and all instructional materials, in addition to the diagnostic instruments and management system.

Selection of Skills

The selection of skills for instruction was based on the importance that we attributed to each skill and the instructional procedures that we adopted. In the program itself, five skills are emphasized and a diagnostic test (criterion referenced) is provided for each. These skills are as follows:

1. Attending to letter order.
2. Attending to letter orientation.
3. Attending to word detail.
4. Sound matching.
5. Sound blending.

However, in teaching these skills several other skills—especially acoustical ones—are taught. For example, sound-matching activities are based on picture—sound associations which are taught in groups of four through songs, games, and stories. The materials for the first set of these activities contain pictures of an angry cat, /f/, a surprised boy, /o/, a snake, /s/, and a child eating cake, /m/ (International Phonetic Alphabet symbols are used here.) These are learned very rapidly by children of all socioeconomic levels and retained with minimal reinforcement through at least the school year. Once learned, they become a mechanism not only for talking about sounds, "Listen for the sound that the mad cat makes," but for self-corrective small-group and individual games. In sorting games for initial sounds, for example, children will sort pictures of common objects into piles according to their initial sounds. The piles for each are marked by the appropriate sound picture, and in addition the sound picture for each object's beginning sound is printed on the reverse side of the object's picture. Once the cards are sorted, they are turned over and checked. Similarly, letter—sound associations are introduced as a basis for blending. They are taught first in association with their corresponding sound pictures, but the sound pictures are quickly faded out. Other skills that are taught include *rhyming* (which is used to introduce sound matching in word-final position) and *same–different* as an introduction to visual matching skills.

Instructional Procedures

The design of instructional procedures was one of the most difficult developmental activities, and the one which revealed most clearly the inadequacy of present-day experimental procedures as aids to instructional design. The most common paradigm for exploring children's skill capabilities is the training–transfer design. Typically, children are introduced to a task through demonstration, and then, using one of several common paradigms, they are given a number of training trials. Those children who reach criterion on the training task (and occasionally, even those who do not) are then given a test which generally utilizes the same paradigm employed for training, but uses new materials. From the results, far-reaching conclusions are usually drawn concerning the age levels at which children develop some particular skill that is assumed to underlie the experimental materials and procedures.

Exactly what can be concluded from such studies beyond the exact materials, paradigms, and subjects involved is not clear. One conclusion should not be made in such a situation: that skills involved cannot be taught to children who are the same age as those children who failed to master the task. A good part of present-day child development research is aimed at disproving the limitations on learning that have been incorrectly inferred from previous studies. A major part of our design efforts (especially for sound skills) was spent in demonstrating that certain skills could, with sufficient effort, be taught to kindergarten children (Venezky *et al.*, 1971).

A second and perhaps more serious limitation to the experimental work of the past two decades on prereading skills is its lack of concern for sustained learning in a classroom setting. Most of what we know about the acquisition of prereading skills derives from brief training and testing paradigms in which an experimenter interacts with one child at a time. Yet the design decisions required in the development of an individualized program relate to sustained learning that takes place over the entire school year and in a variety of instructional groupings—the least frequent of which is the one teacher—one child situation. Questions of optimal group sizes, amounts of repetition and reinforcement, sequencing of instructional activities, and a multitude of other design problems cannot be resolved on the basis of the last 90 years of psychological and educational research, and probably will not be resolved on the basis of the next decade's work unless radical changes are made in experimental methodology.

In the design of the program discussed here, emphasis was placed on drawing the child's attention to the features which were important for a particular task, and in giving him or her strategies for carrying out the more complicated procedures. For order and orientation, for example, the notion of direction is introduced, using an arrow which children learn to manipulate and follow in a variety of activities. The arrow then becomes a prop for determining whether or not two letters (e.g., $b-b$ or $b-d$) point in the same direction or if two letter sequences (e.g., $ab-ab$ or $ab-ba$) have the same order. Activities are sequenced from easy to difficult and, wherever possible, from concrete to abstract. For each skill, activities were designed to incorporate a variety of different paradigms.

The entire program evolved through almost 5 years of tryouts, pilot tests, and field tests. In the research phase of this project, which covered 4 years, diagnostic instruments were developed for assessing particular skills, and some experience was gained in teaching certain less complicated skills, such as relating sounds to pictures. Beginning in the 1970–1971 school year, instructional tasks were designed and tried out in three cooperating kindergarten classes by our experimenters and by the teachers. After extensive feedback from the teachers—and the hiring of one as a full-time staff member—a complete, year-long program was designed and produced in the summer of 1971 and pilot tested in 14 classrooms during the 1971–1972 school year. Pilot-test teachers answered questionnaires, were observed frequently in the classroom, and participated in several feedback sessions during and after the school year.

On the basis of the 1971–1972 data, another major revision was made during the summer of 1972, and field tested in 22 classrooms in Illinois, Wisconsin, and Minnesota in 1972–1973. In addition, one member of our staff taught the program in a cooperating classroom. Using the same feedback techniques as in 1971–1972, data were collected for further revisions for the 1973–1974 school year, when a final tryout was done. In parallel with the 1973–1974 tryout, specifications for the commercial version were drafted for the Encyclopaedia Britannica Educational Corporation, which had been awarded the contract for commercial production and dissemination. During the 1974–1975 school year, different staff-training techniques were tested in about 65 classrooms in seven different states from New England to California, using the commercial version of the program.

What was most evident throughout this work was the number of decisions that had to be made for which supporting data were not obtainable within the constraints of budget and time under which we worked. These varied from the amount of review required for skill maintenance following mastery to the placement of the component number on a practice sheet. Most of these matters were resolved through trial and error, but this is a luxury that few programs can afford.

Evaluation

Several types of evaluation studies have been conducted during program development and are reported in Wisconsin R&D Center Technical Reports (Kamm, Zajano, Hubbard, and Pittelman, 1974; Venezky *et al.*, 1971). Recent studies have examined the effectiveness of the program in teaching the program objectives, retention of skills from end of kindergarten to beginning of first grade, and the relationship of prereading skill mastery to standardized reading readiness scores. The results of these studies (Venezky, Green, and Leslie, 1975), though providing justification for the prereading skill approach and to the program itself, are based upon field-test versions and are too limited in scope to represent a definitive statement of program effectiveness. Furthermore, several issues need to be resolved before an adequate evaluation of this (or any other) program can be made. Although a full discussion is not appropriate here, a brief sampling of these issues should be sufficient to give the flavor of the problems involved.

The objective of any prereading program is to improve reading achievement. However, to assess reading ability at the end of grade one as a measure of effectiveness for a kindergarten program is to confuse program goals with the assumptions upon which the program is based. Program goals relate to what the program provides instruction for: prereading skills, attitudes, etc. The assumption upon which such programs are based is that mastery of certain skills will lead to success in learning to read. Consequently, separate evaluations must be made of the assumptions upon which a program is based and of how well the program meets its instructional goals.

Improving the readiness of children for reading might not lead to a significant increase in average reading scores in a class, but instead might allow the teacher to achieve a desired reading level with less time, effort, and resources than were formerly required. These savings can then be applied to instruction in other subjects. It is conceivable, therefore, that a good prereading program might have a greater effect upon first-grade math scores than first-grade reading scores.

Teachers generally choose their reading programs 6- to 8-months prior to the time they plan to use them. If, due to a prereading program, children come to first grade far better prepared for reading instruction than in former years, the teacher might not be ready to take advantage of the children's advanced preparation. Some teachers will require considerable proof before they are be convinced that the children's preparedness is, in fact, significantly different. Hence, there might be a lag of 1 to 2 years before the first-grade reading program is adapted to the new entry level abilities.

Programs don't teach; teachers do. Therefore, the evaluation of a program must be an evaluation of what the program does for the teacher, and only indirectly what it does for the students. Implied here is an assessment of changes in teacher attitude, utilization of resources, and capabilities for diagnosis and instruction. A program is one of many resources a teacher can utilize to reach a desired goal. It is not like a railroad engine that the engineer controls (today, by push buttons) along a fixed course, according to a fixed time table. A program is more analogous to the blades, creams, powders, and instruction that are provided for the training and use of barbers. We can improve the accoutrements of the trade endlessly, but the end product will still depend upon the skill of the barber.

These are some, but not, all of the problems involved in evaluating a prereading program. They are not insurmountable, but they require serious attention to the goals, resources, and procedures of instruction.

Conclusions

Several major areas require further consideration in the study and instruction of prereading skills. First, the justification for the prereading skills approach to reading readiness rests upon logic and upon a limited experimental base. Long-term learning effects need to be attended to and the viability of discovery techniques within an expanded time scale need to be explored. Short-term achievements may not lead to long-term learning; in fact, it is conceivable that short-term failure through one type of instruction may have a more positive longer-term influence than short-term success through another.

Second, a methodology for studying sustained learning in an instructional setting must be developed. Piaget (1965), borrowing from Claparede, has advocated a technique called "instructional pedagogy" for investigating learning in situ. This approach is based on the manipulation of specific components of an instructional program, with measurement of marginal gain or loss. Whether we pursue this suggestion, or some other, I see no escape from the necessity to develop experimental procedures that use the ongoing classroom in place of the departmental laboratory.

Finally, evaluation of instructional programs requires a sober assessment of the influence of schooling. At present we have little capability for identifying and measuring the relative effects of physical resources, teachers, programs, and parentage on learning. Without knowing the contribution of each, we have no justification for using achievement scores for evaluating programs.

REFERENCES

Bennett, A. An analysis of errors in word recognition made by retarded readers. *Journal of Educational Psychology*, 1942, *33*, 25–38.

Benda, C. E. Psychopathology of childhood. In L. Carmichael (Ed.), *Handbook of Child Psychology*. London: Chapman and Hall, 1954, 1115–1166.

Bereiter, C., & Englemann, S. *Teaching disadvantaged children*. Englewood Cliffs, N.J.: Prentice-Hall, 1966.

Birch, H. G., & Belmont, L. Audio-visual integration in normal and retarded readers. *American Journal of Orthopsychiatry*, 1964, *5*, 852–861.

Bloomfield, L. Linguistics and reading. *Elementary English Review*, 1942, *XIX*, 125–130; 183–186.

Calfee, R., Chapman, R., & Venezky, R. How a child needs to think to learn to read. In L. Gregg (Ed.), *Cognition in learning and memory*. New York: John Wiley & Sons, 1972, 139–182.

Caldwell, E. C., & Hall, V. C. The influence of concept training on letter discrimination. *Child Development*, 1969, *40*, 63–72.

Chapman, R. *Report of the February 1971 version of the Wisconsin Basic Prereading Skill Test*. Technical Report No. 179. Madison: Wisconsin Research and Development Center for Cognitive Learning, 1971.

Cohen, R. Remedial training of first grade children with visual perceptual retardation. *Educational Horizons*, 1967, *45*, 60–63.

Durr, W. K. Computer study of high frequency words in popular trade juveniles. *The Reading Teacher*, 1973, *27*, 37–42.

Durrell, D. D. *Improving reading instruction*. New York: World Book Co., 1956.

Entwisle, D. R. Talk presented to the NIE conference on Title I research, Washington, D.C., June 6, 1974. See also D. R. Entwisle, M. Webster, Jr., & L. Hayduk, *Expectation Theory in the Classroom*. Final Report, USOE Project No. 1.0034 (Baltimore, Maryland, 1974).

Fries, C. C. *Linguistics and reading*. New York: Holt, Rinehart, and Winston, 1963.

Frostig, M. *Developmental Test of Visual Perception*. Palo Alto, Calif.: Consulting Psychologists Press, 1963.

Furth, H. G., & Wachs, A. *Thinking goes to school*. New York: Oxford University Press, 1974.

Gates, A. I. An experimental and statistical study of reading and reading tests. *The Journal of Educational Psychology*, 1921, *12*, 303–314; 378–391; 445–464.

Gates, A. I., Bond, G. L., & Russell, D. H. *Methods of determining reading readiness*. New York: Bureau of Publications, Teachers College, Columbia University, 1939.

Gesell, A. Maturation and the patterning of behavior. In Carl Murchison (Ed.), *A Handbook of Child Psychology*. Worcester, Mass.: Clark University Press, 1933, 209–235.

Gibson, E. J., Farber, J., & Shepela, S. Test of a learning set procedure for abstraction of spelling patterns. *Project Literacy Reports*, 1967, *8*, 21–30.

Gibson, E. J., & Levin, H. *The psychology of reading*. Cambridge, Mass.: M.I.T. Press, 1975.

Gordon, E. W. Characteristics of socially disadvantaged children. *Review of Educational Research*, 1965, *35*, 377–388.

Gruenberg, S. M., (Ed.). *The new encyclopaedia of child care and guidance*. Garden City, N.Y.: Doubleday and Co., 1958.

Hall, V. C., & Caldwell, E. C. *Analysis of young students performance on a matching task*. Research Report, National Laboratory on Early Childhood Education, 1970.

Hill, M. B. A study of the process of word discrimination in individuals beginning to read. *Journal of Educational Research*, 1936, *29*, 487–500.

Huey, E. B. *The psychology and pedagogy of reading.* New York: The Macmillan Co., 1908. (Reprinted, with an introduction by Paul A. Kolers.) Cambridge: M.I.T. Press, 1968.

Jefferey, W. E., & Samuels, S. J. Effect of method of reading training on initial learning and transfer. *Journal of Verbal Learning and Verbal Behavior*, 1967, *6*, 354–358.

Kamm, M., Zajano, N., Hubbard, W. D., & Pittelman, S. *The 1971–72 field test of the Prereading Skills Program.* Technical Report No. 269. Madison: Wisconsin Research and Development Center for Cognitive Learning, 1974.

Klausmeier, H. IGE: An alternate form of schooling. In H. Talmage (Ed.), *Systems of Individualized Education.* Berkeley, Calif.: McCutchan, in press.

Koehler, J., Jr. *Training forms for processing the letter pattern cues of sight words.* Technical Note. Inglewood, Ca.: Southwest Regional Laboratory, 1971.

Marsh, G., & Sherman, M. *Children's discrimination and production of phonemes in isolation and in words.* Technical Memorandum. Inglewood, Ca.: Southwest Regional Laboratory, 1971.

McCutcheon, B. A., & McDowell, E. E. Intralist similarity and acquisition and generalization of word recognition. *The Reading Teacher*, 1969, *23*, 103–107; 115.

Morphett, M. V., & Washburne, C. When should children begin to read? *Elementary School Journal*, 1931, *31*, 496–503.

Muehl, S. The effects of visual discrimination pretraining on learning to read a vocabulary list in kindergarten children. *Journal of Educational Psychology*, 1960, *51*, 217–221.

National Society for the Study of Education (NSSE), Report of the national committee on reading. *Twenty-fourth Yearbook of the NSSE*, Bloomington, Ind.: Public School Pub., 1925.

Otto, W., & Pizillo, C. Effect of intralist similarity on kindergarten pupils' rate of word acquisition and transfer. *Journal of Reading Behavior*, 1970, *71*(3), 14–19.

Paradis, E. E. The appropriateness of visual discrimination exercises in reading readiness materials. *Journal of Educational Research*, 1974, *67*, 276–278.

Piaget, J. [*Science of education and psychology of the child*] (D. Coltman, trans.). New York: Orion Press, 1970 (Original publication, 1965).

Plato. *The dialogues of Plato* (2 vols.) (B. Jowett, trans.). New York: Random House, 1892.

Pryzwansky, B. Effects of perceptual-motor training and manuscript writing on reading readiness skills in kindergarten. *Journal of Educational Psychology*, 1972, *63*, 110–115.

Robinson, J. S., & Higgins, K. E. Young child's ability to see a difference between mirror-image forms. *Perceptual and Motor Skills*, 1967, *25*, 893–897.

Rosen, C. An experimental study of visual perceptual training and reading achievement in first grade. *Perceptual and Motor Skills*, 1966, *22*, 979–986.

Rudegeair, R., & Kamil, M. *Assessment of phonological discrimination in children.* Technical Report No. 118. Madison: Wisconsin Research and Development Center for Cognitive Learning, 1970.

Silberman, H. F. Experimental analysis of a beginning reading skill. *Programed Instruction*, 1964, *3*, 4–8.

Smith, E. E., & Spoehr, K. T. The perception of printed English: A theoretical perspective. In B. H. Kantowitz (Ed.), *Human information processing: Tutorials in performance and cognition.* Potomac, Md.: Erlbaum Press, 1974.

Stern, C. Evaluating language curricula for preschool children, *Monographs of the Society for Research in Child Development*, 1968, *33*.

Thorndike, E. L., *The psychology of learning.* New York: Teachers College, 1913.

Venezky, R. L. Theoretical and experimental bases for teaching reading. In T. Sebeok (Ed.), *Current trends in linguistics* (Vol. 12). The Hague: Mouton, 1974, 2057–2100.

Venezky, R. L., Chapman, R. S., Seegal, J., Kamm, M., & Leslie, R. *The Prereading Skills*

Program: Evaluation of the first tryout. Working Paper No. 81. Madison, Wisc.: Wisconsin Research and Development Center for Cognitive Learning, 1971.

Venezky, R. L., Green, M., & Leslie, R. *Evaluation studies of the Prereading Skills Program.* Technical Report 311. Madison, Wisc.: Wisconsin Research and Development Center for Cognitive Learning, 1975.

Venezky, R. L., & Chapman, R. S. *An instructional program in prereading skills: Needs and specifications.* Working Paper No. 78. Madison, Wisc.: Wisconsin Research and Development Center for Cognitive Learning, 1970.

Venezky, R. L., & Johnson, D. Development of two letter-sound patterns in grades one through three. *Journal of Educational Psychology,* 1973, *64,* 109–115.

Weber, E. *The kindergarten.* New York: Teachers College Press, 1969.

Weber, R. M. First-graders' use of grammatical context in reading. In H. Levin and J. Williams (Eds.), *Basic Studies in Reading.* New York: Harper & Row, 1970. Pp. 147–163.

PART III

Strategies for Improving Classroom Instruction

In the first chapter of Part III, "Strategies for Improving Classroom Instruction," Klausmeier focusses on the teaching of concepts, with particular attention given to the steps essential for the development of an effective instructional design. The design is completely consonant with Klausmeier's theoretical analysis of the four levels or stages in the development of a concept, as reported in Chapter 1. Concepts are important in classroom learning, of course, because of their central role in thinking and, more specifically, in understanding principles and in problem solving.

The author maintains that three major analyses must precede either the actual construction of materials or the development of a strategy for teaching a concept: content analysis, behavior analysis, and instructional analysis. These three analyses are described in detail and, by way of illustrating the steps, in each analysis two concepts are referred to throughout the discussion.

Content analysis of a concept entails determining its place in a more general taxonomy or hierarchy, defining the concept in terms of its attributes, identifying examples and non-examples of it, and identifying illustrative principles and problems involving use of the concept. Behavior analysis refers to identifying the more explicit mental operations involved in learning a concept at each of four levels, as discussed earlier. Instructional analysis refers to delineating the instructional conditions that facilitate concept learning, and therefore takes into account the characteristics of the learners, the level at which the concept is to be taught and learned, the kind of instructional materials and activities needed, and the amount of teacher guidance. Instructional materials that are developed to teach concepts usually take the form of printed materials, either illustrated graphically or supplemented by audiovisual material.

Klausmeier concludes his chapter with a sample instructional lesson developed for use with one of the concepts employed in his research (equilateral triangle). From the sample lesson provided, the reader will gain an appreciation of the rather complex sequence of steps that is needed to produce a set of instructional materials for teaching concepts, and also of the precision with which it is now possible to develop materials to teach particular concepts to particular student populations.

The second chapter in this section reports research and development efforts in the area of creative problem solving with children. Davis, in Chapter 8, first reviews available research relevant to his model of creativity and then describes materials he has developed for training creative thinking of children in the classroom.

Davis maintains that the creative person possesses two important characteristics: creative attitudes or values and techniques or methods for solving problems. Regarding attitudes, the data indicate that the creative person is flexible, open-minded, and receptive to new ideas. Holding such attitudes and values seems to play an important role in facilitating creative thinking. A certain concept of self—namely, belief that one can be creative—appears to be an important factor in facilitating creative thinking. Relevant research is discussed by Davis which demonstrates that a person can intentionally control his production of creative ideas. In one study, for example, subjects who were instructed to be "original" produced many more novel and creative ideas than persons who were instructed to be "practical."

Techniques or methods for creative problem solving is the second important component of creativity, according to Davis' analysis. Researchers in the field of creativity have described several methods that can be used in a conscious and intentional way to produce novel ideas. One well-known technique is "brainstorming," in which a group of persons is encouraged to produce a large number of ideas, without evaluating or criticizing them. Other methods that can be used to increase the production of creative ideas include listing of attributes or new combinations of attributes, idea checklists, and metaphorical thinking. Davis describes several research studies that have tested the effectiveness of some of these idea-stimulating techniques with samples of average persons.

In the final section of his chapter Davis describes three children's workbooks which he helped design. These draw upon research findings pertaining to creative attitudes and methods described above. In all three programs, the attitudes and methods conducive to creative thinking are presented in an interesting and humorous fashion. The first creative-thinking program was presented in a cartoon format; the four cartoon characters were used to convey the desired creative attitudes and problem-solving techniques to the children. At the end of each chapter the children were given exercises which required them to think of new ideas and solve problems. The field evaluation of this classroom-based program showed that it was very effective in increasing children's problem-solving ability. Davis provides an illustrative passage from a second, more general program developed to concentrate entirely upon increasing children's creativity in writing.

The chapter by Davis provides a very good example of the relation between theoretically oriented research and the development of instructional materials. In this case, research led directly to producing curricular materials for the classroom—materials dealing with a very important aspect of children's intellectual performance.

In the final chapter of Part III, Allen discusses a set of techniques that are currently being used very extensively in schools: tutoring of children by other children. The usual tutoring arrangement involves cross-age pairs, with an older child helping a younger child. The idea of using children as tutors is not new, as Allen makes clear in his discussion of the historical origins of tutoring in the British schools of the 19th century. Available evidence suggests that both the tutor (the child who teaches) as well as the tutee (the child being taught) may benefit from the tutoring procedure. Interestingly, it appears that the tutor sometimes may learn even more than the tutee. Particularly intriguing are reports that children who are tutors show improved attitudes toward school and authority and an improved self-concept.

Allen describes a research program concentrating on the effect of tutoring on the tutor (although some research is mentioned dealing with the tutee as well). A series of studies is described investigating: (a) the effect of teaching on the tutor, and (b) the social skills needed in interacting in a tutoring situation. Several field studies in the schools are reported, including a study examining the social and academic behavior of children in an age-heterogeneous school setting—that is, the one-teacher, one-room school.

To effectively teach another person requires that the teacher possess the cognitive and social skills needed in the complex interpersonal situation. These skills are both verbal and nonverbal in nature. Allen reports several experiments in which the nonverbal components of tutoring skills were investigated. For example, one experiment studied the child's intentional and unintentional encoding and decoding of comprehension via nonverbal cues. Children were more accurate than adults in detecting instances of comprehension or noncomprehension of a lesson on the basis of nonverbal cues from another child. Other research explored the child's ability to control his/her nonverbal behavior during a teaching session.

The goal of the research program reported by Allen is to improve our understanding of the basic psychological processes involved in any cognitive or social outcomes produced by the technique of children teaching other children. Therefore, the results of research in this chapter should be applicable across a wide range of subject-matter areas.

All three of the chapters comprising Part III of this book are concerned primarily with the application of knowledge to the classroom setting. By using the knowledge now available (as exemplified by the information reported in these chapters and others in the book), it should be possible to improve substantially the learning of children in the classroom.

CHAPTER 7

Instructional Design
and the Teaching of Concepts[1]

Herbert J. Klausmeier

Concepts, principles, and problem-solving skills have long been recognized as the primary outcomes of learning in the cognitive domain (National Society for the Study of Education, 1950). To these learning outcomes, we should add taxonomic and hierarchical relationships (Klausmeier, Ghatala, and Frayer, 1974). Concepts are the building blocks not only for learning principles, problem-solving skills, and taxonomic and hierarchical relationships, but also of thinking itself (Kagan, 1966). Also, as public entities or word meanings (Carroll, 1964), concepts comprise a substantial part of many subject matters and are the basic unit of instruction.

Knowledge about concept learning has been extended through early experimentation conducted in laboratory settings using experimenter-created populations of concepts (see, for example, Bourne, Ekstrand and Dominowski, 1971; and Bruner, Goodnow and Austin, 1956). More recently, the variables that are relevant to the learning and teaching of subject-matter concepts are being identified and manipulated in school settings (Klausmeier and Feldman, 1975; Klausmeier, Ghatala, and Frayer, 1974; Markle, 1975; Markle and Tiemann, 1969; Tennyson, Woolley, and Merrill, 1972). This knowledge about concept learning, combined with knowledge of instructional design, permits the development of more effective instructional materials and procedures for teaching concepts.

Rapid advances are being made in instructional design (Gagné and Briggs, 1974; Glaser and Resnick, 1972; Merrill, 1971). Three kinds of analyses should precede the actual preparation of either instructional materials or teaching activities to teach concepts to students. A *content analysis* is carried out to determine the substance, that is, the facts, concepts, principles, theories, that students need to learn; this sub-

[1] The author thanks Patricia S. Allen and Susan M. Markle for reading this chapter and providing many helpful comments.

191

stance is incorporated in the terminal objectives of the instruction. A *behavioral analysis* identifies those behaviors, operations, or skills that students must demonstrate in order to learn the substance; these behaviors also are incorporated in the terminal objectives. An *instructional analysis* identifies the instructional procedures to be used in attaining the desired terminal objectives with a particular target population of students. Analysis of the target population of students to determine what they may be capable of learning is assumed to be part of the instructional analysis when the instruction is to be designed for a particular population of students. As will be described in this chapter, developing instructional materials for teaching concepts requires (*a*) analysis of the concepts to be taught—content analysis, (*b*) analysis of the cognitive operations that underlie the learning of the concepts at the particular level at which they are to be attained—behavioral analysis, and (*c*) analysis of instructional procedures that facilitate the attainment of the concept at the desired level—instructional analysis. A general design of instruction incorporating these analyses is reported in Klausmeier, Ghatala, and Frayer (1974) and Klausmeier and Goodwin (1975). In this chapter the design is described more fully.

CONDUCTING A CONCEPT ANALYSIS

Subject matter taught to children, kindergarten through high school, should be selected in the context of the structure of knowledge of the particular discipline or disciplines. This implies that the person conducting a concept analysis should know where the particular concept fits into a taxonomy or hierarchy, how it is defined by experts in the discipline, its use in principles, and its use in solving various kinds of problems.

Conducting a concept analysis includes the following:

1. Outlining the taxonomy or the hierarchy of which the target concept is a part.
2. Defining the concept in terms of its attributes.
3. Specifying the defining attributes and some of the variable attributes of the concept.
4. Indicating illustrative examples and nonexamples of the concept.
5. Identifying illustrative principles in which the concept is incorporated.
6. Formulating illustrative problem-solving exercises involving use of the concept.
7. Developing a list of the key vocabulary words associated with the concept and its defining attributes.

Procedures for carrying out steps 2, 3, and 4 are based on the pioneering work of Markle and Tiemann (1969), while the other steps are related directly to the model of conceptual learning and development developed by Klausmeier, Ghatala, and Frayer (1974), which I summarized in Part I of this volume.

My experience in developing concept analyses indicates that when a particular target population for instruction has not been identified, the analysis should be directed toward the formal level of attaining the concept, and the complete analysis should be expressed in terminology appropriate for senior high school students. The concept analyzer needs the knowledge at this level, even though the instruction may be directed subsequently to a lower level. What is eventually included in a particular set of instructional materials or methods must be related to the level of concept attainment to be taught, and to the level of vocabulary and other characteristics of the target population of students. A description of the procedures for conducting a concept analysis follows, using as examples of each procedure information pertaining to the concepts **equilateral triangle** and **observing scientifically**. Each procedure is described in some detail because a concept analysis provides much of the information needed to develop instructional materials or procedures to teach the concept.

Outlining a Taxonomy or a Hierarchy

A starting point for the analysis of a concept is outlining the taxonomy or the hierarchy of which the concept is a part. A taxonomy involves inclusive–exclusive relationships among classes of things, whereas a hierarchy implies relationships among things ordered by some principle, such as of importance, priority, or dependency. The construct of learning hierarchies as formulated by Gagné (1962, 1968, 1970, 1974) is central in his design of instruction. A learning hierarchy, as defined by Gagné implies that there is only one sequence in which a set of skills can be mastered. (Gagné subsumes concepts and other outcomes of learning also as skills.) In this sense, taxonomics of concepts in various subject matters are clearly not learning hierarchies inasmuch as one can teach either supraordinate or subordinate concepts first. It is essential, therefore, to consider both a learning hierarchy and other hierarchical relationships.

A learning hierarchy results from an analysis of a learning task. Gagné analyzes a learning task into its prerequisite skills. An analysis is begun by asking the question: "What skills must individuals possess to perform the task successfully?" Answering this question yields the hierarchy of skills that are prerequisite to eventually performing the final task, which is also a skill. The hierarchy of skills obtained by the analysis provides the basic information needed to sequence instruction, either in instructional materials or by a teacher. Throughout an instructional sequence, one hierarchical skill is built successively upon another. Three assumptions underlying this kind of analysis, and the concept of learning hierarchy, are: that learning tasks can be analyzed into hierarchical sets of skills, that the prerequisite skills must be learned in order to learn the next successively higher skill, and that the same sequence of instruction will facilitate all persons learning the successive skills.

Figure 1 is a learning hierarchy for subtracting whole numbers that resulted from a task analysis (Gagné and Briggs, 1974). It shows the intellectual skills that are essential for performing the task of subtracting whole numbers of any size. Learning the 10 prerequisite skills should enable individuals to learn to subtract whole numbers of any size. A teacher or writer of instructional material would teach the skills in the order incorporated in the hierarchy. The learning hierarchy also indicates explicitly internal conditions that are prerequisite and essential for learning the successive skills. For example, being able to perform skills I–X is the primary internal condition essential for being able to learn and master Skill XI.

For Gagné (1968, 1970, 1974), the learning hierarchy is the building block in developing an instructional sequence to teach any particular task. Students are placed in an instructional sequence to start the first skill or coordinate set of skills that they have not yet mastered, and they continue through the sequence at their individual rates until the final task is performed successfully. Gagné presumes that most learning tasks can be analyzed into learning hierarchies.

Taxonomic relationships differ from hierarchical relationships. This is reflected in the network of defining attributes of the classes comprising a particular taxonomy and also in the pattern of inclusive and exclusive relationships among the classes comprising a taxonomy. As may be inferred from examining the taxonomy which follows for **equilateral triangle**, a supraordinate concept includes all members of all classes subordinate to it.

Taxonomy for Equilateral Triangle:

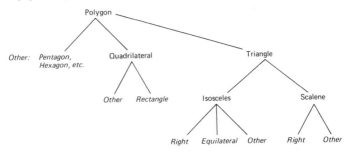

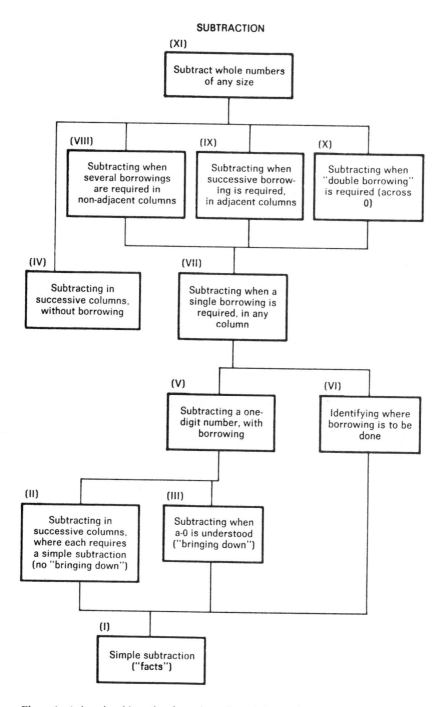

Figure 1. A learning hierarchy for subtracting whole numbers (From Gagné and Briggs, 1974, p. 114.)

Sample Taxonomic Relations involving **equilateral triangle**:

1. Some, but not all, isosceles triangles are equilateral triangles.
2. All equilateral triangles are isosceles triangles.
3. The sum of all right, equilateral, and other triangles is equal to the total possible number of isosceles triangles.
4. Right triangles are not equilateral triangles.

The concepts that are coordinate are at the same level of specificity, and the members of any coordinate class are not members of any other coordinate class. Concepts that are coordinate, for example, **isosceles triangle** and **scalene triangle**, may be either supraordinate or subordinate to other classes, depending on their location in the particular taxonomy. Concepts of a taxonomy, for example, **quadrilateral** and **triangle** subordinate to a given supraordinate concept **polygon**, have all of the defining attributes of the supraordinate concept, but require at least one additional attribute to define them. **Polygon** is defined by the attributes plane, simple, and closed, whereas one of its subordinates, **triangle**, is defined by the attributes plane, simple, closed, and three sides. Concepts that are coordinate may or may not have the same number of defining attributes, depending upon the particular taxonomy of which they are a part.

The hierarchical organization, as shown in Figure 2, for the process concept **observing scientifically** is not a learning hierarchy in the same sense as that dealing with the intellectual skills for subtraction. It results from an analysis of the inquiry skills in science that students should learn to perform during their elementary school years, and not from an analysis of the skills essential to experimenting. However, the arrows do indicate dependency relationships of a noninclusive type among concepts. For example, observing events is essential and prerequisite to drawing inferences about the events and also for classifying the events observed. In this kind of hierarchical organization of concepts, there may or may not be coordinate concepts at certain levels of the hierarchy.

In Figure 2 the solid lines without arrows show a nondependency but not necessarily a coordinate relationship among the concepts. The defining attributes of the concepts and the inclusive—exclusive relationships in a hierarchical organization of concepts are very different from those in a taxonomy.

Bruner (1960) made a useful distinction between the structure of knowledge in a discipline and a structure of knowledge that is learnable by students. However, the latter cannot be derived without the former. Without knowledge of both kinds of structures, one cannot proceed intelligently in the analysis of concepts. At present much of the substance of school subject matters that could be organized into either

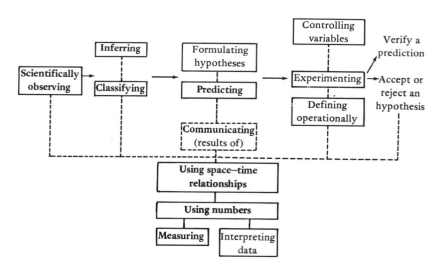

Figure 2. Hierarchy involving observing scientifically (Klausmeier, Swanson, and Sipple, 1976). The process concepts in this figure are drawn from *Science: A process approach* (AAAS Comm. on Science Ed., 1967) however, the figure itself is not. The relationships are presumed to be compatible with the SAPA curricular program. The basic processes as specified by SAPA are boldface, while integrated processes are not. Arrows indicate prerequisite relationships among processes, solid lines connect coordinate or closely-related processes, and dotted lines indicate nonhierarchical linking relationships involving communicating.

taxonomies or hierarchies is not. In the absence of this kind of information, taxonomies and hierarchies are developed by using available printed materials and also by securing assistance from persons with expertise in the particular subject matter. Both the taxonomy and the hierarchy presented in this section were formulated in this manner.

Defining the Concept

Whether or not students will be taught a definition of the word representing the concept, the person conducting an analysis must know or arrive at a societally accepted definition. Further, so that examples and nonexamples may be identified for use in teaching and testing, the meaning of the word should be stated in terms of the defining attributes of the concept represented by the word.

An acceptable definition of a concept that is part of a taxonomy states (a) either the name of the concept supraordinate to the target concept or the defining attributes of the supraordinate concept, and (b) the attributes that are common to all examples of the concept and that distinguish its examples from those of other concepts. In most cases, the name of the concept immediately supraordinate is included as part of the definition. When the supraordinate name does not convey the defining attributes of the supraordinate class (which are also defining attributes of the target concept), it is more appropriate to specify a more inclusive concept name. For example, **geometric figure** may be a more appropriate supraordinate concept than either **isosceles triangle** or **polygon** for the subordinate concept **equilateral triangle**.

Definitions of **equilateral triangle** and **observing scientifically** follow:

Equilateral triangle: A plane, simple, closed figure with three equal sides and three equal angles.

Observing scientifically: Using one or more of the senses in critically examining objects or events and precisely recording data about those objects or events.

The reader will recognize that **observing scientifically** can be treated as a process concept that can be understood, as a process or skill that can be performed, or both. The author treats it as both and presumes that students' understanding it as a concept will facilitate their learning to carry it out as a process. Furthermore, it might be taught to students rotely as a process to be performed without understanding, as Brownell and Moser (1949) found could be done with subtraction.

In generating word definitions we recognize that the same word may represent different concepts, for example, *bear* and *fly;* therefore, one decides the target concept in advance of defining it. Word definitions in terms of defining attributes of concepts cannot always be found in dictionaries. Definitions given in abridged dictionaries are usually synonyms, examples, or uses of the word in context. These also appear in unabridged dictionaries but are useless in determining the defining attributes (Markle, 1975). In arriving at the defining attributes of most concepts the concept analyzer, if not expert in the particular subject matter, uses authoritative printed materials and also may seek the assistance of subject-matter experts.

Specifying the Defining Attributes

The concept analyzer specifies the defining attributes of the concept in order to identify sets of teaching examples and nonexamples (Markle and Tiemann, 1969) and also to teach students an algorithmic strategy for evaluating instances as examples and nonexamples of the concept (to be explained later). Those attributes which are present in every example of a concept and therefore also distinguish the concept examples from examples of all other concepts are called the defining attributes of the concept. Establishing the defining attributes of the concept and arriving at a definition of the word representing the concept proceed simultaneously during a concept analysis.

The defining attributes of **equilateral triangle** and **observing scientifically** follow.

Defining attributes of **equilateral triangle**: (*a*) plane, (*b*) simple, (*c*) closed, (*d*) three equal sides, and (*e*) three equal angles.

Defining attributes of **observing scientifically**: (*a*) using one or more of the senses, (*b*) examining critically, (*c*) recording data precisely.

Specifying the Variable Attributes

The variable attributes of the concept are identified to facilitate the later selection of examples and nonexamples. Examples of the same concept vary widely on their nondefining attributes. For example, reptiles are of many different colors and sizes; fish also vary in color and are of various sizes. The attributes which members of the reptile class and members of the fish class have in common, and which, therefore, may hinder persons in discriminating between the members of the two classes, are called variable attributes. In most previous reports, starting with Bruner, Goodnow, and Austin (1956), they have been called irrelevant attributes.

The first rule for identifying variable attributes is to identify those that are common to the concepts that are coordinate to the target concept. It is these attributes that are present in both the examples and nonexamples of a particular concept and that often lead to errors in classification. The second rule is to identify attributes that may be present in both the target concept and either its supraordinate or subordinate concepts. With concepts that are not part of a taxonomy, one identifies the variable attributes intuitively, selecting those that learners may incorrectly consider as defining attributes of the target concept.

Examples of variable attributes identified for two concepts follow:

Variable attributes for **equilateral triangle**: (*a*) size—small, medium, large, (*b*) orientation on page.

Variable attributes for **observing scientifically**: (*a*) the kinds of objects or events being observed, (*b*) the sense or senses being used, (*c*) the place or situation in which objects or events are being observed, (*d*) the method of recording data.

Selecting Illustrative Examples and Nonexamples

Examples and nonexamples of the concept are needed in teaching the concept and in assessing students' learning of the concept. At least one set (a rational set, as will be described later) of examples and nonexamples is identified during the concept analysis in such a way as to ensure that errors of undergeneralization, overgeneralization, and misconception by the learner will be avoided (Markle, 1975; Markle and Tiemann, 1969). When several concepts of the same taxonomy are taught in a series of lessons, the nonexamples of any one concept are in reality examples of other concepts of the taxonomy. Using examples of concepts of the same taxonomy for nonexamples of the target concept permits the defining attributes to be excluded meaningfully from each nonexample and the variable attributes to be included meaningfully in both the examples and nonexamples.

One cannot deal with examples and nonexamples of concepts in a hierarchy as systematically as in a taxonomy, since there are often neither coordinate nor supraordinate concepts. An intuitive approach is required, and the emphasis is placed more on the selection of examples and nonexamples than on matching the defining and the variable attributes. Descriptions of possible examples and nonexamples of **equilateral triangle** and **observing scientifically** follow:

Examples of **equilateral triangle**: equilateral triangles of various sizes in various spatial orientations.

Nonexamples of **equilaterial triangle**: right triangles, scalene triangles, and quadrilaterals of various sizes in various orientations.

Example of **observing scientifically** (all defining attributes included and explicit): Bill looked at a marshmallow carefully, felt it, tasted it, and smelled it. Then he put it over the flame of a Bunsen burner and watched as it turned from white to black. He smelled it as it burned. After it cooled, he felt it and noticed that it felt crisp. He tasted it and thought that it tasted like charcoal. He recorded these things in his report book.

Nonexample of **observing scientifically** (One or more defining attributes not included): Cecil saw the mailman deliver a box to the principal. Without looking at the label or inside the box, Cecil thought to himself "The principal said he was going to order a new microscope for the school." Cecil saw his friend, Jim, and told him that the new microscope had arrived.

Identifying Illustrative Principles

Concepts are useful to an individual in several ways, as indicated in my earlier chapter in this volume. One especially important use of concepts is in understanding the principles that incorporate the concepts. Understanding principles involving cause-and-effect, correlational, and other relationships among concepts, in turn, makes it possible to explain many events and also, in some cases, to predict and to control (Bruner, 1960; Klausmeier, Ghatala, and Frayer, 1974). Understanding principles facilitates the solution of problems. It is useful, therefore, to identify illustrative principles of which the target concept is a part to promote transfer of concept learning to the understanding of principles. Illustrative principles related to **equilateral triangle** and **observing scientifically** follow.

Illustrative Principles Involving Equilateral Triangle:

1. All equilateral triangles are similar (in shape).
2. If the three angles of a triangle are equal in the number of degrees, the sides of the triangle are of equal length.
3. If the three sides of a triangle are of equal length, the angles of the triangle are equal in the number of degrees.
4. A line that bisects any angle of an equilateral triangle forms two equal angles (and lines) when it intersects the opposite side.
5. The perimeter of an equilateral triangle is three times the length of any side.

Illustrative Principles Involving Observing Scientifically:

1. Observing objects and events is a prerequisite for drawing inferences regarding them.
2. Using more than one of the senses in observing objects and events increases the probability of gaining more precise information.
3. Quantitative observation permits drawing more precise inferences than does qualitative observation.

Examination of the principles indicates that each one expresses a relationship between the target concept and another one in the taxonomy or hierarchy, between the target concept and one or more of its defining attributes, or between the target concept and a less closely related concept. There appear to be no rules for arriving at a set of illustrative principles. However, once a principle is identified, correct applications and misapplications can be identified and used in teaching the principle (Feldman, 1974; Katz, 1976).

Formulating Illustrative Problem-Solving Exercises

As part of a concept analysis, problem-solving exercises are formulated, the solutions of which presumably are facilitated by understanding the target concept and applying knowledge of a principle or a combination of principles. No attempt is made to make the problem-solving exercises of equal difficulty. On the contrary, a range of difficulty is preferable in the analysis so that additional examples of an appropriate level of difficulty can later be prepared for a particular target population of students.

Problem-solving exercises for **equilateral triangle** and for **observing scientifically** follow:

*Illustrative Problem for **Equilaterial Triangle**:*

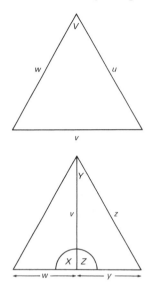

Sides *u*, *v* and *w* are of equal length. How many degrees are in angle *V*?

a. 60°
b. 90°
c. 120°
d. It is impossible to tell without measuring.
e. I don't know.

Line *v* bisects the upper angle of this equilateral triangle. Suppose that side *z* is 2 inches long. How many degrees are in angle *Y*?

a. 30°
b. 60°
c. 90°
d. It is impossible to tell without measuring.
e. I don't know.

*Illustrative Problem for **Observing Scientifically**:*

Below are drawings of a growing plant. It was marked on Day 1 and again on Day 3.

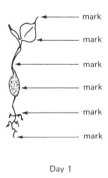

Day 1

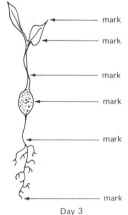

Day 3

Which part grew the most in the two days: (a) the leaf, (b) the stem, (c) the part of the root close to the seed, or (d) the part of the root near the end or tip?

Developing a Vocabulary List

The rule for generating a vocabulary list as part of a concept analysis is to include the name of the concept and the key terms of the defining attributes. The extent to which the terms will be used in teaching a particular concept varies greatly according to the level of attainment desired. None of the vocabulary may be used at the concrete level; all of it must be used at the formal level. Students' knowledge of the name of the concept and the names of its defining attributes has shown a high, positive correlation with the level of concept attainment and also with the uses of concepts (Klausmeier, Sipple, and Allen, 1974a, b). The lists for **equilateral triangle** and **observing scientifically** follow:

Vocabulary for **equilateral triangle**: angle, side, equal, equilateral, triangle, figure, closed, plane, simple.

Vocabulary for **observing scientifically**: observing, scientifically, senses, critically, examine, record, accurately, data, information, precisely.

A BEHAVIORAL ANALYSIS PERTAINING TO CONCEPTS

A behavioral analysis to identify the mental operations prerequisite for attaining concepts has been conducted and reported (Klausmeier, Ghatala, and Frayer, 1974). The mental operations presumed to be essential for attaining concepts at each of four successively higher levels, as given in my earlier chapter, were identified through a behavioral analysis of concept learning tasks and by a review and synthesis of research related to the learning of concepts. The operations are presumed to be the same for all concepts; however, the age at which the operations can be performed on different concepts by the same individual varies markedly (Klausmeier, Sipple, and Allen, 1974a, b). Students are able to perform the operations earlier on concepts for which there are observable examples in the environment, for example, *tree, ant*; and later for concepts which have examples that are represented only symbolically, for example, *noun, numeral.*

To attain a concept at any particular level, learners must be capable of performing the mental operations essential for attaining that level, must have attained the concept at the prior level or be able to do so, and must demonstrate the mental operations of the prior level. These are also considered as the internal conditions that are prerequisite for attaining each level. The specific mental operations for each level are given later when discussing instructional conditions so that the internal conditions pertaining to the levels may be related to the instructional conditions for the same levels.

AN INSTRUCTIONAL ANALYSIS
PERTAINING TO CONCEPTS

An instructional analysis is conducted to identify the instructional conditions that facilitate concept learning. In the analysis, such variables are considered as the characteristics of the learners, the level at which the concept is to be attained, the quality of instructional materials, and the amount of teacher guidance to be provided. Results of relevant research, as well as analyses of learning situations, are incorporated in an analysis. In this section, a brief overview is given of the instructional conditions that facilitate teaching the same concept at successive levels of attainment. The conditions were reported in preliminary form by Klausmeier, Ghatala, and Frayer (1974).

The analysis of instructional conditions led to emphasizing an inductive approach to instruction at the concrete and identity levels. An expository approach receives more emphasis at the formal level.

In an inductive instructional approach, examples and nonexamples of the concept are presented and the learner is instructed to infer either the concept, some of its attributes, or its definition. In an expository approach the learner, early in the instructional sequence, is given the name of the concept and its definition; also, the defining attributes are named and pointed out and some examples and nonexamples are presented. In a combined aproach the learner receives information in an expository manner, processes it, and then proceeds inductively in identifying examples and nonexamples of the concept and in using the concept in understanding principles and in solving problems.

Concrete and Identity Levels

Attaining a concept at the concrete level involves attending to an object, discriminating that object from other objects, and subsequently recognizing the object as the same one experienced before. At the identity level the object is generalized as the same thing when experienced from a different spatio-temporal perspective or when sensed in a different modality. Acquiring the name of the concept and associating the name with the object may come almost simultaneously with learning the concept at these levels.

The following instructional conditions appear to facilitate attainment at these two levels:

1. Present the actual thing—inanimate object, animate object, perceptible event or process, quality or condition—or a pictorial representation of it, and also one or two nonexamples of it.

2. Give the name of the thing and aid the learner to associate the name and the thing.
3. Provide for immediate informative feedback regarding correct identification of the thing and also for correct naming.
4. Present the thing later and elicit the child's response to it.
5. Repeat the preceding sequence as necessary.

Persons who have seen *Sesame Street* recognize that the preceding conditions have been incorporated into the television program. In *Sesame Street*, representations of numerical concepts such as *one* and *two*, the symbols representing the letters of the alphabet, actual examples of conditions such as *above* and *between*, and actual examples of qualites such as *red* and *soft* (as well as other concepts), are taught in a delightful manner. The name of the concept is given orally or in written form almost simultaneously with the presentation of the example. Nonexamples other than examples of other concepts also being taught are used sparingly, apparently to avoid confusing the young viewers. There is feedback to the viewers so that they can determine whether their covert mental responses, or their overt responses, are correct or incorrect. *Sesame Street* provides for a great deal of repetition and practice within each lesson and also across various lessons.

Beginning Classificatory Level

The lowest attainment of a concept at the classificatory level is inferred when a person recognizes two different things as being equivalent in some way. Persons are still at the classificatory level when they can properly identify many instances as examples and nonexamples, but cannot state explicitly the basis of their categorizing in terms of the presence of the defining attributes in the examples and the absence of one or more of the defining attributes in the nonexamples. The new operation involved in attainment at the classificatory level is generalizing that two or more different instances are equivalent in some way. The instructional conditions that facilitate attainment of concepts at the beginning classificatory level follow:

1. Assure that the concept has been attained at the identity level.
2. Present at least two examples and one or two nonexamples of the concept.
3. Give the name of the concept and aid the learner to associate the name of the concept with the examples.
4. Using an inductive method, supplemented with an expository method as necessary, aid the learner to discriminate and name some of the defining attributes of the concept.

5. Using an inductive method, supplemented with an expository method as necessary, aid the learner to define the concept.
6. Provide for informative feedback.
7. Arrange for use of the concept in recognizing newly encountered things as examples or nonexamples.
8. Repeat the preceding sequence as necessary.

With most concepts, several years elapse between the time children first attain a concept at the beginning classificatory level and the time they are capable of the operations essential to attaining the same concept at the formal level. During these years the children will have received formal or informal instruction so that they will be able to identify many different examples, and they will also have formed other concepts of which the nonexamples are members. The kind of instruction that aids students to move from the immature to the more mature phase of the classificatory level through use of printed instruction materials, along with oral instruction and other techniques is described next.

Mature Classificatory Level and Formal Level

Printed instructional materials for teaching concepts can be used effectively with students who can read and who have already attained the target concept at the beginning classificatory level. The materials may be used to aid students to classify more correctly and extensively at the classificatory level, to attain a beginning formal level, and to attain an adult formal level—as research by graduate students and other project staff working with the author at the Wisconsin Research and Development Center for Cognitive Learning has demonstrated. In one controlled classroom experiment that employed two experimental groups and two control groups, McMurray, Bernard, and Klausmeier (1975), prepared and used two lessons to teach fourth-grade students the concept, **equilateral triangle.** Each lesson required about 35 minutes to complete. Of the two experimental groups that received the lessons, 60% and 64% attained the formal level, whereas only 7% and 11% of two control groups did. Two months later the experimental group had maintained this high level of attainment, and the control groups had increased their level of attainment only slightly. The achievement of the two fourth-grade experimental groups compares favorably with that of sixth-grade students participating in a longitudinal study who had not received the lessons (Klausmeier, Sipple, and Allen, 1974a, b). Klausmeier, Schilling, and Feldman (1976) conducted a similar experiment using two lessons dealing with the concept, **tree.** The two experimental groups of second-semester, third-grade students performed significantly higher than two control groups.

Bernard (1976) prepared and used three lessons to teach high school seniors a set of eight concepts organized in a taxonomy dealing with behavior modification procedures. These lessons incorporated the same five procedures as in the earlier mentioned lessons: namely, a concept definition, attribute prompting, rational sets of examples and nonexamples, a strategy for evaluating instances, and feedback. In addition, an advance organizer and within-text questions were used in the experimental lessons. A control group in this study scored 30% correct on the dependent measures; the students receiving the most powerful lesson—one incorporating all the variables mentioned—scored 70%.

Sufficient knowledge has accrued from the preceding studies, and from others so that the guidelines for instruction which follow can be regarded as fully validated. It is also clear that these guidelines can be incorporated into printed materials. Whether teachers can incorporate the guidelines into their instructional procedures without the support of carefully prepared printed materials has not been determined empirically.

1. Establish an intention to learn concepts. An intention to learn concepts is developed before the student tries to learn a particular concept. This is done by telling the students that they will be learning concepts, by pointing out important features of concept learning, or by describing the concept population comprising the taxonomy or hierarchy. Amster (1966), Fredrick and Klausmeier (1968), Kalish (1966), Laughlin, Doherty, and Dunn (1968), and Osler and Weiss (1962) have all reported facilitative effects from instructions designed to establish an intent to learn concepts. Ausubel (1968) has demonstrated the facilitative effects of advance organizers on learning various kinds of new materials and Bernard (1976) has shown the facilitative effects of an advance organizer on learning a taxonomy of concepts.

Establishing an intention to learn concepts (as opposed, for example, to establishing a set to memorize the individual instances) activates several operations essential to attaining concepts at the classificatory and formal levels. First, such instructions may alert the learners that they should attend to and discriminate the attributes of instances. Second, such instructions may engage the learners in an active search for the attributes which distinguish instances from noninstances. At the outset, then, the learner is engaged actively in searching behaviors directed towards learning the particular concept or concepts at a higher level of attainment.

2. Elicit student verbalization of the concept name and the defining attributes. To accomplish this, a vocabulary list is presented at the

beginning of a series of lessons and the students are taught to recognize the words. Having the concept and attribute labels greatly facilitates carrying out both inductive and deductive operations at the formal level of attainment, including formulating, remembering, and evaluating hypotheses and assimilating and processing information that is presented verbally in an expository approach to instruction. Linguistic codes are maximally efficient for carrying out the sequential information processing that is involved in inferring concepts from examples and nonexamples inductively—and also for assimilating the information as presented in a definition, a set of verbal examples and nonexamples of the concepts, and in verbal explanations or descriptions. Clark (1971) reported facilitation of concept attainment through giving the label of the concept and/or the labels of its defining attributes. When printed material is used, the students must not only be able to use the terms orally; they must also be able to read them.

3. Present a definition of the concept in terms of defining attributes, stated in vocabulary appropriate to the target population. Providing students with the concept definition eliminates the operations involved in identifying the defining attributes of the concept and inferring the concept from experiences with examples and nonexamples of the concept. However, simply presenting students with the concept definition does not insure concept attainment—the students may merely acquire a rotely memorized string of verbal associations. To insure that the students acquire a concept and not a string of words, at a minimum they must also be presented with concept examples and nonexamples to classify. Correct classification requires that the students differentiate examples from nonexamples on the basis of the defining attributes contained in the concept definition. Thus, both discriminating the attributes of instances and evaluating instances to determine whether or not they exhibit the defining attributes contained in the definition are operations which the students should perform after they are given the concept definition.

The facilitative effect of a definition is a function of several variables, including the number of rational sets of examples and nonexamples presented. In a controlled experiment with fourth-grade students Klausmeier and Feldman (1975) found a definition to have about the same amount of facilitation as one rational set of examples and nonexamples. A definition combined with one rational set was more effective than a definition or a rational set alone; and a definition combined with three rational sets showed greatest facilitation.

A definition must be stated in appropriate terminology. Feldman and Klausmeier (1974) found a common usage definition to be more effective than a technically stated definition with fourth-graders; whereas the technically-stated definition was more effective with eighth-graders. Feldman (1972), and Merrill and Tennyson (1971) also reported a facilitative effect for definitions.

4. Present at least one rational set of properly matched examples and nonexamples of varying difficulty level.

A rational set of examples and nonexamples was defined initially by Markle and Tiemann (1969). We define a rational set slightly different from Markle and Tiemann to include as many nonexamples as there are defining attributes of the concept and as many examples as there are variable attributes. Each nonexample should have at least one defining attribute and may have only one fewer defining attributes than examples have. Each example should have at least one variable attribute that is also present in one or more nonexamples of the concept and some examples may have more than one variable attribute. A sufficient number of sets should be included so that students learn the concept to the level desired.

In presenting each rational set, each example should be matched with a nonexample having the same variable attribute or attributes. The difficulty level within a set should range from easy to difficult and yet be appropriate to the target population of students. The use of rational sets effectively reduces and eventually eliminates errors of undergeneralization, overgeneralization, and misconception (Feldman, 1972; Markle and Tiemann, 1969; Merrill and Tennyson, 1971; Swanson, 1972; Tennyson, 1973; and Tennyson, Woolley, and Merrill, 1972). It is noted that matching examples and nonexamples in difficulty, and also in both variable and defining attributes cannot be dealt with as precisely with all concepts as with those reported in the preceding experiments.

5. Emphasize the defining attributes of the concept by drawing the students' attention to them. Giving students the names of the defining attributes of the concept in the concept definition is insufficient for teaching them to discriminate the defining attributes and to use them subsequently in differentiating examples from nonexamples of the concept. Frayer (1970) found that emphasizing the defining attributes by verbal cues improved immediate concept learning and later transfer and retention.

Merrill and Tennyson (1971) compared the effects of a concept definition, a definition of the attributes of the concept, a rational set of examples and nonexamples, and attribute prompting singly and in various combinations. Attribute prompting was found to be more facilitative than a definition of the concept or definitions of the attributes. The most effective condition included all four variables. Clark (1971) reported that a large majority of researchers obtained beneficial effects by directing the students' attention to the concept attributes and/or the conceptual rule; also, pointing out the attributes and rules to the students yielded better results than permitting the students to discover them themselves.

6. Provide a strategy for differentiating examples and nonexamples. Bruner, Goodnow, and Austin (1956) described various reception and selection strategies that students learn incidentally, without instruction concerning the strategies. Fredrick and Klausmeier (1968), and Klausmeier and Meinke (1968) reported the facilitative effects of teaching students strategies for attaining concepts. Bernard (1976), McMurray, Bernard, and Klausmeier (1975), and Klausmeier, Schilling, and Feldman (1976), incorporated the same strategy for evaluating instances as examples or nonexamples in their experimental lessons with excellent results. Teaching the efficient strategy in the printed material insures that an effective strategy will be learned and eliminates much trial-and-error learning. Providing for the students to use the strategy in identifying examples and nonexamples and providing feedback promotes active learning of the strategy. In this connection, students of low socioeconomic status do not learn mature conceptualizing skills related to certain subject matters unless they receive appropriate instruction during the school years in those subject matters (Nelson and Klausmeier, 1974).

7. Provide for feedback concerning the correctness and incorrectness of the responses. Clark (1971), Frayer and Klausmeier (1971), Markle (1975), and Sweet (1966) report the desirable effects of feedback to students. Clark (1971), for example, reported that concept attainment improved as the frequency of feedback increased. Frayer and Klausmeier (1971) reported from their survey of research that feedback should be provided after every response, but that it is most important after an incorrect response. Feedback that tells the students not only that a response or hypothesis is wrong, but which also enables them to infer *how* it is wrong and how to correct it is particularly helpful.

Illustrative Lessons

A combined expository–inductive approach to teaching the concept **equilateral triangle** at the formal level follows, to illustrate how the previously described instructional conditions were incorporated into printed materials. Two instructional lessons were developed dealing with the concept **equilateral triangle** for use in an experiment involving fourth-grade children from two elementary schools (McMurray, Bernard, and Klausmeier, 1975).

In the first lesson the children were taught to recognize the words in the vocabulary list and to discriminate and label the defining attributes of the concept. The word list contained all of the words used in the defining attributes and a few others: equilateral, triangle, definition, attributes, angle, length, equal, plane, closed, simple, straight, figure, connect. Teaching the students to discriminate the attributes and to learn the labels followed this sequence: First, the preceding word list was read aloud; second, each word representing an attribute was defined and illustrated through the use of examples and nonexamples; third, the children represented each attribute by connecting dots placed on a page; and fourth, the children were shown drawings of figures and were instructed to indicate whether each figure had a particular defining attribute. Immediate feedback was provided in the material and indicated to the children whether their answers were correct as well as giving the rationale behind the answer.

The beginning of the second lesson was devoted to a review of the previous day's material, after which a definition of the concept was presented and explained. The children were then instructed to draw several equilateral triangles using the defining attributes presented in the definition. Part of a page of a lesson follows to illustrate how the definition was presented:

In this lesson you will learn about a special kind of figure. It is called an equilateral triangle. These figures are equilateral triangles:

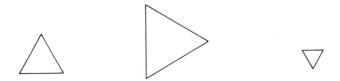

You will learn five important things about equilateral triangles. Equilateral triangles have

1. three straight sides of equal length
2. three equal angles

They are

3. plane
4. closed
5. simple

You will learn about these five things by looking at some figures. You will draw some figures that are outlined in dots. You will also draw some figures by following the numbered dots. You will need to learn and REMEMBER the names of the five important things about equilateral triangles.

Later in the second lesson two rational sets of paired examples and nonexamples were presented that ranged from difficult to easy. Also, explanations were provided as to why particular geometric figures were or were not equilateral triangles. A rational set follows:

Yesterday you learned some things about figures. You learned that some figures have *three straight sides of equal length*.

yes   no

You also learned about angles:

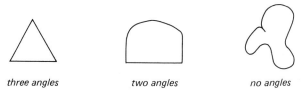

three angles   two angles   no angles

Some angles are the same size. They are equal angles.

equal   not equal

You learned that some figures have *three equal angles*.

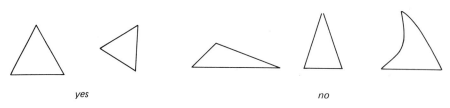

yes   no

You learned that *plane* figures are flat.

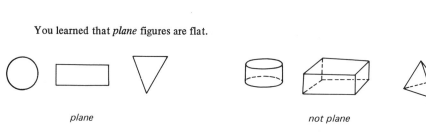

plane   not plane

You also learned about *closed* figures. If you trace them you would come back to where you started.

closed   *not closed*

Remember *simple* figures? Simple figures do *not* have lines or sides that cross.

simple   *not simple*

You learned five important things about a special figure. Say the five things to yourself. What is the name of the figure?

three straight sides of equal length + three equal angles + plane + closed + simple = **equilateral triangle**

Finally, the children were taught a strategy for evaluating examples and nonexamples in terms of whether the instance manifested the five defining attributes of the concept in a conjunctive fashion. The strategy that was taught involved presenting sets of five questions, which the children answered in order to evaluate systematically whether a geometric figure was a member of the class **equilateral triangle**:

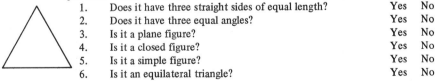

Remember, your job is to tell if the figure is an equilateral triangle. Be sure to circle yes or no to each of the five questions. Then circle yes or no after the question: Is it an equilateral triangle?

		Yes	No
1.	Does it have three straight sides of equal length?	Yes	No
2.	Does it have three equal angles?	Yes	No
3.	Is it a plane figure?	Yes	No
4.	Is it a closed figure?	Yes	No
5.	Is it a simple figure?	Yes	No
6.	Is it an equilateral triangle?	Yes	No

Students were told that they could determine that instances were equilateral triangles when all five questions could be answered affirmatively.

INSTRUCTIONAL PROGRAMMING FOR THE INDIVIDUAL STUDENT

It is probable that nearly all students at all school levels need some instruction from teachers to learn concepts effectively. Printed materials, while helpful to students who can read and can attain concepts at a

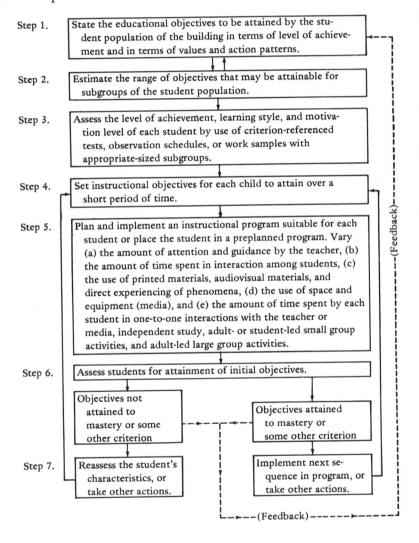

Step 1. State the educational objectives to be attained by the student population of the building in terms of level of achievement and in terms of values and action patterns.

Step 2. Estimate the range of objectives that may be attainable for subgroups of the student population.

Step 3. Assess the level of achievement, learning style, and motivation level of each student by use of criterion-referenced tests, observation schedules, or work samples with appropriate-sized subgroups.

Step 4. Set instructional objectives for each child to attain over a short period of time.

Step 5. Plan and implement an instructional program suitable for each student or place the student in a preplanned program. Vary (a) the amount of attention and guidance by the teacher, (b) the amount of time spent in interaction among students, (c) the use of printed materials, audiovisual materials, and direct experiencing of phenomena, (d) the use of space and equipment (media), and (e) the amount of time spent by each student in one-to-one interactions with the teacher or media, independent study, adult- or student-led small group activities, and adult-led large group activities.

Step 6. Assess students for attainment of initial objectives.

Objectives not attained to mastery or some other criterion

Objectives attained to mastery or some other criterion

Step 7. Reassess the student's characteristics, or take other actions.

Implement next sequence in program, or take other actions.

(Feedback)

Figure 3. Instructional programming model in IGE (Adapted from Herbert J. Klausmeier, Mary R. Quilling, Juanita S. Sorenson, Russell S. Way and George R. Glasrud, *Individually Guided Education in the Multiunit School: Guidelines for Implementation*. Madison, Wisc.: Wisconsin Research and Development Center for Cognitive Learning, 1971, p. 19).

beginning classificatory level, are not sufficient to keep the students motivated or to provide actual examples of concepts. Moreover, students of the same age or grade in schools cannot be taught effectively in classroom-size groups. To provide effectively for individual students to attain concepts and other learning outcomes according to their own varying rates and styles, a model for instructional programming, as shown in Figure 3, was formulated (Klausmeier, Quilling, Sorenson, Way, and Glasrud, 1971; Klausmeier, 1975). Our purpose is not to explain the model fully, inasmuch as sets of multimedia materials dealing with mathematics, science, and social studies have been developed for this purpose (Klausmeier, 1975). It is pointed out that in carrying out Step 5 of the model teachers need high quality printed materials to teach concepts, principles, and problem-solving skills. Accumulated knowledge concerning instructional design and the teaching of concepts appears to be sufficient to start developing these materials in the various curricular areas.

REFERENCES

Amster, H. Effect of instructional set and variety of instances on children's learning. *Journal of Educational Psychology*, 1966, *57*, 74–85.

Ausubel, D. P. *Educational psychology: A cognitive view*. New York: Holt, Rinehart and Winston, 1968.

Bernard, M. E. *The effect of advance organizers and within-text questions on the learning of a taxonomy of concepts*. Technical Report No. 357. Madison, Wisc.: Wisconsin Research and Development Center for Cognitive Learning, 1976.

Bourne, L. E., Ekstrand, B. R., & Dominowski, R. L. *The psychology of thinking*. Englewood Cliffs, N.J.: Prentice-Hall, 1971.

Brownell, W. A., & Moser, H. E. *Meaningful versus mechanical learning: A study in grade III subtraction*. (Duke, University Studies in Education, No. 8.) Durham, N. C.: Duke University Press, 1949.

Bruner, J. S. *The process of education*. Cambridge: Harvard University Press, 1960.

Bruner, J. S., Goodnow, J. J. & Austin, G. A. *A study of thinking*. New York: John Wiley & Sons, 1956.

Carroll, J. B. Words, meanings, and concepts. *Harvard Educational Review*, 1964, *34*, 178–202.

Clark, D. C. Teaching concepts in the classroom: A set of prescriptions derived from experimental research. *Journal of Educational Psychology Monograph*, 1971, *62*, 253–278.

Feldman, K. V. *Instructional factors relating to children's principle learning*. Technical Report No. 309. Madison, Wisc.: Wisconsin Research and Development Center for Cognitive Learning, 1974.

Feldman, K. V. *The effects of number of positive and negative instances, concept definition, and emphasis of relevant attributes on the attainment of mathematical concepts*. Technical Report No. 243. Madison, Wisc.: Wisconsin Research and Development Center for Cognitive Learning, 1972.

Feldman, K. V., & Klausmeier, H. J. Effects of two kinds of definition on the concept attainment of fourth and eighth graders. *Journal of Educational Research*, 1974, *67*, 219–223.

Frayer, D. A. *Effects of number of instances and emphasis of relevant attribute values on mastery of geometric concepts by fourth- and sixth-grade children.* Technical Report No. 116. Madison, Wisc.: Wisconsin Research and Development Center for Cognitive Learning, 1970.

Frayer, D. A., & Klausmeier, H. J. *Variables in concept learning: Task variables.* Theoretical Paper No. 28. Madison, Wisc.: Wisconsin Research and Development Center for Cognitive Learning, 1971.

Fredrick, W. C., & Klausmeier, H. J. Instructions and labels in a concept attainment task. *Psychological Reports,* 1968, *23,* 1339–1342.

Gagné, R. M. Learning hierarchies. *Educational psychologist,* 1968, *6,* 1–9.

Gagné, R. M. *Essentials of learning for instruction.* Hinsdale, Ill.: Dryden Press, 1974.

Gagné, R. M. The acquisition of knowledge. *Psychological Review,* 1962, *69,* 355–365.

Gagné, R. M. *The conditions of learning* (2nd ed.). New York: Holt, Rinehart & Winston, 1970.

Gagné, R. M., & Briggs, L. J. *Principles of instructional design.* New York: Holt, Rinehart & Winston, 1974.

Glaser, R., & Resnick, L. B. Instructional psychology. In P. Mussen & M. Rosenzweig (Eds.), *Annual review of psychology.* Palo Alto, Ca.: Annual Reviews, Inc., 1972. Vol. *23,* pp. 207–276.

Kagan, J. A developmental approach to conceptual growth. In H. J. Klausmeier & C. W. Harris (Eds.), *Analyses of concept learning.* New York: Academic Press, 1966, Pp. 97–116.

Kalish, P. W. *Concept attainment as a function of monetary incentives, competition, and instructions.* Technical Report No. 8. Madison, Wisc.: Wisconsin Research and Development Center for Cognitive Learning, 1966.

Katz, Selena. *The effects of each of five instructional treatments on the learning of principles by children.* Technical Report No. 381. Madison, Wisc.: Wisconsin Research and Development Center for Cognitive Learning, 1976.

Klausmeier, H. J. IGE: An alternative form of schooling. In H. Talmage (Ed.), *Systems of individualized education,* The National Society for the Study of Education series on contemporary educational issues. Berkeley: McCutchan Pub., 1975, 48–83.

Klausmeier, H. J., & Feldman, K. V. Effects of a definition and a varying number of examples and nonexamples on concept attainment. *Journal of Educational Psychology,* 1975, *67,* 174–178.

Klausmeier, H. J., Ghatala, E. S., & Frayer, D. A. *Conceptual learning and development: A cognitive view.* New York: Academic Press, 1974.

Klausmeier, H. J. & Goodwin, W. *Learning and human abilities: Educational psychology* (4th ed.). New York: Harper & Row, 1975.

Klausmeier, H. J., & Meinke, D. L. Concept attainment as a function of instructions concerning the stimulus material, a strategy, and a principle for securing information. *Journal of Educational Psychology,* 1968, *59,* 215–222.

Klausmeier, H. J., Quilling, M. R., Sorenson, J. S., Way, R. S., & Glasrud, G. R. *Individually guided education and the multiunit elementary school: Guidelines for implementation.* Madison, Wisc.: Wisconsin Research and Development Center for Cognitive Learning, 1971.

Klausmeier, H. J., Schilling, J., & Feldman, K. V. *The effectiveness of experimental lessons in accelerating children's attainment of the concept tree.* Technical Report No. 372. Madison, Wisc.: Wisconsin Research and Development Center for Cognitive Learning, 1976.

Klausmeier, H. J., Sipple, T. S., & Allen, P. S. *First cross sectional study of attainment of the concepts equilateral triangle, cutting tool, and noun by children age 5 to 16 of city A.* Technical Report No. 287. Madison, Wisc.: Wisconsin Research and Development Center for Cognitive Learning, 1974(a).

Klausmeier, H. J., Sipple, T. S. & Allen, P. S. *First cross sectional study of attainment of the concepts equilateral triangle and cutting tool by children age 5 to 16 of city B.* Technical Report No. 288. Madison, Wisc.: Wisconsin Research and Development Center for Cognitive Learning, 1974(b).

Klausmeier, H. J., Swanson, J. E., & Sipple, T. S. *Analysis of basic process concepts of elementary science.* Working Paper No. 167. Madison, Wisc.: Wisconsin Research and Development Center for Cognitive Learning, 1976.

Laughlin, P. R., Doherty, M. A., & Dunn, R. F. Intentional and incidental concept formation as a function of motivation, creativity, intelligence, and sex. *Journal of Personality and Social Psychology,* 1968, *8,* 401–409.

Markle, S. M. They teach concepts, don't they? *Educational Researcher,* 1975, *4,* 3–9.

Markle, S. M. & Tiemann, P. W. *Really understanding concepts: Or in frumious pursuit of the jabberwock.* Champaign, Ill.: Stipes, 1969.

McMurray, N. E., Bernard, M. E., & Klausmeier, H. J. *An instructional design for accelerating children's attainment of the concept equilateral triangle.* Technical Report No. 321. Madison, Wisc.: Wisconsin Research and Development Center for Cognitive Learning, 1975.

Merrill, M. D. (Ed.). *Instructional design: Readings.* Englewood Cliffs, N.J.: Prentice-Hall, 1971.

Merrill, M. D., & Tennyson, R. D. *Attribute prompting errors as a function of relationships between positive and negative instances.* Working Paper No. 28. Provo, Utah: Instructional Research and Development, Brigham Young University, 1971.

National Society for the Study of Education. *Learning and instruction,* Forty-Ninth Yearbook, Part I. Chicago: University of Chicago Press, 1950.

Nelson, G. K., & Klausmeier, H. J. Classificatory behaviors of low-socioeconomic-status children. *Journal of Educational Psychology.* 1974, *66,* 432–438.

Osler, S. F., & Weiss, S. R. Studies in concept attainment: III. Effect of instructions at two levels of intelligence. *Journal of Experimental Psychology,* 1962, *63,* 528–533.

Page, E. B. Teacher comments and student performance: A 74 classroom experiment in school motivation. *Journal of Educational Psychology,* 1958, *49,* 173–181.

Swanson, J. E. *The effects of number of positive and negative instances, concept definition, and emphasis of relevant attributes on the attainment of three environmental concepts by sixth-grade children.* Technical Report No. 244. Madison, Wisc.: Wisconsin Research and Development Center for Cognitive Learning, 1972.

Sweet, R. C. *Educational attainment and attitudes toward school as a function of feedback in the form of teachers' written comments.* Technical Report No. 15. Madison, Wisc.: Wisconsin Research and Development Center for Cognitive Learning, 1966.

Tennyson, R. D. Effect of negative instances in concept acquisition using a verbal-learning task. *Journal of Educational Psychology,* 1973, *64,* 247–260.

Tennyson, R. D., Woolley, F. R., & Merrill, M. D. Exemplar and nonexemplar variables which produce correct concept classification behavior and specified classification errors. *Journal of Educational Psychology,* 1972, *63,* 144–152.

CHAPTER 8

Research and Development
in Training Creative Thinking

Gary A. Davis

The research and development activities described here are based upon two very important features of creative thinking and of the creative person. First, we assume that the single most important characteristic of the highly creative individual is creative *attitudes*. The concept of creative attitudes is broadly defined to include purposes, values, and a number of personality traits which together predispose an individual to think in an independent, flexible, and imaginative way. As explained below, these attitudes are absolutely essential for creativity and in fact lie at the core of every creative problem-solving course or program, from Torrance's elementary school exercises (Myers and Torrance, 1965, 1966; Torrance and Myers, 1970) to the Lockheed—Georgia (1971) courses for engineering and design.

The second component of creativity is *techniques.* There is a substantial literature stemming from professional problem solving in advertising (Osborn,[1] 1963), invention design (Alexander, 1965; Gordon, 1961; Prince, 1971), journalism (Crawford, 1954), and other areas which describes conscious methods for producing new idea combinations. Most of these creative thinking techniques, such as brainstorming, attribute listing, checklisting, and the metaphor-based synectics methods, were initially derived from the introspective reports of creative individuals. Essentially, these procedures are "unconscious" methods that have been specified and operationalized. We normally use such "forced" techniques to supplement our intuitive supply of problem solutions.

The global goal of the creativity project, then, was to: (*a*) identify important and perhaps trainable attitudes and related affective dimen-

---

[1] Alex Osborn, inventor of brainstorming, was a cofounder of Batten, Barton, Durstin, and Osborn, successful New York advertising agency, and founder of the Creative Education Foundation.

sions of creativity, (*b*) simplify and evaluate some professional creative thinking techniques, and (*c*) incorporate these into three attractive workbooks designed for upper elementary and junior high school students. Preliminary basic research with college student subjects examined mainly the effectiveness of different creative thinking techniques.

CREATIVE PROBLEM-SOLVING MODEL

Creative Attitudes

One of our basic assumptions is that using one's imagination in creative problem-solving is in part a voluntary act. Probably all creative people use their imaginations consciously and deliberately, try to be flexible and open-minded, and typically show a keen interest in new ideas, far-fetched or not. One experiment examined the deliberate control which individuals have over their creativeness (Manske and Davis, 1968). Thirty college students listed unusual uses for a wire coat hanger, a screwdriver, or an automobile tire under different instructional constraints. The subjects were allowed 10 minutes to list their ideas for a given product. Each idea was rated according to how "original" and how "practical" it was. Every subject thus received an average originality and practicality score, along with a frequency (number of ideas) score. Briefly, we found that college students could voluntarily and significantly adjust their creativity test responses in accord with the instructions. When asked to "be original" the students tended to give original answers. When the same students were instructed to "be practical" their ideas tended to be rated as more practical. When they were instructed to "be wild" their ideas turned out not to be more original than those produced under neutral instructions, but they listed almost twice as many. Wallach and Kogan (1965) similarly concluded that highly intelligent but not highly creative students were disinclined rather than unable to use their imaginations. There does indeed seem to be a conscious predisposition of creative people to regularly and voluntarily use their creative imaginations. One of the single most important purpose of the creativity training materials described below is to strengthen students' tendencies deliberately and consciously to think in a more creative and flexible fashion.

The creative person also may be aware of *barriers* to creative thinking that prevent him/her from taking a fresh and innovative approach to a problem. Compared with the average person, the creative person usually is more conscious of conformity pressures, regulations, traditions, habitual ways of perceiving and responding, and generally "doing things the way they have always been done." It is accepted by creativity-oriented educators, such as E. Paul Torrance and Sidney Parnes, that the processes of "proper" education and socialization work counter to open, and often playful, creative development. There is a strong need for creative exercises, activities, and a heightened "creative awareness" to compensate for this loss.

Turning to other attitudes and traits of creative thinkers, the highly creative person almost by definition is a one-of-a-kind, unique individual. Nonetheless, there is a fairly recurrent syndrome which most creative people seem to share. For example, one who innovates necessarily must be willing to try out new ideas, to gamble on their feasibility and acceptability. The further he/she departs from standard methods, the greater is the risk of failure. It is not surprising that research has shown the highly creative person to be strong in independence, self-confidence, nonconformity, and willingness to take risks. Playfulness, too, and a good sense of humor often characterize the creative thinker. Many imaginative ideas come from toying with a seemingly ridiculous solution to make it workable, from looking at a problem upside down, or from climbing inside the problem in order to think like an electron, a canning machine, a piccolo, or a blob of oil paint (e.g., Gordon, 1961; Prince, 1971). It is said that ". . . in the creative adult, the child remains fully alive [Barron, 1969]." The problem is that most of us grow up and lose our fresh childlike view of the world.[2]

All three of our training programs use humor not only to maintain interest but to encourage a playful and an unhibited approach to creative thinking. A *creative atmosphere* depends almost totally upon a sense of freedom to innovate and explore without fear of evaluation. If students believe they will be criticized, ridiculed, or otherwise threatened, they will simply turn off their creative expressions. At the very least they will delay their creative activity until they find a safer environment—perhaps a basement workshop, a public library, the privacy of their own rooms, or someone else's more receptive classroom. Carl Rogers used the term *psychological freedom* to describe this basic attitudinal prerequisite to creative activity.

It would appear difficult to strengthen such major personality traits as independence, self-confidence, unconventionality, or risk-taking with any sort of short-term creativity training episode. However, Parnes (1971) reports changes in precisely these traits after a short course in creative problem-solving attitudes and methods. It seems likely then, that a student who becomes more "creativity conscious," more appre-

---

[2] For a more extensive discussion of attitudes and other personological traits of creative individuals, see Davis (1975).

ciative of innovative ideas, and who becomes willing to toss out wild ideas in a group problem-solving session would in fact be displaying what we normally mean by independence, self-confidence, and other creativity-related traits.

There are many other fairly reliable traits of the creative person which may not readily lend themselves to training; our programs do not directly seek to alter such characteristics. For example, the creative thinker typically displays high energy and enthusiasm, adventurousness, and spontaneity. It is thus common for the creative person to do things on the spur of the moment, to become highly involved in ideas and projects and to stay up half the night developing them. The creative person enjoys the challenging and is attracted to the complex, the asymmetrical, the mysterious, and the ambiguous. One study (Davis, Peterson and Farley, 1974) showed that more creative college students tended to be stronger believers in ESP, mental telepathy, flying saucers, and other psychical phenomena. The creative person also may show a tendency to be artistic and to have aesthetic interests. He/she might also be cynical and idealistic, characteristics which may not be endearing to the average schoolteacher.

One important yet teachable attitude related to the student's self-concept is simply the notion that he or she *can* learn to become a more imaginative problem solver. By practicing creative thinking exercises and activities and by internalizing attitudes related to flexible thinking, individuals should become more optimistic about their creative capabilities.

One final attitude conducive to creative behavior has been named *constructive discontent* (Osborn, 1963), referring to the notion that any man-made object or process may be changed for the better. The creative thinker simply does not believe in the impossible. Guilford's (1967) concept of *problem sensitivity,* measured by tests which ask for improvements for kitchen appliances or for institutions, overlaps with the concept of constructive discontent. With these attitudes the thinker is both sensitive to difficulties and assumes that they can be corrected with a constructive, creative approach.

Overall, the affective component of creativity is extremely important. Studies of the affective, cognitive, and even biographical characteristics of highly creative individuals have repeatedly confirmed that these persons possess the attitudes and traits described above (Barron, 1969; Davis, 1975; Mackinnon, 1971). They appreciate creative ideas and consciously seek novel problem solutions. They are above average in self-confidence and in the risk-taking attitudes needed for creative innovation. They are aware of negative influences (barriers) to creative thought, such as restrictive rather than creative atmospheres. They often possess a good sense of humor and are willing to try new ideas and experiences. In our training programs many of these attitudes and predispositions are modeled by the characters in the various story lines. Furthermore, some particular attitudes and their role in creative thinking are clearly identified and explained, and exercises are constructed which usually demand a humorous, far-fetched, and necessarily original response.

Creative Thinking Techniques

In addition to the attitudinal side of creativity, we have further assumed that a working knowledge of several creative thinking techniques would both: (a) increase students' understanding of the nature and source of many creative ideas, and (b) provide them with some comprehendable methods for generating new combinations of ideas, thereby improving their capability for producing imaginative problem solutions. That is, the conscious use of these techniques should supplement their intuitive use of unspecified strategies.

Brainstorming is one popular creative thinking method. Basically, brainstorming is based upon attitudes. The core principle is the concept of *deferred judgment,* the notion that criticism and evaluation are postponed. The goal of the brainstorming group is to generate a long list of fanciful, perhaps wild, problem solutions. The greater the number of ideas, the greater the probability of finding some good ones. In the classroom, brainstorming can be used as a purely fanciful creative thinking activity intended to stretch young imaginations. Problems such as "How do we keep the trolls out of the pumpkin patch?" or "What do you say to a man from Venus?" can stimulate only imaginative and quite preposterous ideas. Brainstorming also may be used to generate solutions for real school problems, such as keeping the school grounds tidy, improving the taste of steam-table cafeteria food, or traffic safety. The procedure also may be used to stimulate analysis of local problems such as spring flooding or unemployment, or even international problems of pollution, overpopulation, food shortages, and war. Brainstorming is basically very simple. The rules of deferred judgment and suspended criticism are explained, a problem is presented, and students work individually or, most commonly, as a group to list lots of possible solutions to the problem. Brainstorming provides a free and creative atmosphere and gives students worthwhile practice in stretching their imaginations.

Another more specific creative thinking technique is called *attribute listing.* In our training programs we preferred the less cumbersome name *part-changing.* Attribute listing (or part-changing) is both a theory of creative thinking and a teachable strategy for producing new ideas.

The originator of attribute listing, the late Professor Robert Crawford of the University of Nebraska, proposed that all—absolutely all—instances of creative innovation amount to either: (*a*) modifying important attributes of the problem, or (*b*) transferring attributes from one situation to a new context. For example, students may pretend that they are executives in the prepared foods industry and are searching for ideas for new varieties of breakfast cereals. They would begin by identifying important attributes or "parts" of the product, for example, *flavor, shape, color, name, extra ingredients, packaging* and perhaps others. Specific ideas for each of these could be listed on the blackboard and interesting combinations noted for further elaboration and evaluation. The attribute listing method may be used not only to invent an infinite variety of consumer products but may be applied to more aesthetic and artistic creations as well. Attributes of a painting, a short story, a sculpture, or a dramatic play may be identified, and then creative ideas for each of the listed attributes could be suggested.

Attributes also may be transferred from one situation to another. Probably every great composer borrowed melodies from folk tunes, modifying and transforming these into great music. For example, the waltzes of both Brahms and Beethoven were modifications of German peasant dances. All 15 of Liszt's Hungarian Rhapsodies were "borrowed" from Hungarian gypsies. A fashion designer might transfer ideas from civil war uniforms, ancient Egypt, colonial times, or other periods in history to more contemporary fashions. If students are planning booths or demonstrations for a "parents' night," ideas for creative displays could be borrowed from unrelated settings, such as gambling casinos, funeral parlors, Frankenstein movies, a showboat or carnival, and so on. Attribute modifying and attribute transferring are simple yet effective means for producing ideas for a large variety of problems.

There are other forced combinations procedures which can suggest creative problem solutions. The *morphological synthesis* method, which we renamed the *checkerboard* method, is an extension of attribute listing. Basically, two or three dimensions of the problem are identified. After ideas for each dimension are listed, all possible combinations are examined. For example, students might be looking for solutions to the energy crises. One axis of a two-dimensional checkerboard matrix could be *source of power*, eliciting such ideas as wind power, solar energy, ocean tides, geothermal energy, and so on. Each of these specific ideas could be combined with each idea along the other axis for *uses of the power*, such as heating homes, transportation, cooking, manufacturing, running the TV set, or plowing the fields. Surprising and interesting combinations always result. Students come to better understand the idea-combining nature of much creative thinking and also understand how they and others can produce novel idea combinations.

One also may use *idea checklists* to help stimulate new idea combinations. Very generally, whenever we browse through a pet store for a new tropical fish, consult a *Thesarus* to find the right word, read the Yellow Pages to locate the nearest TV repairman, or scrutinize a catalogue, we are using idea checklists. Thus as the name implies, the checklist strategy simply amounts to examining some kind of "list" that could suggest nonobvious solutions for a given problem. Students in one sixth-grade class who were studying one of our workbooks consulted books on China and Japan which they used as idea checklists to suggest ways to decorate their classroom in an oriental mode. An idea checklist essentially stimulates unusual and nonhabitual idea combinations. A person acquainted with the checklist method might quickly search out a helpful list of ideas rather than rely entirely upon his/her own imagination.

Some idea checklists have been designed especially for creative problem solving. Osborn (1963) devised his "73 idea-spurring questions" to inspire individual and group brainstormers. Consider as you read through this checklist how a mousetrap, can opener, or some other common objects might be reshaped by Osborn's hints.

Put to other uses? New ways to use as is? Other uses if modified?

Adapt? What else is like this? What other idea does this suggest? Does past offer parallel? What could I copy? Whom could I emulate?

Modify? New twist? Change meaning, color, motion, sound, odor, form, shape? Other changes?

Magnify? What to add? More time? Greater frequency? Stronger? Higher? Longer? Thicker? Extra value? Plus ingredient? Duplicate? Multiply? Exaggerate?

Minify? What to subtract? Smaller? Condensed? Miniature? Lower? Shorter? Lighter? Omit? Streamline? Split up? Understate?

Substitute? Who else instead? What else instead? Other ingredient? Other material? Other process? Other power? Other place? Other approach? Other tone of voice?

Rearrange? Interchange components? Other pattern? Other layout? Other sequence? Transpose cause and effect? Change pace? Change schedule?

Reverse? Transpose positive and negative? How about opposites? Turn it backward? Turn it upside down? Reverse roles? Change shoes? Turn tables? Turn other cheek?

Combine? How about a blend, an alloy, an assortment, an ensemble? Combine units? Combine purposes? Combine appeals? Combine ideas?

Metaphorical thinking (see Davidson's chapter in this volume) lies at the heart of many forms of creative thinking, particularly creative writing. Indeed, one mark of every outstanding author or poet is a genius for colorful, metaphorical word play. It also is true that metaphorical thinking may be used deliberately in problem solving, as when we transfer a solution from an old problem to some new, apparently similar problem context. There is a group of metaphorical thinking techniques, all devised by William J. J. Gordon (1961), which may be used to stimulate highly imaginative ideas. Three of Gordon's pet analogical devices are the *direct analogy, personal analogy,* and *fantasy analogy* methods.

With the *direct analogy* approach the problem solver looks for remote problem parallels, especially from natural, biological systems. Such metaphorical activity—asking how animals, birds, insects or flowers have solved similar problems—provides the combinatory play which may lead to new solutions. For example, the problem of automobile safety could be approached by thinking about how bats, fish, birds, grasshoppers, etc. avoid smashing into each other. Could these ideas be applied to reducing auto accidents?

The *personal analogy* method would also seem to guarantee an original point of view. With this strategy one imagines oneself to be part of the problem or problem object. For example, if a class were working on the problem of keeping the school grounds clean, students could imagine that they themselves were soda pop cans, paper scraps, and cigarette butts. What would they feel like? How would they like being tossed about on the school grounds? How can they get safely into a trash can?

The *fantasy analogy* strategy seems to be a form of Freudian wish fulfillment. The users of fantasy analogy would search for ideal problem solutions, regardless of how ridiculous. For example, having a problem solve itself would be an ideal solution which may stimulate a number of possibilities. To illustrate, years ago someone probably asked how to make a refrigerator defrost itself, how to make tires repair their own leaks, or how to make an oven clean itself. Asking students to think about perfect or ideal problem solutions leads to a considerable amount of imaginative speculation.

Research on Idea-Stimulating Techniques

Most adult-level creative thinking courses include instruction in brainstorming, attribute listing, matrix (checkerboard) methods, using idea checklists, and sometimes in using Gordon's metaphorical thinking techniques. With the exception of brainstorming, there have been virtually no laboratory evaluations of the effectiveness of these methods. Prior to designing simplified forms of these creative thinking techniques for the schools, the author and his colleagues conducted a series of experiments with college students to determine if, in fact, one's imagination could be extended with a few minutes instruction in some of these techniques.

Our first effort, an attempt to demonstrate that idea checklists could stimulate idea production, was a complete failure (Train, 1967). In the first of three experiments, Train provided subjects in the checklist group, but not subjects in the control group, with a list composed of 55 of Osborn's "73 idea-spurring questions" in order to stimulate ideas for changing or improving either a car, an office desk or a kitchen sink. All subjects worked for 10 minutes on each of the three problems. The results indicated that subjects in the control group produced a slightly greater number of ideas than did subjects in the checklist group. Also, ideas produced by control subjects were rated as slightly more original, on the average. An examination of the subjects' responses suggested that most subjects in the checklist group largely ignored the not-too-helpful checklist of ideas.

We believed that these results were due to the high complexity of the problem objects (car, desk, and sink), and that less complex problem objects would perhaps elicit fewer ready ideas for changes or improvements; subjects should then be more likely to draw ideas from the checklist. In a second experiment, Train (1967) required subjects to list changes or improvements for a simple problem object (a cup) and a more complex object (kitchen sink). She also allowed 20 minutes per problem instead of 10 minutes, believing that the additional time would exhaust the intuitive idea supply and encourage subjects to consult the checklist. Once again, however, the availability of the checklist did not stimulate idea production—even with a simpler object (which elicited as many ideas as did the complex object) and with the longer problem-solving time. The quantity and quality of ideas produced by subjects in the *checklist group* were virtually identical to that of subjects in the *control group*.

Experiment III was the final attempt by Train to facilitate idea production with the checklist procedure. Train speculated that a more detailed checklist should provide more specific suggestions for ideas and idea combinations. Therefore, some of the general terms on Osborn's checklist were greatly expanded and presented in detail: *Change form* became *new form (square, triangle, oval, rectangle, sharp corners, round corners, asymmetrical, doughnut shape, other forms?); change color* became *new color (silver, gold, copper, bronze, brass, red, purple, green, white, black, gray, blue, plaid, striped, polka-dots, op art, other colors or patterns?);* and so on. Again a cup and a kitchen sink were used as problem objects and 20 minutes per problem were allowed. Consistent with the result of experiments I and II, the availability of the checklist influenced neither quantity nor quality of idea production. The conclusion from this series was clearly that college students resist drawing ideas from a ready-made checklist when they are capable of generating their own. In an unpublished report, Torrance also described how adults sometimes resist using unfamiliar thinking and problem solving methods.

In a related study, Davis and Roweton (1968) proposed that the idea checklist used in Train's experiments did not fully motivate or challenge the capabilities of college students. They devised a brief seven-item checklist containing only general categories of ideas. It was predicted that this idea checklist would better stimulate and challenge the associative capabilities of college students. Subjects in the checklist group received the following brief checklist entitled "Aids in Thinking of Physical Changes":

add and/or subtract something
change color
change the materials
change by rearranging the parts
change shape
change size
change design or style

The checklist subjects also received a brief explanation of the meaning of the checklist items and how these items could suggest ideas for modifying virtually any problem object. Subjects in the control group were not provided with the idea checklist. All subjects received 10 minutes to work on each of two problems, listing changes or improvements for a thumb tack or a kitchen sink.

The results of this study were quite positive and dramatic. First, the checklist subjects produced no fewer than 2.5 times the number of ideas generated by subjects in the control group. Second, although the mean creativity ratings were not especially high for either group, ideas produced by subjects in the checklist group were rated as significantly more creative, on the average, than ideas produced by subjects in the control group. Third, compared with subjects in the control group, checklist subjects produced five times as many ideas which were rated as "highly creative." Apparently, the brief seven-item checklist motivated subjects by providing a few general categories of problem solutions that stimulated a large number of specific ideas. While providing hints, this checklist permitted subjects to think in their own familiar and fluent fashion.

A third study in this series (Warren and Davis, 1969) compared the idea-generating effectiveness of: (*a*) Osborn's long 73-item checklist; (*b*) the short Davis and Roweton 7-item checklist; (*c*) the morphological synthesis (checkerboard) method, and (*d*) no aids at all (control group). Since Wallach and Kogan (1965) suggested that time pressure disrupts the natural flow of creative thought, subjects in this experiment were allowed unlimited time to think of ideas for changing or improving a doorknob. They could leave "when finished," but were asked not to be influenced by others who might leave considerably earlier. After the general instructions were presented, subjects were assigned to one of the four treatment conditions by the simple expedient of randomly distributing four sets of specific written directions. The subjects knew that different sets of written instructions were distributed, but they did not know the nature of the other instructions nor how many sets of instructions were used.

Subjects in two of the four treatment groups were taught the checklist technique. These printed instructions explained that:

1. Lists such as the Yellow Pages or the classified ads of a newspaper can be used as idea sources.
2. Idea checklists often help a person become more open-minded about a problem.
3. Even though a final solution may not be found in a list, valuable hints might be.

Subjects in the *short-checklist group* were provided with the brief seven-item checklist. Subjects in the *long-checklist group* were given copies of Osborn's (1963) "73 idea-spurring questions." A third group of subjects was instructed in the morphological synthesis technique. This explanation emphasized that:

1. A good way to think of variations and improvements for something is to analyze the "thing" into its various dimensions and then combine the values of these dimensions into new arrangements.
2. The very large number of ideas found in this fashion may be good in themselves, or may act as hints for producing still other ideas.

Examples were provided to clarify the procedure. The subjects in the control group received no instructions regarding idea-generating techniques.

The problem that all subjects solved was presented as follows:

"Produce as many ideas as you can that may be used as physical changes and/or improvements for a door knob. Some of your ideas may be rather complete changes or improvements, while others may be only a starting point. Don't worry about your ideas being too silly, wild or useless. If you have a thought that might apply to this problem, write it down."

Completion times were recorded as each subject turned in his or her booklet.

The results confirmed that the short checklist is indeed stimulating and motivating. Subjects in the short checklist group tended to work longer than subjects in the *morphological synthesis group* who, in turn, spent more time on the problem than subjects in the long checklist and control groups. Furthermore, subjects in the short checklist group produced roughly double the number of ideas generated by subjects in the long checklist or control groups. However, in accord with the general expectation that the morphological synthesis procedure would lead to large numbers of idea combinations in relatively short periods of time, subjects in the morphological synthesis group listed the greatest mean number of ideas. A derived measure of ideas-per-minute showed that subjects with instructions in the morphological synthesis procedure also produced ideas considerably faster than subjects under any of the other training conditions. The four groups did not differ significantly in the mean rated "originality" of their ideas.

Together, the Davis and Roweton (1968) and the Warren and Davis (1969) studies confirmed that the short idea checklist can stimulate new idea combinations with college students. The list provides seven general categories of solutions which stimulate a large number of specific ideas suited, of course, to the particular task of thinking of physical changes for a simple object such as a doorknob. More generally, we concluded that an intermediate level of idea-stimulating cues is most ideal. If a problem situation provides no particular suggestions or cues for ideas, creative thinking will be depressed. On the other hand, if a list of ready-made solutions is *handed* to the active thinker, as in the case of our long checklist groups, he/she may not be inclined to use that list as an idea source. Finally, with the double qualification that a particular technique must be both suitable to the problem at hand and teachable in the time allowed, this series of experiments supports the feasibility of increasing creativive output by teaching "artificial" techniques for generating new combinations of ideas.

MATERIALS FOR TRAINING CREATIVE THINKING

Our concepts of creative attitudes and creative problem-solving techniques were incorporated into three sets of materials for training creative thinking which were designed for the upper elementary and lower junior high school grades. All three programs seek to encourage creative and problem-solving behaviors: (a) by instructions and illustrations dealing with creative attitudes and techniques, (b) by exercises that allow the learner to actively create new ideas while practicing the strategies, and (c) by example, in that the story lines and content of the three materials—especially the professionally written *Imagination Express*—were intended to be models of flexibility and imagination.

Thinking Creatively: A Guide to Training Imagination

Our first effort to structure creative problem-solving principles was *Thinking Creatively: A Guide to Training Imagination* (Davis and Houtman, 1968; see also Davis, 1969, 1973). Prepared for sixth-, seventh-, and eighth-grade students, the 150-page workbook takes the form of humorous dialogue among four cartoon characters. Mr. I., an eccentric, backyard scientist—inventor (Figure 1), instructs the younger characters in the importance of open-minded, creativity-conducive attitudes and in using various problem-solving techniques. He engages in unusual activities consistent with a creative atmosphere, such as preparing a carrot sandwich, or honey-flavored ice cream, or some other surprising delight. Dudley Bond, a distant relative of a very famous secret agent, is the eager young male character. While awkward at times, Dudley displays a fine sense of humor and quite enjoys the challenge of finding new ideas for solving problems. Maybelle is a curious but slightly naive young lady who needs help in finding zesty ideas for her English themes. As Maybelle explains, "I get tired of writing about Hambone, my pet iguana." Finally we have Max, the professional bear and resident clown of the program, who rarely understands anything very clearly. He often displays his lack of creativity by criticizing the "nutty" ideas, allowing

Figure 1. "Max, Maybelle, Dudley, and Mr. I" (from *Thinking Creatively*, Davis and Houtman, 1968).

his friends frequent opportunity to reemphasize the critical role of flexible, free-thinking attitudes.

Throughout the program, the four friends attack many simple and complex problems. Mr. I. explains the creative procedures and attitudes likely to help solve a given problem, and Dudley, Maybelle, and sometimes Max use the principles to produce novel problem solutions. At the end of each of 10 chapters, important principles are reviewed and exercises are presented which allow the student readers to solve problems similar to those solved by the cartoon quartet within the story line. Active practice in solving problems and thinking of new ideas is extremely important. We assume that the skills of imagination, like those of arithmetic and violin playing, may be strengthened through exercise.

The program recognizes that pressures exist that often inhibit an easy flow of "ridiculous" or "silly" ideas. Therefore, to create an atmosphere in which the wildest ideas may be freely suggested, *Thinking Creatively* deliberately uses humor. The story characters readily propose outlandish problem solutions and at the same time engage in slapstick comedy. In addition to building a creative atmosphere, the humor helps maintain student interest by the ancient technique of entertainment.

The creative problem-solving content of the program focuses upon the creative attitudes described above and upon such idea-stimulating techniques as attribute listing (*part-changing* method), the morphological synthesis procedure (*checkerboard* method), *checklisting*, and many of the metaphor-based synectics methods (one of which, *direct analogy*, we renamed the *find-something-similar* method).

In addition, we sought to increase students' understanding of problem solving by describing four problem-solving steps: First, one must clearly understand the problem and define it in general terms ". . . to open our minds to more kinds of solutions." For example, one problem was originally stated as "Think of ways to give your pet hamster a bath. He thoroughly dislikes water, to say nothing of soap! [Davis and Houtman, 1968, p. 134]." Stated more generally, the "real" problem was ". . . to separate the dirt from the hamster." The second step is to think of different main approaches to solving the problem. In the hamster problem, vacuuming would constitute one approach; soap-and-water tactics would be another. Third, one thinks of different specific ideas for each main approach (for example, different ways to vacuum and different ways to apply soap-and-water to the hamster—or the hamster to soap-and-water). The fourth step is to evaluate and select the best ideas.

Regarding the effectiveness of *Thinking Creatively*, we ideally would hope for long-term improvement in problem solving and creative skills in the students' personal and educational lives and eventually in their chosen careers. In our two field evaluations we necessarily resorted to attitude surveys, divergent thinking tests, and informal student and teacher reactions. Briefly, a small pilot evaluation with middle-class seventh-grade students showed that 23 students using the program produced an average of 65% more ideas on three divergent thinking tasks (ideas rated as significantly more "creative") than 32 control students who were enrolled in a creative writing course. The attitude survey indicated that the experimental students were significantly more confident of their creative ability, more appreciative of unusual ideas, and more aware of the importance of creative innovation in society (Davis, Houtman, Warren and Roweton, 1969). A larger field test with inner-city students (two sixth-grade and two eighth-grade classes) showed less, but still reliable improvement in creative attitudes and idea-producing capabilities (Davis, 1970a, 1970b; Davis, Houtman, Warren, Roweton, Mari and Belcher, 1972). With the exception of one teacher, whose severe discipline problems prevented group problem solving and discussion, all teachers felt the program provided beneficial information and experiences for both students and teachers. One class, at the students' suggestion, used the checkerboard (morphological synthesis) method to generate theme-writing ideas for every person in the class. As noted above, students in this class also used the checklist method to find ideas for decorating their room in an Oriental mode.

Imagination Express

Two considerations regarding *Thinking Creatively* led to the development of another creative thinking and problem-solving program, *Imagination Express: Saturday Subway Ride* (DiPego, 1973). First of all, concepts in *Thinking Creatively* drew heavily from professional creative problem-solving principles, emphasizing inventing and product design. Creative writing was touched upon very lightly, and such areas as music, artwork, entertainment, and social problems had been omitted entirely. Second, there was reason to believe that a group of highly talented professional writers might be better able to teach creative thinking by example, by modeling what "being creative" is like.

A group of Chicago-based writers calling themselves "The Creative Establishment" was therefore commissioned by the Wisconsin Research and Development Center to write *Imagination Express*, basing it upon the main principles and content of *Thinking Creatively*. It is noteworthy that these unusually creative individuals agreed fully with the concepts of creativity—attitudes and techniques—taught in the workbooks.

Like *Thinking Creatively, Imagination Express* is not tied to any one curriculum area. Rather, both sets of materials teach general principles of flexible thinking and problem solving relating to creative attitudes and idea-finding strategies. Brainstorming, part-changing, the checkerboard method, and the find-something-similar strategy are explained, and appropriate exercises are provided. Unlike *Thinking Creatively,* however, most exercises are not tied to a particular "forced" creative thinking technique. Rather, students practice writing songs, dialogue, advertising slogans, and thinking of inventions and problem solutions by using intuitive, unknown thinking methods. *Imagination Express* differs from its predecessor in several other respects. Its audience reasonably could be "students" of any age, beginning with fifth- or sixth-grade. The booklet may be used at even lower grades with the aid of an interested and enthusiastic teacher. And again, the scope of *Imagination Express* is considerably broader than *Thinking Creatively.* The professionally prepared *Imagination Express* also has been commercially published, while *Thinking Creatively* exists only in an unpublished form.

The content and flavor of *Imagination Express* might best be presented in a few illustrative passages:

Let me tell you about last Saturday.
I took a ride on a new super subway that travels a fast circle from Kansas City to Pittsburgh to Dublin to Tokyo to Santa Monica and back.
What's wrong?
You say there's no such subway, and you're about to close the book and stare out the window?
Well, maybe you're wrong. Maybe I zipped around the world on an underground thought, a daydream, a nightdream, or a superfastspecialfivecityidea.
That's what this book is all about.
Ideas.
You may say my subway ride is just a wild idea and pretty silly, and you'd rather pitch pennies?
Well, what about flying? People said that men flying around in machines was a wild idea and pretty silly. Then the Wright brothers took off and ZIP!
People once thought that TV was just a wild idea and probably wouldn't work—and bicycles, too, and life insurance and polio vaccine.
A wild idea is something that people find hard to accept because it's new and sounds strange and looks funny and maybe it's light green suede and smells of paprika. Anyway, it's something people haven't seen before, and that makes them afraid.
Some people only feel safe with old, comfortable, tried-out ideas. I guess those people never learned to stretch their minds.
That's what this book is all about, too—learning to stretch your mind, learning to reach out for big, new, different, and even wild ideas.
Why?
So you can solve problems and create new things and improve old things and have more fun. Ideas are good anywhere, anytime, in any climate and even underwater.

Now, you've gotten me way off the subway track. Let's get back to Saturday. Last Saturday I took a ride on a super subway.

I bought my ticket in Kansas City, Mo., but they wouldn't take money.

"What can you do?" the ticket-seller asked me.

"What do you mean?"

"In order to ride this subway, friend, you have to do something musical. Can you sing?"

I can't sing. I can't dance very well either. And I only had two months of lessons on the B-flat clarinet before I gave it up. I couldn't think of anything musical I could do. But I really wanted that ticket to Pittsburgh.

"Well, can you write me a song?"

"You mean make something up?"

"Yes," he said.

"Now?"

"Well . . ." He scratched a sideburn and said, "Tell you what. You can get on the subway and ride to the first stop—Pittsburgh. When you get to Pittsburgh, you better have a song ready or we'll have to send you right back here. . . ."

"How long before we get to Pittsburgh?" was my next question.

"That depends," he said. "We'll get to Pittsburgh as soon as you can lean back in your seat and close your eyes and not think about Pittsburgh. As long as you're thinking about Pittsburgh, we won't get there. Could take days or minutes. . . ."

"Well, I can't help thinking about having a song ready for Pittsburgh. How do you write a song?"

He looked very thoughtful and squinty and smart and said to me, "I don't know." I thanked him for being honest. Some people never admit they don't know something. "Excuse me." I left my seat and walked up the aisle.

I met an old woman with blue hair and a radio cane. "That's a good idea," I said, "a transistor radio built right into your cane."

"I'm an inventor," she said. "I'm paid by the job with an advance on royalties based on thousands of items sold. What do you need?"

"A song."

"Oh." She nodded and smiled. "Well, that has to come from your own mind," she said, and turned off her cane.

"But I don't even know where to start."

"Start with rhythm," she said. "A song has to have a beat."

"Where do I find it?"

She only said, "Shhhhhhhhh."

I shut up. I even closed my eyes. But all I heard were the wheels of the subway:

> clackaty clackaty chugity
> clackaty clackaty chugity
> clackaty clackaty chugity

"Clackaty clack . . . hey! That's the rhythm I need!"

She said, "Yes, now comes the melody. Why don't you borrow one, just for now?"

"Like 'My Darlin' Clementine'?"

"Yes, or 'Old Man River.' "

We settled on "You Are My Sunshine."

"Whatever you need for a song is around you and inside of you all the time," she said.

Well, I knew I needed words, so I looked around. Above the subway windows were advertising posters. You've seen them—ads for shaving cream, hair lotion, insurance, concerts, how to get a job, where to go to electronics school, etcetera. Well, when you're desperate for a song, why not? Here it goes—to the tune of "You Are My Sunshine," and the clackaty clackaty beat of the subway.

(CLACKATY CLACKATY CHUGITY)
Don't drop out of school
Don't drop out of school
Remember al-ways
To look your best
Elect Polinski
As County Sheriff
And the zoo will o-pen in May.

Well, what do you think? Oh, it's not that bad. It might get me to Pittsburgh. Okay, you try it. But take your time. Maybe you can make your words really mean something, tell a story, or just tell how you feel, or what kind of day it is outside the window. Anyway, take a stab at it. And remember what this book is about—stretching your mind, reaching out a little, bending your brain. Go ahead. What you need to write a song is around you and inside you all the time. . . .
"Hey! Wow! Yow! Hey!"
It was the conductor, screaming and running down the aisle, his eyes wide, his hat off.
"Hey! Eeeeyah!"
People got their tickets ready in a hurry, figuring the conductor was awfully excited about his job.
"Gaa! Yow! Wow!"
But he wasn't collecting tickets, just running and yelling.
"Wow! It's coming! Run for your lives! Nobody move! Look out! It's coming!"
"What's coming?" people asked. "What is it?"
But he wouldn't answer and he wouldn't stop. When we blocked the aisle, he jumped up and ran along the tops of the seats. "It's coming! Run! Don't make a move! Look out! Save yourselves! Eeeeyah!"
We were all pretty excited and scared. I'd call it a semi-panic.
"What is it?" I yelled. "Hey, tell us!"
The conductor stuck his head out of the window, pulled it back in and looked at me. I could say he was the color of milk, but there's chocolate milk and buttermilk. I could say chalk, but there are all colors of chalk. There is even dirty snow and brown sugar and off-white . . . So I'll just say he was pale and let it go. He was pale.
"Oh my gosh, it's coming, and it hates subway trains," he said. He stuck his head out again. "It eats subway trains for breakfast! Help!"
Everybody crowded around him. What is it? What does it look like? He was still looking out the window. "It's coming closer!"
"Describe it!"
He did. "It flies . . . and it tunnels underground. It has pockets."
"What?"
"Pockets. One hundred and seventeen pockets. And it loves to dance."
"Is that important?"
He just went on. "It can swim too, and it carries a pocket watch."
"Which pocket?" I said, but nobody paid attention.
"It's hungry and it has a can opener and a temper—it's part Scotch and part Bolivian and it's coming! Lock the windows! Everybody run! Don't make a sound! Help!"
Wow. You can guess what was going through my head at that moment. I was picturing it . . . that big hungry Scotch-Bolivian giant of a . . . Well, why don't you

picture it yourself? Picture it in your mind, let your imagination put it together, using any colors, shapes, ideas you want. Then take a peek into your mind and see what it looks like. Draw it on the next page. . . .
The passengers were crunched in a bunch, all yelling at once.
All I could hear were pieces of sentences: What is . . . How can . . . Please tell . . . Stop the . . . Save . . . Help . . . Then the conductor pulled his head back in, and he wasn't pale. I mean, I would say he was normal flesh color, but there are a lot of different colors for flesh and faces, right? So I'll just say he wasn't pale and let it go. He wasn't pale. And he was smiling!
"Relax," he said.
"Is it gone?"
"There isn't any it. I made it up."
"Why? Why!"
The conductor smiled and took out his pocket watch. "So you would all forget about Pittsburgh, and we could get here. And it worked." He looked at his watch. "Right on time. Pittsburgh!" And he went down the aisle calling out the word as though nothing had happened. "Pittsburgh!" Come to think of it, nothing much had happened, except in my head [Abridged from DiPego, 1973, pp. 1–13] .

Throughout *Imagination Express* exercises are interspersed at appropriate points. For example, in the excerpts above the student is asked to write a song, and later to draw a picture of "it." Elsewhere in *Imagination Express,* the student is exposed to a fanciful dialogue, play script, or "tall tale," and then is asked to write his or her own dialogue, play script, or tall tales. After a vivid war scene, students are asked to discuss as a class the meaning and significance of the scene.

In nearly all cases, the frequent exercises provide an intermediate level of hints or cues which elicit creative ideas almost spontaneously. For example, the following is an exercise in dialogue writing:

1. Two astronauts are orbiting the moon. Suddenly there is a knock on the spaceship door.
Astronaut 1. ⸺⸺⸺⸺⸺⸺⸺⸺⸺⸺⸺⸺
Astronaut 2. ⸺⸺⸺⸺⸺⸺⸺⸺⸺⸺⸺⸺

The readers of *Imagination Express* should become more receptive to creative ideas, more oriented toward using their creative capabilities, and should have a better understanding of methods for producing new idea-combinations. Especially, with the workbook itself serving as a model, they will have a keen feel for what "being creative" is like.

"Write? Right!" A Program For More Creative Writing[3]

Susan Houtman incorporated principles of creative thinking and problem solving into a creative writing workbook entitled *Write? Right!*

[3] This section was prepared in collaboration with Susan E. Houtman.

(Houtman, 1970a), prepared for upper elementary school students. In addition, by serving as a supplement to the more traditional grammar-oriented approach to language arts, the workbook provides a relevant context—writing itself—in which the rules of grammar may be learned.

As with *Thinking Creatively* and *Imagination Express,* Houtman designed *Write? Right!* to be enjoyed, to make learning and thinking fun, and to open the student to his or her own creative potential. A young writer's first attempts should be an adventure and a challenging game, not a dry academic chore.

Hoping to shape such intrinsic motivation, *Write? Right!* exposes the student to a variety of writing and thinking experiences—for example, short stories, advertising campaigns, rhymed and unrhymed poetry, inventing descriptive character names (e.g. "Bertha Bulgover") and story titles, songs, interviews, word games, cartoon captions, mystery plots, and letters. Entertaining demonstrations are followed by exercises. The student is urged to try all of the exercises, no matter how new or strange they may seem (such as composing a letter his dog might write—à la Snoopy). The teacher is asked not to grade students at this point. Rather, he or she should encourage and smilingly accept whatever is produced. Students thus learn to trust their own written feelings and thoughts first, and only later worry about writing them well.

Along the way, students are shown some idea-generating techniques adapted to creative writing to help them over the "but-I-can't-think-of-anything-to-say" barrier. Some of these techniques, such as the checklist and the part-changing methods, have been described earlier. Other strategies are a bit more unusual, such as a metaphor-based "learning to think like a rock." Using "the old iceberg approach to ideas," a student learns to find unusual ideas by putting aside the first rush of ideas (the tip of the iceberg which everyone sees) and searching for unique ideas that are hidden beneath the surface. These techniques reinforce such creative attitudes as "being different is not the same as being right or wrong." That is, originality is a virtue.

Throughout *Write? Right!* the student is urged to visualize and verbalize in his/her own way. Many of the exercises are structured so that students may pick a literary, artistic, or sometimes even a musical or scientific mode of self-expression. Furthermore, the *Teachers' Manual* (Houtman, 1970b) provides several variations for approaching and handling the exercises, as well as for extending the creative thinking and writing principles to other classroom contacts.

In conclusion, all three of our Wisconsin programs try to amplify creative potential by fostering attitudes (including awarenesses, sets, predispositions) conducive to imaginative behavior, by teaching techniques for actually producing new idea-combinations, and by strengthening intuitive thinking abilities through practice. We are confident that the creativity concepts in these materials are sound and can truly add creative flexibility to students' long-term thinking and problem-solving growth.

REFERENCES

Alexander, T. Synectics: Inventing by the madness method. *Fortune*, 1965, 72(2), 165–168; 190; 193–194. (Reprinted in G. A. Davis & J. A. Scott, eds., *Training Creative Thinking.* New York: Holt, 1971. Pp. 1–13.)

Barron, F. *Creative person and creative process.* New York: Holt, 1969.

Crawford, R. P. *Techniques of creative thinking.* New York: Hawthorn, 1954.

Davis, G. A. Training creativity in adolescence: A discussion of strategy. In R. E. Grinder (Ed.), *Studies in adolescence. II.* New York: Macmillan, 1969, 538–545.

Davis, G. A. *Problems in assessing the effectiveness of creative thinking.* Paper presented in a symposium entitled, "Assessing creativity: Progress in both directions," at the American Educational Research Association, Minneapolis, March, 1970(a).

Davis, G. A. *Training creative thinking: In the suburbs and the inner city.* Paper presented at the Eighth Creativity Conference, Buffalo, June, 1970(b).

Davis, G. A. *Psychology of problem solving: Theory and practice.* New York: Basic Books, 1973.

Davis, G. A. In frumious pursuit of the creative person. *Journal of Creative Behavior,* 1975, *9,* 75–87.

Davis, G. A., Peterson, J. M., & Farley, F. H. Attitudes, motivation, sensation-seeking, and belief in ESP as predictors of real creative behavior. *Journal of Creative Behavior,* 1974, *8,* 31–39.

Davis, G. A., & Houtman, S. E. *Thinking creatively: A guide to training imagination.* Madison, Wisc.: Wisconsin Research and Development Center for Cognitive Learning, University of Wisconsin, 1968.

Davis, G. A., Houtman, S. E., Warren, T. F., & Roweton, W. E. *A program for training creative thinking: I. Preliminary field test.* Technical Report No. 104. Madison, Wisc.: Wisconsin Research and Development Center for Cognitive Learning, University of Wisconsin, 1969.

Davis, G. A., Houtman, S. E., Warren, T. F., Roweton, W. E., Mari, S. K., & Belcher, T. L. *A program for training creative thinking: II. Inner city evaluation.* Technical Report no. 224. Madison, Wisc.: Wisconsin Research and Development Center for Cognitive Learning, University of Wisconsin, 1972.

Davis, G. A., & Roweton, W. E. Using idea checklists with college students: Overcoming resistance. *Journal of Psychology,* 1968, *70,* 221–226.

DiPego, G. *Imagination express: Saturday subway ride.* Buffalo, N. Y.: D.O.K. Publishers, 1973.

Gordon, W. J. J. *Synectics.* New York: Harper & Row, 1961.

Guilford, J. P. *The nature of human intelligence.* New York: McGraw-Hill, 1967.

Houtman, S. E. *Write? Right!* Madison, Wisc.: Wisconsin Research and Development Center for Cognitive Learning, University of Wisconsin, 1970(a).

Houtman, S. E. *Write? Right! Teachers' Manual.* Madison, Wisc.: Wisconsin Research and Development Center for Cognitive Learning, University of Wisconsin, 1970(b).

Lockheed-Georgia, Value Engineering Department. Value engineering. In G. A. Davis & J. A. Scott (Eds.), *Training creative thinking.* New York: Holt, 1971, 143–161.

Mackinnon, D. W. Educating for creativity: A modern myth? In G. A. Davis & J. A. Scott (Eds.), *Training creative thinking.* New York: Holt, 1971, 194–207.

Manske, M. E., & Davis, G. A. Effects of simple instructional biases upon performance in the unusual uses test. *Journal of General Psychology,* 1968, *79,* 25–33.

Myers, R. E., & Torrance, E. P. *Can you imagine?* Boston: Ginn, 1965.

Myers, R. E., & Torrance, E. P. *For those who wonder.* Boston: Ginn, 1966.

Osborn, A. F. *Applied imagination.* New York: Scribner's, 1963.

Parnes, S. J. Can creativity be increased? In G. A. Davis & J. A. Scott (Eds.), *Training creative thinking.* New York: Holt, 1971, 270–275.

Prince, G. The operational mechanisms of synectics. In G. A. Davis & J. A. Scott (Eds.), *Training creative thinking.* New York: Holt, 1971, 30–42.

Torrance, E. P., & Myers, R. E. *Creative learning and teaching.* New York: Dodd, Mead, 1970.

Train, A. J. *Attribute listing and use of a checklist: A comparison of two techniques for stimulating creative thinking.* Unpublished master's thesis, University of Wisconsin, 1967.

Wallach, M. A., & Kogan, N. *Modes of thinking in young children.* New York: Holt, 1965.

Warren, T. F., & Davis, G. A. Techniques for creative thinking: An empirical comparison of three methods. *Psychological Reports,* 1969, 25, 207–214.

CHAPTER 9

Children Helping Children: Psychological Processes in Tutoring

Vernon L. Allen

By these means a few good boys, selected for the purpose, as teachers of the repective classes, form the whole school, teach their pupils to think rightly, and mixing in all their little amusements and diversions, secure them against the contagion of ill example, or the force of ill habits; and, by seeing that they treat one another kindly, render their condition contented and happy [Andrew Bell, 1797].

My school is attended by three hundred scholars. The *whole* system of tuition is almost entirely conducted by boys . . . This system of tuition is mutually for the advantage of the lads who teach, and those who are taught; by it the path of learning is strewed with flowers . . . [Joseph Lancaster, 1803].

The 'discovery' of Dr. Bell was not what he called his *system*, but the carrying into practice and the school room of an old, old truth, which in the present day we are all of us a little apt to forget. LEARNING IS A SOCIAL ACT: it is best carried on under social conditions [J. M. D. Meiklejohn, 1881; capitals in original].

Qui docet discit. [He who teaches, learns; an ancient dictum].

TUTORING: OLD AND NEW

As the quotations from Bell (1797) and Lancaster (1803) make clear, the use of children to teach other children in the schools is not by any means a recent innovation; the idea has had a long and lively past. Perhaps we are destined always to rediscover ideas from the past when seeking to make improvements on the present. Nevertheless, old though an idea may be, it frequently benefits from the revision and refurbishment afforded by reexamination in the light of contemporary scientific and educational knowledge. Some old ideas do indeed contain a kernel of truth in spite of their antiquity. And tutoring in the schools is not a new idea. The technique of children teaching children attained wide

241

popularity, particularly in British schools, almost 200 years ago; the present revival of interest in these techniques should not be dismissed, however, as merely being old wine in new bottles.

Problem

A large number of tutorial programs involving children teaching children are currently in operation in the United States and in other countries. Recently, a report emphasized the appropriateness and the particular value of peer tutoring for use in underdeveloped countries (Klaus, 1973). Unfortunately, only sparse and generally unobjective information is available concerning the evaluation and analysis of the diverse types of programs now extant. A great deal of systematic information will be needed if schools are to organize tutorial programs that maximize the beneficial consequences for both tutors and tutees. No single tutorial program is likely to be optimal for all schools and all students; programs should be designed to fit the particular needs of a wide and heterogeneous population of students.

The general goal of the research program reported in the present chapter is to contribute toward a better understanding of the underlying psychological processes responsible for any change in academic achievement and in social behavior that results from the use of children as teachers of other children in the school setting. The present research program has focused primarily on the child who does the teaching (tutor), although much of the research has also examined the effect of tutoring on the child being taught (tutee).

Historical Perspective

Before discussing the theoretical framework of the research and factors involved in contributing to the effectiveness of tutoring, it may be illuminating to pause for a brief backward glance through social history. Two points are worth our attention: first, the historical background of age gradation in schools—the practice of assigning same-age students together in a class or grade; and, second, the nature of tutorial programs that existed in the British schools almost two centuries ago. To discuss the former issue first, questions such as the following can be raised: What are the origins of the present-day practice of segregating children in the schools on the basis of their biological age? How does our conception of the period of childhood differ from that held by persons in earlier historical periods? How has the conception of childhood affected the interaction between children and adults and between younger and older children?

Origins of Age Differentiation

Light is thrown on these questions by a fascinating historical study written by the French social philosopher, Philippe Ariès (1962). Ariès documents his contention that the idea of childhood as a separate category of life did not exist prior to the sixteenth or seventeenth century. In medieval society there was no conception of childhood as we know it today; after infancy the child was dressed like a miniature adult and, indeed, was treated like an adult in most respects. As soon as the child could live without the constant care of his mother he became a member of adult society, going directly into the great world of work and behaving as an adult. The modern conception of childhood as a special stage of life which is characterized by innocence and which is allocated to preparation for later adult life was foreign to the Middle Ages.

In Europe prior to the seventeenth century childhood was not a period of quarantine during which the child was sheltered and kept apart from the adult world. In work and play children mixed freely with older companions and adults. Once past the age of 5 to 7 years, the child was absorbed into the world of adults, participating as equals in all aspects of adult life, even, as Ariès notes, ". . . in taverns of ill repute. . . ." Acquisition of work skills was transmitted from generation to generation by the apprenticeship system; the art of work and the art of living were in like manner acquired through direct contact with older children and adults.

Ariès contends that up until modern times, that is, about the seventeenth century, there was extensive free and easy mingling among persons of all ages. The portrayal of the life of children in the late Middle Ages and up to the modern era represents a dramatic and remarkable contrast to the relative lack of contact across ages nowadays. How can such an evolution in social behavior be explained?

One of the basic sources for the origin of age-differentiation—and hence age-segregation—stems from the institution of the school, according to Ariès. The school of the Middle Ages presents a sharp contrast to our current conception. A crucial difference was the absence of the concept of gradation of difficulty of material, with an attendant lack of differentiation among students according to their age or intellectual development. Students simply memorized their textbooks; there was no difference in the level of difficulty of the material being studied. Thus, school subjects were not separated into different levels ranging from easiest to most difficult. Another difference was that all students were taught simultaneously, the older students being distinguished from younger ones only by virtue of having repeated the same material a greater number of times. Therefore, students of all ages—mostly boys and men of from 10 to 20 years of age—were mixed together in the same classroom. Robert of Salisbury describes a school he visited in the twelfth century: "I saw the students in the schools. Their numbers were great. I saw there men of diverse ages: puerso, adolescentes, juvenes, senos." (That is, all ages of life were represented.) The mixing of diverse ages in the classroom apparently continued in out-of-school hours as well.

Toward the end of the Middle Ages changes began to appear that were to contribute strongly toward the eventual sharp differentiation among ages that is so characteristic of current society. Apparently some teachers began grouping together in one area of the large schoolroom those students studying the same lessons. This seems to have been the beginning of changes that eventually developed into the principle of separation of students by classes or grades on the basis of age. With the significant increase in the school population in the fifteenth century, the usefulness for disciplinary purposes of small classes—as compared to the normal 100 or 200 students—became readily apparent. The next step was the isolation of each small class in a separate room. Thus, by the seventeenth century the classroom or grade as we know it was well established.

In spite of separate physical premises for each class, children were still not allocated to a classroom on the basis of their age. Age as an important criterion for membership in a classroom came to be recognized only gradually. Data presented by Ariès (1962) reveal the age composition of classrooms of two French schools, one in the early seventeenth century and a comparable school in the early nineteenth century. For illustrative purposes, I have calculated the data from these two schools in terms of the percentage of students of a particular age in each class. As shown in Figure 1, in the seventeenth century school there was a wide range of ages represented in each class or grade. For instance, in the third class (third most advanced) there were children from 9 to 24 years of age; the age distribution for this class was almost rectangular. By contrast, as can be seen in Figure 1, the data from the early nineteenth century showed a much narrower range of ages at each class (and also a greater number of classes); the close correspondence between school class and age of students in this school begins to approximate the present-day pattern of age homogeneity.

In summary, the analysis by Ariès (1962) suggests that the school contributed significantly to age-consciousness and age-segregation by evolving the system of school classes formed on the basis of age of

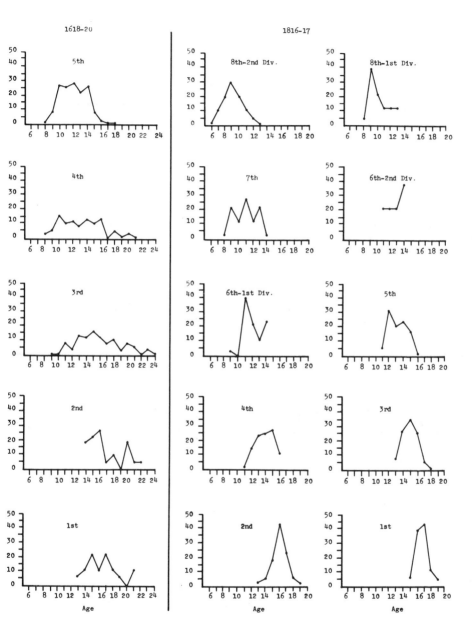

Figure 1. Age of children (%) in two schools in France in the seventeenth century (Jesuit college of Châlons, 1618–20) and in the nineteenth century (Sainte-Barbe, 1816–17). (The "first" class is the most advanced.) [Adapted from data provided by Ariès (1962).]

students. Coinciding with this organizational development in the schools was the concomitant evolution of the conception of the nature of childhood. The modern characterization of childhood as a special stage of life, a period of innocence and a time for preparation for the later serious business of life, was a conception of childhood that evolved slowly from the time of the Middle Ages. We see that a sharp differentiation across age groups did not always exist in western society; its historical roots can be located in the not-so-distant past.

The Bell–Lancaster System

Having taken one short excursion into social history, we will pick up another relevant thread from the past and weave it into the texture of our discussion. In the early nineteenth century a system based upon the use of children as teachers of other children was the object of widespread public attention and acclaim, and was adopted in many schools. A brief description of this movement—for movement it became in the intensity of belief of its adherents—will perhaps place in perspective similar systems currently being introduced in many schools.

The Bell–Lancaster system (as it may be called) had a strong impact on education in Britain in the early nineteenth century. A Scotsman, Andrew Bell, became superintendent of a school ("Asylum") in Madras, India, established for orphans who were, for the most part, sons of British soldiers and Indian mothers. Bell experienced a great deal of frustration in efforts to teach these students; they were ". . . in general, stubborn, perverse, and obstinate [Bell, 1797, p. 19]." Finally, Bell devised a system which had as its basic and most novel component the use of older children to teach other children. Not only did this system appear to be successful as a means of providing elementary instruction, but it also brought about a marked improvement in the behavior of the students. Using this system transformed the school; in Bell's (1797) words: "The school is thus rendered a scene of amusement to the scholars, and a spectacle of delight to the beholder. . . . For months together it has not been found necessary to inflict a single punishment [p. 32]." Bell's (1797) description of his system is none too clear, but its basic feature seems to have been some one-to-one tutoring by the boys and, in addition, the teaching of entire classes by one older boy with the aid of younger boys as assistants. The extent of the involvement of students in the teaching process is indicated by Bell's report that in 1791 a boy of 11 years of age was in charge of his school of 300 students. The children seemed to be quite successful in their teaching efforts, as exemplified by this passage from Bell's 1797 report of his Madras school: "Friskin, of twelve years and eight months, with his assistants of seven, eight, nine and eleven years of age, has taught boys of four, five, and six years, to read the Spectator distinctly, and spell every word accurately as they go along, who were only initiated into the mysteries of their A, B, C, eight months before... [p. 21]." After having learned to read the *Spectator,* there would seem to be few worlds left for these students to conquer!

Published in 1797, the report of Bell's system as practiced at the Madras school was enthusiastically accepted by a professional educator in England, Joseph Lancaster. Embellishing Bell's basic idea of using children as teachers, and adding new elements of his own, Lancaster (1803) vigorously publicized the system. In England and Wales alone, around 100,000 children were being taught by the Bell–Lancaster system in 1816, according to Bell (1817). Lancaster was perhaps the most avid public advocate of the "monitorial" system. He asserted that by the use of this system up to 1,000 students could be taught by only one adult teacher. Such a remarkable feat required the maintenance of strict order and discipline, and entailed a table of organization that might be envied by many an Army battalion. All the students were seated in neat and symmetrical rows in a large classroom. Teaching was conducted mechanically and with great precision. First, the teacher drilled older children in the lesson; then these older children taught groups of younger children, who in turn might drill still other children younger than themselves. By this ripple or multiplicative effect, efforts of a single "master" (teacher) could be increased manyfold.

Proponents of the system of using children for teaching were well aware that it had social, as well as cognitive, benefits for both the learner and the teacher. Both Bell and Lancaster commented explicitly on the improvement in behavior due to younger children's emulating the positive behaviors of older children who were placed in a position of trust and responsibility as teachers. A not insignificant social–psychological feature of this system is that the individualized instruction afforded close surveillance of each child's behavior, a point mentioned by Lancaster (1803) and Laborde (1815) as being an important factor in reducing disciplinary problems.

The fame of the student-teaching-student system for inexpensively educating poor children spread beyond the borders of Britain and attracted attention in other countries. A Frenchman visiting England in the early nineteenth century wrote a book recording his impressions of the Bell–Lancaster schools and advocated establishing a similar system in France (Laborde, 1815). As he noted, mothers who have children of different ages realize that they like to teach and help each other:

Toutes les mères de famille qui ont des enfans de differens ages, ont observé combien ils aiment à se reprendre l'un l'autre, à se corriger, et combien les grands jouissent avec une sorte de protection et de bonté des maladresses des petits [p. 51].

Labord then expresses his amazement that such an obvious phenomenon has not been used in public education:

> Il est extraordinaire qu'un spectacle que tout le monde a toujours sous les yeux,
> n'ait pas donné plus tot l'idée de l'appliquer à l'education publique [p. 30].

Popularity of the Bell–Lancaster system gradually waned over the
years, apparently for several reasons. It appears that the basic weakness
of such schools was the generally low standard of teaching by the
untrained children, who were often only 8- or 9-years old (Dures,
1971). In addition, in the early nineteenth century facilities were not
adequate for training professional teachers to use these techniques
effectively. Interest in the Bell–Lancaster system also diminished as the
state began to provide money for public education; the low cost of the
tutorial schools as a means of educating the poor was a point frequently
emphasized by its proponents. (Notice the title of Lancaster's 1805
pamphlet: *Improvements in Education as it respects the Industrious
Classes of the Community, Containing, Among Other Important Particulars, an Account of the Institution for the Education of one Thousand
Poor Children.*) One can speculate, finally, that the growth of profes-
sionalism among teachers also contributed to the decline of the tutorial
schools. A self-conscious teaching profession is likely to look with
disdain and derision upon the idea that untrained young children can
perform the skilled function of teacher.

Previous Research

A wide variety of tutoring programs now exist that use children as
tutors for other children in the schools (Gartner, Kohler, and Riessman,
1971; Thelen, 1969). Although these programs are claimed to be
beneficial in many ways for both tutors and tutees, the supporting
evidence has often been inconclusive. It is quite common for anecdotal
reports, rather than rigorous data, to constitute the information
obtained from tutorial programs in the schools (e.g., Bell, Garlock and
Colella, 1969; Costello and Martin, 1972; Goodman, 1971; Moskowitz,
1972; Office of Education, 1967; Swett, 1971). Yet some well controlled research studies have been reported in the area (e.g., Ellson,
Barber, Engle, and Kampwerth, 1965; Klosterman, 1970; Robertson,
1971). Encouraged by the prospect of positive effects for both tutors
and tutees (especially when using older children to teach younger
children), a large number of schools have recently inaugurated some
form of tutorial program. It should be emphasized, however, that there

is a surprising paucity of systematic theory and research available in this area: Application has outpaced understanding.

In a recent paper we critically reviewed the available research on tutoring, examining both long-term programs operating in the school and short-term experiments investigating specific variables that affect the outcome of tutoring (Feldman, Devin-Sheehan, and Allen, 1974). Only a limited amount of data is available—and it often inconclusive— concerning many crucial variables that may determine the outcome of a tutoring program, such as characteristics of the tutor and tutee, (sex, race, and socioeconomic status), age differential between tutor and tutee, time spent in tutoring, and type of training received by the tutor. These and other variables are discussed in our review; it will suffice at this time to make only a few generalizations. A wide range of types of children appear to benefit from the experience of tutoring, including children with behavior problems, low-achievers, and institutionalized children. As for whether same- or opposite-sex tutor and tutee pairing is more effective, available data are inconclusive. Surprisingly, there is only a small amount of data on race, socioeconomic status, and age differential between tutor and tutee. Nor did we locate any studies that compared the effect of varying amounts of time spent in tutoring. Some research has attempted to evaluate the effect of training on the tutor, but the data do not indicate clearly that any one particular training method is superior to others; there is very little research showing that tutor training has a beneficial effect at all.

Most of the available research on tutoring can be characterized as evaluation research; thus, the typical study simply attempts to demonstrate that a particular tutoring program causes a positive change for tutees or tutors. Mere evaluation research—which does not systematically vary the multitudinous variables involved in a tutoring program—is not likely to lead to a deeper understanding of tutoring. Moreover, from our review of the literature, it is quite clear that numerous problems of methodology are quite common in much of the research in the area of tutoring.

Some of the most frequently encountered methodological problems deserve mentioning. Failure to collect rigorous data from tutoring programs is a common practice in research in this area. Even more important, many studies simply do not employ pertinent control groups (e.g., Hassinger and Via, 1969; Klein and Niedermeyer, 1971; Schoeller and Pearson, 1970). It is often difficult, of course, to obtain appropriate control groups when research is conducted in the context of an ongoing school program. In spite of such difficulty, the importance of control groups cannot be overemphasized; they are simply indispensible for arriving at a definitive conclusion about a tutoring

250   Vernon L. Allen

program. Interpretation of results of any tutoring program will remain equivocal without appropriate control conditions.

Difficulty in the method used to select tutors and tutees is related to the issue of appropriate control groups. For example, in one study an experimental group of volunteers was compared to a control group of nonvolunteers (Lucas, Gaither, and Montgomery, 1968). Unfortunately, for obvious practical reasons this is not an uncommon practice in tutoring research. Such problems in design may produce apparently inexplicable results, as in the study by Weitzman (1965). In this study high school juniors and seniors tutored 25 other high school students who volunteered for the program. The controls were matched with experimentals by sex, age, and scores on an aptitude test. Paradoxically, the participating volunteer students were rated by their teachers as having *less* motivation than students in the control group. On being asked at the conclusion of the program why they joined the program, 36% of the "volunteers" said they were asked by teachers or felt compelled to join. Results showed that although tutored students did not show greater improvement on classroom examinations and quizzes than nontutored students, they did improve more than the controls in study habits, motivation and interest, and in homework and classroom exercises. These data may well be biased, since the pre- and post-ratings on which they are based were made by the students' teachers—who had helped develop the program and who were thus aware of the identities of tutees and of control students.

In contrast, a study that stands out as a model of well controlled research is Klosterman's (1970) experiment. One of the four schools in low socioeconomic districts was randomly selected as a control school; children from two randomly selected fourth-grade classrooms from this school were designated the school control group. In the other three schools, fourth-graders were either assigned randomly to be tutored individually, tutored in a small group, or to be members of the control group for the class. This is the only study we located that included control groups both for the classroom and for the school. The school control group is particularly important, since it is likely that the existence of a tutorial program in a school would affect control students in that school—especially if they are in a classroom that has tutors or tutees participating. This study found that tutoring did significantly increase reading achievement scores. It is of methodological interest to note that results showed no difference between the classroom control and the school control conditions.

Two important variables that are frequently not controlled in tutoring research are the role of friendship between tutor and tutee and the total amount of instructional time received. Most studies have compared the effects of tutoring plus classroom instruction to classroom instruction alone. When tutoring is supplementary to classroom instruction (as it usually is), any obtained benefits may be attributable to the increased instruction time rather than to the tutoring itself. One study that did take this factor into account used more able second- and third-grade students as tutors for their slower learning classmates (Mollad, 1970). The control group (three classes in each of the two grades) spent 2½ hours weekly on word knowledge and 4 hours weekly on reading comprehension in their classrooms. The tutored experimental group (also three classes from each grade) spent half the specifically allotted time receiving class instruction and the other half being tutored. After 4 months, tutees in both grades made significantly greater gains than the controls in word knowledge (though not in reading comprehension). Tutors improved at least as much or more than tutees.

For an objective evaluation of a tutoring program, it is clear that controls are needed for several obvious factors of the sort mentioned above. One additional factor that has not been controlled in any study is the special attention and extensive personal contact that tutors and tutees (especially tutors) receive from teachers and other adults in the course of the operation of the program. Many of the controls mentioned as being important are probably integral components of tutoring programs as most are now constituted. Yet it is still important to try to disentangle the critical variables from the many unessential ones; in order to understand any change in behavior and achievement, it is imperative to isolate the variables responsible. In the absence of appropriate control groups, one cannot say with confidence whether any effects can be attributed to the tutoring, per se, or to other factors that are merely associated with the program.

Having made these methodological criticisms, at the same time it should be emphasized that some well-conducted studies of tutoring programs have obtained positive results. Moreover, subjective reports of teachers and children, coupled with the intuitive plausibility that this technique is beneficial for both tutors and tutees, are criteria deserving serious consideration in any comprehensive and balanced assessment.

Of perhaps even more fundamental importance than inadequate statistical controls and lack of rigorous research design are substantive and theoretical issues in tutoring research. All too often in this area there has been only minimal attention devoted to conceptualizing the research program in theoretical terms. If available psychological and educational theory are not utilized in formulating problems, the resulting research on tutoring is likely to be rather fragmented, inconclusive, and noncumulative. The wider use of systematic theory should lead to the investigation of problems of more basic significance, thereby contributing to a better understanding of the practical question of how one should organize an effective tutoring program to meet the individual needs of many different types of students.

THEORETICAL ANALYSIS

In applied research, there are advantages to be gained from approaching a problem with a general theoretical framework in mind. First, a theory helps identify relevant independent and dependent variables for investigation—a procedure likely to be more efficient and productive than selecting variables by trial and error or by intuition. Second, intervening psychological processes will usually be specified by a theory, thereby suggesting an explanatory scheme for the behavior in question. And, third, the conceptual framework of a theory provides units of analysis and a corresponding terminology for communicating about the phenomena in a coherent and systematic manner. (See also Ghatala and Levin's discussion of theory in Part I of this volume.)

Our research uses a role theory framework for the conceptual analysis of the cross-age tutoring situation in which an older child helps a younger child with school work. "Social role" is a concept used to designate the set of expectations that are associated with a particular position in the social structure, such as father or mother, teacher or student. These expectations always define the rights and duties of any person who occupies a given social position. Role expectations can be specified only in relation to complementary roles; thus, for example, the role of teacher consists of expectations relative to the complementary role of student. The basic datum of role theory is role enactment—the behavior appropriate to the social position that an individual occupies. To resort to a dramaturgic metaphor, according to role theory social behavior adheres to the part and not to the actor.

In the role theory conceptualization of social behavior, several variables are recognized as affecting one's role enactment, such as role location, accuracy of role expectations, involvement in the role, congruence between self and role, role demands, and cognitive and motoric skills. Space does not permit a discussion of these factors here; they are explicated in some detail by Sarbin and Allen (1968). Role theory also provides an account of the bases of self or social identity and deals with the effect of role enactment on self-concept and social identity. In everyday life, one enacts more than a single role; multiple role enactment often leads to complex problems of conflict between roles. Since so much of our behavior consists of enactment of social roles, concepts taken from role theory can be profitably employed to interpret a substantial amount of social behavior.

Role theory is employed in the present research project because it appears to be particularly appropriate for analysis of cross-age tutoring. The macro-social roles of teacher and student are also involved in the micro-social system of tutoring. The molar units of analysis used by role theory appear to render it especially amenable to the analysis of complex ongoing social behavior and applied research problems in general. Moreover, role theory explicitly recognizes the interactive and complementary nature of social behavior. The theory has the further advantage of linking the individual to the social system by means of the concept of social position. It is unfortunately true that many psychological theories view the individual as an entity totally encapsulated from the surrounding social system. It should be pointed out that our research uses role theory primarily as a heuristic device—as a framework for suggesting questions and for analyzing the tutoring situation—and is not basically directed toward deriving specific predictions about role theory that can be formally tested.

The Tutor

One intriguing finding from existing research is that the tutor may benefit from tutoring even more than the tutee in many cases. For instance, Cloward (1967) found that over a 7-month period tenth- and eleventh-graders who had tutored younger children showed a significantly greater increase in reading achievement scores than a comparable control group that did not tutor. Furthermore, the gain in reading scores by the tutors was even greater than the tutees' improvement. In addition, abundant anecdotal evidence suggests that the tutor may profit in a variety of ways from his involvement in teaching: The tutor's motivation, sense of responsibility, and attitude toward school appear to show a positive shift. Accepting such claims for the moment, how can one explain the apparently beneficial effect of tutoring on the tutor?

A role theoretical analysis would seem to be directly applicable to this question. It is a basic tenet of role theory that enactment of a role produces changes in self-concept, attitudes, cognitions, and behaviors in a direction consistent with expectations associated with the role. A substantial amount of empirical evidence demonstrates that role enactment does produce behavioral and attitudinal changes in the person enacting a role (Lieberman, 1956; Waller, 1932). Role theory would account for the effects of tutoring on the tutor as the consequence of enacting the role of teacher, in much the same way that enacting any role produces behavioral and cognitive changes congruent with role expectations.

Let us look closely at the role of teacher in terms of possible effect on learning. Successful enactment of the role of teacher (or tutor) requires that a person engage in behavior clearly distinguishable from the behavior of a person enacting the role of student (or tutee). First, it is necessary for a teacher to adopt a completely different point of view from that taken by a student. It is thus likely that a restructuring and reorganizing of the material to be taught will occur when a person enacts the role of teacher. There are cognitive benefits from having to find examples and illustrations, and in explaining things to the younger child in an uncomplicated way: By being forced to explain something in very simple terms the tutor also comes to understand the material better himself. By comparing their abilities and competencies with those of younger children, tutors find that they may know more than they realized and gain in confidence as a consequence of self-reinforcement. Another critical aspect of the teacher role is the requirement that one thoroughly master the material to be taught, which gives the tutor the opportunity to practice and relearn material before and during the session that he/she may have incompletely mastered in school. An important motivational factor is added by the possibility of embarrassment in the presence of the student if the teacher were not to know the material well. Also, since teachers are generally understood to be respected, prestigious, authority figures, role enactment may increase self-esteem and produce positive attitudes toward school and teacher due to identification with the teacher. Being a tutor should enhance the child's role-taking ability—to understand better the teacher's point of view by cognitively placing himself in the teacher's position—when he is back in the classroom. All these factors intrinsic to the role of teacher should facilitate the learning of material when one enacts the role of teacher.

Turning now to more general aspects of the role, the most pervasive characteristic of the role of teacher is that of helping another person. It is interesting to note that the helping relationship often seems to be as beneficial to the helper as it is to the help-recipient. Across diverse areas of behavior, it has been observed repeatedly that an individual who helps others experiences positive dividends of a psychological nature. Evidence from several areas in addition to tutoring supports this conclusion. For instance, research has shown that young persons engaged in various types of volunteer service (e.g., community service or overseas service such as the peace corps) derive personal benefits from the experience of helping others (Gillette, 1968). In the mental health field, several programs have employed college students to visit and socialize with patients in mental hospitals. Quite apart from any effects such programs have on the patients, it has been found that the students are positively affected by the experience of being useful (Holzberg, Knapp, and Turner, 1966).

It is clear that in a variety of settings the process of helping another person also results in beneficial psychological changes taking place in the person providing the help. Unfortunately, children are typically the recipients of help from others, rather than the givers of help. Thus, any program such as tutoring, which allows children to help other persons, would contribute significantly to their feeling useful and needed. The feeling of being helpful to others is particularly important for adolescents who—being caught between childhood and adulthood—realize that they are not yet actually useful and needed members of society.

The social relationship between the tutor and the tutee is another source of potential benefit for the tutor. When tutoring a younger child, the older child can learn to be nurturant and to take responsibility for another person, which may foster more mature behavior in general. Being emulated and respected by a younger child enhances the tutor's self-esteem and at the same time promotes positive social behavior. Thus, older children should be less likely to engage in undesirable and antisocial behavior, realizing that a younger (and unsophisticated) children may imitate their actions; being a role model for a younger child constrains one's behavior along socially desirable directions. In summary, from interacting in a tutorial setting with a younger child, the older child may derive a number of outcomes that contribute toward more positive social behavior both in and out of school.

The Tutee

Several factors can be mentioned that probably contribute to any impact that tutoring may have on the tutee. First of all, tutoring is an eminent example of individualized instruction. By virtue of the one-to-one situation, the material to be learned can be matched closely to the learner's interests and ability, and immediate feedback can be provided. In terms of a role theory analysis, it is interesting to point out that the tutor–tutee relationship possesses an important element that is lacking when an adult is the teacher. In the child-teaching-child situation, it is more likely that an affective relationship will develop between the tutor and tutee. This emotional component may be a very important contributory factor in the learning by the tutee.

Some of the possible beneficial consequences for the younger child in a different-age tutoring interaction are quite apparent. The natural respect and emulation that younger children display for older children can be utilized to the advantage of learning in the tutoring situation. Older children can play an important part in the social development of younger children by influencing and reinforcing their prosocial behaviors. It is plausible to believe that communication during teaching between children who are close in age could be more effective and satisfying to the tutee than communication between adults (e.g., teachers) and children, with the result that material may be learned more efficiently. Both cognitive and motivational aspects of learning may be more acceptable to the tutee when coming from another child rather than from an adult.

Age seems to be particularly salient at the younger stages of life because it is highly related to noticeable and valued characteristics such as size and strength. A younger child can use an older tutor as a role model—as a source for setting level of aspiration for achievement. Research shows that older age is positively valued by younger children (Lohman, 1970). Being a friend of a prestigious older child can enhance a younger child's self-esteem. It can be maintained, then, that the younger child stands to gain in many ways from social interaction in the context of a benevolent or helping relationship such as the tutoring situation.

From Theory to Research

Four objectives of the present research project on cross-age tutoring can be specified:

1. To delineate in a systematic manner the cognitive, social, and affective consequences of tutoring for both the child serving as teacher and the child who is the learner.
2. To provide an understanding of the psychological factors that mediate any effects of tutoring on the participants.
3. To attain a better understanding of the social interaction processes occurring between the tutor and tutee in the tutoring situation.
4. To specify, on the basis of theoretical analysis and empirical findings, the particular techniques of tutoring that will result in optimal benefit for tutors under any set of conditions.

The general strategy of the present research program was planned to maximize the benefits derived from a reciprocal relation between theory and empirical findings, and to enable the research to proceed by using diverse though complementary research methods. Several phases or stages of research were planned. First, some early studies were conducted as field studies in school settings, from which detailed firsthand observations of cross-age tutoring procedures could be made. The purpose of these early studies was not merely to demonstrate the existence of the phenomenon of interest (many such studies already existed), but to gain firsthand familiarity with the tutoring process. Several components of behavior were examined as dependent variables for both the tutor and tutee: academic achievement, self-esteem and motivational variables, attitudes toward various aspects of school, role-taking ability, identification with authority, and several behavioral measures. These studies were quite exploratory—being designed as validation research and also as a means of hypothesis-finding under naturalistic conditions.

In a second stage research was directed toward a systematic exploration of the variables affecting the outcome of the peer-teaching techniques. These studies have practical utility in providing information for schools concerning the most efficient conditions for peer-teaching. In addition, such parametric studies are useful theoretically in demonstrating the range of potent variables affecting the outcome of tutoring, and thereby suggesting underlying psychological processes that may be responsible for any positive effects. Both short-term and longer duration studies were conducted in the school and in the laboratory setting.

A third stage, or component, of the research strategy involved a somewhat different research methodology. This research overlapped in time with the other stages, but was concentrated primarily in the early phases of the research program so that any suggestive findings could be tested more systematically by controlled studies. To a certain extent, research during this stage was directed toward hypothesis-finding. Methodology in this stage of research consisted of techniques that permitted the collection of data in a more exploratory, unstructured, unconstrained, and yet more intensive manner. Included in the research at this stage were studies utilizing interviews, questionnaires, and self-report measures of a structured and semistructured nature. Information was obtained from both children and teachers.

A fourth stage in the research overlapped somewhat with the other stages. Several studies instigated under more controlled conditions investigated selected hypotheses having theoretical (and practical) interest. We attempted here to separate certain components from the complex ongoing interaction process by systematically manipulating particular variables while holding others constant. In this way, causal effects could be ascertained to a degree utterly impossible to attain in the context of the more complex natural process of the multifarious correlated variables existing in the school setting. These studies were usually of shorter duration than the field studies, but varied in length from a single session to repeated sessions lasting over a period of several weeks. The particular purpose of the investigation dictated the duration of the study.

In summary, the research strategy was designed to pursue investigations among four substantive fronts: validation and hypothesis-finding studies in the school, parametric studies in the school and laboratory, hypothesis-finding studies by self-report techniques, and hypothesis-testing studies by the experimental method. Different, though complementary, research methodologies were utilized, and findings at one stage were related to research at other stages. The research unavoidably overlapped in time to a considerable extent, of course, and not all stages received the same amount of research attention. Most of the studies investigated specific hypotheses of theoretical interest or of practical importance by way of studies of fairly short duration in the laboratory setting.

FIELD STUDIES OF TUTORING

Several of our investigations have been concerned with obtaining relatively general information about tutoring, using fairly naturalistic and unstructured research techniques. Discussed in this section will be a self-report study on tutoring and cross-age interaction in the one-room school and a questionnaire study dealing with childrens' preferences for various tutoring arrangements.

The One-Room School

If one looks for a setting that would appear to offer the optimal possibility for cross-age interaction within a setting conducive to positive behavior, the one-room school of the not-so-distant past would seem to provide an ideal paradigm. The one-teacher village school which was once very common is now found only in sparsely populated rural areas. Within a single room children of a wide range of ages attended school.

Being present in the same room with both older and younger children enabled students to overhear lessons the teacher gave to children who were more and less advanced than themselves. In addition to the advantages of review and preview of material made possible by this arrangement, there were other advantages, such as the older children helping the younger with their lessons. The burden of being the sole teacher to several levels of students often made it necessary for the teacher to turn to the older children for assistance with the younger. On the playground the lack of substantial numbers of children of the same age forced all ages to play together to a greater extent than in a traditional school.

In order to explore students' behavior and attitudes in the one-room school setting, we administered separate questionnaires to teachers and students in 110 one-teacher schools in the state of Nebraska (Allen and Devin-Sheehan, 1974). Responses were obtained from 1405 students and 110 teachers. The focus of the study was primarily on the extent and nature of cross-age contacts in these schools. The study investigated the use of children as tutors and helpers for other children, interaction across ages in academic and social settings, and teachers' views of the academic and social advantages and disadvantages of one-teacher schools as compared to graded schools. In addition, the study also assessed the children's attitudes about school, themselves, and older and younger children.

According to teachers' reports, some form of student or peer tutoring took place on a fairly regular basis in 31% of the schools, and in another 25% of the schools there was some kind of informal tutoring program. Moreover, 77% of the students stated that they sometimes asked other students for help with schoolwork when they were at their desks, and 88% reported working together with other students. In these schools it is clear that other students are important learning resources for a child. Students from all grades were used as tutors. Teachers reported that in the lower grades (one through three) boys and girls were tutors equally often; but in the upper grades (four through eight) girls were much more likely than boys to be tutors. This seems to be at least partially due to the teachers' preferences, for in 82% of the schools having a formal program the tutors were selected by the teacher.

Most of the formal tutoring was on a one-to-one basis, with some being on a one-to-two or one-to-three basis. Tutors had more than one tutee in 79% of the cases, and usually worked with their students each day, or two to three times a week. There was an equal number of same-sex and opposite-sex tutoring pairs. Various age differences existed between tutor and tutee, ranging from same-age to as much as 5 years difference. The most frequent age difference between tutor and tutee was 2 years, followed by 3 and 4 years' difference. The students who were tutored felt positively about the experience, with the younger students expressing more enthusiasm than the older. Student responses to questions about school were also generally favorable. On one item 59–64% of the students in each grade stated that they would not prefer being in a school where all the children in the room were the same age as the respondent.

One item in the student questionnaire stated: "When you are working at your seat and you can hear the teacher giving a lesson to *older* students, do you ever listen? How many new things do you learn when you listen?" Results are presented in Table 1. Of interest is the large

TABLE 1
Responses to the Item: "When You Are Working at Your Seat and You Can Hear the Teacher Giving a Lesson to *Older* Students, Do You Ever Listen?"[a]

Grade	Boys' responses (%)				Girls' responses (%)			
	I don't listen	I don't learn any new things	I learn some new things	I learn many new things	I don't listen	I don't learn any new things	I learn some new things	I learn many new things
1	05	04	29	62	04	01	47	48
2	07	02	39	52	03	04	47	46
3	09	03	44	44	10	01	52	37
4	04	05	49	42	04	02	61	33
5	04	03	61	32	03	01	66	30
6	09	03	58	30	09	03	64	24
7	10	04	62	24	06	00	67	27
8	35	06	41	18	20	06	65	09
Mean	10	04	48	38	07	02	59	32

[a] $n = 1405$

proportion of students who indicated that they did listen to older students' lessons and felt doing so was useful to them. Similar data are shown in Table 2 for students' responses to a related question: "When you are working at your seat and you hear the teacher giving a lesson to *younger* students, do you ever listen? Does this help you with things you've already learned?" Again, it is noteworthy that most students said they listened to and benefited from other (younger) students' lessons. Older students listened less than younger, as would be expected, but even among the oldest students (eighth graders) 80% of the boys and 92% of the girls reported that they listened and were helped by the lessons.

A large amount of social interaction seems to occur across different age levels in these one-room schools. In response to a question asking how much time was spent talking with various age groups, students reported that they talked about the same amount with other students who were older, younger, and the same age as themselves. Consistent with these data, 76% of the students stated that it was easy to be friends with children of all different ages. According to data obtained from both teachers and students, it is clear that the older children felt a strong sense of responsibility for the younger children. When the older students (grades four through eight) were asked if they felt they should help take care of the younger children at school, 94% of the girls and 87% of the boys replied affirmatively.

Some information was obtained concerning role models. Among the older students 45% of the boys and 37% of the girls reported that younger children tried to act like them; one-third of the older students thought that the younger children did not use them as role models. Furthermore, 23% of the older students indicated that they themselves tried to act like students older than themselves, as compared with 39% of the younger boys and 31% of the younger girls.

Teachers were asked to list (separately) the academic and social advantages and disadvantages of the one-teacher schools. In order of descending frequency, the 103 teachers who responded to this item mentioned the following as academic advantages: A teacher can give more individualized attention (54); children learn from each other (37); the younger children learn from the older children (36); students can progress at their own rate (34); and the older students get review from the younger students' lessons (27). As academic disadvantages teachers listed most frequently: not enough materials (30); not enough time for teacher to get around to everyone in every subject (17); and lack of competition from students' own age group (10). As for advantages for social and character development of students, the following were listed most often: Students learn to work and play with children of all ages

TABLE 2
Responses to the Item: "When You Are Working at Your Seat and You Hear the Teacher Giving a Lesson to Younger Students, Do You Ever Listen?"[a]

Grade	Boys' responses (%)				Girls' responses (%)			
	I don't listen	Listening doesn't help me	Listening helps me a little	Listening helps me a lot	I don't listen	Listening doesn't help me	Listening helps me a little	Listening helps me a lot
1	14	13	22	51	08	14	27	51
2	16	13	30	41	10	07	49	34
3	13	20	37	30	15	17	36	32
4	20	14	45	21	14	13	45	28
5	28	22	37	13	14	16	55	15
6	16	19	48	17	12	20	57	11
7	20	13	56	11	08	10	58	24
8	20	10	50	20	08	05	75	12
Mean	18	15	42	25	11	13	50	26

[a] $n = 1405$

(78); older students learn to take responsibility for and to understand younger students (51); and a feeling of family-like closeness and togetherness prevails (19). The two most frequent social disadvantages mentioned were: social shyness of students (9); and less adequate social opportunities for seventh and eighth graders (9). The open-ended responses given by teachers indicated strong enthusiasm about their schools, and they believed that the advantages greatly outweighed the disadvantages. Perhaps the limiting case of the one-room school would closely approximate a large family (Bossard and Boll, 1956). In fact, one teacher reported that a student had recently stated to her, "We are just like a big family and you are the mommy." The teacher asked us, "Is this an advantage?"

Attitudes and Preferences

As part of our general role theory orientation to understanding the effect of tutoring on the tutor, we measured role perceptions and expectations by assessing the preferences of 865 children regarding a variety of tutoring arrangements, both from the vantage point of tutor and tutee. The students ranged in grade from first through eighth, and came from schools in a large city, a suburb, and a rural area. Each student received one of the two forms of the questionnaire—the tutor or the tutee version. The nature of the peer-tutoring situation was described to the students before administering the questionnaire. The students indicated whether he—she would rather teach (or be taught by) a boy or girl, by someone he—she knew or didn't know, alone or with one or two others. Other questions asked for the preferred amount of time to be spent in tutoring, level of difficulty of the lesson, frequency of grading, and preferred age and level of ability of the tutee (or tutor).

Results for both boys and girls indicated preference for having same-sex tutors and tutees. The students also preferred to teach children younger than themselves, and to be taught by children older than themselves. Other results revealed a slight preference for being taught alone instead of with one or two other tutees. Being taught on a one-to-one basis was preferred by 42% of the children, with about equal percentage of the remaining saying they would like to be taught by one or by two other tutees. Interestingly, about 60% of the younger children (grades 1--3) said they would rather teach three children at the same time. For older white children (grades 4–6), about equal preference (40%) was given for teaching either one child or three together, whereas older black children expressed a strong preference for teaching three children at the same time (74%).

One item on the questionnaire assessed the grading preference of children when teaching and learning. Students who answered the learner questionnaire were asked how often they would like their "child teacher" to give them grades: either none at all, a grade every time they met, or a grade only at the end of the teaching program. As shown in the top half of Table 3, most learners expressed a preference for receiving grades rather than not being graded at all (23% of the younger rural students said they would not like to be graded at all). Most students preferred being graded at the end of the tutoring program rather than at every meeting. As can be seen in the bottom half of Table 3, most of the children said that if they were teaching another child they would prefer giving grades at the end of the tutoring program, just as learners did. But among the younger white students, about 55% stated they would rather give grades at each meeting.

On another item three-quarters of the students who responded as learners expressed a preference for their teacher to be "much smarter than me"; yet more than half the students responding as tutors said they would like to teach a child who was "just as smart" or "much smarter" than themselves.

TABLE 3
Preferred Grading Frequency of Tutors and Tutees (in Percentages)

| | (A) Tutees | | | | | | |
| | Grades 1–3 | | | | Grades 4–6 | | |
	(N)	None	Each	End	(N)	None	Each	End
Rural	(159)	23	36	41	(87)	02	36	62
Suburban	(68)	08	41	52	(27)	07	07	85
Urban								
(black)	(115)	08	31	63	(114)	09	25	67
Mean		13	35	52		06	22	72

| | (B) Tutors | | | | | | |
| | Grades 1–3 | | | | Grades 4–6 | | |
	(N)	None	Each	End	(N)	None	Each	End
Rural	(94)	09	56	35	(41)	07	41	51
Suburban	(20)	55	55	45	(42)	07	21	71
Urban								
(black)	(58)	19	19	76	(44)	07	20	73
Mean		05	43	52		07	27	66

THE ROLE OF THE TUTOR

As noted earlier, one of the most interesting results to emerge from research on tutoring concerns its effects on the older child who teaches or helps the younger child; the improvement is not only in learning but also in social, motivational, attitudinal, and self-concept changes (Gartner, Kohler and Riessman, 1971). The positive effects of tutoring have seemed impressive to teachers and other observers over the years. Turning to the nineteenth century for an example, Joseph Lancaster remarked in his book published in 1803:

> . . . I have ever found, the surest way to cure a mischievous boy was to make him a *monitor*. I never knew anything succeed much better, if as well [p. 31; italics in the original].

By the term "monitor," Lancaster means "tutor." And Lancaster did have some extreme cases. In one instance a boy's truancy was so severe that

> . . . his father got a log and chain and chained it to his foot, and in that condition, beating him all the way, followed him to school repeatedly . . . [Lancaster, 1803, p. 32].

In-School Studies

In an earlier section several psychological processes were mentioned that may contribute toward the social and personal benefits for the tutor resulting from the tutoring situation: The older child is looked up to and emulated by the younger child; being a role-model may influence the older child's behavior in socially desirable ways; the tutor feels that he/she is doing something important and valuable that will truly help a younger child; and the tutor perceives himself/herself as enacting the prestigious and responsible role of teacher. In short, it seems that when a child is placed in this responsible role he discovers that he must live up to its expectations.

The role of teacher represents prestige, authority, and suggests competence. It would seem reasonable that enactment of this role would increase self-esteem and produce positive attitudes toward school and teachers for the child who tutors. How can one maximize the positive consequences to the child enacting the role of teacher? According to role theory, a number of factors contribute to the degree of individual change produced by enacting a role, including involvement in the role, clarity of role expectations, and so on (Sarbin and Allen, 1968).

Following the line of thinking suggested by role theory, in our studies of ongoing tutoring in the schools we have attempted to incorporate those factors that should enhance the positive effects of tutoring for the tutor. To increase involvement and provide greater clarity of role expectations, we supplied appropriate symbolic cues that would increase visibility of the role for the tutor, tutees, and other children. Distinctive appurtenances were provided, such as a certificate designating the tutor as a "student teacher," a portfolio for keeping a daily log and lesson plans, and other equipment typically possessed by a teacher. Tutors consulted with their classroom teacher on their tutee's needs; they were given some responsibility for developing a curriculum for their tutee; they had disciplinary responsibility for their tutee; and they were not closely monitored. All these "symbols and tokens of position" should have enhanced involvement in the role and helped clarify role expectations—factors that should increase the likelihood of behavioral and attitudinal changes consistent with expectations for the role of teacher.

It is interesting to note that a very consistent and almost unanimous response of the children who have participated in our tutoring programs has been a very positive reaction to the experience. Older children almost invariably reported that they enjoyed teaching the younger children; and the younger children also liked being taught in the one-to-one situation by a student who is 2 or 3 years older. Both tutors and tutees said they would like to participate in a similar program in the future. Many older children were very enthusiastic, in particular, about being able to teach younger children. It is not hard to understand why children are so enthusiastic about teaching other children. There are many very attractive elements that comprise the teacher role: increased responsibility, prestige, and status in the eyes of other students, attention and reward from adults, and respect from a younger child. Our studies in schools also provided suggestive data indicating positive responses by tutors on self-judgments of competence in intellectual and school-related areas; perhaps this was due to the tutors' having the opportunity to discover that they knew more than they realized and that they could be effective in teaching younger children.

The positive effects of tutoring on the tutor have frequently been so impressive that some schools have used it as a means of improving the academic work, motivation, and social interaction in the case of underachievers and children with behavior problems in school. Enacting the role of teacher may be a particularly effective means of producing an increase in learning for low-achieving children, who have probably repeatedly experienced failure and tend to be passive participants in any learning situation. An experiment was designed to investigate the learning of low-achieving children when placed in the role of teacher, in comparison to spending the same amount of time studying alone (Allen and Feldman, 1973). It was expected that both the tutee and tutor would benefit from tutoring, but that the relative superiority of tutoring over studying alone would be even greater for the tutor than for the tutee. To provide a rigorous test of this hypothesis, a short-term laboratory study was designed that allowed a much greater degree of control over extraneous factors than would have been possible in an actual school setting.

The control condition used for assessing the effect of tutoring in the present study differed from that usually employed in tutoring research. Typically, the effects of tutoring are evaluated by comparing results with a group of children not receiving any special treatment at all. A more reasonable comparison would be a group that spends the same amount of time studying the material by themselves. Certainly this control condition imposes a more strenuous test for evaluating the outcome of tutoring than found in the control condition traditionally used in this area. Moreover, for purposes of application to the school setting, one would like to know whether tutoring produces performance that is superior to solitary study of the same material.

Tutors were 10, low-achieving fifth-graders and tutees were 10, randomly-selected third-graders (8 males and 2 females in both cases). The children participated for 10 consecutive weekdays over a 2-week period. On alternate days, the fifth-grade tutor either taught the same third-grade tutee for 20 minutes or spent an equivalent period of time studying the material alone. The younger children were taught the day's lesson by the tutor or spent the same amount of time studying the material independently. At the conclusion of each day's lesson both children were given a test on the content of the material. Content of the lessons were counterbalanced, and included elementary scientific topics, language, and reading, all adapted from textbooks.

Results showed that over the 2-week period the tutors' performance improved while they were enacting the role of teacher; yet performance deteriorated slightly during the same period of time when they were studying the material alone (Figure 2). Moreover, on the last two sessions performance in the tutoring condition surpassed the level of any previous performance in the tutoring or studying alone conditions. As the tutors acquired more practice in enacting the role of teacher, they became increasingly successful in learning the material when tutoring. In the case of the learners (tutees), there was a weak interaction ($p < .10$): Initially they learned more when being taught, but by the end of the 2-week period they did slightly better when studying alone (Figure 3).

The results reveal a trend which, if borne out in further research, suggest an interesting dilemma. Ironically, conditions that provide opti-

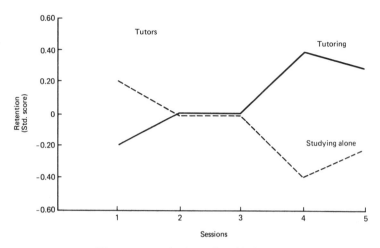

Figure 2. Learning by underachieving tutors.

mal benefits for low-achievers (tutoring) may be gained at the ultimate expense of the tutees, who might have profited more from spending the same amount of time studying the material by themselves. Low-achieving children may simply be poor tutors for other children. Therefore, tutees may suffer when included in a tutoring program designed to help low-achieving tutors. This point should not be pressed too strongly in view of only tentative results. These data are not conclusive by any means, but they should serve as a warning indicator, alerting one to the

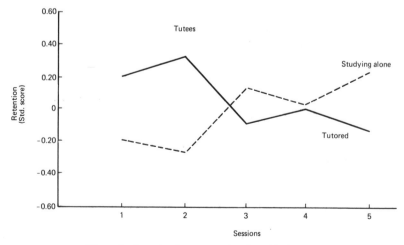

Figure 3. Learning by tutees of underachieving tutors.

possibility of a potential problem when designing long-term tutoring programs.

Evaluation

One interesting and perhaps central aspect of the role of teacher is evaluating and grading one's student. Data from the questionnaire study reported earlier indicated that both tutors and tutees felt that tutors should evaluate and grade the learners quite frequently. It may well be that evaluation and power over the student are attractive components of the teacher role for children who serve as tutors. This could be one aspect of the role that contributes to the tutor's feelings of importance, authority, and confidence. Students' statements of preferences in connection with the teacher role should not, however, be completely accepted in the absence of congruent behavioral data. Therefore, a tutoring situation was devised in which the degree of evaluation and importance of the evaluation required of tutors was systematically varied (Towson and Allen, 1970).

Subjects were male and female fifth- and third-grade children; a total of 39 tutor–tutee pairs participated in the experiment. The same-sex tutors and tutees were randomly assigned to three conditions: evaluation with reward, evaluation but no reward, and no evaluation at all. In the evaluation–reward condition, each fifth-grade "teacher" completed a written evaluation of his (or her) third-grade "student" after each of the six daily tutoring sessions. On the basis of this evaluation the fifth-grade teacher determined the size of the reward deserved by the third-grade student for that lesson. This condition was included so that the grades given by the tutor would appear to have important (or, in any case, pleasant) consequences for the tutee. In the evaluation–no-reward condition, the tutor also evaluated the tutee's performance after each session, but had no power to allocate rewards. In the no-evaluation condition the tutor neither evaluated the tutee nor determined amount of reward. Reading material was used as the content of the lessons.

In the evaluation–reward and evaluation–no-reward conditions each fifth-grade tutor completed a "report card" concerning the tutee at the end of each tutoring session. Grades were given both for performance and for effort. The third-grade tutees knew that they were being graded, but they were not actually shown the report cards, since knowledge of the evaluation would influence performance differentially across experimental conditions. (The tutors believed that the tutees saw the grades.) The report cards were not used in the control (no-evaluation) condition.

Upon completion of each tutoring session, each fifth-grade tutor in the evaluation–reward condition also decided how many small pieces of candy ("candy corn") his third-grade student deserved. So that the students' actual performance would not be affected differentially by the amount of reward received, the experimenter arranged always to give the same amount of candy to learners in all three conditions. Thus, any effect of reward was held constant. The fifth-grade tutors also received a standard amount of candy from the experimenter after each tutoring session.

Data concerning the tutors' reactions to the teaching role after their six days of experience as a teacher are presented in Table 4. Differences among the three experimental conditions were very clear and consistent. From the pattern of results shown in the table, it is obvious that tutors in the evaluation–reward condition were significantly less satisfied with their teaching experience than tutors in the other two conditions. Thus, for example, in comparison to the control condition, tutors in the evaluation–reward condition indicated that they believed they did less well as a tutor, thought the teaching was more difficult, and did not feel as important as a consequence of the teaching. When the evaluation carried important consequences for the tutee—namely, determined the number of candies he received—the task of evaluating the tutee seems to have been especially unpleasant and unsatisfying for the tutor. The relatively greater dissatisfaction expressed by tutors in the evaluation–reward condition may have been due to their discovering that the role of teacher was more difficult and stressful than they had

TABLE 4
Effects of Evaluation and Reward Components of the Role of Teacher[a]

Item	Evaluation plus reward	Evaluation no reward	No evaluation
1. Being a teacher was easy.	3.15	4.15	4.69
2. I was a good teacher.	3.69	4.16	4.08
3. Teaching made me feel important.	3.69	4.23	4.15
4. I would have liked teaching more if I could have given my student tests.	2.85	4.00	4.00
5. Correcting my student's reading mistakes made me feel important.	3.31	4.15	3.77
6. Filling out my student's report cards made me feel important.	3.31	4.15	—

[a]Agree very much = 5; Disagree very much = 1.

anticipated. Having the power to influence the outcome for another person was no doubt less enjoyable than the tutors could have believed before experiencing it. Certainly not all elements of the role of teacher are pleasant!

Being Imitated

Another factor that may contribute to the changes that tutoring brings about in the tutor concerns the concept of role model. Older children who serve as tutor for younger children may see that their behavior influences the tutee, both in cognitive and social areas. Thus tutors may serve as role models for younger children; that is, younger children may imitate tutors and try to be like them. If the older children realize that their own behavior has an effect on the younger children's behavior—that younger children use them as a models to copy—the older children may feel obligated to behave in socially desirable ways. With greater age discrepancies between the older and younger children, the effect on the older children of being role models should be stronger.

We have investigated experimentally the effect on sixth-grade tutors of being imitated in varying degrees by younger children (Allen and Devin-Sheehan, 1973). Tutors were 65, sixth-grade male and female students; tutees were 65, second-grade males and females. The tutoring materials were lists of sight words and reading games. The study was conducted in an elementary school over a period of 3 weeks. Three levels of imitation on a series of opinion statements (low, medium, and high) were experimentally controlled in order to determine if the tutors' reactions would differ as a function of varying degrees of imitation. In addition, amount of tutee liking for the tutor was either medium or high. Since imitation probably also normally implies liking, lack of this control would make it difficult to attribute any results solely to the imitation variable.

Results showed that female tutors' liking for their same-sex tutees increased the more they thought they had been imitated. But for male tutors, as the amount of imitation increased, a decrease in liking for their tutees was shown. These results suggest that the optimal level of perceived imitation for children may depend upon the sex of the child. In a school situation that provides opportunity for a considerable amount of out-of-class contact between older and younger children, the tutor's being a role model for the younger child to imitate and look up to may exert a very powerful influence in constraining the tutor's behavior along socially desirable channels. The present study provides information only on the tutor's affective reaction to being imitated;

research on the important behavioral consequences of being imitated by a younger child or a tutee has not yet been conducted.

TUTOR'S ATTRIBUTIONS ABOUT THE TUTEE

The reactions made by the tutor concerning his/her tutee—such as judgments about ability and liking—may have important effects for both the tutor and the tutee. In a series of studies we have investigated one factor likely to influence the attitudes and attributions of ability made by the tutor: the pattern of apparent success and failure of the tutee in learning the material.

Ongoing Behavior

Both reinforcement theory and role theory suggest that the degree of student success over a period of time will affect both the tutor's perception of the student's ability and the tutor's liking for the student. Thus, a student who does consistently well should be perceived as more intelligent and likeable than one who does consistently poorly. Likewise, a tutor should enjoy the teaching experience more when the student does consistently well than when the student does consistently poorly. These predictions are straightforward and not surprising. Role theory suggests further, however, that the order or sequence of a tutee's success or failure over time is a critical determinant of the tutor's perceptions. The impact of tutoring on the tutor should be affected by his/her perceived success in enacting the teacher role, that is, by success in actually helping the tutee.

In the tutoring situation, it is congruent with the role of teacher for a student to do poorly on a task initially but to later show improvement in performance. For one to enact appropriately and effectively the role of teacher, then, the learner should show an improvement in performance over time. The converse of this pattern of performance for one's student (initially doing well but then deteriorating over time) should be perceived as ineffectual and inappropriate enactment of the role of teacher. Thus, with an equivalent amount of objectively successful learning, the direction of change in the tutee's performance should lead to different consequences in terms of the tutor's satisfaction with his/her role enactment.

In our first study, the pattern or sequence of performance of a learner in the tutor—tutee learning situation was varied according to degree of congruence of the learning to expectations of the teacher role (Allen and Feldman, 1974a). Tutors were 81, eleven-year-old children who taught a concept-formation task to an 8-year-old confederate who was role-playing during a 45-minute session. Over the one-session teaching period the tutee's performance on the task varied according to one of four patterns: success throughout the session, failure throughout, success in the first half and failure in the second half, or failure in the first half and success in the second half. For conditions of changing performance by the tutee (success–failure, failure–success) the absolute level of performance remains identical, of course; only the sequence of success or failure differs across the two conditions. Under the learning situation more closely approximating expectations of the teacher role (poor initial performance then improvement), the tutor should respond more positively about his/her own performance as a teacher and express more positive attitudes and attributions about the learner.

Results showed clearly that the sequence of the tutee's success or failure, rather than absolute amount of learning, per se, determined the tutor's reactions. Figure 4 shows that the tutor's attributions about intellectual ability, liking of the tutee, and general reactions to the situation were disproportionately influenced by the tutee's performance early in the session. In other words, a strong and consistent primacy effect was found: The tutee's early performance exerted a significantly greater impact than later performance on several aspects of the tutor's reactions toward the tutee. The same primacy effect was also obtained for the tutor's own enjoyment of the tutoring session.

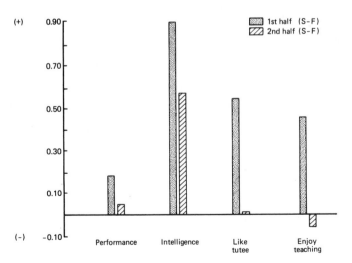

Figure 4. Reactions of tutors as a function of the sequence of ongoing performance by tutees (primacy effect). [Data indicate the difference between conditions of success and failure by the tutee (Success minus failure), when occuring at the first or second half of the session.]

Thus, results showed, contrary to the role theory prediction, that the condition more closely approximating the role of teacher (initial poor learning followed by improvement) did not result in more positive responses by the tutor. Even so, this finding led us to several more studies on the primacy effect in ability attributions and attitudinal response.

Would the primacy effect have occurred even if successful and unsuccessful learning were separated by an interval of a few days? Many actual tutoring programs in the schools are arranged on a schedule of two or three meetings a week. The temporal separation might be sufficient to destroy the initial expectation established by the tutor. In an attempt to eliminate the primacy effect in a subsequent study, the lesson was structured in some conditions as two discrete units temporally (Feldman and Allen, 1974a). Elementary school students either viewed the two parts of a lesson contiguously, or observed the second part 2 days after seeing the first part. In this study, subjects merely observed a tutoring session on videotape and then made judgments about the tutee's performance, instead of serving as tutors themselves. Results showed that separating the two parts of the lesson by a period of 2 days still did not eliminate the primacy effect: Early performance had a significantly greater effect on attribution concerning the tutee's ability and learning than later performance. A clear primacy effect under conditions of this study attests to the strength and persistence of initial expectations about a learner's performance.

Practical implications of these findings for cross-age tutoring in the schools are obvious. It is important that the first learning task be easy enough to ensure that the tutee can perform well, since initial learning strongly affects the tutor's attributions about the tutee's ability, liking of the tutee, and reaction to tutoring. And we know from other research that a teacher's expectations about a student can indeed influence the tutee's subsequent learning (Rubovits and Maehr, 1971). Moreover, the nature of the tutor's initial reactions to the tutoring situation may determine how much he/she will benefit from the potentially valuable experience of teaching a younger child.

Completed Behavior

We have discovered that it is possible to eliminate the primacy effect if one devises a completely different situation. The most satisfactory explanation for the primacy effect in ability attribution has been suggested by Jones, Goethals, Kennington, and Severance (1972). Jones *et al.* argue that in the case of attributions of stable traits such as ability, early performance sets up an initial expectation or anchor to which later changes in performance are assimilated. Assimilation presumably occurs through a process of memory distortion, with later performance being recalled as more consistent with early performance than is objectively true. It follows, according to this interpretation, that one way of eliminating the primacy effect is to insure that a person can accurately recall the entire pattern of performance.

An experiment was conducted to test this hypothesis (Feldman and Allen, 1974b). College students were given a questionnaire containing a chart showing the performance of a third-grade tutee who was tested on a trapezoid-identification task by a fifth-grade tutor. The chart indicated whether the tutee answered correctly or incorrectly on each of the 28 trials. Each subject received one of four charts, which differed in the proportion of correct and incorrect answers in the two halves of the test (success–success, failure–failure, success–failure, failure–success). The subject estimated how well the tutee did overall, and his/her level of intellectual ability. Since the complete record of the learner's performance was available to the subject, an initial expectation about the learner could not be established nor could the memory of later performance be distorted in any way.

As we expected, under these conditions the primacy effect did not materialize. To our surprise, however, a recency effect was obtained instead! That is, level of the second-half learning exerted a significant impact on judgment of performance and attribution of ability, though first-half learning did not.

To reassure ourselves that this finding was indeed a reliable phenomenon, the experiment was replicated with slight modifications. Results again revealed a strong recency effect both for attribution of ability and perception of performance, as indicated in Figure 5. Subjects' judg-

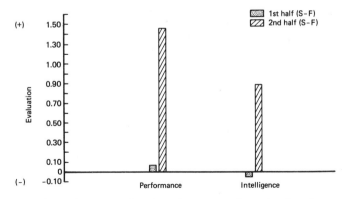

Figure 5. Reactions of tutor as a function of sequence of completed performance by tutee (recency effect). [Data indicate the difference between conditions of success and failure by the tutee (success minus failure), when occurring at the first or second half of the session.]

ments were disproportionally influenced by how well the tutee did in
the last part of the lesson.

It seems, then, that the tutor may be susceptible to either a primacy
or a recency effect in judgments about the learner, depending upon the
nature of the situation. Observation of on-going behavior as it unfolds
on a trial-to-trial basis results in early performance exerting a greater
impact than later performance on the attitudes and attributions made
about the student. By contrast, when the record of the learner's
sequence of completed performance is available for inspection, the level
reached on later performance seems to be taken as most indicative of
amount of learning and underlying ability. These findings should reduce
concern about the practical implications of the primacy effect observed
in attributions of ability. According to present data, a primacy effect
will not appear if the cumulative record of a person's performance is
available. Our studies indicate that when the entire sequence of performance is present, attribution of ability is more strongly affected by
most recent performance than by earlier performance. Certainly, then,
under such conditions the fear of biased effect of first impressions due
to early performance is not as serious a problem as our earlier findings
suggested. Availability of an objective record of the entire sequence of
learning is thus important if the primacy effect in attribution of ability
and perception of quality of learning is to be avoided.

ROLE SKILLS IN TUTORING:
NONVERBAL BEHAVIOR

To enact any role effectively and convincingly, an individual must
possess the requisite role skills. For example, in the case of the tutor it
is necessary to constantly monitor the ongoing behavior of the tutee
during the teaching session in order to determine whether the tutee
understands the material that is being taught. Both verbal and nonverbal social skills are used in the course of interaction with the tutee.
Several of our studies have dealt with role skills relevant to the tutoring
situation; in this section I shall focus primarily on studies concerning
nonverbal behavior.

Nonverbal Monitoring

Studies reported earlier showed clearly that the degree and pattern of
success or failure displayed by a tutee will influence the attributions
and reactions made by the tutor. Yet it is also likely that overt
behavioral responses as well as attitudinal reactions and attributions will

occur. Research was extended into the area of the tutor's overt responses by a study investigating the behavioral concomitants of the tutor's affective reactions toward the tutee. According to our earlier findings, when the tutee performs well the tutor will be more satisfied with the role of teacher than when the tutee performs poorly. These attitudes held by the tutors might very well be reflected in verbal and nonverbal behavior vis-à-vis the tutee. There is a good deal of empirical evidence showing that the nonverbal behavior of adults reflects one's affective state (Argyle, 1969; Mehrabian, 1972). For instance, smiling, nodding, and greater eye gaze generally signify positive affect. Conversely, negative affect is demonstrated by frowns, grimaces, and head-shaking. Thus, it is probable that the success or failure of the tutee will lead to differential nonverbal behavior.

In addition, the tutor's verbal behavior is likely to be affected by the performance of the tutee. Instances of failure will no doubt lead to corrective verbal statements and further explanation, and success will elicit responses of a different sort. It is reasonable to assume that the affective tone of the tutor's verbal responses will also be affected by the tutee's performance.

Subjects for the study were some of the children who participated in the first attribution study (Allen and Feldman, 1974a). While tutors were interacting with their tutee (a role-player) their behavior was being recorded on video and audiotape. It will be recalled that the tutee performed either well or poorly on the two halves of a 24-item test. For purposes of the present study, verbal and nonverbal results from the first half of the test only were analyzed. Thus, there were two conditions: (a) successful performance, in which the tutee answered correctly on 9 of the 12 items, and (b) failing performance, in which the tutee answered incorrectly on all except 3 questions.

The affective content of the tutor's speech was determined from typed transcripts of the tutoring sessions. Three categories were used to assess the tutors' verbalizations: positive, negative, and neutral affective tone. Logical phrases (usually statements) were used as the unit of analysis. Examples of phrases coded as representing positive affect are "That's right" or "You're really catching on." Examples of phrases coded as negative are: "You're wrong," "It isn't," or "You better try getting these." Each subject thus received two scores: proportion of positively toned statements and proportion of negatively toned statements. Nonverbal behavior of tutees was analyzed by trained coders using a set of 20 different categories of behavior. In addition, direction and amplitude of eye gaze were recorded by a coder.

Results showed that tutors in the successful performance condition used a significantly higher proportion of positive affective phrases than tutors who taught a tutee who performed poorly. Conversely, tutors in the successful performance condition used significantly fewer negatively toned phrases than did subjects in the failure condition. Thus, the affective tone of the tutors' verbalizations were affected by experimental manipulation: Positive affect was greater in the successful performance condition than in the failure condition.

Nonverbal behavior also differed according to tutee performance. Results showed that under conditions of tutee success there were significantly fewer instances of pursing lips, headshakes, forward leaning, reaching toward tutee, and fidgeting; there were significantly more headnods and erect posture. Eye gaze was also affected by tutee performance. The measure of number of gazes directed at the tutee showed a significant difference for tutee performance, indicating that tutees who were doing poorly (failure condition) were looked at more frequently than tutees who were doing well (42% versus 34%, respectively). Parallel results were found for amount of time spent looking at the tutee. Again, tutors spent a somewhat greater proportion of time looking at the tutee when he/she was doing poorly (32%) than when the tutee was succeeding (25%). Thus, the two measures of eye gaze consistently showed that there was significantly greater eye contact under conditions of unsuccessful than under successful performance.

The present results show quite clearly that both the verbal and nonverbal behavior of tutors were affected by the performance of their tutees. These findings have important practical implications. Thus, it is reasonable to assume that if a tutee is able accurately to assess the tutor's affective reactions, this might well have an impact on the tutee's motivation and enjoyment of the tutoring experience.

Decoding

In a teaching situation it is often necessary for the teacher to rely heavily on nonverbal cues to determine how much the student really understands about the material that is being taught. Little is known, however, about the accuracy of an observer's estimate of the degree of understanding of another person on the basis of nonverbal cues alone. This question concerns the ability of a person accurately to decode another's nonverbal behavior. Both peer teachers as well as adult teachers who work with younger children need to be adept in decoding of children's nonverbal responses. Although a great deal of interest has been shown recently in research on decoding and encoding of nonverbal behavior, there is still a paucity of evidence concerning developmental trends (that is, age differences) for this type of behavior. According to the few studies that have directly investigated developmental trends, accuracy in decoding of nonverbal responses apparently increases with age (Dimitrovsky, 1964; Gates, 1923). Unfortunately, in these studies adults were used as the stimulus persons, that is, children were asked to indicate the nature of an emotion on the basis of an adult's facial expressions. Thus, it is unclear whether the same result would be found if the stimulus persons were children.

Two opposing predictions can be made about children's ability to decode nonverbal behavior, depending on the assumptions one makes about the nature of the encoding (i.e., the original production) of children's nonverbal behavior. If the process of encoding (producing) nonverbal behavior is different in some fundamental way (qualitatively or quantitatively) for children and adults, then children should be superior to adults in decoding nonverbal cues of other children. The rationale for this prediction is clear: Children interact more with other children than adults do, so children should be more adept at decoding the nonverbal behavior of their peers. The opposite prediction can be made if the process of encoding nonverbal behavior is similar for children and for adults. If this is the case, adults should be more accurate than children in decoding nonverbal responses, since adults have had much greater experience in interacting with people in general and more practice in interpreting nonverbal cues.

A study was designed to examine systematically the accuracy of children and adults in decoding of nonverbal behavior, that is, in drawing inferences about underlying cognitive states on the basis of children's overt nonverbal responses (Allen and Feldman, 1974b). A set of 20 silent samples (30 seconds each) were prepared of stimulus persons who had been videotaped while listening to two 4-minute lessons. The stimulus persons were 10 third-graders (5 males and 5 females). On the basis of preliminary testing, two lessons were selected; one lesson was very easy for the child (first-grade level) and the other was very difficult (fifth-grade level). Then the two samples from each of the 10 stimulus persons were placed in random order on a new videotape. Thus, the videotape contained 20 short segments: each of 10 children listening to an easy lesson, and each of the same 10 children listening to a difficult lesson.

These samples of nonverbal behavior were then shown to groups of adults, sixth-graders, and third-graders. The adult observers (12 males and 24 females) were almost all experienced teachers enrolled in graduate education classes at the University of Wisconsin. The 51, sixth-grade children (26 males and 25 females) and 45, third-grade children (28 males and 17 females) all attended suburban Wisconsin elementary and middle schools.

Observers were told that they would be shown several short film segments of children listening to an arithmetic lesson. It was explained that each film segment would be shown without any sound, and that after seeing each 30-second film clip they would be asked to estimate on a 6-point Likert scale how much the student understood about the lesson. (The scale ranged from "understood everything" to "did not understand at all.") Hence, observers rated the degree of understanding of each stimulus person based only on the meager nonverbal cues available on the 30-second film. Data were analyzed by a 3 X 2 X 2 X 2 X 2 X 10 analysis of variance, using as factors the age and sex of subjects, order of presentation of the tape, difficulty of the lesson, sex of the stimulus persons, and the 10 stimulus persons.

Although results were complicated by a number of higher-order interactions, the main findings were quite clear. The most important finding was a significant interaction involving age of observer and type of lesson (easy or difficult), which indicated differential accuracy in estimated understanding of the stimulus persons according to age of the observer. As can be seen in Figure 6, observers in all age groups rated the stimulus persons who were listening to the easy lesson as understanding more than stimulus persons listening to the difficult lesson. But the third- and sixth-graders were more accurate—more discriminating—in their ratings than the adults. In fact, analysis of the ratings of understanding within each age group showed that only the third- and sixth-graders significantly perceived differences in degree of understand-

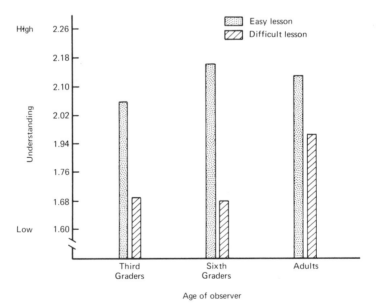

Figure 6. Ratings of understanding by age of observer and type of lesson. Higher numbers indicate inferences of greater understanding.

ing of the stimulus person as a function of level of difficulty of the lesson. Thus, only the children were able to decode accurately the nonverbal behavior of the stimulus persons. Interestingly, it seems that the difference between adults and children was due to over-estimation by adults of the degree of understanding revealed in the difficult lessons, in comparison to the rating made by the children.

A higher order interaction indicated that the sex of the stimulus person did produce differences in rating of understanding. Although sixth-grade subjects were equally accurate in their perception of male and female stimulus persons, both the third-graders and the adults were more accurate in decoding responses of the male stimulus persons than of the females. Moreover, some stimulus persons were quite consistently more discriminable than others. These interaction effects did not, however, modify the basic finding that children were superior to adults in decoding the degree of understanding revealed by minimal nonverbal cues.

Two important positive features of the present experiment should be pointed out. First, our study used 10 children as stimuli, which begins to approach what Brunswik (1956) has called representative sampling of the social ecology. Most work in the nonverbal behavior area has employed only one stimulus person, which seriously limits the generalizability of results. Second, in our study nonverbal behavior of the stimulus children was obtained under natural conditions of listening to a lesson, whereas most previous studies have used actors who were instructed to behave in a specified way.

To repeat, results of the present experiment disclosed a difference in decoding accuracy between adults and children: Third- and sixth-graders could discern a difference in understanding between children who were listening to an easy versus a difficult lesson, but adults were unable to do so. Consistent with our findings, other investigators have found that when shown films of students in the classroom, teachers could not accurately judge the comprehension of the students (Jecker, Maccoby, and Breitrose, 1964). Although our results were very clear, alternate explanations can be offered. First, children's nonverbal encoding may be different from that of adults; perhaps frequent interaction with peers facilitates the ability of children to decode the nonverbal behavior of other children. Alternatively, it is possible that children and adults may encode in the same manner but that the adults misinterpreted the meaning of children's nonverbal behavior due to believing that adults and children encode differently. Although the precise explanation for the finding cannot be stated with certainty, it is clear that children were better than adults in decoding subtle nonverbal cues that indicate degree of a child's comprehension.

Encoding

A question closely related to the accuracy of nonverbal decoding of children is whether children are able successfully to encode a given cognitive state by the intentional use of nonverbal responses, that is, by role playing. The children who served as stimulus persons in the study just discussed (encoding) had responded quite naturally; they were not cognitively aware of the nonverbal behavior that they were emitting. Would their nonverbal behavior have been different had the children made an intentional effort to convey to other persons that they understood or did not understand the material? It is of interest both for theoretical and practical reasons to know whether children are able accurately to convey their true level of comprehension by intentionally deploying nonverbal responses. In addition, it would be interesting to know if children are capable of simulating that they understand or do not understand a lesson. If a students can simulate successfully, it would be possible for them to control the teacher's perception of their comprehension of material. Put another way, can a person successfully "present self" to others in a cognitive sense, as well as in a social sense?

In an experiment designed to investigate these questions, we used as subjects a total of 22, third- and sixth-grade children (Allen and Feldman, 1974c). After having listened to the easy and hard lessons, the children were told to pretend that they were: (a) first listening to a very hard lesson that they did not understand, and (b) then hearing a very easy lesson that they did understand. (The order was balanced across subjects.) The children were instructed not to say anything, but simply to try to show by way of their nonverbal behavior that they did or did not understand the lesson they were hearing. During this 4-minute period they were actually listening to a tape-recorded story, and their nonverbal responses were being recorded on videotape for later analysis.

The nonverbal behavior that occurred during the two role playing situations was coded into one of 15 categories by two experienced coders. Data were analyzed in terms of the mean frequency of responses occuring during a 10-second period for the first 80 seconds of the session. Using a 2 × 2 analysis of variance, we compared the nonverbal responses under the role play condition to similar but naturally occurring nonverbal behavior that had been collected earlier while the subjects were actually listening to a hard and an easy lesson.

Results shown in Table 5 indicated that on each of the 15 categories assessing nonverbal responses there was either a significant main effect or interaction involving the natural versus the role play conditions. A multivariate test combining all measures revealed significant main

TABLE 5
Frequency of Nonverbal Behavior under Natural and Role Play Conditions

	Natural		Role play				
Category	Easy	Difficult	Easy	Difficult	Significance		
1. Shrug	.00	.45	.41	4.00	(A)[a]	(B)	(C)
2. Body fidget	2.77	.91	.23	.64	(A)	(B)	(C)
3. Hand to hair	.36	.55	.23	2.09	(A)	(B)	(C)
4. Hand to face	2.95	.14	.04	.00	(A)	(B)	(C)
' 5. Nervous hand movement	.55	.18	4.68	3.45	(A)	(B)	−
6. Relaxed posture	1.23	.00	.09	.41	−	(B)	(C)
7. Rigid posture	.36	.18	1.86	2.41	(A)	−	−
8. Smile-positive affect	.09	.00	.00	.32	−	−	(C)
9. Frown-grimace	.23	3.45	2.23	.18	(A)	−	(C)
10. Nodding head	.00	1.77	.32	.36	(A)	(B)	(C)
11. Shaking head	.04	1.82	3.45	.32	(A)	−	−
12. Pursing lips	.05	.00	.50	.36	(A)	−	−
13. Eyes away from blackboard	3.77	2.91	.73	.00	(A)	(B)	−
14. Eyes roaming	.41	2.45	.14	.09	(A)	(B)	(C)
15. Eyes closed	1.14	4.95	.05	.14	(A)	(B)	(C)

[a](A) = significant main effect for natural-role play; (B) = significant main effect for easy–difficult; (C) = significant interaction; All significances are beyond the .05 level.

effects for natural versus role play ($p < .0006$), for easy versus difficult ($p < .02$), and for the interaction ($p < .001$).

Thus, the data reveal that the deliberate nonverbal responses of the children were quite different from nonverbal responses that occurred unintentionally. For example, there was less body fidgeting under difficult than easy conditions when role playing, but the opposite in the natural state; there was less roaming of the eyes in the difficult than in the easy condition when role playing, but the opposite when nonverbal behavior was natural. In general, under role playing many of the children's nonverbal responses seemed to be exaggerated and emitted at a higher rate than when they were responding naturally.

Based on the present results we can say, therefore, that if children attempt purposely to convey to another person (e.g., a teacher) that they do or do not understand the material, the resulting pattern of nonverbal responses will be likely to differ from nonverbal responses that are emitted naturally. Although role playing and natural behavior resulted in different nonverbal responses at the encoding stage, it is still important to examine the decoding stage as well. On the basis of nonverbal cues alone, can observers accurately perceive the distinction in cognitive state (understanding or not understanding) in the way that was intended by the children when they were role playing?

To investigate this question, groups of third-grade children were shown 20 samples (30-seconds each) from the videotapes of the third-grade children who had attempted to convey understanding or lack of understanding by role playing. After viewing each sample on a television screen, the observers indicated on a 6-point rating scale the degree of understanding they thought was shown by the child just observed.

Results showed that when the children role played understanding, they were rated by observers as understanding significantly more than when they role played lack of understanding. Thus, despite the existence of objective differences in nonverbal responses under the natural and role-play conditions, children were still able to convey quite accurately to other children the intended cognitive state of comprehension or lack of comprehension by way of nonverbal responses.

Nonverbal Leakage

Another aspect of role skills connected with tutoring requires tutors to differentiate and control the relation between their verbal and nonverbal behavior. In tutoring programs the tutors are typically told to praise and encourage their tutees at all times, regardless of actual performance. Now if the learner performs poorly, positive verbal responses from the tutor are inconsistent with the tutor's private knowledge about the situation. Under such circumstances the tutor's true feelings might be revealed through nonverbal cues that could easily be detected by the learner. That is to say, nonverbal "leakage" may occur which reveals the true nature of one's underlying belief or affect. Children do seem to be capable of controlling their nonverbal responses to a certain extent, as indicated by the role playing study reported above. At the same time, there are data showing that people will sometimes reveal information through nonverbal responses that they did not intend to reveal. For instance, Ekman and Friesen (1969) provide some data in support of their hypothesis that individuals who are being deceptive will unintentionally disclose that they are not being truthful by means of their nonverbal behavior.

An experiment was designed to test more directly the nonverbal "leakage" hypothesis (Allen, Feldman, and Devin-Sheehan, 1974). A situation was arranged in which 45 male and female tutors (8- and 11-year-olds) were told that they should always say "good" after responses made by the younger tutee on a 20-item test—regardless of whether the tutee's responses were actually correct or not. In every case the tutee was a confederate who performed either very well (90% correct answers) or very poorly (90% wrong). Thus, tutors were either being predominantly truthful (successful performance) or untruthful (failing performance) when they were saying "good" to their tutees. Appropriate role skills in this situation require that tutors monitor their own verbal and nonverbal behavior and be able to inhibit nonverbal cues that might disclose negative reactions to the tutee's poor performance. Are tutors of 8 and 11 years of age able to conceal nonverbal cues that express their true dissatisfaction with the tutee's poor performance? In other words, will nonverbal "leakage" occur?

Videotape recordings were made of each tutor's nonverbal behavior while he or she was giving positive verbal feedback to the tutee. Experienced coders categorized the tutors' nonverbal responses. Results indicated a number of statistically significant differences in the objective nonverbal responses of the tutor in the good and poor performance conditions—though in both conditions the tutor was always giving positive verbal feedback consistently. Tutors in the poor performance condition exhibited, for example, fewer smiles, more stares, more pauses in speech, and more raising of the eyebrows. These data are presented in Figure 7. Thus, nonverbal "leakage" did occur, unintentionally revealing the discrepancy between the tutor's overt verbal responses and his/her own private knowledge.

Are other children capable of discerning the tutor's underlying affective reactions to the tutee on the basis of the "leaked" nonverbal cues? To answer this question we constructed a new videotape using samples

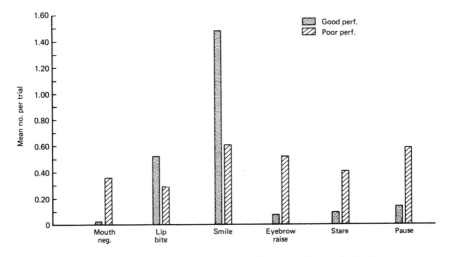

Figure 7. Unintentional nonverbal responses by tutors (nonverbal leakage).

taken from the videotapes of the 8-year-old subjects in the two conditions of the nonverbal leakage experiment. The tape consisted of 32
(silent) 30-second samples from the tutors' nonverbal behaviors. Fifty-
five same-age observers were shown each segment in turn, and were
asked to rate for each one how "satisfied" the tutor appeared to be
with his tutee.

Results disclosed that tutors in the poor performance condition—
where the tutor's positive feedback was inconsistent with the tutee's
performance—were judged as being significantly less satisfied with their
tutees than tutors in the good performance condition. Thus, not only
did nonverbal "leakage" occur in terms of objective behavior, but other
children were able to detect the existence of negative reactions on the
part of the tutor from observing their subtle and unintended nonverbal
responses. These data show that when the tutor's praise is not veridical,
nonverbal signs of dissatisfaction will appear which can be accurately
decoded by the tutee. Therefore, constant but nonveridical praise from
the tutor which disregards the tutee's actual performance—as recommended by many tutoring programs—may have a detrimental effect on
the tutee's motivation and feelings of satisfaction.

CONCLUSIONS

Research reported in this chapter has been directed toward increasing
our understanding of the psychological processes involved in interage
tutoring by children. Of particular interest have been those factors
responsible for any positive changes associated with the older child's
enacting the role of tutor for a younger child. As a general conceptual
framework for analyzing the tutoring situation, we have utilized role
theory.

The present research has not been concerned with developing a
tutoring program and curriculum with its accompanying instructional
materials, training procedures for tutors, and other aids. Several such
programs have been developed by others; some of the programs focus
on specific content (e.g., reading or mathematics) and others are
designed to be used with any subject matter. Several current programs
are mentioned in our review paper (Feldman, Devin-Sheehan, and
Allen, 1974).

Numerous mundane questions of praxis have not yet been addressed
or have received only cursory attention by available research in tutoring. For example: How often should tutoring take place? What are the
advantages and disadvantages of maintaining the same tutor–tutee pair
for a long period of time versus switching frequently? What is the
optimal age difference between tutor and tutee? Should tutors be

allowed a great deal of freedom in preparing and organizing their lessons, or is a well-structured procedure preferable? These and a great many other obvious practical questions can be raised immediately. And for each such question, information needs to be obtained concerning the effect of tutoring on the tutor and the tutee and for social–personal as well as for academic outcomes.

Nor have we even begun to understand the tutoring situation from a theoretical point of view. Cross-age tutoring is a very complex interactive process that involves the expression of cognitive, social, and affective behavior on the part of both the tutor and the tutee. Thus, for instance, research on tutoring shows that not all children are equally effective as tutors; and, according to recent findings (Cloward, 1974), the differential effectiveness of tutors cannot be accounted for by differences in intelligence or school achievement. This suggests that effective and ineffective tutors interact differently with their tutees. A better understanding of the psychological processes involved in the interaction between the tutor and tutee—including verbal and nonverbal responses—might enable one better to predict outcomes for tutees. Such information should have relevance to the problems faced by practitioners in designing effective tutoring programs.

Perhaps one of the important advantages of cross-age tutoring is simply that it provides a context in which children can interact in socially constructive ways with other children of quite different ages (Coleman, 1974). Interaction between children of different ages is likely to bring benefits to both the younger and the older child. In our society, with its heavy emphasis on age-grading, children are not provided with many opportunities—particularly benign and structured opportunities—to interact in a responsible and helpful manner with children much older or younger than themselves. One of the characteristics of present-day life is an increasing degree of isolation and segregation of persons on the basis of their age roles; little contact seems to occur even between persons fairly close in age, such as younger and older children. As Bronfenbrenner (1970) has said, "We are coming to live in a society that is segregated not only by race and class, but also by age [p. 100]."

Most schools are currently still highly segregated according to age, though signs of increasing flexibility are becoming apparent. Tutoring or informal helping of some sort has been adopted by a large number of schools, as was mentioned earlier; most tutoring programs do involve an older child helping a younger child in some way. Another recent development is the multi-unit school, initiated by our own Wisconsin Research and Development Center for Cognitive Learning. The multi-unit school has as one of its central features the organization of students in groups on the basis of their level of attainment in the subject matter, rather than on the basis of age per se. Usually children of two or three adjacent ages are included together within a single instructional group. This age range may be too narrow to expect much in the way of psychological advantages from the arrangement; nevertheless, it does have the advantageous effect of breaking the rigidity of the age–grade system in the schools.

It is more than obvious that at this point the empirical information provided by our research is insufficient to specify precisely the conditions under which tutoring will produce optimal academic and social benefits for the tutor and the tutee. Confronted with the stresses and strains of everyday academic life with students, it is inevitable that school personnel would initiate a promising program such as tutoring without waiting patiently for empirical research to answer the many questions that one might like to ask. Nevertheless, taking the long view will serve to remind us that with this problem, as with others, there is also something to be said for putting the horse before the cart!

REFERENCES

Allen, V. L., & Devin-Sheehan, L. *On being a role model.* Unpublished manuscript, Department of Psychology, University of Wisconsin, Madison, 1973.

Allen, V. L., & Devin-Sheehan, L. *Cross-age interaction in one-teacher schools.* Unpublished manuscript, Department of Psychology, University of Wisconsin, Madison, 1974.

Allen, V. L., & Feldman, R. S. Learning through tutoring: Low-achieving children as tutors. *Journal of Experimental Education,* 1973, *42,* 1–5.

Allen, V. L., & Feldman, R. S. Tutor attribution and attitude as a function of tutee performance. *Journal of Applied Social Psychology,* 1974, *4,* 311–320.

Allen, V. L., & Feldman, R. S. *Decoding of nonverbal behavior by children and adults.* Unpublished manuscript, Department of Psychology, University of Wisconsin, Madison, 1974(b).

Allen, V. L., & Feldman, R. S. *Encoding of comprehension by role playing.* Unpublished manuscript, Department of Psychology, University of Wisconsin, Madison, 1974(c).

Allen, V. L., Feldman, R. S., & Devin-Sheehan, L. *The unintentional expression of nonverbal cues.* Unpublished manuscript, Department of Psychology, University of Wisconsin, Madison, 1974.

Argyle, M. *Social interaction.* Chicago: Aldine-Atherton, 1969.

Ariès, P. *Centuries of childhood* (R. Balkick, trans.). New York: Knopf, 1962. (Originally published under the title *L'enfant et la vie familiale sous l'ancien regime,* by Librairie Plon, Paris, 1960.)

Bell, A. *An experiment in education made at the male asylum of Madras: Suggesting a system by which a school or family may teach itself under the superintendence of the master or parent.* London: Cadell and Davis, 1797.

Bell, A. *Instructions for conducting schools through the agency of the scholars themselves; comprising the analysis of an experiment in education, made at the male asylum, Madras, 1789–1796.* London: G. Roake, 1817.

Bell, S. E., Garlock, N., & Colella, S. C. Students as tutors: High schoolers and elementary pupils. *Clearing House,* 1969, *44,* 242–244.

Bossard, J. H. S., & Boll, E. S. *The large family system.* Philadelphia: University of Philadelphia Press, 1956.

Bronfenbrenner, U. *Two worlds of childhood.* New York: Russell Sage, 1970

Brunswik, E. *Perception and the representative design of psychological experiments.* Berkeley: University of California Press, 1956.

Cloward, R. D. Studies in tutoring. *The Journal of Experimental Education,* 1967, *36,* 14–25.

Cloward, R. D. *Predictors of change in a tutorial program.* Unpublished manuscript, Rhode Island College, 1974.

Coleman, J. S. *Youth: Transition to adulthood.* Chicago: University of Chicago press, 1974.

Costello, J., & Martin, J. One teacher-one child, learning together. *Elementary School Journal,* 1972, *73,* 72–78.

Dimtrovsky, L. The ability to identify the emotional meaning of vocal expressions at successive age levels. In J. Davitz (Ed.), *The communication of emotional meaning.* New York: McGraw-Hill, 1964.

Dures, A. *Schools.* London: Batsford, 1971.

Ekman, P., & Friesen, W. Nonverbal leakage and clues to deception. *Psychiatry,* 1969, *32,* 88–109.

Ellson, D. G., Barber, L., & Kampwerth, L. Programmer tutoring: A teaching aid and a research tool. *Reading Research Quarterly,* 1965, *1,* 71–1127.

Feldman, R. S., & Allen, V. L. Determinants of the primacy effect in attribution of ability. *Journal of Social Psychology,* 1975, *96,* 121–133.

Feldman, R. S., & Allen, V. L. Attribution of ability: An unexpected recency effect. *Psychological Reports,* 1975, *36,* 59–66.

Feldman, R. S., Devin-Sheehan, L., & Allen, V. L. *Research on children tutoring children: A critical review.* Unpublished manuscript, Department of Psychology, University of Wisconsin, Madison, 1974.

Gartner, A., Kohler, M. C., & Riessman, F. *Children teach children: Learning by teaching.* New York: Harper & Row, 1971.

Gates, G. S. An experimental study of the growth of social perception. *Journal of Educational Psychology,* 1923, *14,* 449–461.

Gillette, A. *One million volunteers: The story of volunteer youth service.* Middlesex, England: Penguin, 1968.

Goodman, L. Tutoring for credit. *American Education,* 1971, *7,* 26–27.

Hassinger, J., & Via, M. How much does a tutor learn through reading? *Journal of Secondary Education,* 1969, *44,* 42–44.

Holzberg, J. D., Knapp, R. H., & Turner, J. L. Companionship with the mentally ill: Effects on the personalities of college student volunteers. *Psychiatry,* 1966, *29,* 395–405.

Jecker, J., Maccoby, N., & Breitrose, H. S. Teacher accuracy in assessing cognitive visual feedback from students. *Journal of Applied Psychology,* 1964, *48,* 393–397.

Jones, E. E. Goethals, G. R., Kennington, G. E., & Severance, L. J. Primacy and assimilation in the attribution process: The stable entity proposition. *Journal of Personality,* 1972, *40,* 250–274.

Klaus, D. J. *Students as teaching resources.* (Project no. 931-17-690-570). Pittsburgh: American Institutes for Research, 1973.

Klein, S. P., & Niedermeyer, F. C. Direction sports: A tutorial program for elementary school pupils. *Elementary School Journal,* 1971, *72,* 53–61.

Klosterman, R. The effectiveness of a diagnostically structured reading program. *The Reading Teacher,* 1970, *24,* 159–162.

Laborde, Le Comte Alexandre de. *Plan d'education pour les enfans pauvres, d'apres les deux methodes combinees du docteur Bell et M. Lancaster.* Paris: H. Nicolle, 1815.

Lancaster, J. *Improvements in education, as it respects the industrious classes of the community.* London: Darton and Harvey, 1803.

Lancaster, J. *Improvements in education, as it respects the industrious classes of the community, containing, among other important particulars, an account of the institution for the education of one thousand poor children.* London: Darton & Harvey, 1805.

Lieberman, S. The effects of changes in roles on the attitudes of role occupants. *Human Relations,* 1956, *9,* 385–402.

Lohman, J. E. Age, sex, socioeconomic status and youth's relationships with older and younger peers. *Dissertation Abstracts International* 1970, *31*(5-A), 2497.

Lucas, J. A., Caither, G. H., & Montgomery, J. R. Evaluating a tutorial program containing volunteer subjects. *Journal of Experimental Education,* 1968, *36,* 78–81.

Mehrabian, A. *Nonverbal behavior.* Chicago: Aldine-Atherton, 1972.

Meiklejohn, J. M. D. *Dr. Andrew Bell: An old educational reformer.* Edinburgh and London: Blackwood, 1881.

Mollad, R. W. Pupil-tutoring as part of reading instruction in the elementary grades. *Dissertation Abstracts International,* 1970, *31*(4-B), 2260.

Moskowitz, H. Boredom? No More! 7th graders try teaching. *Science and Children,* 1972, *10,* 14–15.

Office of Education. Pint-size tutors learn by teaching. *American Education,* 1967, *3,* 20; 29.

Robertson, D. J. The effects of inter-grade tutoring experience on tutor attitudes and reading achievement. *Dissertation Abstracts International,* 1971, *32*(6-A), 3010.

Rubovits, P. L., & Maehr, M. L. Pygmalion analyzed: Toward an explanation of the Rosenthal-Jacobson findings. *Journal of Personality and Social Psychology,* 1971, *19,* 197–203.

Sarbin, T. R., & Allen, V. L. Role theory. In G. Lindzey & E. Aronson (Eds.), *The handbook of social psychology* (Vol. 2). Reading, Mass.: Addison-Wesley, 1968. Pp. 488–567.

Schoeller, A., & Pearson, D. A. Better reading through volunteer reading tutors. *The Reading Teacher,* 1970, *23,* 625–636.

Swett, M. This year I got my buddy to laugh. *Childhood Education,* 1971, *48,* 17–20.

Thelen, H. Tutoring by students. *School Review,* 1969, 77, 229–244.

Towson, S., & Allen, V. L. *The effect of evaluation of tutee on tutor's reaction to tutoring.* Unpublished manuscript, Department of Psychology, University of Wisconsin, Madison, 1970.

Waller, W. *The sociology of teaching.* New York: Wiley, 1932.

Weitzman, D. L. Effect of tutoring on performance and motivation ratings in secondary school students. *California Journal of Educational Research,* 1965, *16,* 108–115.

Subject Index

A 6
B 7
C 8
D 9
E 0
F 1
G 2
H 3
I 4
J 5